Creating the
PEACEABLE
SCHOOL

Creating the PEACEABLE SCHOOL

A Comprehensive Program for Teaching Conflict Resolution

Program Guide
Second Edition

Richard J. Bodine ✦ Donna K. Crawford ✦ Fred Schrumpf

Research Press   2612 North Mattis Avenue   Champaign, Illinois 61822   (800) 519-2707   www.researchpress.com

Cover design by Linda Brown, Positive I.D. Graphic Design, Inc.
Composition by Jeff Helgesen
Printed by Malloy
ISBN 0-87822-476-9
Library of Congress Control Number 2002105393

To the children and youth
who become peacemakers

Contents

Tables

Preface

This second edition of *Creating the Peaceable School* reflects our continuing commitment to a vision of peace and our awareness of the educator's responsibility for creating an environment where students can learn and accept their power to create peace within themselves and within the world. If not in our schools, then where will youth learn to create peace?

The program described in this revision derives from the original book (Bodine, Crawford, & Schrumpf, 1994) and is influenced by three other publications: the revised edition of *Peer Mediation: Conflict Resolution in Schools* (Schrumpf, Crawford, & Bodine, 1997), *The Handbook of Conflict Resolution Education: A Guide to Building Quality Programs in Schools* (Bodine & Crawford, 1998), and *Developing Emotional Intelligence: A Guide to Behavior Management and Conflict Resolution in Schools* (Bodine & Crawford, 1999). Specifically, the present volume expands the responsibility education program of the original with concepts from *Developing Emotional Intelligence* and extends the program development information with ideas from *Peer Mediation* and *The Handbook of Conflict Resolution Education*. The concepts of peacemaking and the three strategies of conflict resolution education—mediation, negotiation, and group problem solving—are retained and refined. We believe this Program Guide and the accompanying Student Manual represent a truly comprehensive program for teaching conflict resolution at the elementary and middle school levels. We further believe that the skills associated with peacemaking, negotiating, and group problem solving are as viable for use with high school students as is the now widely accepted skill of mediation.

We are grateful for all those thousands of educators who attended our training workshops, returned to their teaching responsibilities, and provided opportunities for young people to experience and learn conflict resolution. We have received valuable feedback from these educators and have even had occasion to work with some of their students. We again express our deepest appreciation to the group of elementary-age peer mediators who, prior to the original publication of *Creating the Peaceable School,* taught us valuable lessons about the potential of conflict resolution at the elementary level, about the capability of students this age, about the training required for mediators, about developmentally appropriate expectations for the conflict resolution process, and about the ability to celebrate diversity:

Brandon Baker	Brendan Kibbee	Travis Stephens
Rose Barnes	Kamiel Marion	Laura Stewart
David Bellmore	Denny Marsh	Rebecca Tabb
Sara Castle	Nadja Michel-Herf	Alex Thaler
C. J. Eaton	Nicole Murrah	Jama Thomas

Will Eckenstein	Daniel Nelson	Jay Ward
Rennee Eiscamp	Lauryl Newell	Natasha Viedenbaum
Mario Grady	Sarah Odeh	Blake Wetzel
Elizabeth French	Ashley Powell	Andy Williamson
Eric Ho	Katie Schrepfer	Drew Winterbottom
Patricia Ho	Kaveri Rajaraman	Ariel Zodiates
Grace Jones		

We also acknowledge two major partnerships—with the states of Illinois and Tennessee—that allowed us to sustain and expand our training programs. Although we have provided training in the *Creating the Peaceable School* program in nearly every state, plus Canada and Australia, these two partnerships have deepened over time and grown in quality. We thank Mike Kotner, of the Illinois State Board of Education; Dennis Rendelman, of the Illinois State Bar Association; Mike Hermann, of the Tennessee Department of Education; and Suzanne Stampley, of the Tennessee Legal Community Foundation, for their confidence in our program and the energy they put forth in implementing it. We also express our appreciation of and admiration for the work of Dr. Diane Powell, of the Washington, DC, public schools, whose vision and leadership has challenged and is challenging an entire urban school district to move toward peaceable schools.

Thanks to the Research Press staff, especially Ann Wendel, for believing in us and our ideas, and Karen Steiner, for her editing queries and dedication to clarity. A special thank you to Topper Steinman and Vernessa Gipson for their continued association, support, and friendship—and for being the excellent trainers they are. We also thank our colleagues Russell Brunson and Katy Woodward for their efforts in collecting and processing much of the information that appears in Appendix A, the summary of implementation results for Creating the Peaceable School and other conflict resolution programs.

Our gratitude is deep and abiding to all those too numerous to list who have provided us with inspiration and harmonious support in our mission to create peace. Thank you! Thank you! Thank you!

Finally, we honor the mysteries and challenges that cause our souls to evolve—it has been a quality journey.

Introduction

Imagine a school or classroom where learners manage and resolve their own conflicts, both with and without adult assistance. Picture a place where diversity and individuality are celebrated . . . a place where people listen in order to understand others' viewpoints and perceive conflict as an opportunity to learn and grow . . . a place where adults and children cooperate instead of acting aggressively or coercively . . . a place that supports everyone's rights and encourages everyone to exercise his or her responsibilities . . . a place where peace is viewed as an active process, made day by day, moment by moment. This is our vision—a vision of the peaceable school.

Creating the Peaceable School presents a comprehensive plan for achieving this vision. Central to the plan is the creation of a cooperative school context, achieved through the institution of a rights and responsibilities approach to discipline and the liberal use of cooperative learning. The conflict resolution strategies of mediation, negotiation, and group problem solving are also pivotal: Through them, students learn to recognize, manage, and resolve conflict in peaceful, noncoercive ways.

The goal of students as peacemakers is ageless, and students at all levels will benefit from the establishment of the peaceable school environment. Students at the earliest grade levels can begin to assimilate the concepts and learn the conflict resolution skills presented in this book. The time it takes to introduce these concepts and skills is time well invested. The return on that investment is greater acceptance of responsibility by students, resulting in less need for adult involvement in student behavior management activities. If effort is not expended early on with young learners, the adults in the system will spend considerably more time trying to gain compliance to rules as students move through the system from year to year. Teachers who choose not to spend time early in the school term to develop student responsibility will spend more time throughout the year on problems associated with student behavior. The issue is not whether a part of the school's mission is responsibility education, for which conflict resolution training for students is a valuable tool. The issue is timing—pay now or pay later. As with nearly every other example in life, if one chooses to pay later, one must also pay more—interest accrues.

This Program Guide presents a theoretical overview of the principles associated with conflict resolution and includes detailed instructions for conducting activities to help students master the skills and knowledge needed to apply these ideas. The accompanying Student

Manual, recommended for each learner, summarizes important concepts and presents forms and worksheets designed to reinforce student learning.

As is the case for all learning activities, teachers will need to adapt the content of the activities described here to their students' developmental level and experience. In particular, teachers will need to consider the appropriateness of activity length for learners' attention spans, use developmentally appropriate language to define the words needed to discuss central concepts, and vary the degree of adult involvement to guide learners through the activities. In addition, they will need to assist the learners in using the mediation, negotiation, and group problem solving strategies. Once teachers understand the basic principles involved in creating the peaceable school, they can readily adapt the activities as necessary.

TOWARD THE GOALS OF THE PEACEABLE SCHOOL

As used in this book, *peaceable* means being inclined or disposed to peace, promoting calm. Peace is that state in which, in any specific context, each individual fully exercises his or her responsibilities to ensure that all individuals fully enjoy all the rights accorded to any one individual in that context. Peace is that state in which every individual is able to survive and thrive without being hampered by conflict, prejudice, hatred, antagonism, or injustice. Peace is not a static state of being, but rather a continual process of interaction based on a philosophy that espouses nonviolence, compassion, trust, fairness, cooperation, respect, and tolerance. It is important to realize that peace is not the absence of conflict. When conflict occurs, as it inevitably will, it is recognized, managed, and resolved in ways that allow each individual to satisfy his or her basic needs.

In the peaceable school, the pervasive theme touching the interactions between children, between children and adults, and between adults is the valuing of human dignity and self-esteem. According to Kreidler (1990), "Peace is a realistic and attainable goal. It is also an inspiring ideal" (p. xvi).

Kreidler (1984) defines the peaceable classroom as a warm and caring community in which five qualities are present:

1. *Cooperation.* Children learn to work together and trust, help, and share with each other.

2. *Communication.* Children learn to observe carefully, communicate accurately, and listen sensitively.

3. *Tolerance.* Children learn to respect and appreciate people's differences and to understand prejudice and how it works.

4. *Positive emotional expression.* Children learn to express feelings, particularly anger and frustration,

in ways that are not aggressive or destructive, and children learn self-control.

5. *Conflict resolution.* Children learn the skills of responding creatively to conflict in the context of a supportive, caring community. (p. 3)

When the goals of the peaceable school are met, students—and likely teachers, too—gain life skills that will benefit them not just in school but also at home, in their neighborhoods, and in their present and future roles as citizens in a democratic society. In addition, the school becomes a more peaceful and productive environment, where students and teachers together can focus on the real business of learning and having fun.

In the peaceable school, the classroom is the place where students gain the knowledge base and the skills needed to resolve conflicts creatively. The classroom is also the place where the majority of conflicts will be resolved. The peaceable classroom is therefore the unit block of the peaceable school.

The classroom teacher is the key player in providing the learning opportunities required to create a peaceable environment in the school and in exemplifying the behaviors expected of a peacemaker. However, every adult in the school environment—principal, subject specialist, counselor, social worker, psychologist, secretary, supervisor, and so on—is a potential teacher of the concepts and behaviors of peace. As used in this book, the term *teacher* refers both to the classroom teacher and to others in the school environment who are in a position to teach, if not didactically, then by their example. Students will learn from whatever they observe: either appropriate and desirable behavior or inappropriate and undesirable behavior. Each person in the school must be diligently cognizant of his or her responsibility in this regard.

If adults are not consistently modeling the behaviors they are teaching young people to exhibit, then they are actually teaching the behaviors that the adults are exhibiting. Teachers, all of them, must behave as learners are expected to behave. This is especially true regarding conflict resolution.

RATIONALE FOR TEACHING CONFLICT RESOLUTION

For a school to become a peaceable place, the coercive behaviors of both adults and children must be replaced with the skills and strategies of conflict resolution. These skills and strategies are the tools for building the peaceable school.

Whatever all the elements of the multifaceted purpose of schools, their ultimate mission is to prepare young people to participate fully and responsibly in our democratic society. These young people must be able to do that on their own through the exercise of responsible behavioral choices. Our society is not constructed, nor do we wish it to be constructed, with some authority always directing an individual's actions. The ability to deal constructively with the ever-present conflicts of life is central to one's future success as a citizen of this social order. Without the ability to resolve conflicts constructively, one will be constantly at the mercy of others (Bodine & Crawford, 1998).

The ability to express and resolve conflicts is central to the peaceful expression of human rights. The skills and strategies of conflict resolution are also the skills of peace. Conflict resolution and peacemaking can be viewed as responsibilities inherent in citizenship in a democratic society. When children peacefully express their concerns and seek resolutions to problems that take into account common interests, they not only promote the values of human dignity and self-esteem, they also advance democracy. The teacher whose classroom and teaching enable the learner to behave peacefully truly serves the highest ideals of the educational system.

Strong, valid reasons exist for teaching conflict resolution strategies in the school environment. Davis and Porter (1985) articulate some of the more important ones:

Conflict is a natural human state and can be a constructive force when approached with skill.

Using mediation, negotiation, and group problem solving to resolve school-based disputes can improve the school climate.

Conflict resolution strategies can result in reduced violence, vandalism, chronic school absence, and suspension.

Conflict resolution training helps students and teachers deepen their understanding of themselves and others.

Conflict resolution training provides the recipient of the training with important life skills.

Training in mediation, negotiation, and group problem solving encourages high-level citizen activity.

Negotiation and mediation, in particular, provide a forum for promoting interest in and understanding of the American legal system.

Shifting the responsibility for solving some school conflicts to students frees adults to concentrate more on teaching and less on discipline.

Behavior management systems more effective than detention, suspension, or expulsion are needed to deal with conflict in the school setting.

Conflict resolution training increases skills in listening, critical thinking, and problem solving—skills basic to all learning.

Negotiation and mediation emphasize the ability to see others' points of view and the peaceful resolution of differences—skills that assist one to live in a multicultural world.

Negotiation and mediation are problem-solving tools that are well suited to the problems that young people face, and those trained in these approaches often use these tools to solve problems for which they would not seek adult help.

Some of the outcomes just described can be realized even if only portions of the program suggested in this book are applied. Broader outcomes will be realized when the program is applied consistently on a schoolwide basis, building on knowledge and skills each year as students progress from grade level to grade level. The time it takes to teach the skills and to develop understanding of the concepts is time well spent. The return on the investment is a greater acceptance of responsibility on the part of students for their behavior—and a corresponding decrease in the need for adult involvement in the management of student behavior.

It is important to stress that the skills and concepts of conflict resolution should not be taught in isolation. The traditional curriculum of our schools includes many issues of conflict. Teachers should look for opportunities to integrate learning about conflict into learning about traditional subjects. Literature, social studies, science, and the arts are especially replete with conflict situations that provide a natural forum for many of the activities in creating a peaceable school.

ORIGINS OF CONFLICT

The conflict resolution strategies described in this book are designed to help learners—both adults and students—become aware of their choices in conflict situations and to enable them to resolve the conflicts in their lives with confidence and independence. Central to this goal is an understanding of the underlying origins of conflict.

As William Glasser (1984) explains in his exposition of control theory, conflict originates from within. Control theory explains why (and to a great extent how) all living organisms behave. According to this theory, everything we do in life is behavior; all of our behavior is purposeful, and the purpose is always to attempt to satisfy basic needs that are built into our genetic structure. The theory is called control theory because all behavior is our best attempt at the moment to control ourselves (so that we can control the world around us) as we continually try to satisfy one or more basic, inborn needs. In other words, no behavior is caused by any situation or person outside of the individual.

Accepting this idea requires a shift in thinking on the part of those who view life according to a stimulus-response paradigm. According to the stimulus-response paradigm, we answer the telephone because it rings, and we stop the car because the traffic light is red. Likewise, students stop running down the hall because we tell them to walk. From the stimulus-response perspective, behavior is caused by someone or something (the stimulus) outside the individual: The action that follows is the response to that stimulus. According to the control theory paradigm, people or events outside us never stimulate us to do anything. Rather, our behavior always represents the choice to do what most satisfies our need at the time. From this perspective, we follow the rules of a game to achieve a meaningful outcome. We answer the phone because we choose to do so in order to communicate, not because we react to the ring. We stop at a red light because we choose to avoid risking a traffic ticket or an accident, not because the light turned red. Likewise, if students stop running down the hall, it is because they choose to walk, in the belief that walking is more need fulfilling at the moment. When we repeat a choice that is consistently satisfying, we exercise less and less deliberation in making that choice. Even a quick action is chosen and not automatic.

All individuals are driven by genetically transmitted needs that serve as instructions for attempting to live our lives. These basic needs are the physiological need to survive and the four psychological needs that follow:

1. The need for *belonging*—fulfilled by loving, sharing, and cooperating with others

2. The need for *power*—fulfilled by achieving, accomplishing, and being recognized and respected

3. The need for *freedom*—fulfilled by making choices in our lives and being safe

4. The need for *fun*—fulfilled by laughing and playing

The needs are equally important, and all must be reasonably satisfied if individuals are to fulfill their biological destiny. The individual has no choice but to feel pain when a need is frustrated and pleasure when it is satisfied. When any need goes unsatisfied, there is a continual urge to behave. This urge is as much determined by human genetic instructions as is eye color. Instructions related to survival—such as hunger, thirst, and sexual desire—are relatively distinct. Individuals quickly learn that the particular discomfort is attached to this need, and it is plain what they must do to satisfy the survival instructions. The nonsurvival, or psychological, needs are challenging because it is often less clear what an individual must do to satisfy them. Psychological needs, like biological needs, have their source in the genes, even though they are much less tangible and the behaviors that fulfill them are more complex than the physical behaviors used to fulfill the survival needs.

Glasser holds that we are essentially biological beings, and the fact that we follow some of our genetic instructions psychologically rather than physically makes neither the instructions less urgent nor the source less biological. The four needs seem to conflict with one another, and the constant challenge to satisfy them requires continual renegotiation of balance. For example, when a person chooses to work long hours, his accomplishments may help to meet his power need, but he may not be involved with his friends and family in a need-fulfilling way. Perhaps another individual derives a sense of freedom from living alone but loses a sense of belonging when exercising this choice. Everyone knows a golfer who struggles to balance the need for fun and the need for belonging, met by spending time on weekends with family.

Even though individuals may not be fully aware of their basic needs, they learn that there are some general circumstances that relate strongly to the way they feel. For example, people behave lovingly with their parents because it feels good, they realize that when people pay attention to their words or actions they feel powerful, by making choices they feel the importance of freedom, and through laughter they learn about fun.

Even though human needs are essentially the same for everyone, the behaviors through which individuals choose to satisfy those needs may be quite different. Beginning at birth, individuals have unique experiences that feel either pleasurable or painful. Through these experiences, individuals learn how to satisfy their needs. Because individuals have different experiences, the things they learn to do to satisfy their needs will be different as well. Each individual has memories of need-fulfilling behaviors specific to his or her unique life experiences. These pleasurable memories constitute the individual's quality world and become the most important part of the person's life. For most people, this quality world is composed of pictures (or, more accurately, perceptions) representing what they have most enjoyed in life. These perceptions become the standard for behavior choices. Unlike the basic survival needs, which are the same for everyone, the perceptions in each person's quality world are completely individual. Individuals choose to behave in different ways to fulfill their needs because their quality worlds are different. It is important to realize that the choice the individual makes in each situation is the choice he or she believes offers the best potential to meet basic needs. In short, each person is doing the best he or she knows how to do to satisfy basic needs. One individual's choice, however, may limit or disrupt another's choice. This is one significant source of conflict, especially in social situations like school, where the choice not to associate with one another is nearly nonexistent. To be in effective control of one's life means integrating this knowledge into the way one deals with others.

To satisfy the basic needs, a person must behave. This means acting, thinking, feeling, and involving the body, all of which are components of the *total behavior* generated in the effort to get what is wanted. Whenever there is a discrepancy between what one wants and what one has, the internal behavioral system is activated. This is because all humans function as control systems: Their motivation is always to control not only for present needs but, after those are satisfied, for future needs. People innately reject being controlled by others because they are capable of fulfilling their own needs—indeed, that is the purpose of the control system. Loss of control to another is dysfunctional and runs counter to the fulfillment of needs.

To satisfy needs, people must be able to sense what is going on both around and within them, then be able to act on that information. When we sense a discrepancy between what we have and what we want, we behave by acting upon the world and upon ourselves as a part of the world. If we examine this behavior, it may seem to be composed of four different behaviors, but these are actually four components of what is always a total behavior. These four components, which always occur synchronously, are as follows:

1. Doing (for example, walking, talking)

2. Thinking (for example, reasoning, fantasizing)

3. Feeling (for example, angering, depressing)

4. Physiology (for example, sweating, headaching)

The feeling component of behavior is typically the most obvious. However, the more a person can recognize that feelings are just one component of total behavior, the more the person will be in control of his or her life. The value of recognizing total behavior is that doing so enables a person to control behavior to satisfy his or her needs more effectively. In most situations, a person is more in tune to feelings than to actions, thoughts, or physiology. By recognizing that the feeling component is just one of four that make up total behavior, a person can be more in control of his or her life.

When people begin to think in terms of total behavior, they can see that they choose these behaviors and have the option to change them. The way to change a total behavior is to change the behavior's doing and thinking components. One has almost total control over the doing component of behavior and some control over the thinking component—less control over the feeling component and almost no control over physiological phenomena. Behavior in its totality ultimately gives one control over all components. When what we are doing changes, our thoughts, feelings, and physiological responses change as well.

The message is that, because people always have control over the doing component of behavior, if they change that component, they cannot avoid changing the thinking, feeling, and physiological components as well. To get their needs met effectively, people must realize that they always have control over the doing component and can choose to do something more effective than their present behavior. Each individual, in every situation, has a choice to behave differently. One can always choose a new behavior.

Thus, even though all people are driven by the same four needs, each person's wants are unique. Wants are like pictures in an album: It is impossible for two people to have the same picture album because it is impossible for two people to live exactly the same life. If a person wishes to understand conflict and perceive it positively, the knowledge that no two people can have exactly the same wants is central. For example, if two individuals wish to satisfy their need to belong through a friendship, they must learn to share their commonalities and respect and value their differences.

As long as people have differing wants and as long as an individual's needs can be satisfied in ways that may conflict, the need to renegotiate balance will exist. Thus, driven by our genetic instructions, we will inevitably experience conflict.

SCOPE OF THE PROGRAM

This book presents a comprehensive program, the goal of which is to create a peaceable school. We believe the ideas presented are best applied on a schoolwide basis. However, an individual teacher in a self-contained classroom or a group of teachers in a particular school unit can accomplish what is suggested here in their own environment of responsibility. It is possible to develop a peaceable classroom in any school. Those who do so have our commendation—they see the need and the potential for peace, and they accept no excuse for not pursuing what they believe is required to achieve it. Specific recommendations for organizing and implementing the program outlined here are included in Section 7.

Foundation Abilities for Conflict Resolution

In the problem-solving strategies of conflict resolution, certain attitudes, understandings, and skills are facilitative and/or essential. For problem solving in conflict situations to be effective, attitudes and understandings ultimately must be translated into behaviors—that is, into foundation abilities. Although considerable overlap and interplay exist, these foundation abilities involve the following clusters of behaviors.

Orientation Abilities

Orientation abilities encompass the values, beliefs, attitudes, and propensities compatible with effective conflict resolution. They include the following:

Nonviolence

Compassion and empathy

Fairness

Trust

Justice

Tolerance

Self-respect

Respect for others

Celebration of diversity

Appreciation of controversy

These values, beliefs, attitudes, and propensities can be developed through teaching activities that promote cooperation and prejudice reduction. Orientation abilities culminate in an internalization that every conflict presents an opportunity to learn and grow if one chooses to approach it constructively and creatively.

Perception Abilities

Perception abilities encompass the understanding that conflict does not lie in objective reality but in how people perceive that reality. Perception abilities include the following:

Empathizing in order to see the situation as the other side sees it

Self-evaluating to recognize personal fears and assumptions

Suspending judgment and blame to facilitate a free exchange of views

Reframing solutions to allow for face-saving and to preserve self-respect and self-image

These abilities enable one to develop self-awareness and to assess the limitations of one's own perceptions. They also enable one to work to understand others' points of view. The culminating notion is that differences in point of view exist for many reasons and that labeling points of view in a polarized fashion is not helpful in resolving issues between individuals.

Emotion Abilities

Emotion abilities encompass behaviors to manage anger, frustration, fear, and other emotions. These abilities include the following:

Learning the language of emotions and developing the courage to make emotions explicit

Expressing emotions in nonaggressive, noninflammatory ways

Exercising self-control in order to control one's reaction to others' emotional outbursts

These abilities enable one to gain the self-confidence and self-control needed to confront and resolve the conflict. The basis for these behaviors is acknowledging that emotions—often strong ones—are present in conflict, that these emotions may not always be expressed, and that emotional responses by one party may trigger emotional responses from another party.

Communication Abilities

Communication abilities encompass behaviors of listening and speaking that allow for the effective exchange of facts and feelings. These abilities are as follows:

> Listening to understand
>
> Speaking to be understood
>
> Reframing emotionally charged statements into neutral, less emotional terms

These abilities include the skills of active listening, which allow one to attend to another person and that person's message; summarize that message to check out what was heard and advise the other person of the message received; and ask open-ended, nonleading questions to solicit additional information that might clarify the conflict. Also included are the skills of speaking to be understood rather than to debate or impress, speaking about yourself by describing the problem in terms of its impact upon you, speaking with clarity and conciseness to convey your purpose, and speaking in a style that makes it as easy as possible for the other party to hear. The skill of reframing, coupled with acknowledging strong emotions, is highly useful in conflict resolution. Participatory conflict resolution, in which those who own the conflict work for resolution, is simply a communication process.

Creative Thinking Abilities

Creative thinking abilities encompass behaviors that enable people to be innovative in problem definition and decision making. These abilities are as follows:

> Contemplating the problem from a variety of perspectives
>
> Approaching the problem-solving task as a mutual pursuit of possibilities
>
> Brainstorming to create, elaborate, and enhance a variety of options

Included is the skill of uncovering the interests of the parties involved in a conflict through questioning to identify what the parties want, as well as probing deeper by seeking to understand why they want what they want. The skill of problem definition involves stating the problem, and thus the problem-solving task, as a pursuit of options to satisfy the interests of each party. Flexibility in responding to situations and in accepting a variety of choices and potential solutions is an essential skill in decision making. The behavior is brainstorming—separating the process of generating ideas from the act of judging them. Also critical to success is the ability to elaborate potential solutions and to enhance and embellish existing solutions.

Critical Thinking Abilities

Critical thinking abilities encompass the behaviors of analyzing, hypothesizing, predicting, strategizing, comparing and contrasting, and evaluating. Included are the following:

Recognizing and making explicit existing criteria

Establishing objective criteria

Applying criteria as the basis for choosing options

Planning future behaviors

These foundation abilities are necessary for the utilization of the problem-solving strategies of conflict resolution. Since most, if not all, are also abilities central to learning in general, they can be developed in schools in a variety of ways, many of those ways separate from the issue of personal conflict.

Conflict Resolution Strategies

The strategies of mediation, negotiation, and group problem solving are central to the creation of the peaceable school. These strategies give students a way to deal with differences without aggression or coercion. Mediation and negotiation are strategies helpful in situations in which individuals are involved; group problem solving is an approach designed to help a group reach a consensus decision about a problem concerning the group. The six steps in each of these conflict resolution strategies are generally as follows:

Step 1: Agree to participate; accept ground rules

Step 2: Gather points of view

Step 3: Focus on interests

Step 4: Create win-win options

Step 5: Establish criteria to evaluate options; evaluate options

Step 6: Create an agreement

Teachers, administrators, and other staff in schools charged with managing student behavior are all too aware of interpersonal and intergroup conflict. A considerable amount of these adults' responsibilities to the school community concerns managing conflict. Indeed, to advise that schools not have in place methodologies to manage behavior arising from conflict would be unconscionable. However, the conflict resolution strategies presented here differ from typical school problem resolution efforts.

There are many possibilities for problem solving between people or groups of people. The use of arbitration as a problem-solving strategy is widely employed. Arbitration is the process whereby a party not involved directly in the conflict determines a solution to the conflict; the arbitrator rules, and the disputants are expected to comply with the ruling. This is the process that is characteristic of adult involvement in most conflicts between students in schools. However, conflict resolution programs, based on principled negotiation theory, differ from the pervasive practices for managing student conflict. Conflict resolution involves cooperative, collaborative problem-solving methodologies in which those with ownership of the problem participate directly in crafting a solution to the problem, with or without involvement of others. Table 1 illustrates those differences.

Prevalent practices for managing conflict in schools mostly entail arbitration, with the adult authority serving as arbitrator to settle the dispute for the parties. Conflict resolution involves bringing the parties of the dispute together; providing them the processes to resolve the dispute; and expecting them to do so, with or without the involvement of others. The problem-solving strategies of conflict resolution are future directed. *The disputants craft and commit to a plan of action to behave differently from this point forward.*

Fundamental Skill Areas

The first six sections presented in this book address six skill areas fundamental to the achievement of a peaceable school. These six sections comprise the training component for implementing the peaceable school. Each section offers a theoretical overview of the skill area, then a number of activities and strategies to engage students in developing a knowledge base and acquiring critical skills. The seventh section gives an overview of issues in program development and implementation.

Section 1: Building a Peaceable Climate

Responsibility and cooperation are the foundation on which all other skills in the peaceable school are built, and they are the focus of this first section. In order to manage student behavior without coercion, the adults in the school must view acceptable behavior as the responsibility of each student, and each student must accept this responsibility.

TABLE 1   Prevalent Practice Versus Conflict Resolution

Relies on a third party to settle disputes.	Directly involves the conflicting parties in both resolution process and outcome.
Reactively offers services after the conflict occurs.	Proactively offers skills and strategies to participants prior to their involvement in the conflict.
Focuses on conflict after a school rule has been broken; often offers advice to ignore problem if it is thought not to be major or serious.	Intervenes in conflicts and prevents their escalation into the broken-rule stage or violence.
Uses arbitration almost exclusively to settle disputes.	Maximizes the use of negotiation and mediation processes to resolve disputes.
Requires adults to spend a disproportionate amount of time dealing with minor student conflicts.	Uses teacher and virtually unlimited student resources to handle such conflicts and learn essential decision-making skills in the process.
Relies on disciplinary codes that are ineffective at helping students reconcile interpersonal and intergroup differences.	Focuses attention not on the disciplinary offense but on how to resolve the interpersonal and intergroup dimensions of a conflict.

This occurs only when behavioral expectations are clearly delineated and when those to whom the expectations apply have been fully educated about responsible behavior.

The first five activities in Section 1 focus on developing students' knowledge about responsibility—what choices define responsibility and what rights correspond to it. The first of these activities introduces the class meeting instructional format. As used here and in other sections, the class meeting is a vehicle for students to internalize the knowledge base and skills they need to become peacemakers.

The second building block of the peaceable school is cooperation. Although cooperating is a natural human tendency, doing so in school may seem unnatural to students who have become acclimated to the predominant competitive educational practices. The last three activities in Section 1 are designed to help students define and experience cooperation in ways that will make that idea come alive in the classroom.

Section 2: Understanding Conflict

A shared understanding of the nature of conflict is a prerequisite for students to engage in successful conflict resolution. Section 2 provides information and activities designed to instill a shared understanding of the nature and causes of conflict, as well as of possible responses to conflict and its potential benefits. The idea that psychological needs are the underlying cause of conflict is particularly useful to students as they seek common interests to resolve disputes. The activities of Section 2 develop orientation abilities, seeking to change how one views conflict and one's ability to choose responses to conflict.

Section 3: Understanding Peace and Peacemaking

Section 3 provides information and activities to help students look at the concept of peace and put this concept into practice. Pursuing interests rather than positions allows students to accept diversity and to view diversity as an asset in the peaceable school. Activities in this section are designed to help students learn the specific behaviors associated with peacemaking and to evaluate their own performance as peacemakers.

The first four activities of Section 3 develop orientation abilities, seeking to change how one views peace and one's role as a peacemaker. The rest of the activities of Section 3 develop the remaining foundation abilities of perception, emotion, communication, creative thinking, and critical thinking. These activities provide training in the specific skill areas required to employ any of the three conflict resolution strategies.

Section 4: Mediation

Section 4 explores the concept of mediation, defined as assisted conflict resolution between disputants. Mediation is presented both as a strategy for use within the classroom and as a schoolwide vehicle for resolving conflicts. Training activities cover a six-step mediation process designed to allow students to gain the skills to act as neutral third parties in facilitating conflict resolution between disputants. Mediation is the first strategy presented not because it is more important than the others but because it is the most efficient training strategy for developing understanding of the six steps of conflict resolution.

Section 5: Negotiation

Section 5 explores the concept of negotiation, defined as unassisted conflict resolution between disputants. It provides training activities in skills designed to help disputants state their individual needs, focus on their interests rather than their positions, and generate options for mutual gain. Training activities focus on a six-step negotiation process paralleling that presented for mediation. The hallmark of a peaceable school is that a critical mass of students and adults possess the ability to negotiate.

Section 6: Group Problem Solving

Section 6 presents group problem solving as a creative strategy to deal with disputes involving a significant percentage of the classroom population. In this strategy, the teacher uses the class meeting format to facilitate the group problem solving process. Although the teacher's role is central, the group itself is responsible for working to achieve a consensus decision that they can implement to resolve the conflict.

Section 7: Program Development and Implementation

Section 7 presents information about various strategies for starting and sustaining a peaceable school. This section provides the program development component for implementing the peaceable school.

Learning Format Options

The training activities can be offered in a variety of learning formats—the greater the variety, the greater the enjoyment for the learners and the teacher. One or more of the format options described in the following pages have been specified for each activity. The creative teacher will be able to use formats other than the ones suggested and to encourage products other than those specified in the activities—perhaps audio and/or video productions, Web pages, power point presentations, skits, dioramas, photo essays, research projects, community outreach efforts, and the like.

Whole Class Discussion/Participation

This format, in which the entire class is involved, is the one most familiar to teachers and students. In the activities, a choice is often given between this and the class meeting format. If the activity procedures involve grouping and regrouping of students, then whole-class discussion/participation may be most workable. If the activity procedures suggest mostly interactions involving the whole class, then use of the class meeting format is encouraged.

Learning Center

If an activity is suitable for a classroom learning center, individual students may pursue the activity independently or in small groups. In this format, the interaction of class members is not essential. Students may pursue the activity at different times, and direct teacher involvement is not required.

Cooperative Learning

Cooperative learning experiences help students understand what it means to reach a group goal or shared outcome. Cooperation in problem-solving ventures is the foundation of conflict resolution. In cooperative learning activities, group members interact with one another to solve problems. Cooperative learning assumes that no group member already has a solution to the common problem; a true cooperative learning activity requires the resources of each member of the group to arrive at a solution. A cooperative context is established by structuring the majority of learning situations cooperatively.

The most prevalent cooperative learning strategies are the Learning Together strategies, developed by David Johnson and Roger Johnson (1975, 1993) and colleagues at the University of Minnesota; the Student Team Learning techniques, developed by Robert Slavin (1987) and colleagues at Johns Hopkins University; and the Group Investigation method, developed by Yael Sharan and Shlomo Sharan (1990) of Tel Aviv University. The classroom teacher may choose ideas from the plethora of cooperative learning idea books available (some specific titles are included in the suggested reading list following the Section 1 overview).

Class Meeting

Glasser (1969) refers to this teaching format as the open-ended meeting, in which "children are asked to discuss any thought-provoking question related to their lives, questions that may also be related to the curriculum of the classroom. The difference between an open-ended meeting and ordinary class discussion is that in the former the teacher is specifically not looking for factual answers" (pp. 134–135).

In the peaceable school, the class meeting serves two functions: First, in its general use, the format appears as a teaching option throughout all sections of the book. As such, it helps students acquire the knowledge and skills they need to be peacemakers. Discussion questions for use in additional class meetings are also provided at the end of the overviews for Sections 1, 2, and 3. Second, the class meeting is the forum for the specific strategy of group problem solving. The more general use of the class meeting is discussed here; guidance for applying the class meeting format in the context of the group problem solving approach is provided in Section 6.

Ground rules for the class meeting. The ground rules for the class meeting are as follows:

1. Participants sit in a circle.

2. Every member of the class is responsible for communication (listening and speaking).

3. The "Rule of Focus" applies to all discussion. This means that whoever is speaking will be allowed to talk without being interrupted.

4. Participants show respect for others. This means no criticism or sarcasm toward group members or their ideas.

5. Each time someone in the group finishes making a statement, another group member summarizes and clarifies it before anyone else goes on to a new idea.

The first two rules establish an equality base within the group—each group member is valued, and all have similar status. The circle allows visual contact among members, which contributes to good listening behavior and affords no one person any special status because of placement in the group. (The teacher should be careful not to sit in the same location or by the same students at each class meeting.) The remaining rules ensure that a group member is heard and understood and encourage discussion to continue.

Role of the teacher-facilitator. As facilitator of the class meeting, the teacher helps students think and relate what they know to the topic being discussed. The open-ended nature of the discussion allows for seemingly disparate ideas and helps make the topic of discussion relevant to students with a wide range of interests and abilities. The concepts of responsibility, cooperation, conflict, and peacemaking—along with the specific skills involved in communication and conflict resolution—easily fit into the format of an open-ended class meeting. Specifically, the teacher-facilitator does the following:

1. *Determines the purpose of the meeting and develops a question map for it.* The facilitator's original question or directive frames the purpose of the class meeting, communicates that purpose to the group, and initiates discussion. The rest of the question map, or plan for stimulating or redirecting discussion, is designed to extend discussion if it lags or focus it if it strays nonproductively from the original purpose. Ideally, the students will pursue the purpose of the meeting without getting stuck or off track. However, the question map should account for either possibility. Intervention is also often required to help meet time constraints.

2. *Reviews and enforces ground rules.* Group acceptance of ground rules is essential. The facilitator reviews basic ground rules and specifies any special ground rules that might be needed (for example, to protect confidentiality or to preserve students' self-esteem). During the deliberations, the facilitator ensures that all ground rules are followed.

3. *Establishes a positive, optimistic tone.* Students are encouraged to participate by the facilitator's enthusiasm and interest in the discussion. The facilitator should be alert to guard against a few students' dominating the discussion. If this is the case, the facilitator should encourage quieter members to speak.

4. *Summarizes the proceedings.* By summarizing key ideas gleaned from the discussion, the facilitator is able to refocus the group on the stated purpose of the class meeting and help move the group through the process in a timely manner.

5. *Avoids dominating the discussion or pressing his or her point of view.* The successful facilitator orchestrates the class meeting with as little verbal involvement as possible. In other words, the facilitator starts the process and monitors progress, intervening only when absolutely necessary. The more the session flows without the facilitator's direct intervention, the more the students will feel ownership of the process. The facilitator should remain impartial and should not attempt to steer the discussion unless the discussion significantly digresses from the purpose, and the digression does not seem to reflect a meaningful alternate purpose. The facilitator's ideas are best framed as questions to be considered by the group.

6. *Expresses appreciation for the efforts and accomplishments of the group.* The group should hear that the facilitator knows that learning through class meetings is hard work and that all contributions, successful or not, are worthy of praise. Providing specific feedback to the group about those things that worked particularly well is important. Such feedback should focus on the process of the discussion. In brief, the facilitator conveys to the group that he or she really believes that group members represent an important source of information and that this collective information contributes significantly to the fund of knowledge in the classroom. It is important that students have an opportunity to express and challenge ideas.

Suggested Readings

Crawford, D. K., Bodine, R. J., & Hoglund, R. G. (1993). *The school for quality learning: Managing the school and classroom the Deming way.* Champaign, IL: Research Press.

Glasser, W. (1969). *Schools without failure.* New York: Harper & Row.

Glasser, W. (1984). *Control theory.* New York: Harper & Row.

Glasser, W. (1986). *Control theory in the classroom.* New York: Harper & Row.

Building a Peaceable Climate

OVERVIEW

To bring the vision of the peaceable school to fruition, the teacher must first develop a classroom environment conducive to constructive conflict management. The development of such an environment is contingent upon the implementation and application of two interrelated structural and behavioral concepts: establishment of a cooperative context for the classroom and management of student behavior without coercion. As Johnson and Johnson (1993) assert:

> It makes no sense to talk of constructive conflict management in schools structured competitively. The first step in teaching students the procedures for managing conflicts, therefore, is creating a cooperative context in which conflicts are defined as mutual problems to be resolved in ways that benefit everyone involved. (p. 8)

Constructive conflict management is this paradigm shift—cooperate; don't coerce.

The importance of creating a conducive environment cannot be overstated. Learners need a friendly, supportive atmosphere to engage productively in self-evaluation and to risk trying new behaviors. This atmosphere depends heavily upon a system of sensible, predictable rules and expectations. Only when the teacher in the peaceable school succeeds in creating a facilitative environment does he or she turn attention to developing in students the knowledge base and skills they need to manage conflict constructively.

To reiterate, the creation of the peaceable school environment hinges on two preconditions: a cooperative context in the classroom and a responsibility education program, including a supporting classroom discipline program, that allows the teacher to manage student behavior without coercion.

A COOPERATIVE CONTEXT

In the classroom, as with any collection of individuals, there are two possible contexts for conflict—cooperative and competitive. In competition, rewards are restricted to the few who perform the best. Competitors usually have a short-term orientation and focus all their energies on winning, paying little if any attention to the longer term interest of maintaining good relationships. Competitors typically avoid communication with each other (except for hostile "trash talk" intended to demean or incite the other individual), misperceive the positions and motivations of the others involved, are suspicious of others, and deny the legitimacy of the needs and feelings of others in favor of their own interests. A competitive context creates a win-lose approach to resolving conflict.

In contrast, a cooperative context involves goals that all are committed to achieving. Outcomes beneficial to everyone involved are sought. Cooperators typically have a long-term orientation and focus energies both on achieving goals and on maintaining good relationships with others. Cooperators tend to perceive the positions and motivations of others accurately, communicate accurately and thoroughly, hold a positive and trusting attitude toward others, and see conflicts as mutual problems for which solutions that benefit all involved can be found.

Johnson and Johnson (1993) proclaim that "it makes little sense to teach students to manage conflicts constructively if the school is structured so that students have to compete for scarce rewards (like grades of 'A') and defeat each other to get what they want" (p. 1). The nature of the reward system is an extremely important dimension because it affects both the establishment of a cooperative classroom context and the management of student behavior without coercion.

The primary reward system of nearly every classroom is grades—primary in importance to the recipient, that is. The practice of awarding grades is the ultimate coercive practice. Grades exemplify a competitive context. Defenders of the grading system often argue that competition is fundamental to our society and that participating in a competitive system early on prepares the learner for the realities of life. This argument is based on several myths about competition: that competition is part of human nature and is an inevitable fact of life; that competition motivates one to do one's best; that without competition one would cease to be productive; that competition in the form of contests is the best way to have fun. Competition in the learning environment, as in any endeavor, creates winners and losers. It also suppresses learners' inclination to work cooperatively. On the other hand, when learners are encouraged to cooperate, combining their talents and energies so that as many as possible can achieve the desired result, the system becomes a win-win system. Learning by all individuals is the outcome of a win-win system; in the win-lose system, grades, not learning, are the outcome.

Johnson and Johnson (1993) also advance that a cooperative context is best established by structuring most learning situations cooperatively. The teacher in the peaceable school implements cooperative learning activities that require collaboration and promote interdependence among class members. The teacher fosters a community-of-learners atmosphere that evokes the feeling that "we are all in this together" and that requires learners to help one another actively. Collaboration is the rule; competition is minimized or eliminated. All learners strive to be the best they can be and to do the best they can do.

The teacher builds a collaborative atmosphere by promoting the following simple notions among the students:

1. If one learner in the group can do something, everyone can learn to do it.

2. Learners working together can accomplish greater results than learners working independently.

3. If you can do something another cannot, you can help that other person reach the same level of success if you exercise patience and provide encouragement and assistance.

4. In any group (two or more individuals) situation—be the problem mental, physical, or social—"we" are smarter and more creative than "me."

Surely the goal of school is for all to learn. Cooperation enables that goal, whereas competition yields the "scarcity mentality" embedded in the notion that there is not enough opportunity for all to be winners; therefore, there must be losers: nonlearners.

MANAGING BEHAVIOR WITHOUT COERCION

The success of each learner in achieving quality depends above all else on the absence of coercion. To coerce is to compel or force another to act or think in a given manner—to dominate, restrain, or control another through the use of actual or implied force. The teacher in the peaceable school abandons as counterproductive the inclination to exercise forceful authority over the learners. Forceful authority is counterproductive to the cooperative context and to successful conflict resolution. The teacher in the peaceable school transfers the responsibility for acceptable behavior to the students—not through force or domination but through reason and support.

The successful creation of the peaceable school hinges upon each learner's fully accepting the responsibility to develop quality behavior. Only the teacher who abandons coercion can help students realize this goal. As Haim Ginott (1972) observes:

> I've come to the frightening conclusion that I am the decisive element in the classroom. It's my personal approach that creates the climate. It's my daily mood that makes the weather. As a teacher, I possess tremendous power to make a child's life miserable or joyous. I can be a tool of torture or an instrument of inspiration. I can humiliate or humor, hurt or heal. In all situations, it is my response that decides whether a crisis will be escalated or de-escalated and a child humanized or dehumanized. (pp. 15–16)

In any conflict situation an individual has only two choices for seeking basic need satisfaction—to problem solve toward a resolution of the conflict or to continue the conflict. By choosing not to problem solve, either as a conscious choice or due to the absence of problem-solving knowledge and ability, one chooses to attempt to gain need satisfaction by forcing others in the conflict to do what one wants them to do. This force may be either active aggression or passive aggression, but either is coercion. Because the individual is constantly seeking need satisfaction, coercion is the only behavior choice available when he or she chooses to continue the conflict.

Because behavior management is always within a conflict situation, it is imperative that adults model problem solving rather than coercion as they seek to create a constructive learning environment.

Rights and Responsibilities

To build the foundation for learners to make responsible behavioral choices in the classroom and school, and to develop a culture where human dignity and self-esteem are valued, all individuals must understand their basic human rights, respect those rights for self and others, and learn how to exercise their rights without infringing upon the rights of others. This is the foundation for peace. Teaching respect for human rights and the responsibilities inherent in those rights begins with the adoption of rights and responsibilities to govern the school and the classrooms in it. These rights and responsibilities become the constitution under which the rules and conventions of management and interaction are generated.

Rights are guaranteed conditions—privileges or freedoms that are given to everyone all the time. They are what you should always expect. *Responsibilities* are something one is always expected to do, a way one is always expected to act, and a way one is expected to treat someone else. There is a simple and direct relationship between rights and responsibilities in any social context: Enjoying a right requires everyone to accept and exercise certain responsibilities. A rights and responsibilities document that visually displays the relationship between each right and the related responsibility provides an easy tool for discussing behavioral expectations. Table 2 is a prototype of such a document, which may be applied in any setting.

This prototype is only an example; rights and responsibilities will likely vary from place to place. It is important only that the same rights and responsibilities govern all within a given place. Table 3 is a document that shows how one school, Leal Elementary School in Urbana, Illinois, stated its behavioral expectations when Richard Bodine served as principal.

In the context of our democratic culture, the notion of rights and related responsibilities makes sense to everyone. These behavioral expectations apply to all members of the school environment—adults or children, teachers or learners.

TABLE 2   Rights and Responsibilities

Rights	**Responsibilities**
I have the right:	**I have the responsibility:**
To be treated with respect and kindness: No one will tease me, demean me, or insult me.	To treat all others with respect and kindness by not teasing, demeaning, or insulting them.
To be myself: No one will treat me unfairly because of looks, abilities, beliefs, or gender.	To honor individual differences by treating all others fairly, regardless of looks, abilities, beliefs, or gender.
To be safe: No one will threaten me, bully me, or damage or remove my property.	To help make the environment safe by not acting dangerously, by securing my property, by not threatening or bullying others, and by respecting the property of others.
To be heard: No one will yell at me, and my opinions will be considered.	To listen to others, consider their opinions, and allow others to be heard.
To be free to express my feelings and opinions without criticism and to learn about myself through constructive feedback.	To express myself respectfully in ways others can hear me and to allow others to express themselves and to provide others with constructive feedback.
To learn and to be given assistance to do so.	To accept assistance when given in the spirit of increasing my opportunity to learn and grow and to unconditionally provide assistance to others whenever I can do so.
To a comfortable, supportive, challenging, and appropriate learning environment.	To contribute to, and not detract from, the learning environment.
To expect that all rights will be mine in all circumstances and to receive assistance from those in charge when that is not the case.	To protect my rights and the rights of others by exercising my full responsibilities at all times and by helping others to do the same.

TABLE 3 Rights and Responsibilities at Leal School

My Rights	My Responsibilities
I have the right to be happy and to be treated with compassion in this school: This means that no one will laugh at me or hurt my feelings.	I have the responsibility to treat others with compassion: This means that I will not laugh at others, tease others, or try to hurt the feelings of others.
I have the right to be myself in this school: This means that no one will treat me unfairly because I am . . . black or white fat or thin tall or short boy or girl adult or child.	I have the responsibility to respect others as individuals and not to treat others unfairly because they are . . . black or white fat or thin tall or short boy or girl adult or child.
I have the right to be safe in this school: This means that no one will . . . hit me kick me push me pinch me threaten me hurt me.	I have the responsibility to make the school safe by not . . . hitting anyone kicking anyone pushing anyone pinching anyone threatening anyone hurting anyone.
I have the right to expect my property to be safe in this school.	I have the responsibility not to take or destroy the property of others.
I have the right to hear and be heard in this school: This means that no one will . . . yell scream shout make loud noises or otherwise disturb me.	I have the responsibility to help maintain a calm and quiet school: This means that I will not . . . yell scream shout make loud noises or otherwise disturb others.
I have the right to learn about myself and others in this school: This means that I will be free to express my feelings and opinions without being interrupted or punished.	I have the responsibility to learn about myself and others in this school: This means that I will be free to express my feelings and opinions without being interrupted or punished and I will not interrupt or punish others who express their feelings and opinions.
I have the right to be helped to learn self-control in this school: This means that no one will silently stand by while I abuse my rights.	I have the responsibility to learn self-control in this school: This means that I will strive to exercise my rights without denying the same rights to others and I will expect to be corrected when I do abuse the rights of others, as they shall be corrected if my rights are abused.
I have the right to expect that all these rights will be mine in all circumstances so long as I am exercising my full responsibilities.	I have the responsibility to protect my rights and the rights of others by exercising my full responsibilities in all circumstances.

Note. From *Leal School Staff Handbook* by R. J. Bodine, unpublished manuscript, n.d., Leal School, Urbana, Illinois.

With such a constitution in place, the teacher in the peaceable school is in a position to establish expectations for work and behavior in the learning environment. For example, an expectation for work may state that learners must choose activities to pursue; they may not elect to do nothing. An expectation for behavior might be that when a fellow learner asks for help, you should provide whatever assistance you can. Such expectations, as simple and few as possible, are designed to guarantee that all learners will be engaged in learning activities and will not disrupt one another's learning opportunities. The teacher is responsible for promoting acceptable and successful behaviors from every learner. Each learner is expected to strive for quality—do the best he or she can do and be the best he or she can be. Because no student who feels threatened or coerced can engage in quality learning or quality behavior, and because coercion is counter-productive to the cooperative context and a poor model for conflict resolution, the teacher must be unconditionally committed to managing the classroom without coercion. This commitment, enacted through the kind of sense-based behavior management system discussed in the following pages, is the foundation of the classroom discipline program.

Punishment Versus Discipline

Are the idea of a discipline program and the notion of behavior management without coercion contradictory? The answer is a resounding no, but the question is certainly understandable. Many existing discipline programs are misnamed. It would be more accurate to call them punishment programs. Punishment is coercive; discipline is educational. Table 4 contrasts punishment and discipline.

Punishment is a poor deterrent to undesirable behavior. It often results in an angry recipient who focuses on revenge behaviors or a compliant one who attempts to follow the rules out of fear. Because punishment does not teach appropriate behaviors, it frequently leads to repetition of the undesirable (punished) behavior or the exhibition of an equally undesirable behavior.

Compliance is the recourse of the learner who wishes to avoid punishment. The learner acquiesces to an authority. Behavior change, if any, is usually predicated on fear—either fear of the person in authority or fear of the consequences of not doing as expected. Perhaps one of the main reasons that many school discipline programs no longer work with many students is that those students have no fear—they have already experienced things far worse than the school can or would do to them. A tendency to yield to others runs counter to the philosophy of the peaceable school. Compliance negates thinking: The learner accepts, at least temporarily, the logic of the authority. The compliant learner does not examine alternative behaviors to find the one that would be most need fulfilling in the given situation. Compliant behavior is also contrary to conflict resolution. Because compliance rarely fulfills one's needs, the compliant behavior tends to

TABLE 4 Punishment Versus Discipline

Punishment	Discipline
Expresses power of an authority; usually causes pain to the recipient; is based upon retribution or revenge; is concerned with what has happened (the past).	Is based on logical or natural consequences that embody the reality of a social order (rules that one must learn and accept to function adequately and productively in society); concerned with what is happening now (the present).
Is arbitrary—probably applied inconsistently and unconditionally; does not accept or acknowledge exceptions or mitigating circumstances.	Is consistent—accepts that the behaving individual is doing the best he or she can do for now.
Is imposed by an authority (done to someone), with responsibility assumed by the one administering the punishment and the behaving individual avoiding responsibility.	Comes from within, with responsibility assumed by the behaving individual and the behaving individual desiring responsibility; presumes that conscience is internal.
Closes options for the individual, who must pay for a behavior that has already occurred.	Opens options for the individual, who can choose a new behavior.
As a teaching process, usually reinforces a failure identity; essentially negative and short term, without sustained personal involvement of either teacher or learner.	As a teaching process, is active and involves close, sustained, personal involvement of both teacher and learner; emphasizes developing ways to act that will result in more successful behavior.
Is characterized by open or concealed anger; is a poor model for the expectation of quality.	Is friendly and supportive; provides a model of quality behavior.
Is easy and expedient.	Is difficult and time-consuming.
Focuses on strategies intended to control behavior of the learner.	Focuses on the learner's behavior and the consequences of that behavior.
Rarely results in positive changes in behavior; may increase subversiveness or result in temporary suppression of behavior; at best, produces compliance.	Usually results in a change in behavior that is more successful, acceptable, and responsible; develops the capacity for self-evaluation of behavior.

be inconsistently displayed in the presence of the authority and to disappear in the absence of the authority. In a school setting, it is true that a teacher can easily manage a group of compliant learners. However, the teacher in the peaceable school must accept that quality learning and quality behavior bear little relationship to compliance.

Punishment frustrates all of the recipient's basic psychological needs (belonging, power, freedom, and fun). The relationship between the recipient and the person administering the punishment is diminished, stymieing the recipient's ability to meet the need for belonging. Because of punishment's negative focus, the recipient is likely to be ostracized by appropriately behaving peers and will seek out inappropriately behaving peers in an effort to belong. Punishment obviously restricts freedom and is not pleasurable—it causes emotional and sometimes physical pain. Punishment diminishes the power of the recipient, who typically blames the punisher for causing the problem and does not view himself or herself as being in a position to solve it. The punisher is viewed as the one with the power to control behavior, and the recipient of punishment sees no reason to engage in self-evaluation of behavior, a strategy critical to conflict resolution.

Discipline, on the other hand, helps promote self-evaluation of behavior. By learning to behave consistently in an acceptable manner, one earns freedom because those with the authority to manage choices trust that acceptable choices will be made and appropriate actions will follow. The more learners are in effective control of their behavior, the more powerful they feel. The more successful they are in choosing acceptable behaviors, the more likely they are to be engaged by others who behave appropriately. Thus, life in school becomes more need fulfilling and pleasurable. The learner grows in self-confidence and self-esteem and becomes increasingly able to participate in creative and constructive conflict resolution.

Sense-Based Versus Rule-Abundant Behavior Management Systems

In the peaceable school, the teacher knows that discipline is a positive learning experience based on the learner's self-evaluation and choice. Both the self-evaluation of behavior and the generation and evaluation of alternative behavioral choices are fundamental to success in conflict resolution processes. The teacher develops a plan to engage learners in activities that promote responsibility education and quality behavior. A *sense-based system* for defining and managing behavior is fundamental to this plan.

Each learner must fully understand the behavioral expectations of the school and the classroom. Such understanding is simplified when expectations make sense to the learner. Expectations make sense when there is a logical, age-appropriate explanation for their existence; when rules are few and simple; when expectations are predictable and can be applied to new situations; and when the consequences for inappropriate behavior are known, nonpunitive, and consistently applied. The rights and responsibilities concept is understandable to students because it is based on a logical system of thought—a system fundamental to our democratic traditions. Rules within such a framework simply serve to let everyone know his or her responsibilities and safeguard the rights of all: In other words, rules make explicit the relationship between responsibilities and rights. Such a logical and fundamentally simple notion provides students with a framework they can use even without adult intervention to determine what is and is not acceptable behavior. This type of independent assessment is crucial to the school-wide implementation of a conflict resolution program. In brief, the sense-based system for determining acceptable and unacceptable behavior reduces rule confusion and concerns regarding the uniform enforcement of rules.

A *rule-abundant system* is the antithesis of the sense-based approach. In a rule-abundant system, the various rules appear to be unconnected and unrelated, rules are many and complex, expectations are not easily applied to new situations, and the consequences for inappropriate behavior—usually punitive—are neither understandable nor consistently applied. In such a system, rules proliferate with each new problem because those in charge of the system depend on rules to solve problems (conflicts). These rules become sacred—often more important than the problems they were designed to solve. The abundance of rules results because each crisis may require more than one rule to resolve. Often the need for extra rules becomes apparent only when the original rule is challenged by those whose behavior it was intended to control. Because rules are generated to address a specific crisis, often there is no rational, systematic basis for them as a whole.

A significant number of conflicts between students occur because of confusion regarding behavioral rules. When expectations are unclear, one learner is likely to attempt to satisfy a basic need in a way that thwarts another learner's attempt to satisfy a basic need. Even if the individual learner knows all the rules, he or she may still feel unjustly singled out. Complaints like "But Susie did the same thing, and she wasn't punished" or "I was just doing what I've been told to do when John picked on me. Why don't you reprimand John?" are common.

Under a sense-based system, questions such as "What right did you violate?" "Do you think anyone's rights were denied in this situation?" "Did you exercise your responsibility?" and "Did you do the best you know how to do?" serve to help the learner evaluate his or her own behavior in a context of reason and logic rather than in the context of adult authority. It is difficult for a learner to evaluate his or her own behavior when rules seem arbitrary and the justification is "because I [the adult] said so." From the child's viewpoint, the rules of the system exist without justification. It is the adult's responsibility to provide this justification.

Table 5 contrasts the main characteristics of a sense-based behavior management system with those of a rule-abundant system. Clearly, the goals of the peaceable school will be best served if any rules cre-

TABLE 5   Characteristics of Sense-Based Versus Rule-Abundant Behavior Management Systems

Sense-Based System	Rule-Abundant System
Has a logical organization.	Lacks organization.
Rules are few and simple, predictable, and generalizable.	Rules are many and complex, lack predictability, and cannot be generalized (situation specific).
Consequences for inappropriate behavior are known and consistently applied.	Consequences for inappropriate behavior are unknown and/or inconsistently applied.
Authority derives from system.	Authority derives from those in charge.
Reduces rule confusion.	Is characterized by rule confusion.

ated are sensible and generalizable. Students cannot resolve behavioral conflicts within a system absent of behavioral norms. If the authority and justification for rules are the domain of the adults in the system, students cannot engage successfully in unassisted conflict resolution.

Fundamentals of a Classroom Discipline Program

As a framework for managing learner behavior without coercion, a discipline program includes educational strategies for promoting responsible behavior and intervention strategies for helping individual learners achieve quality behavior. The components of a classroom discipline program presuppose a rights and responsibilities constitution for the school and include the following: class meetings, life rules, CARE (Communication About Responsibility Education) time, and time-out. The conflict resolution strategies outlined in Sections 4, 5, and 6 (mediation, negotiation, and group problem solving) are also central to the overall approach.

The first two components of the noncoercive discipline program, class meetings and life rules, may be sufficient for most learners to internalize appropriate behaviors. Others will need additional attention and support from the teacher to understand expectations and to learn behaviors consistent with those expectations. The latter two components of the noncoercive discipline program, CARE time and time-out, help learners take effective control of their behavior in two distinct problem areas. Specifically, CARE time is used when the student is not producing quality work or following work guidelines, and time-out is used with the student who is disrupting the learning environment of others.

Class Meetings

As described in the introduction, class meetings are open-ended discussions, usually involving the entire class and facilitated by the teacher. They have two important and related uses with regard to the classroom discipline program: They provide an excellent environment in which to develop the knowledge and skill base required to make appropriate choices, and they are the vehicle for a conflict resolution process for social problem solving. Their specific functions include the following:

1. They introduce behavioral expectations and help learners understand the reasons for rules in the social setting.

2. They help learners understand their basic psychological needs, as well as appropriate choices they can make to meet their needs.

3. They help learners understand diversity, conflict, and problems.

4. They provide a forum for addressing individual and group educational and behavioral problems at both the classroom and school levels.

5. They help learners discover that everyone has both individual and group responsibilities for learning and for behaving in a way that fosters learning.

6. They help learners understand that, although the world may be difficult and may at times appear hostile and mysterious, they can use their minds to solve their problems.

7. They help learners see the relevance of the expected school and classroom behavior to behavioral expectations in real-life settings.

The class meeting can be a most effective vehicle for responsibility education. Although meetings are time-consuming, they are critical to the success of the classroom in promoting responsible behavior. As a rule, such meetings require considerable time during the early weeks of the school term because this is the time for orientation, teaching, and reteaching. However, the real payoff comes when meetings are scheduled regularly throughout the school term. Meeting activities are consistent with the desired learner outcomes of the responsibility education program. The activities provide a systematic way for learners to gain an understanding of and respect for self and others, to develop an understanding of behavior and of conflict, and to develop the social problem solving skills they will need in life. These are outcomes learners will not realize unless they have opportunities to explore behavioral alternatives and practice problem solving. Learners of every age experience difficulties in getting along with one another and find interpersonal problems most difficult to solve. Without help resolving these difficulties, learners tend to evade the problems, lie their way out of situations, depend on others to solve their problems, or just give up. None of these courses of action is constructive conflict resolution.

The class meeting is an appropriate forum for reviewing school rights and responsibilities, as well as any related rules and reasons behind those rules. It is also a forum for discussing the consequences of not following the rules, helping an individual or the group determine alternative behaviors to replace unacceptable ones, suggesting strategies to help an individual deal with someone who is creating a problem for him or her, and exploring a variety of ways to meet expectations. The class meeting can be a vehicle for generating expectations for the classroom—in other words, class rules.

Later in this section, there is a list of questions that may be used in class meetings to promote general understanding of rights and responsibilities, expectations, and their connecting relationships. Other class meeting questions are suggested in Sections 2 and 3 to promote understanding of the concepts of understanding conflict and understanding peace and peacemaking, respectively. Section 6 presents a special application of the class meeting format as a problem-solving strategy.

Rules for Rules

A rule is a statement that attempts either to clarify the relationship between a right and a responsibility or to emphasize the importance of a particular responsibility. To be consistent with a plan to manage behavior without coercion, rules generated must meet certain conditions:

A rule must make sense to those expected to abide by it and must fit under the general purview of the school constitution (in other words, rights and responsibilities). The rights and responsibilities provide the justification for rules. Whenever a rule is generated that might appear to students to be an exception to the constitution, an age-appropriate, sensible reason for the rule is required. Either a link to the rights and responsibilities is provided, or some other sensible justification is given.

There should be few rules. No one, especially children, can remember many rules. Many rules are implicit in the rights and responsibilities document. Specific rules are needed only to emphasize the seriousness of a behavior or to cover conditions not inherent in the rights and responsibilities. When an additional rule appears needed, determine whether a present rule can be eliminated. Perhaps a rule has achieved its purpose and no longer needs to be emphasized.

A rule is stated in the positive. Rules are more effective and meaningful when they describe desired rather than undesired behavior. A rule actually defines or describes behavior. Why would we want to define or describe unwanted behavior? Might that suggest a behavior to someone that he or she had not yet thought of?

A rule must be enforceable. A rule is useless unless it can be enforced in all circumstances in which it applies, regardless of the individuals involved in the circumstance. Consistency in the management of behavior is paramount. Unenforceable rules or selective enforcement of rules creates confusion regarding expectations. When a rule is not consistently applied, a significant number of individuals may be willing to risk not following the rule. If the rule is then enforced with those individuals, they can and will claim unfair treatment.

Rules are not sacred. A rule can be, must be, changed if it is not working to create the desired sense of community.

Breaking a rule results in a consequence. In a management system without coercion, the logical consequence that is always applicable in all circumstances for each individual is the requirement to choose another behavior that is acceptable within the social context—a responsible behavior. If it is deemed through the consensus process of constructing the management system that additional consequences are appropriate, those consequences must not be punitive or coercive. They also must be logical consequences. The characteristics of logical consequences are as follows:

1. *They are known in advance.* The rule and the consequence for not following the rule are clearly linked, and that link has been explained. The axiom is "If you choose not to follow the rule, you choose the consequence." If it is clearly communicated that choosing to fight at school results in a suspension of school privileges when one fights, one chooses the suspension when one chooses to fight. This clear relationship facilitates the questioning process "What are you doing?" and "What are you choosing when you do that?"

2. *They do not cause actual physical pain and do not involve public humiliation.* Logical consequences respond to the misbehavior in ways that preserve the behaver's dignity—the behavior is the problem, not the person exhibiting the behavior.

3. *They are related to the problem behavior.* A logical consequence reinforces an acceptable behavior. For example, the requirement to clean graffiti from a bathroom wall is related to drawing the graffiti on the wall. Rules also reinforce respect for public property.

Life Rules

With the rights and responsibilities constitution in place, the teacher as manager is in a position to establish expectations for work and behavior in the learning environment. Because the rights and responsibilities provide a framework to do so, learners can participate in establishing those expectations and will therefore have ownership. For example, an expectation for work may state that learners may choose learning activities to pursue; they may not elect to do nothing. An expectation for behavior might be that when a fellow learner asks for help, you should provide whatever assistance you can. Such expectations, as simple and few as possible, are designed to guarantee that all learners will be engaged fully in learning activities and that each will contribute actively to building the community of learners within the classroom. The teacher is responsible for promoting acceptable and successful behaviors from every learner. Each learner is expected to strive for quality—to do the best he or she can do and be the best he or she can be.

Obviously, classroom expectations must be congruent with those of the school, and discussions and other learning activities should be designed to help learners see the relationship between the two sets of expectations. Each classroom teacher develops—it is hoped with learner participation—any specific rules that might be needed because of special classroom circumstance (a gym class, a science lab, a machine shop, etc.) or special population circumstance, which would dictate that a rule be stated age appropriately (a kindergarten class, a class for mentally challenged learners, a program for severely emotionally challenged students, etc.). Any specific rules generated for specific locales within the school must be complementary to the rights and responsibilities and should meet the rules for rules. However, the rules may differ from locale to locale within the school. Rules for the gym may focus on safety issues; for the computer lab, on the respect for property; and for the classroom, on respect for one another and the learning environment.

Rules for the school and the classroom are the rules for success in any life venture. Helping learners make this connection is the ultimate goal of the responsibility education program. One possible focus for classroom expectations could be on life rules. The teacher could orchestrate a discussion of behavior expected in the real world that allows people to succeed and to get their needs satisfied. For example, when adults are responsible, prompt, prepared, participate, and show respect, their chances for success and satisfaction increase. Once these life rules are identified, the teacher facilitates discussions and activities designed to enable the class to translate each rule into a desired classroom behavior. Table 6 shows how life rules and classroom expectations relate.

Rules need to be flexible to accommodate genuine mitigating circumstances. Life rules are rarely rigid. For example, in real life, there are probably few absolute deadlines. Generally a deadline can be extended so that a quality result will be obtained. The life rules of the school and the classroom also must be reasonably flexible. The goal is to help learners comprehend the value of life rules. People of all ages tend to follow rules that enable them to get along and be safe. For example, games require rules that let all players play in the same manner to achieve a meaningful outcome; traffic signs enable drivers to travel with greater safety and a minimum of fear. The real reason a driver stops at a stop sign is not the possible consequence of getting a ticket but the belief that stopping is in the driver's best interest and in

TABLE 6   Life Rules and Classroom Expectations

Life Rules	Classroom Expectations
Be prompt.	Meet deadlines.
Be prepared.	Have materials. Listen for instructions. Follow directions.
Participate.	Be a part of discussion. Complete work. Stay engaged.
Show respect.	Honor self and others. Value property.
Be responsible.	Accept ownership. Plan more effective behavior.

the interest of others. A consequence in and of itself will not change a behavior. A consequence works only when learners find value in the relationship with the person asking them to do something or when they see value in what they are being asked to do.

Life rules are one "sense-based" foundation for rules—the rules make sense because valid reasons for them exist. Whatever validating base beyond rights and responsibilities is selected, adherence to the "rules for rules" is strategic. Involvement of learners in the creation of these rules for specific circumstances provides them a sense of ownership and solidifies understanding of the necessity for and desirability of the rules.

CARE Time

CARE (Communication About Responsibility Education) time is a brief period for the teacher and the learner to communicate about completion of work and engagement in classroom activities. This communication can be woven into the natural interactions of the teacher and learner within the classroom setting, or it can occur at a scheduled time during or outside the school day. The primary purpose of CARE time is to help learners focus on how they are acting, thinking, and feeling and on what they want; to help learners evaluate whether their chosen behaviors are helping them get their needs met effectively; and to help learners develop and commit to plans for effective, quality behavior.

During CARE time, the teacher poses questions such as the following:

1. *What are you doing?* Focus on total behavior—that is, how the learner is thinking, acting, and feeling. Help the learner understand that all behaviors are chosen.

2. *What do you want?* Focus on the learner's present picture and expand it to the learner's quality world—the way he or she wants life to be.

3. *Is the present behavior going to get you what you want?* Focus on getting the learner to evaluate his or her behavior.

4. *What can you do to get what you want?* Focus on developing a plan that has a good chance of success.

It is important to keep in mind that the learner who fails to complete work often sees no purpose in completing the work other than to avoid unpleasant consequences. Thus, work completion becomes a compliant behavior, not a need-fulfilling behavior. When compliance is the reason for completing work, work will rarely be of quality, nor will it be done consistently.

Even when learners see relevance to the work in progress and truly desire to do well, they may fail to meet agreed-upon deadlines. This situation requires feedback and counseling from the teacher. Learners typically miss deadlines because they lack experience with time management, underestimating either the time required to complete the activity or the scope of the job—it is more complicated or detailed than he or she thought. Learners may also underestimate quality—they do not fully visualize the goal (a quality product) until the learning activity is well under way. Self-evaluation and planning during CARE time will help the learner become a more efficient time manager.

The convention should exist that either the teacher or the learner may request CARE time. Students need to know that frustration is a part of learning and that it is permissible and advisable to request a conference with the teacher for help in addressing the problem.

Time-Out

The primary purpose of time-out is to temporarily remove the learner from a situation where he or she is disrupting the learning environment of others. It is not intended as punishment. Self-evaluation is the only way to promote long-term change in learner behavior. When used properly, time-out will encourage the learner to self-evaluate and make better behavioral choices. In the peaceable school, the process follows a sports analogy: As in sports, school time-out is used to break the momentum, evaluate the situation, and formulate a plan. The message should be "Something is out of sync, and we need to work it out." The plan that the learner develops in time-out emphasizes the positive behavior that he or she is willing to engage in when the learning activity is resumed—for example, "I will do my work and not disrupt others who are working" or "I'll keep my hands and feet to myself."

Time-out is an effective strategy only when the learner and the teacher perceive it as a favorable method for working out problems. If this is to happen, both the classroom atmosphere and the time-out must be positive and noncoercive. Time-out is in essence an opportunity for the learner to evaluate his or her behaviors. It is a process that enables the learner to determine that he or she is responsible for behavioral choices. In addition, time-out gives the learner a chance to develop the skills for making more effective behavioral choices.

The time-out location should be comfortable and conducive to problem solving. It may be an area of a classroom or another, separate place in the school. When taking a time-out, the learner needs a place to become calm, think about the situation, and develop a plan to return to classroom activities. The duration of the time-out is up to the learner. The teacher may set a minimum time to avoid further disruption of classroom activities, but ideally the learner returns to the group when he or she has an acceptable plan of action. The idea is to keep the learner in class and engaged in learning activities, not to interrupt his or her education.

Time-out is, in a sense, a last resort. When a behavior problem occurs in the classroom, the teacher first attempts to work it out with the learner, using an in-class intervention. When a learner disrupts the class, the preferred approach is for the teacher to ask questions to encourage the learner to evaluate his or her behavior. The questions focus the learner's attention on the behavior. The teacher can ask one question and continue with other classroom activities, perhaps without waiting for a verbal response. The intent is to have the learner answer the question for himself or herself. It is very difficult for the learner to avoid thinking about the question. The number and types of questions the teacher asks are determined by the severity of behavior, the activity under way, the learner involved, and so on. The tone of the questioning must always be noncoercive. The following specific questions are helpful:

1. *To identify the expected and/or target behavior:* "What are you doing?" "Could you please find a space to work on your own?" or "Are you following our rules?"

2. *If the learner continues the unacceptable behavior:* "What is the rule about [specific behavior being challenged]?" "Are you following our rule about this?" or "Is what you're doing against the rules?"

3. *If the learner still does not stop the unacceptable behavior:* "Are you choosing time-out?" or "Do you know what you need to do to stay in this classroom?" and "Will you do it?"

If the disruptive behavior continues after two or three interventions, it is best to talk briefly with the learner in private. If that isn't possible, the learner should go to the classroom time-out area. To end the time-out and return to classroom activities, the learner must formulate an action plan. The plan may be either verbal or written, depending on the skill and ability of the student and the preference of the teacher.

Verbal plan. The learner unobtrusively signals the teacher that he or she has a plan and would like to rejoin the group. As soon as possible the teacher goes to the time-out area and asks what the plan is. If the plan is acceptable, the learner returns to the classroom activities; if not, the learner stays in time-out to develop another plan. If possible, the teacher should talk with the learner about the plan. It is especially useful to relate the learner's plan—acceptable or unacceptable—to the behavior that triggered the time-out. A good way to do this is by asking questions—often the same questions the teacher asked before sending the learner to time-out.

A sometimes effective alternative to the teacher's visiting the learner in the time-out area to discuss the plan is for the teacher to signal the learner to return to the group. The learner's ability, or lack thereof, to participate appropriately testifies to the plan. It is especially important to talk to the learner about the plan at a later, more convenient time.

Written plan. If the student has the skills to write a plan, and the teacher prefers that approach, forms for these plans are kept in the time-out area. (See the STAR form on page 40 for an example.) The learner must complete the form before signaling the teacher and returning to classroom activities. The teacher should approve the plan and, if possible, discuss it briefly with the learner. If the learner has trouble completing a plan, the teacher should help by raising the same questions used for CARE time: "What do you want?" and "Is what you are doing helping you get what you want?"

When a learner disrupts classroom activities while in the time-out area or fails to follow the plan developed in time-out, he or she may need to take time-out outside the classroom. If possible, the teacher should first discuss behavioral choices with the learner and ask if he or she is choosing time-out outside the classroom. If the unacceptable behavior still does not cease, the learner should be sent to the out-of-class time-out area.

The out-of-class time-out area should be supervised by an adult who will encourage the learner to discuss what is happening that resulted in a time-out and assist the learner in devising an alternative to the problem behavior in order to return to the classroom as soon as possible. The duration of time-out will vary for each learner. There is no benefit in holding a learner for a set length of time. Such a practice tends to breed resentment, anger, and a desire for revenge. The learner should be allowed to rejoin the class when he or she has developed a satisfactory plan.

In most schools there is a schoolwide time-out room, although it is probably not labeled as such. A learner who exhibits unacceptable behavior is usually referred to the principal's office and engaged by either the principal or another staff member designated to handle discipline problems. This system can rather easily be adapted to the time-out practices described here. It is recommended that the learner be required to have an acceptable written plan before returning to class. A plan sheet similar to the in-class form can be used, and the time-out

STAR Plan (Success Through Acting Responsibly)

My behavior (What am I doing?)

_____

_____

_____

_____

My plan (I will . . .)

_____

_____

_____

_____

Name _____ Date_____

supervisor can help the learner develop the plan and complete the form. A conference with the classroom teacher is also called for—not to punish the learner but to ensure that the plan has been thought through and that the learner has evaluated the previous behavior. This conference also reestablishes the teacher's and the learner's shared responsibility to preserve the learning environment and to strive for quality.

The importance of the peaceable school environment to the success of a conflict resolution program cannot be overemphasized. Learners need a friendly, supportive atmosphere to engage productively in self-evaluation and to risk trying new behaviors. A relationship of mutual appreciation and trust between the teacher and each learner is required for the development of quality behavior. This relationship depends heavily on a system of rules and expectations that is sensible and predictable. The success of each learner in achieving quality depends above all else on the absence of coercion: The teacher's most important challenge in the peaceable school is to relate consistently in a noncoercive way to each learner. The disciplinary interactions between teacher and learner provide a most obvious and important opportunity for the teacher to model constructive conflict resolution.

QUESTIONS FOR CLASS MEETINGS

The following questions and statements, given in no particular order, may be used in class meetings to promote understanding of the content of this section.

Responsibility Education

1. What is responsibility?
2. Give examples of occasions when you felt you exhibited responsible behavior.
3. Can you give an example of a situation in which someone else behaved in a manner that you thought was responsible?
4. Describe an action you have taken that you are proud of.
5. What is right?
6. What is wrong?
7. How do you decide right from wrong?
8. How do you help someone who is having difficulty following the rules? How can someone help you?
9. Describe something someone else did that made you feel proud of him or her.
10. What is a friend?
11. What does freedom mean?
12. What would you like to change about yourself?
13. What would you not like to have to change about yourself?
14. What motivates you to do your best?
15. Who understands you?
16. How do you feel about yourself?
17. How do you think others see you?
18. Whom do you understand?
19. Describe your most cherished privilege.

Cooperation

1. What is cooperation?
2. What is competition?
3. Give examples of occasions when you felt you showed cooperative behavior.
4. How did you feel when you cooperated?

5. How do you think others felt when you cooperated?

6. Can you give an example of a situation in which someone else behaved in a manner that you thought was cooperative?

7. How do you feel when you compete and win? Compete and lose?

8. Describe situations or activities where you believe cooperation is essential.

9. Describe situations or activities where you believe cooperation would not be helpful.

10. Is cooperation ever harmful?

11. When is competition essential?

12. Is competition ever harmful?

Suggested Readings

Bodine, R. J., & Crawford, D. K. (1999). *Developing emotional intelligence: A guide to behavior management and conflict resolution in schools.* Champaign, IL: Research Press.

Crary, E. (1984). *Kids can cooperate.* Seattle: Parenting Press.

Crawford, D. K., Bodine, R. J., & Hoglund, R. G. (1993). *The school for quality learning: Managing the school and classroom the Deming way.* Champaign, IL: Research Press.

Girard, K., & Koch, S. J. (1996). *Conflict resolution in the schools: A manual for educators.* San Francisco: Jossey-Bass.

Glasser, W. (1965). *Reality therapy.* New York: Harper & Row.

Johnson, D. W., & Johnson, R. T. (1975). *Learning together and alone: Cooperation, competition, and individualization.* Englewood Cliffs, NJ: Prentice Hall.

Lantieri, L., & Patti, J. (1996). *Waging peace in our schools.* Boston: Beacon.

Rhoades, J., & McCabe, M. E. (1992). *The cooperative classroom: Social and academic activities.* Bloomington, IN: National Educational Service.

Schniedewind, N., & Davidson, E. (1987). *Cooperative learning, cooperative lives: A sourcebook of activities for building a peaceful world.* Dubuque, IA: William C. Brown.

Schrumpf, F., Crawford, D. K., & Bodine, R. J. (1997). *Peer mediation: Conflict resolution in schools* (Rev. ed.). Champaign, IL: Research Press.

1 Introduction

PURPOSE To learn what the peaceable school is about and to become familiar with the class meeting strategy and its ground rules

MATERIALS Student Manuals

FORMAT OPTION Class meeting

PROCEDURE

1. Welcome students and explain that what they learn in the forthcoming activities will help them work together to create a peaceable school. Discuss the ideas on pages 3–4 of the Student Manual, "Introduction," summarizing what students will learn to help them create a peaceable school.

2. Next explain that the class meeting is an open-ended discussion and a strategy that will be used to help build a peaceable school. Refer students to "Ground Rules for the Class Meeting" on page 5 in the Student Manual.

3. To illustrate Rule 1, have class members arrange themselves in a circle. Discuss why the circle arrangement might be advantageous (for example, it allows each person to see every other person, and it confers no special status on any one person).

4. Discuss Rule 2 by asking the following questions:

   > In a discussion, what can we assume about the person who is silent?

   > Can we expect others to know what we are thinking or feeling if we don't speak up?

5. To explain Rule 3, demonstrate interrupting by asking a volunteer to tell about a playground problem. As the student talks, frequently interrupt: Tell your view of the problem, ask questions, agree and disagree often with the student.

6. Explain Rule 4 by asking another volunteer to tell about a playground problem. As the student talks, interrupt and tell the student you think he or she is wrong, the idea is silly, and so forth. Discuss with the group the effect of criticism or sarcasm. Ask what feelings and behaviors this evokes in others—for example, anger, resentment, withdrawal.

7. Explain Rule 5 by asking another volunteer to talk about a playground problem. Summarize what the student says as a way of modeling what is expected.

8. Allow several pairs of students to demonstrate Rule 5 by having one person speak and the other listen and summarize. Ask why this behavior is important. Possible responses are that it allows the speaker to know he or she was heard and allows the group to hear each idea twice.

Student Manual
page 3

Introduction

IMAGINE . . .

♦ A school where you and your peers peacefully resolve your conflicts

♦ A classroom where you work together with peers . . . trusting, helping, and sharing

♦ A lunchroom where you observe carefully, communicate accurately, and listen to understand

♦ A playground where you respect, appreciate, and celebrate your differences

♦ A principal's office where you express feelings, particularly anger and frustration, in ways that do not hurt others

This is the vision of the peaceable school.
In the peaceable school, all of these
behaviors happen in each of these places.

3

Student Manual
page 4

WHAT YOU WILL LEARN

To help you build a peaceable school, you will learn about:

- ♦ The class meeting

- ♦ Rights and responsibilities

- ♦ Rules

- ♦ Cooperation

To help you understand how to get along, you will learn about:

- ♦ Conflict

- ♦ Peace and peacemaking

To help you resolve problems, you will learn about:

- ♦ Negotiation

- ♦ Mediation

- ♦ Group problem solving

4

Student Manual
page 5

Ground Rules for the Class Meeting

RULE 1   Participants sit in a circle.

RULE 2   Every member of the class is responsible for communication (*listening and speaking*).

RULE 3   The *"Rule of Focus"* applies to all discussion. This means that whoever is speaking will be allowed to talk without being interrupted.

RULE 4   Participants show respect for others. This means no criticism or sarcasm toward group members or their ideas.

RULE 5   Each time someone in the group finishes making a statement, another group member summarizes and clarifies it before anyone goes on to a new idea.

The class meeting is a strategy that will help build a peaceable school.

5

A CTIVITY

2 Responsibility Is . . .

PURPOSE To understand responsibility as a behavior

MATERIALS Student Manuals
Newsprint
Markers

FORMAT OPTIONS Whole class discussion/participation
Class meeting

PROCEDURE
1. Refer students to page 6 in their Student Manuals, "What Responsibility Means to Me." Explain that the idea of responsibility is important to people who live and work together.

2. Divide the class into groups of four or five. Give each group a few sheets of newsprint and some markers. Ask each group to discuss the chores or jobs they are expected to do at home. Have each group make a list of these chores or jobs.

3. Invite the groups to share their lists, then post them in the room.

4. Explain that each chore or job that we are expected to do regularly is a responsibility and that others must be able to trust that we will do our chores and jobs—that we will exercise our responsibilities.

5. Ask the class to share ways they are expected to behave at home. Give examples, such as saying thank you or excuse me, cleaning up your own mess, and showing respect for adults. Once the class has the idea, invite the small groups to create a second list of these expectations.

6. Ask the groups to share their lists; post them next to the chores and jobs lists for each group. Explain that the way we are always expected to behave is a responsibility.

7. Examine the posted lists and find some common at-home responsibilities for class members.

8. Ask each group to develop five rules for a home that would tell a stranger what the responsibilities would be if he or she moved into that home.

9. Have the groups share their ideas with the class.

10. Draw out ideas from the class to define responsibility. Be sure the following concepts are included:

    Something you are always expected to do

    A way you are always expected to act

    A way you are expected to treat someone else

11. Have the students write or draw their own ideas about responsibility on page 6 of their Student Manuals, then discuss.

*Student Manual
page 6*

What Responsibility Means to Me

INSTRUCTIONS: In the boxes, write words or draw pictures that come to mind when you think of responsibility.

RESPONSIBILITY

Peace is a responsibility.

6

Activity

3   What Is a Right?

PURPOSE   To understand that a right is a guaranteed condition

MATERIALS   Student Manuals
Easel pad and marker

FORMAT OPTION   Class meeting

PROCEDURE

1. Arrange the students in the class meeting circle. Explain that the purpose of this class meeting is to understand what a right is.

2. Tell the class to think about the word *privilege* and the word *freedom*. Ask the class to give examples of privileges (for example, being allowed to use the computer if other work is completed ahead of time) or freedoms (for example, choosing your own friends) given to students during the school day.

3. On the easel pad, list the privileges and freedoms students generate. After several examples are recorded, ask:

   What is a privilege?

   What is a freedom?

   How are they different or the same?

   Elicit the idea that freedom and privilege are synonymous. Young children may be more familiar with the word *privilege,* but it is important for them to understand the word *freedom* as well.

4. Tell the class that privileges or freedoms that are given to everyone all the time are called *rights.* Ask students to write or draw some things they think students have the right to do on page 7 of their Student Manuals, "What Rights Mean to Me."

5. Compile students' ideas on the easel pad under the heading "Students Have the Right to . . ." Reduce the list to those items the group agrees should be rights for everyone, all the time.

6. Ask what other rights the group thinks students have in school. Add these to the list on the easel pad.

7. Post the list and tell the class to think on their own about the rights of students. If they think of other ideas, they should tell you, and you will ask the group at the next meeting if the ideas could be added. (Note: The rights poster will be used again in Activity 4.)

Student Manual
page 7

What Rights Mean to Me

INSTRUCTIONS: In the boxes, write words or draw pictures that come to mind when you think of rights.

RIGHTS

Peace is a right.

7

ACTIVITY

4   Rights and Responsibilities

PURPOSE   To understand the relationship between rights and responsibilities

MATERIALS   Student Manuals
Rights poster (saved from Activity 3)
Newsprint
Markers
Rights and Responsibilities chart (See p. 54 of this guide; one copy for each student. Use your school's own Rights and Responsibilities chart if one exists.)

FORMAT OPTIONS   Whole class discussion/participation
Class meeting

PROCEDURE
1. Refer students to page 8 in their Student Manuals, "Rights and Responsibilities." Review the definition of responsibility and the idea that rights are guaranteed conditions.

2. Review the rights poster students created in Activity 3. Ask about any additional ideas for rights and add those the class agrees should be included. Emphasize the idea that, even though rights are guaranteed conditions, enjoying rights requires everyone to accept certain responsibilities.

3. Give each group of four or five students some sheets of newsprint and markers. Assign each group an equal number of the rights listed on the poster. Ask the group to draw a picture or list words to describe a responsibility to correspond to each right assigned to the group. For example: "We said students have the right to be safe in school. One responsibility to help preserve that right would be that no one should throw rocks at anyone else."

4. Invite the groups to explain their drawings or word collections. Allow other students to ask for clarification.

5. Refer students to "My Rights and Responsibilities" on page 9 in their Student Manuals. Encourage them to make a list of their own personal rights and responsibilities.

6. Discuss the personal lists, making sure students understand the main idea that rights are guaranteed conditions (what you should always expect) but that enjoying rights requires everyone to accept

certain responsibilities (always doing something or acting in a certain way).

7. Give each student a copy of the Rights and Responsibilities chart. Explain that, in a peaceable school, everyone has the same rights and the same responsibilities: "These are the rights and responsibilities for our school. These rights and responsibilities apply to all persons, at all times, and in all places in our school. The responsibilities are the behaviors expected from us all so that we all will enjoy the rights."

Student Manual
page 8

Rights and Responsibilities

RIGHTS ARE . . .

◆ Guaranteed conditions
(what you should always expect)

RESPONSIBILITIES ARE . . .

◆ Something you are always expected to do

◆ A way you are always expected to act

◆ A way you are expected to treat someone else

Enjoying a right requires everyone to
accept certain responsibilities.

8

Student Manual
page 9

My Rights and Responsibilities

INSTRUCTIONS: Write some of your own rights and responsibilities.

RIGHTS	**RESPONSIBILITIES**
Example: I have the right to be myself and be respected.	*Example:* I have the responsibility to respect others, even if they are different from me.

9

Rights and Responsibilities

Rights

I have the right:

To be treated with respect and kindness: No one will tease me, demean me, or insult me.

To be myself: No one will treat me unfairly because of looks, abilities, beliefs, or gender.

To be safe: No one will threaten me, bully me, or damage or remove my property.

To be heard: No one will yell at me, and my opinions will be considered.

To be free to express my feelings and opinions without criticism and to learn about myself through constructive feedback.

To learn and to be given assistance to do so.

To a comfortable, supportive, challenging, and appropriate learning environment.

To expect that all rights will be mine in all circumstances and to receive assistance from those in charge when that is not the case.

Responsibilities

I have the responsibility:

To treat all others with respect and kindness by not teasing, demeaning, or insulting them.

To honor individual differences by treating all others fairly, regardless of looks, abilities, beliefs, or gender.

To help make the environment safe by not acting dangerously, by securing my property, by not threatening or bullying others, and by respecting the property of others.

To listen to others, consider their opinions, and allow others to be heard.

To express myself respectfully in ways others can hear me and to allow others to express themselves and to provide others with constructive feedback.

To accept assistance when given in the spirit of increasing my opportunity to learn and grow and to unconditionally provide assistance to others whenever I can do so.

To contribute to, and not detract from, the learning environment.

To protect my rights and the rights of others by exercising my full responsibilities at all times and by helping others to do the same.

Creating the Peaceable School (2nd ed.) © 2002 by R. L. Bodine, D. K. Crawford, and F. Schrumpf. Research Press (800) 519-2707.

5   Rules

PURPOSE To learn that the real purposes of rules are (a) to let everyone know his or her responsibilities and (b) to safeguard the rights of all

MATERIALS Student Manuals
Easel pad and marker
Rights and Responsibilities chart (from Activity 4)

FORMAT OPTION Class meeting

PROCEDURE 1. Explain that a rule usually makes clear the relationship between a right and a responsibility. For example:

Rule 1: Show Respect for Others

Implies that each person has the right to be himself or herself and that each has the responsibility to treat others fairly and with compassion.

Implies that each person has the right to be physically and emotionally safe and that each has the responsibility not to hurt others.

Rule 2: Be Prepared to Learn

Implies that each person has the right to take maximum advantage of the learning opportunities offered and that each has the responsibility to be ready by having the materials needed so that others don't have to wait.

Implies that each person has the right to expect that activities will proceed as planned and that each has the responsibility to listen for instructions and follow directions.

2. Encourage students to suggest rules for the classroom. Discuss the implicit relationship between rights and responsibilities in each of the rules students propose. (There may be several implicit relationships for each rule.)

3. Have students narrow the list to five rules that will help everyone in the classroom. Write these rules on the easel pad. When the five rules are agreed upon, ask if each can be justified through the school's Rights and Responsibilities. Modify the list until the rules are justifiable by the school's Rights and Responsibilities. Post this final list in the classroom.

4. Have students copy these five rules to page 10 of their Student Manuals, "Rules for Our Class." Explain that these rules are all founded on the school's Rights and Responsibilities. However, other rules may also be founded on the same Rights and Responsibilities. Indicate that these are the rules that this class will emphasize, but other classes may have different rules.

5. Discuss some different rules that might exist for the gym, the playground, the library, and so forth.

Student Manual
page 10

Rules for Our Class

INSTRUCTIONS: Write five rules for our class.

RULE 1 _____
_____
_____

RULE 2 _____
_____
_____

RULE 3 _____
_____
_____

RULE 4 _____
_____
_____

RULE 5 _____
_____
_____
_____

Rules let everyone know his or her responsibilities
and safeguard the rights of all.

10

A C T I V I T Y

6   Cooperation Is . . .

PURPOSE   To understand cooperation as a behavior

MATERIALS   Student Manuals
Butcher paper
Tape
Markers
Writing paper and pencils

FORMAT OPTIONS   Whole class discussion/participation
Cooperative learning

PROCEDURE
1. Prepare a large banner of butcher paper and post it on a wall in the classroom. Write the word *cooperation* in the middle of the banner.

2. Ask class members to share an example of a time when they had to cooperate with another person to accomplish a task.

3. Ask several members of the class to define cooperation. Elicit the idea that cooperation means to share, to work together, to help one another, and so on. It may help to raise the idea that cooperation is different from competition.

4. Divide the class into groups of three students each. Have the three students face one another, each holding a clenched fist: Students shake their fists up and down together four times and count, "One, two, three, four." On the count of four, each one puts out any number of fingers from zero to five. The goal is for students to put out a total of 11 fingers. Each group keeps trying until they succeed in having 11 fingers out. The group may not talk during this time.

5. Next have each group try to total 23 fingers, with each person using both hands.

6. Discuss the activity by asking the following questions:

   What made this activity difficult?

   What helped your group to succeed?

   Did you do better the second time, when you tried to total 23 fingers? If so, why?

7. Ask students to pair up with someone they don't know very well. Ask each pair to get one pencil and one sheet of paper. Tell students that they cannot talk during this exercise. Ask students to grip the pencil together and, without talking, write the word *cooperate* and draw a peace symbol on the sheet of paper. Encourage the pairs to try this twice.

8. Discuss this activity, using the following questions:

   What made this activity difficult?

   What helped you to succeed?

   Did you do better the second time? If so, why?

9. Refer students to the "Cooperation" illustration on page 11 of their Student Manuals. Ask students to describe what they see in these drawings and what they think the drawings mean.

10. Point out that cooperation is a behavior that allows each person involved to succeed or to get his or her needs satisfied. Cooperation allows everyone involved to win, and no one loses. Therefore, cooperation is called a win-win behavior. When problems are solved by cooperating, everyone involved can feel good.

11. Instruct students to draw pictures on the banner that show cooperation, as the cooperation illustration in their Student Manuals does. Tell the class they can work as pairs or groups of four to five students to develop the pictures.

12. Leave the banner up for at least a week; encourage students to add pictures to it at any time.

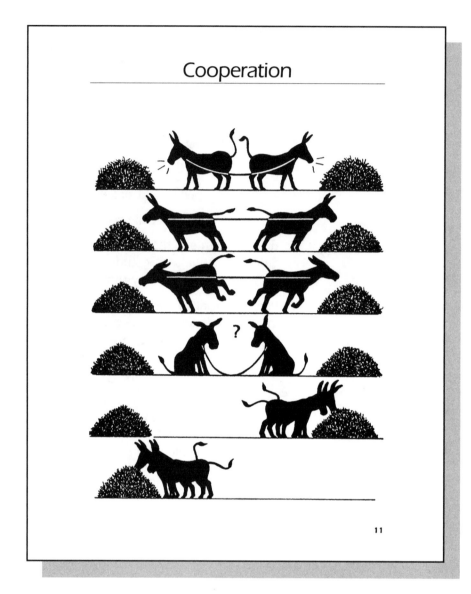

A C T I V I T Y

7   What's in the Box?

PURPOSE   To experience group cooperation in problem solving

MATERIALS   Two shoe boxes, each containing 25 assorted small objects—for example, keys, comb, knife, checker, book of matches, glue stick, scissors, guitar pick, paper clip, toothpick, golf ball, quarter. (The two boxes should not contain exactly the same items.)
Paper and pencils

FORMAT OPTION   Cooperative learning

PROCEDURE

1. Divide the class into groups of four. Each group member needs a pencil and sheet of paper.

2. Tell the class that you have 25 items in a shoe box and that you are going to give each group 30 seconds to look in the box. After the time is up, each group will compile a list of the items they saw in the box.

3. Give the groups a few minutes to plan how they will approach the problem. Have each group come to the first box separately and silently view the contents for 30 seconds. Then instruct them to return to their seats and begin compiling their lists.

4. After 3 to 5 minutes, hold up each item and ask each group to consult their list to see if they remembered it. After you have held up all the items, ask each group how well they did at the task.

5. Discuss how the groups decided to approach the problem:

   > What was their plan?

   > How well did their plan work?

   > What would they do differently next time?

   > What did they learn from the exercise?

6. Tell the class that they will have another chance to do the same activity but with a different box of items. Give the groups 5 minutes to plan.

7. Allow each group 30 seconds to look in the second shoe box. Then have them record their observations.

8. Hold up each item and have groups check off the items they remembered.

9. Ask each group how their plan was different the second time and how well it worked. Discuss what students might do differently if they had a third chance.

CTIVITY

8   Key Concept Review

PURPOSE   To understand the meaning of key concepts related to responsibility education and cooperation

MATERIALS   Butcher paper
Magazines
Comic books
Scissors
Glue
Markers

FORMAT OPTIONS   Cooperative learning
Class meeting

PROCEDURE

1. Ask students to define in their own words the following concepts. Solicit several definitions for each. Discuss the different definitions until the group displays a common understanding of each of the concepts.

RESPONSIBILITY	FREEDOM
TRUST	RULE
RIGHT	COOPERATION
PRIVILEGE	COMPETITION

2. Divide the class into eight groups of equal numbers. Assign each group one of the words and instruct them to use the art materials to develop a poster that shows the meaning of the concept—draw a picture, write a definition, create a collage, and so forth.

3. Display the posters in the classroom.

SECTION 2

Understanding Conflict

OVERVIEW

Conflict is a natural, vital part of life. When conflict is truly understood, it can become an opportunity to learn and create. The synergy of conflict can create new alternatives—something that was not possible before. Examples of such synergy exist everywhere in nature: In the forest, the nutrients provided by decaying leaves support the growth of enormous trees. In the sea, a beautiful pearl is the synergistic result of sand irritating a sensitive oyster inside its shell.

The challenge for people in conflict is to apply the principles of creative cooperation that can be learned from nature in their human relationships. When differences are acknowledged and appreciated—and when the conflicting parties build on one another's strengths—a climate is created that nurtures the self-worth of each individual and provides opportunities for fulfillment to each.

PERCEPTIONS OF CONFLICT

Without conflict, there would likely be no personal growth or social change. Unfortunately, when it comes to conflict, the perceptions of most people are quite negative. When asked to list words or phrases associated with conflict, most adults, as well as most children, respond negatively: "Get rid of it," "It's harmful," "War," "Hate," "Get even," and so forth. These negative attitudes about conflict are likely the result of assimilated messages from the media, parents, teachers, friends, government officials, and most others with whom one encounters conflict.

Negative perceptions and the reactions they provoke are extremely detrimental to successful conflict resolution. However, before they can be replaced, they must first be understood. To start, think about your own attitudes toward conflict:

Does denying the existence of conflict help you resolve it?

Does accusing or defending help you to cooperate?

Can you make a conflict go away by not thinking about it?

Are you really able to force another person to change?

Does assuming there will be a winner and loser help?

The answers to these questions reveal that everyone in every conflict has a choice—to be driven by negative perceptions or to take control of the situation and act in a positive way. With more personal awareness and better understanding of available choices, one becomes able to approach conflict knowing that it can have either destructive or constructive results. When conflict is perceived as a positive life force, those in conflict become responsible for producing a result in which relationships are enhanced and individuals are empowered to control their own lives in ways that respect the needs of others. In brief, the power to create resolution lies within each person.

It is important to realize that children's success in developing an awareness of the positive potential of conflict is an outgrowth of their teachers' own endeavors and commitment to approach conflict in a positive way. Teachers who integrate positive ways of resolving conflict into their classrooms and schools will see results that have a powerful effect on their own lives and work, as well as on the lives and work of their students.

ORIGINS OF CONFLICT

Diagnosing the origins of a conflict can help define a problem, and a definition of the problem is the starting point in any attempt to find a solution. As discussed in the introduction, almost every conflict involves an endeavor by the disputants to meet the basic psychological needs for belonging, power, freedom, and fun (Glasser, 1984). Limited resources and different values may appear to be the cause of conflicts, but unmet needs are truly at their root.

Unmet Psychological Needs

Conflict resolution is next to impossible as long as one side believes its psychological needs are being threatened by the other. Unless unmet needs are expressed, the conflict will often reappear even when a solution is reached regarding the subject of the dispute. In short, psychological needs are satisfied more often by people than by things.

Limited Resources

Conflicts involving limited resources (time, money, property) are typically the easiest to resolve. People quickly learn that cooperating instead of competing for scarce resources is in their best interests. In cooperation, disputants share in problem solving, recognize each other's interests, and create choices. This process usually provides satisfaction because the psychological needs of belonging and power, perhaps even of freedom and fun, are addressed in the equitable allocation of limited resources.

It is important to realize how conflicts over unmet psychological needs are played out against the backdrop of limited resources. For instance, the student who is upset over the fact that his friend has not repaid a loan may really want to know his friend respects him (a power need). He may not easily accept a payment solution unless his need for recognition is addressed in the process.

Different Values

Conflicts involving different values (beliefs, priorities, principles) tend to be the most difficult to resolve. When a person holds a value, he or she has an enduring belief that a specific action or quality is preferable to an opposite action or quality. This belief applies to attitudes toward objects, situations, or individuals. The belief becomes a standard that guides the person's actions.

When the terminology used to express a conflict includes words such as *honest, equal, right,* and *fair,* the conflict is typically one of values. Many times disputants think in terms of "right/wrong" or "good/bad" when values are in opposition. Even conflicts over differing goals can be viewed as value conflicts: The source of a goal conflict relates either to the goal's relative importance for each disputant or to the fact that the disputants highly value different goals.

When values are in conflict, the disputants often perceive the dispute as a personal attack. They tend to personalize the conflict because their whole sense of self feels threatened. When people feel attacked, they typically become defensive and stubbornly cling to their own convictions. Strong stances on principle are therefore characteristic of values conflicts. The conflict exists because the disputants are governed by different sets of rules. Because the disputants evaluate the problem and each other according to conflicting criteria, resolution can be especially difficult.

Again, psychological needs are enmeshed in values conflicts. For example, a person may be in conflict when a friend does not keep a promise. The person's picture of a friend is that of someone who is reliable, and her sense of belonging is threatened because her value system includes the assumption that friends do not make promises they cannot keep.

Rigid value systems can severely restrict one from meeting the need to belong. The more one adheres to any value, the more one's belonging is limited to others who hold the same beliefs. Inflexible values are also almost always destructive to our need to be free. We see others as wrong if they do not hold our beliefs, and we see situations as bad if they do not meet our standards. When this is the case, our options in life, as well as our choice of friends, become limited.

Resolving a values conflict does not mean the disputants must change or align their values. Often a mutual acknowledgment that each person views the situation differently is the first step toward resolution. If the disputants can learn not to reject each other because of differences in beliefs, they will be better able to deal with the problem on its own merits. This is the essence of the strategy of separating the people from the problem (Fisher, Ury, & Patton, 1991).

RESPONSES TO CONFLICT

Responses to conflict can be categorized into three basic groups: soft responses, hard responses, and principled responses. In both soft and hard responses, participants take positions or stands on the problem. They negotiate these positions, either trying to avoid or win a contest of will. Soft and hard negotiations either bring about one-sided losses to reach an agreement or demand one-sided gains as the price of the agreement. In principled responses, participants use conflict resolution strategies designed to produce wise agreements. A wise agreement is one that addresses the legitimate interests of both parties, resolves conflicting interests fairly, is durable, and takes contextual interests into account—how others besides the disputants will be affected by the agreement.

Soft Responses

Soft responses usually involve people who are friends or people who just want to be nice to each other because it is likely the contact between the parties will continue in the future. In any case, they want to agree, and they negotiate softly to do so. Avoiding conflict is often the first soft response. People attempt to avoid conflict altogether by withdrawing from the situation, ignoring it, and denying their emotions or the fact that the conflict or their emotions even matter. When people choose to avoid conflict, it is usually because they are not interested in maintaining the relationship or they lack the skills to negotiate a resolution. Accommodation, when one party adjusts to the position of the other without seeking to serve his or her own interests in the relationship, is a common soft response.

When soft negotiating attempts are made, the standard moves are to make offers and concessions, to trust the other side, to be nice and friendly, and to yield as necessary to avoid confrontation. Soft responses, especially avoidance responses, may have some merit in the immediate situation—for example, they may help a person control anger or offer protection from the responses of someone who responds aggressively. However, the soft response typically results in feelings of disillusionment, self-doubt, fear, and anxiety about the future.

Hard Responses

Hard responses to conflict usually involve adversaries whose goal is victory. Hard responses to conflict are characterized by confrontations that involve threats, aggression, and anger. Hard negotiators demand concessions as a condition of the relationship and insist on their position. They often search for a single answer to the problem—the one the other side will give in to. Hard negotiators frequently apply pressure in trying to win a contest of will. They use bribery and punishment (for example, withholding money, favors, or affection). When these intimidating tactics cause the other side to yield, the hard negotiator feels successful. Hostility, physical damage, and violence often result from this response to conflict. Furthermore, this attitude is always detrimental to cooperation.

Principled Responses

Principled responses involve people who view themselves as problem solvers. Their goal is a wise outcome reached efficiently and amicably. These problem solvers have developed communication and conflict resolution skills. Principled negotiators understand that communication is fundamental to cooperative interaction and comprehend what it means to develop a common understanding. Principled responses to conflict are characterized by first seeking to understand the other side, then seeking to be understood. Principled negotiators are skilled, active, empathic listeners. They listen with the intent to understand. Principled negotiators get inside the other person's frame of reference to see the problem as that person does and to comprehend the person emotionally and intellectually.

Principled negotiators focus on the interests of both sides and invent options for mutual gain. Principled responses to conflict create the opportunity for each participant to meet his or her needs. Principled responses to conflict are proactive, not reactive. When people behave proactively, they do not feel victimized or out of control—they do not blame other people or circumstances when in conflict. Instead, they take charge of their actions and feelings and use their negotiation skills to make resolution a possibility.

Outcomes of Soft, Hard, and Principled Responses

Adults and children alike engage in soft and hard positional bargaining in response to everyday conflicts. As participants in soft and hard negotiation, they take a position, argue for it, and make concessions to reach a compromise. In their book *Getting to Yes,* Fisher et al. (1991) describe positional bargaining as a method in which each disputant tends to get locked into a position by arguing for it and defending it against attack. The more a negotiator attempts to convince the other side of the impossibility of changing position, the more difficult it becomes to do so. Egos become identified with the position, and saving face becomes a new interest in reconciling future actions. Holding on to positions makes it less and less likely that an agreement, let alone an agreement that is satisfactory to each side, will be reached:

> As more attention is paid to positions, less attention is devoted to meeting the underlying concerns of the parties. Agreement becomes less likely. Any agreement reached may reflect a mechanical splitting of the difference between final positions rather than a solution carefully crafted to meet the legitimate interests of the

parties. The result is frequently an agreement less satisfactory to each side than it could have been. (Fisher
et al., 1991, p. 5)

In addition, arguing over positions is inefficient because each side
starts with an extreme position in order to reach a favorable settle-
ment. Positional negotiators stubbornly hold to the extreme position,
deceive the opposing side as to their true point of view, and make
small concessions only to keep the process from breaking down.
Negotiation in this situation is a difficult, frustrating, time-consuming
process:

> Dragging one's feet, threatening to walk out,
> stonewalling, and other such tactics become common-
> place. They all increase the time and cost of reaching
> agreement as well as the risk that no agreement will be
> reached at all. (Fisher et al., 1991, p. 6)

Arguing over positions endangers relationships because the interaction becomes a contest of will. Disputants assert what they will and
will not do, each attempting to force the other to change position:

> Anger and resentment often result as one side sees
> itself bending to the rigid will of the other while its
> own legitimate concerns go unaddressed. Positional
> bargaining thus strains and sometimes shatters the rela-
> tionship between the parties. The process may produce
> an agreement, although it may not be a wise one.
> (Fisher et al., 1991, p. 6)

The three types of responses to conflict produce different outcomes. Soft positional bargaining is considered a lose-lose approach to
conflict. People give in on their positions for the sake of the relationship. They do not reconcile the interests at the root of the problem;
consequently, neither person gets what he or she wants—in other
words, they both lose. In those situations where one side accommo-
dates the other, a win-lose situation may result. A person who avoids a
conflict by accommodating the other person loses in the sense that he
or she has little courage to express personal feelings and convictions
and is intimidated by the other. When conflicts are avoided, basic psychological needs are not acknowledged or met. Thus, people who
avoid conflicts are not in effective control of their lives; they see themselves as victims, and their relations with others invariably suffer.

Hard positional bargaining is considered a win-lose approach to
conflict, where the more aggressive party wins and the adversary
loses. Sometimes hard positional bargaining becomes lose-lose when
the desire to punish or get even provokes adversaries to take vindic-
tive actions that are self-destructive as well as destructive to the oppo-
nent. Hard positional bargaining produces stressful situations when
the disputants are required to continue to interact in some manner,
perhaps even to continue to work together toward common goals.

Principled responses to conflict change the game and the outcome. Principled methods produce wise outcomes efficiently and amicably. This kind of response to conflict focuses on interests instead of positions and brings people in conflict to a gradual consensus on a joint resolution without the costs of digging into positions or destroying relationships. Principled negotiation is a win-win response to conflict.

The challenge in conflict resolution education is to replace, through comprehensive training followed by ample practice opportunities, commonly held myths about conflict with a view more in line with reality. This, for most youth and adults, is a major paradigm shift. Table 7 exhibits the desired shift in understanding of conflict.

The actions people choose when they are involved in a conflict will either increase or decrease the problem: When the conflict escalates, the problem remains unresolved and the effects can be destructive. As a conflict escalates, threats usually increase and more people become involved in the conflict and take sides. Anger, fear, and frustration are expressed, sometimes violently. As a conflict escalates, people become more and more entrenched in their positions. Conflicts de-escalate when differences and interests are understood. People remain calm and are willing to listen to opposing viewpoints. Those involved focus on the problem rather than on one another and create the opportunity for resolution.

In summary, conflict in and of itself is neither positive nor negative. Rather, the actions we choose turn conflict into a competitive, devastating battle or into a constructive challenge where there is opportunity for growth. We always have the choice, when in conflict, to work for resolution. If a conflict remains unresolved, some possible outcomes are:

> Threats and blame continue.
>
> Feelings are hurt; relationships are damaged.
>
> Self-interest results; positions harden.
>
> Emotions increase; tempers get out of hand.
>
> Sides are drawn; others get involved.
>
> People do not get what they want or need.
>
> Violence may result.

If people work together for agreement, the following outcomes are possible:

> Better ideas are produced to solve the problem.
>
> Relationships and communication are improved.
>
> Views are clarified; problems are dealt with.
>
> People listen to and respect one another.
>
> There is cooperation.

TABLE 7   Conflict Myths and Conflict Realities

Myth	Reality
Conflict is always bad.	Conflict is neither good nor bad—the behaviors we choose in conflict situations turn conflict into a destructive or constructive force.
Conflict is a contest.	Many conflicts can be resolved win-win: Nearly every conflict can be approached win-win.
There is one right way to approach conflict.	There are a variety of ways to respond to a conflict; each different type of response has benefits and limitations.

People get what they want and need.

Fairness and peace are achieved.

QUESTIONS FOR CLASS MEETINGS

The following questions and statements, given in no particular order, may be used in class meetings to promote understanding of the content of this section.

1. What is conflict?

2. What happens at school that satisfies your need to belong? Outside of school?

3. What happens at school that satisfies your need for power? Outside of school?

4. How does the school environment allow you to satisfy your need for fun? What changes in school do you think would make school more fun?

5. What choices do you make in school? Outside of school?

6. Share with the group a pleasurable experience: Tell us what you were doing, thinking, and feeling, and how your body reacted.

7. Share with the group an experience that was painful or uncomfortable: Tell us what you were doing, thinking, and feeling, and how your body reacted.

8. Can you think of examples of conflicts that involved you in which limited resources were part of the issue?

9. Can you think of examples of conflicts that involved you where different values were part of the issue?

10. How do you feel when you are at odds with another person and that person gives in to you? How do you feel when you give in to another person?

11. How do you react when another shows anger or hostility toward you? How do you feel in that situation?

12. What makes you angry? How do you let another person know you are angry?

13. If you were really upset with a friend, how could you handle that and still be friends?

14. How do you draw the line between "giving up" and "fighting back"?

15. Can you remember any conflicts you have had that turned out really good?

Suggested Readings

Glasser, W. (1984). *Control theory.* New York: Harper & Row.

Glasser, W. (1986). *Control theory in the classroom.* New York: Harper & Row.

Kreidler, W. J. (1984). *Creative conflict resolution: More than 200 activities for keeping peace in the classroom.* Glenview, IL: Scott Foresman.

Levin, D. E. (1994). *Teaching young children in violent times: Building a peaceable classroom—A pre-school to grade 3 violence prevention and conflict resolution guide.* Philadelphia: New Society.

Porro, B. (1996). *Talk it out: Conflict resolution for the elementary classroom.* Alexandria, VA: Association for Supervision and Curriculum Development.

Prutzman, P., Stern, L., Burger, M. L., & Bodenhamer, G. (1988). *The friendly classroom for a small planet.* Philadelphia: New Society.

Sadalla, G., Henriquez, M., & Holmberg, M. (1987). *Conflict resolution: A secondary school curriculum.* San Francisco: The Community Board Program.

Sadalla, G., Holmberg, M., & Halligan, J. (1990). *Conflict resolution: An elementary school curriculum.* San Francisco: The Community Board Program.

Schrumpf, F., Freiburg, S., & Skadden, D. (1993). *Life lessons for young adolescents: An advisory guide for teachers.* Champaign, IL: Research Press.

Shure, M. B. (1992). *I Can Problem Solve (ICPS): An interpersonal cognitive problem-solving program for children.* Champaign, IL: Research Press.

Wichert, S. (1989). *Keeping the peace: Practicing cooperation and conflict resolution with preschoolers.* Santa Cruz, CA: New Society.

ACTIVITY

1   Conflict Is . . .

PURPOSE   To learn that conflict is a natural part of everyday life

MATERIALS   Student Manuals
Newsprint
Markers
Tape

FORMAT OPTIONS   Whole class discussion/participation
Class meeting
Cooperative learning

NOTE   Before beginning, prepare six sheets of newsprint by writing one of the following headings at the top of each:

Conflicts on the playground

Conflicts in the cafeteria

Conflicts in the classroom

Conflicts with brothers or sisters

Conflicts with friends

Conflicts in the world

PROCEDURE   1. Refer students to page 15 in their Student Manuals, "What Conflict Means to Me." Ask them what comes to mind when they hear the word *conflict*. Typical responses include *fight, war, hit, hate, argue, push,* and so forth. Give students some time to write or draw their responses on this page.

2. Form groups of four or five students. Give each group one of the prepared sheets of newsprint and a marker. Encourage each group to compile a list or draw pictures of conflicts for their assigned topic.

3. Invite each group to share their list, then post these around the room. As examples are shared, ask one or two members of the group to talk in more detail about some of the conflicts they listed.

4. Review the lists and point out that most of the conflicts were probably handled in negative ways. Explain that we usually think of conflict as something we do not like and that we generally try

to avoid conflict. Discuss the consequences of handling conflict by avoiding it or by blowing up. Typical responses include the following:

> We feel sad and rejected.
>
> The conflict continues.
>
> The problem gets worse.
>
> We feel angry and afraid.
>
> Violence and fights happen.
>
> People get hurt.

5. Point out that conflicts can be handled in positive ways. Ask students to look at their lists and think about positive ways of dealing with conflict. Write these responses on a sheet of newsprint. Typical responses include talking, listening, staying calm, cooperating, and sharing.

6. Discuss what happens when conflicts are handled positively. Possible outcomes include the following:

> We become better friends.
>
> We feel respected.
>
> Everyone's ideas are understood.
>
> Good solutions are possible.

7. Refer students to page 16 of their Student Manuals, "Ideas About Conflict." Amplify the concepts as follows:

> Conflicts are a natural part of everyday life. (The concern is not that we will experience conflicts but how we will handle them.)
>
> Conflicts can be handled in positive or negative ways. (Depending on how conflicts are handled, the outcomes will be creative or destructive.)
>
> Conflicts are an opportunity to learn and grow. (Friendships and relationships can be built when we respond positively to conflicts.)

Student Manual
page 15

What Conflict Means to Me

INSTRUCTIONS: In the boxes, write words or draw pictures that come
to mind when you think of conflict.

CONFLICT

15

*Student Manual
page 16*

Ideas About Conflict

♦ Conflicts are a natural part of everyday life.

♦ Conflicts can be handled in positive or negative ways.

♦ Conflicts are an opportunity to learn and grow.

16

ACTIVITY

2 Conflict Collage

PURPOSE   To explore the concept of conflict further

MATERIALS   A story illustrating conflict
Comics
Magazines
Newspapers
Scissors
Glue
Butcher paper

FORMAT OPTIONS   Whole class discussion/participation
Learning center
Cooperative learning

PROCEDURE
1. Read a story where characters are in conflict. Discuss the conflict and how it was resolved in the story. A good one to try for the primary level is *Moose and Goose,* by Marc Brown (Dutton, 1978); for older students, try *The Pennywhistle Tree,* by Doris Buchanan Smith (Putnam, 1991). Other books for children are listed in Appendix B.

2. Give students comics, magazines, and newspapers and instruct them to look for and cut out headlines or pictures of conflict. Encourage students to glue these cutouts to butcher paper to create "conflict collages."

3. Discuss the collages.

4. After the discussion give learners the opportunity to write their thoughts and feelings about conflict on their collages.

ACTIVITY

3 Basic Needs

PURPOSE To learn that most conflicts between people involve the attempt to meet basic needs for belonging, power, freedom, and fun

MATERIALS Student Manuals

FORMAT OPTIONS Whole class discussion/participation
Cooperative learning

PROCEDURE

1. Refer the group to "Basic Needs," on page 17 of their Student Manuals, and discuss. Emphasize that most disputes between people involve the attempt to meet basic needs for belonging, power, freedom, and fun.

2. Refer the group to "How We Meet Our Basic Needs," on page 18 of their Student Manuals. Discuss the idea that, although we all share the same basic needs, the things each of us chooses to do to meet these needs are different. For example, everyone has a need for power. However, Paul gets this need met by developing his music skills. Elizabeth gets this need met by being on the soccer team. Darrin gets this need met by being able to draw cartoon heroes.

3. Refer the group to the "How I Meet My Basic Needs" form on page 19 of their Student Manuals. Give students time to record some of the things they do to get their basic needs met.

4. In small groups, have students discuss the examples they recorded and compare how they are alike and how they are different.

5. Repeat the idea that basic needs are usually the origin of conflict: For instance, suppose you are upset because your friend is going to a party you were not invited to. You might get into a conflict with this friend because you are not getting your belonging need met. Suppose someone calls you a name and you get into an argument. Name-calling shows a lack of respect, which is related to the power need.

6. Refer the group to the "Looking at My Conflicts" form on page 20 of their Student Manuals. Ask students to record examples of conflicts they have experienced in each need shape.

7. Have students get back into the same small groups to talk about each need and the conflicts they have experienced.

8. Summarize that being aware of our basic needs helps identify unmet needs as the origin of conflict: When we understand the origin of a conflict, we have a better chance of resolving it.

Student Manual
page 17

Basic Needs

BELONGING

POWER

FREEDOM

FUN

Understanding how to resolve a conflict begins with identifying the origin of the conflict. Most every conflict between people involves the attempt to meet basic needs for belonging, power, freedom, or fun.

17

Student Manual
page 18

How We Meet Our Basic Needs

♦ Our **BELONGING** need is met by developing relationships with others where we have the opportunity to love, share, and cooperate.

♦ Our **POWER** need is met by achieving, accomplishing, and being recognized and respected.

♦ Our **FREEDOM** need is met by making choices in our lives.

♦ Our **FUN** need is met by laughing and playing.

We are all born with the same basic needs. However, the things we each choose to do to meet these needs may be different from what others choose.

18

Student Manual
page 19

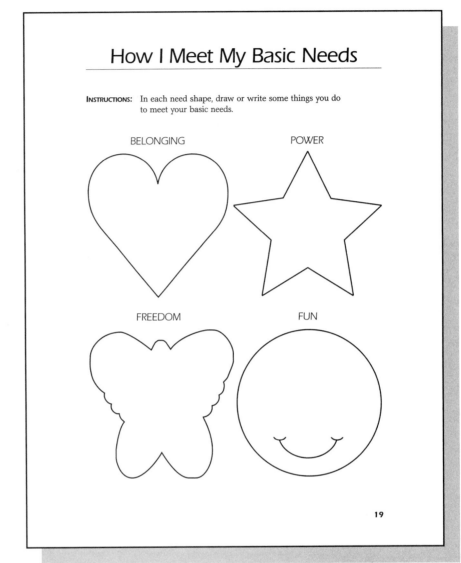

Student Manual
page 20

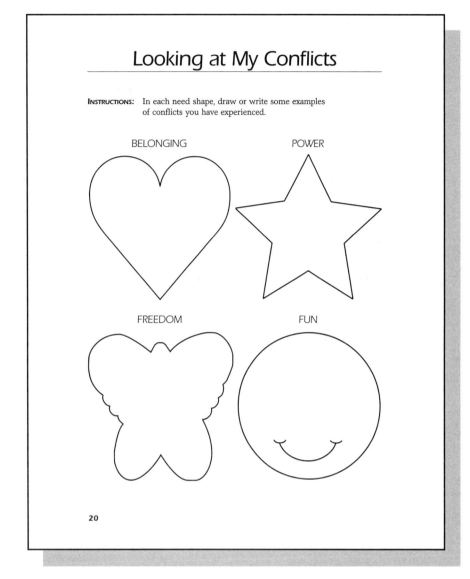

Looking at My Conflicts

INSTRUCTIONS: In each need shape, draw or write some examples of conflicts you have experienced.

BELONGING

POWER

FREEDOM

FUN

20

ACTIVITY

4 Enough Is Not Enough

PURPOSE To learn that conflicts can be caused by limited resources as well as by basic needs not being met

MATERIALS Student Manuals

FORMAT OPTIONS Whole class discussion/participation
Class meeting

PROCEDURE 1. Explain that *limited resources* may appear to be the cause of some conflicts. Ask students to think of situations where conflicts resulted from not having enough of something—for example, not enough pieces of pie or slices of pizza, not enough time with an adult or friend, not enough balls or jump ropes at the playground, not enough space for two kids in the front seat of the car.

2. Refer the group to the "Enough Is Not Enough" form on page 21 of their Student Manuals. Ask students to draw two conflicts they have experienced that were caused by limited resources.

3. Discuss how these conflicts usually get resolved:

   Does an adult decide?

   Does the older person get what he or she wants?

   Is there a compromise?

   Do the people involved decide on a fair way to share?

4. Ask students to look at their drawings of limited resources conflicts again and think about which basic needs were not getting met in these situations. Have students make lines from their drawings to the basic needs that were also the cause of the conflict.

5. Discuss students' responses. Summarize by restating the idea that conflicts involving limited resources can also be caused by basic needs not getting met.

Student Manual
page 21

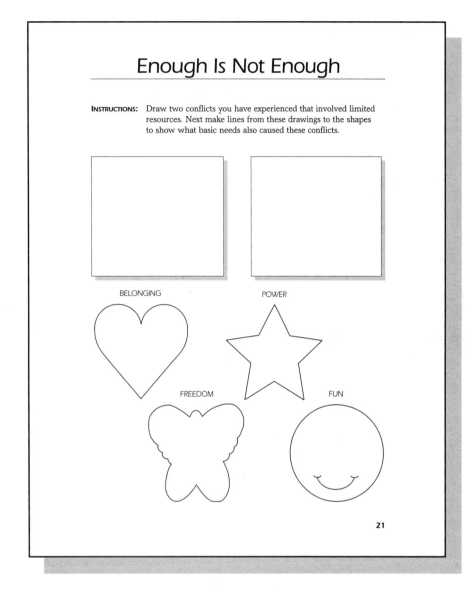

Enough Is Not Enough

INSTRUCTIONS: Draw two conflicts you have experienced that involved limited resources. Next make lines from these drawings to the shapes to show what basic needs also caused these conflicts.

BELONGING

POWER

FREEDOM

FUN

21

5 Different Values

PURPOSE To learn that conflicts are caused by different values as well as by basic needs not getting met

MATERIALS Student Manuals
Newsprint
Markers
Tape

FORMAT OPTIONS Whole class discussion/participation
Class meeting
Cooperative learning

NOTE Before beginning, choose three pairs of sentence stems from the following group. Prepare six sheets of newsprint by writing a sentence stem at the top of each.

> A woman would make a good president of this country because _____.
>
> A woman would not make a good president of this country because _____.
>
> Chewing gum should be allowed in school because _____.
>
> Chewing gum should not be allowed in school because _____.
>
> Children should have the right to vote at age 10 because _____.
>
> Children should not have the right to vote at age 10 because _____.
>
> Children should watch only an hour of TV each week because _____.
>
> Children should not be restricted to watching only an hour of TV each week because _____.

PROCEDURE   1. Have students line up in a semicircle according to the following physical characteristics:

> *First:* Tallest to shortest
>
> *Second:* Darkest hair to lightest hair
>
> *Third:* Shortest hair to longest hair
>
> *Fourth:* Lightest skin to darkest skin

2. Discuss how it felt to be placed in a line based on physical characteristics. (Students may report feeling uncomfortable about being grouped in this way, especially with regard to skin color. However, their discomfort can help sensitize them to the importance of underlying differences.)

3. Explain that it is easy to see physical differences but that other differences are not so easy to see—for example, things we believe in, attitudes, or religious preferences.

4. Divide the class into six small groups. Pass out one of the prepared sheets of newsprint to each group. Ask group members to number their sheet of newsprint from one to five and give five reasons that complete the statement given on their sheet.

5. Ask each group to tape their sheet of newsprint to the wall, then share their reasons. Compare the sheets for each of the paired sentences. Ask who is right and why. After students have responded, clarify that no one is right and no one is wrong—that these statements represent different *values.*

6. Refer the group to the "Different Values" form on page 22 of their Student Manuals. Ask students to draw two conflicts they have experienced that were caused by different values.

7. Next ask students to look at their drawings and think about which basic needs were not getting met. Have students make lines from their drawings to the basic needs that also caused the conflicts. Discuss these responses.

8. Summarize that conflicts involving differences in values are also caused by basic needs not getting met. Conflicts involving values tend to be more difficult to resolve because when values are different, people often perceive the dispute as a personal attack. Resolving a values conflict does not mean the disputants must change their values. If they can agree that having different views is OK, they may still be able to cooperate to find a solution that allows each to satisfy his or her needs.

Student Manual
page 22

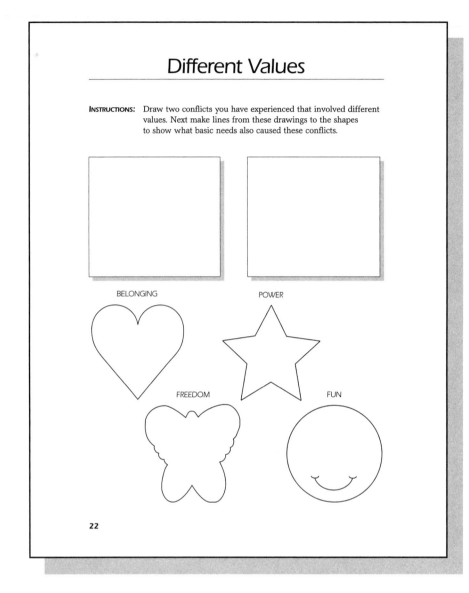

Different Values

Instructions: Draw two conflicts you have experienced that involved different values. Next make lines from these drawings to the shapes to show what basic needs also caused these conflicts.

BELONGING

POWER

FREEDOM

FUN

22

6   Origins of Conflict

PURPOSE   To practice identifying origins of conflict

MATERIALS   Student Manuals

FORMAT OPTIONS   Whole class discussion/participation
Class meeting

PROCEDURE

1. Refer the group to page 23 in their Student Manuals, "Origins of Conflict," where a diagram of the relationship between conflict and unmet basic needs, limited resources, and different values appears.

2. Review the idea that limited resources and different values can be the causes of conflict:

   > Conflicts can be about limited resources (a lack of time, money, or property). For instance, two classmates are having a conflict over property when they are arguing about who will get to use a certain book they both want for a report.

   > When people in conflict talk about honesty, rights, or fairness, the conflict is probably about different values. For instance, a student who values honesty in her friends will probably be very upset and angry if a friend lies to her.

3. Review the idea that unmet needs are also a part of conflicts over limited resources and different values:

   > The two classmates fighting over the book they both want for a report are really attempting to get their power needs met. If they fail the class or do not write a quality report, they will not be accomplishing or achieving, and they may not be recognized or respected by themselves or others.

   > The student who is angry because her friend lied to her is attempting to get her belonging need met. She finds it difficult to share and cooperate with someone who is not honest.

4. Refer the group to the "Origins of My Conflicts" form on page 24 of their Student Manuals. Ask students to draw or write about conflicts they have experienced that were caused by basic needs not getting met. Then have them check to see if any of these conflicts were also caused by limited resources or different values.

5. Ask the following questions about several student conflicts:

Who was involved in the conflict?

How did you feel?

What did the other person want?

What did you want?

Were limited resources or different values involved in the conflict? If so, how?

What unmet basic need or needs caused the conflict?

Student Manual
page 23

Origins of Conflict

LIMITED RESOURCES	UNMET BASIC NEEDS	DIFFERENT VALUES
Time	Belonging	Beliefs
Money	Power	Priorities
Property	Freedom	Principles
	Fun	

CONFLICT

Limited resources and different values
can be the causes of conflict. Unmet needs
are also a part of conflicts over limited
resources and different values.

23

Student Manual
page 24

Origins of My Conflicts

INSTRUCTIONS: In each need shape, draw or write examples of conflicts you
have experienced where you did not get your basic needs met.

BELONGING

POWER

FREEDOM

FUN

♦ Were any of these conflicts also caused by limited resources
(time, money, property)?

♦ Were any of these conflicts also caused by different values
(beliefs, priorities, principles)?

24

A CTIVITY

7 What's My Response?

PURPOSE To examine one's typical responses to conflict

MATERIALS Student Manuals

FORMAT OPTIONS Whole class discussion/participation
Class meeting

PROCEDURE
1. Explain that when we are in conflict with another person we have certain responses. These responses may vary depending on who the other person is and the situation.

2. Invite students to share examples of conflicts they have had recently with a brother, sister, or friend. How did they respond? Ask for examples of conflicts with adults. What were their responses?

3. Refer the group to the "How I Respond to Conflict" form on page 25 of their Student Manuals and have them complete it as the instructions direct.

4. Divide students into small groups and ask them to discuss the responses they use most often. Have each group share their conclusions with the class as a whole.

5. Discuss which responses help students get their basic needs met and which do not. The following questions may help:

    Does avoiding or ignoring a friend you are mad at help you get your belonging need met? Why?

    Does letting an adult decide who is right help you get your power or freedom needs met? Why?

    Do talking and finding ways to agree help you? How?

Student Manual
page 25

How I Respond to Conflict

INSTRUCTIONS: Put a check mark in the boxes that show the responses that are most typical for you when you are in conflict with another person. Then circle the three responses you normally make first in a conflict.

	OFTEN	SOMETIMES	NEVER
Yell back or threaten the person	☐	☐	☐
Avoid or ignore the person	☐	☐	☐
Change the subject	☐	☐	☐
Try to understand the other side	☐	☐	☐
Complain to an adult	☐	☐	☐
Call the other person names	☐	☐	☐
Let the person have his or her way	☐	☐	☐
Try to reach a compromise	☐	☐	☐
Let an adult decide who is right	☐	☐	☐
Talk to find ways to agree	☐	☐	☐
Apologize	☐	☐	☐
Hit or push back	☐	☐	☐
Cry	☐	☐	☐
Make it into a joke	☐	☐	☐
Pretend my feelings are not hurt	☐	☐	☐

25

8 Soft, Hard, or Principled Responses

PURPOSE   To understand soft, hard, and principled responses to conflict and the different results of these responses

MATERIALS   Student Manuals
Paper
Markers

FORMAT OPTIONS   Whole class discussion/participation
Class meeting

PROCEDURE

1. Refer the group to page 26 in their Student Manuals, "Soft Responses to Conflict." Ask what comes to mind when students hear the word *soft.*

2. Explain that ignoring a conflict and hoping it will go away, denying that it really matters, withdrawing from a situation and not sharing what you are feeling, and giving in just to be nice are examples of *soft responses* to conflict.

3. Invite students to share times when they gave a soft response to a conflict. In the space at the bottom of page 26, have students write or draw an example of a conflict in which they gave a soft response.

4. Refer the group to page 27 in their Student Manuals, "Hard Responses to Conflict." Ask students what they think of when they hear the word *hard.*

5. Explain that sometimes we have a *hard response* to conflict. Threats, pushing, hitting, and yelling are examples of hard responses.

6. Invite students to share their experiences. In the space at the bottom of page 27, have students write or draw an example of a conflict in which they gave a hard response.

7. Refer the group to page 28 in their Student Manuals, "Principled Responses to Conflict." Explain that a third type of response to conflict is a *principled response.* Principled responses include listening with the intent to understand the other person's point of view,

showing respect for differences, and looking for ways to resolve the problem that will help everyone involved.

8. To review, discuss the top portion of "Responses to Conflict" on page 29 of the Student Manual. Next have students work in small groups to answer the questions for each possible response to conflict.

9. Reassemble in the larger group to discuss and review main ideas.

Student Manual page 26

Soft Responses to Conflict

Sometimes we have a soft response to conflict. Have you ever:

♦ Ignored a conflict, hoping it would go away?

♦ Denied that a conflict mattered?

♦ Withdrawn from a situation and not shared what you were feeling?

♦ Given in just to be nice?

INSTRUCTIONS: Write or draw an example of a conflict in which you responded in a soft way.

SOFT

26

Student Manual
page 27

Hard Responses to Conflict

**Sometimes we have a hard response to conflict.
Have you ever:**

- ◆ Threatened?

- ◆ Pushed?

- ◆ Hit?

- ◆ Yelled?

INSTRUCTIONS: Write or draw an example of a conflict in which you
responded in a hard way.

HARD

27

Student Manual
page 28

Principled Responses to Conflict

A third type of response to conflict is a principled response. Have you ever:

◆ Listened with the intent to understand the other person's point of view?

◆ Showed respect for differences?

◆ Looked for ways to resolve the problem that will help everyone involved?

PRINCIPLED

28

Responses to Conflict

SOFT RESPONSE	HARD RESPONSE	PRINCIPLED RESPONSE
Withdrawing	Threatening	Listening
Ignoring	Pushing	Understanding
Denying	Hitting	Respecting
Giving in	Yelling	Resolving

INSTRUCTIONS: Answer the questions below for each possible response to conflict.

RESPONSES	Are basic needs getting met?	How do people feel?	Will things get better or worse?
Soft			
Hard			
Principled			

29

ACTIVITY

9 Getting to Win-Win

PURPOSE To learn that soft, hard, and principled responses to conflict achieve losing or winning outcomes

MATERIALS Student Manuals
A few inflated balloons

FORMAT OPTION Whole class discussion/participation

PROCEDURE 1. Refer the group to page 30 in their Student Manuals, "Outcomes of Conflict." Explain that conflicts result in winning or losing outcomes, depending on the responses we choose:

> *Lose-lose* is when neither person gets what he or she wants. Neither person gets his or her needs met. Both people lose.

> *Win-lose* is when one person gets what he or she wants and the other person does not. Only one person gets his or her needs met. One person wins, and the other person loses.

> *Win-win* is when the people in the conflict invent options that help both people get their needs met. They both win.

2. Ask for two student volunteers to act out the five scenes on pages 31–32 of the Student Manual. As the volunteers finish each scene, ask the group the questions pertaining to it. If necessary, refer students to the form on page 29 of their Student Manuals ("Responses to Conflict") to help them determine their answers.

Scene I (Win-Lose)

Did Eric have a soft, hard, or principled response to the conflict? (Soft: Giving in.)

What about Tanya's response? (Soft: Ignoring.)

What was the outcome of their responses?
(Win-lose: Tanya got her needs met, but Eric did not.)

Scene 2 (Lose-Lose)

Did Tanya have a soft, hard, or principled response to the conflict? (Soft: Giving in.)

What about Eric's response? (Soft: Giving in—because he didn't follow after Tanya to try to play with her.)

What was the outcome of their responses?
(Lose-lose: Neither person got his or her needs met. Eric wanted to play with Tanya, and Tanya wanted to play with the balloon by herself.)

Scene 3 (Win-Lose)

Did Eric have a soft, hard, or principled response to the conflict? (Hard: Yelling and threatening.)

What about Tanya's response?
(Hard: Pushing and yelling.)

What was the outcome of their responses?
(Win-lose: Tanya got her needs met, but Eric did not.)

Scene 4 (Lose-Lose)

Was Tanya's response soft, hard, or principled?
(Hard: Pushing and grabbing.)

What about Eric's response?
(Hard: Pushing and grabbing.)

What was the outcome of their responses?
(Lose-lose: No one got his or her needs met.)

Scene 5 (Win-Win)

Was Tanya's response to the conflict soft, hard, or principled?
(Principled: Listening, understanding, respecting, resolving.)

What about Eric's response? (Principled: Listening, understanding, respecting, resolving.)

What was the outcome of their responses?
(Win-win: Both got their needs met.)

3. Summarize the possible outcomes of the three types of responses:

   Soft: Lose-lose or win-lose

   Hard: Lose-lose or win-lose

   Principled: Win-win

4. Have students fill in these outcomes on the page titled "Summary: Responses and Outcomes," on page 33 of their Student Manuals.

Student Manual
page 30

Outcomes of Conflict

LOSE-LOSE

WIN-LOSE

WIN-WIN

Conflicts result in winning or losing outcomes
depending on the responses we choose.

30

Five Scenes

SCENE 1

Tanya: *(Tosses balloon in the air, having fun by herself.)*

Eric: I want to play with you. *(Tries to join Tanya by tapping balloon up in the air.)*

Tanya: *(Calmly)* I had it first. *(Ignores Eric and continues to hit the balloon.)*

Eric: *(Watches Tanya, looks sad, and walks away.)*

SCENE 2

Tanya: *(Tosses balloon in the air, having fun by herself.)*

Eric: I want to play with you. *(Tries to join Tanya by tapping balloon up in the air.)*

Tanya: *(Calmly)* I had it first.

Eric: *(Calmly)* You always have everything first.

Tanya: *(Hands the balloon to Eric and walks away.)*

SCENE 3

Tanya: *(Tosses balloon in the air, having fun by herself.)*

Eric: I want to play with you. *(Tries to join Tanya by tapping balloon up in the air.)*

Tanya: *(Angrily)* No, I had it first, and it's mine.

Eric: *(Angrily)* You always have everything first. I'm not going to play with you anymore if you don't let me play right now.

Tanya: *(Pushes Eric away and yells.)* Go away! I don't want to play with you!

Eric: *(Hits the balloon hard and angrily stomps away.)*

31

Student Manual
page 32

SCENE 4

Tanya: *(Tosses balloon in the air, having fun by herself.)*

Eric: I want to play with you. *(Tries to join Tanya by tapping balloon up in the air.)*

Tanya: *(Angrily)* No, I had it first, and it's mine.

Eric: *(Angrily)* You always have everything first. I'm not going to play with you anymore if you don't let me play right now.

Tanya: *(Pushes Eric away and yells.)* Go away! I don't want to play with you!

Eric: *(Pushes Tanya back.)*

Tanya and Eric: *(Both grab the balloon, which pops.)*

SCENE 5

Tanya: *(Tosses balloon in the air, having fun by herself.)*

Eric: I want to play with you. *(Tries to join Tanya by tapping balloon up in the air.)*

Tanya: I want to play with the balloon by myself.

Eric: Why do you want to play with the balloon by yourself?

Tanya: I'm practicing. This is the first step to learning how to juggle.

Eric: I still want to play with you.

Tanya: I want to play with you, too. I only need to practice a few more minutes. Will you watch and tell me how I'm doing?

Eric: Okay. *(Watches Tanya.)* You're good. Will you teach me how to juggle?

32

Student Manual
page 33

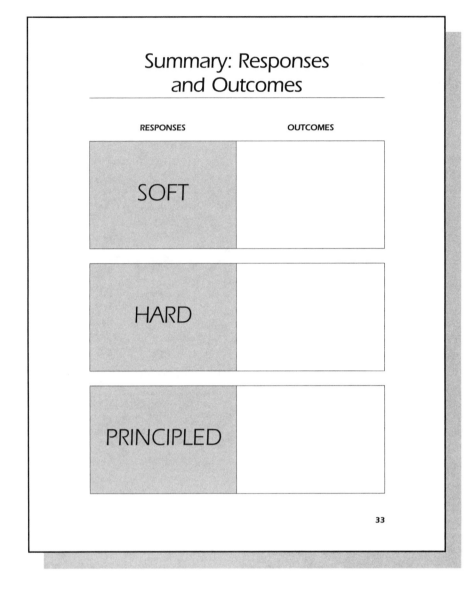

ACTIVITY

10 Conflict Review

PURPOSE To identify origins, responses, and outcomes of a personal conflict

MATERIALS Student Manuals

FORMAT OPTIONS Class meeting
Learning center

PROCEDURE
1. Refer students to the "Understanding Conflict" diagram appearing on page 34 of their Student Manuals. Review and discuss all the concepts presented thus far relating to the origins of and possible responses to conflict.

2. Next refer students to the "Sample Conflict Review" on page 35 of their Student Manuals. Explain how to fill out the form, using this page as a model if necessary.

3. Encourage students to fill out the blank "Conflict Review" form on page 36 of their Student Manuals, using a recent personal experience.

4. Invite students to share their responses on this form with the group.

Student Manual
page 34

Understanding Conflict

ORIGINS OF CONFLICT		
LIMITED RESOURCES	**UNMET BASIC NEEDS**	**DIFFERENT VALUES**
Time	Belonging	Beliefs
Money	Power	Priorities
Property	Freedom	Principles
	Fun	

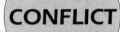

CONFLICT

RESPONSES TO CONFLICT		
SOFT	**HARD**	**PRINCIPLED**
Withdrawing	Threatening	Listening
Ignoring	Pushing	Understanding
Denying	Hitting	Respecting
Giving in	Yelling	Resolving

34

Student Manual
page 35

Sample Conflict Review

INSTRUCTIONS: Think of a conflict you recently had with a friend and tell about it in the boxes below.

WHAT WAS THE CONFLICT?		
What happened?		
Pete and I were riding bikes. I hit a rock and wiped out. Pete called me a crybaby and mama's boy. I got mad and punched him. We fought.		
What did you want?		**What did the other person want?**
I didn't want him to make fun of me. Sympathy.		*I don't know.*

WHAT WERE THE ORIGINS OF THE CONFLICT?		
Resources (time, money, property)	**Basic Needs** (belonging, power, freedom, fun)	**Values** (beliefs, priorities, principles)
	To be friends. Respect.	*Friends don't bully each other.*

HOW DID YOU RESPOND?		
Soft	**Hard**	**Principled**
	Punched him.	

WHAT WAS THE OUTCOME?		
Lose-Lose	**Win-Lose**	**Win-Win**
We haven't played together since the fight.		

35

Student Manual
page 36

Conflict Review

INSTRUCTIONS: Think of a conflict you recently had with a friend
and tell about it in the boxes below.

WHAT WAS THE CONFLICT?	
What happened?	
What did you want?	**What did the other person want?**

WHAT WERE THE ORIGINS OF THE CONFLICT?		
Resources (time, money, property)	**Basic Needs** (belonging, power, freedom, fun)	**Values** (beliefs, priorities, principles)

HOW DID YOU RESPOND?		
Soft	**Hard**	**Principled**

WHAT WAS THE OUTCOME?		
Lose-Lose	**Win-Lose**	**Win-Win**

36

11 Negative-Positive

PURPOSE To understand that conflict in and of itself is neither negative nor positive

MATERIALS Student Manuals
Newsprint
Markers

FORMAT OPTION Cooperative learning

PROCEDURE
1. Have students work in small groups. Provide half of the groups with sheets of newsprint with a negative sign (–) and the other half with sheets of newsprint with a positive sign (+) written at the top.

2. Ask the groups having sheets with negative signs: "Think of times when conflicts go unresolved. What happens?" Ask the groups having sheets with positive signs: "Think of times when people work together for win-win agreements. What happens?"

3. Have each group list at least five possible outcomes, either positive or negative.

4. Invite the small groups to share their results, then post the lists in the room.

5. Ask students to record positive and negative outcomes they have personally experienced on page 37 of their Student Manuals, "My Conflicts: Negative and Positive Outcomes." Discuss the outcomes students describe.

6. Refer students to page 38 of their Student Manuals, "Summary: Negative and Positive Outcomes," to review the main outcomes.

7. Stress the idea that conflict in and of itself is neither positive nor negative. Rather, the actions we choose turn conflict into a competitive, devastating battle or into a constructive challenge where there is opportunity for growth. We always have the choice, when in conflict, to work for resolution.

Student Manual
page 37

My Conflicts:
Negative and Positive Outcomes

INSTRUCTIONS: Think of times when conflicts in your life have gone
unresolved. Tell about what happened.

_____

_____

_____

_____

_____

_____

_____

INSTRUCTIONS: Think of times when you and other people have worked
together to resolve conflicts. Tell about what happened.

_____

_____

_____

_____

_____

_____

_____

37

Student Manual
page 38

Summary: Negative and Positive Outcomes

NEGATIVE (-)

If a conflict remains unresolved, some possible outcomes are:

- Threats and blame continue.
- Feelings are hurt; relationships are damaged.
- Self-interest results; positions harden.
- Emotions increase; tempers get out of hand.
- Sides are drawn; others get involved.
- People do not get what they want and need.
- Violence results.

POSITIVE (+)

If people work together for agreement, some possible outcomes are:

- Better ideas are produced to solve the problem.
- Relationships and communication are improved.
- Views are clarified; problems are dealt with.
- People listen to and respect one another.
- There is cooperation.
- People get what they want and need.
- Fairness and peace are achieved.

> We have the choice when in conflict to work for a positive resolution.

38

ACTIVITY

12   Key Concept Review

PURPOSE   To understand the meaning of key concepts related to conflict

MATERIALS   Butcher paper
Magazines
Comic books
Scissors
Glue
Markers

FORMAT OPTIONS   Cooperative learning
Class meeting

PROCEDURE

1. Ask students to define in their own words the following concepts. Solicit several definitions for each. Discuss the different definitions until the group displays a common understanding of each of the concepts.

CONFLICT	LIMITED RESOURCES
BELONGING	DIFFERENT VALUES
POWER	PRINCIPLED RESPONSE
FREEDOM	RESOLUTION

2. Divide the class into eight groups of equal numbers. Assign each group one of the words and instruct them to use the art materials to develop a poster that shows the meaning of the concept—draw a picture, write a definition, create a collage, and so forth.

3. Display the posters in the classroom.

SECTION 3

Understanding Peace and Peacemaking

OVERVIEW

Just as conflict is a natural, vital part of life, so is peace. Peace is essential to human survival (both individually and collectively), inherent in human development, and within each of us. Peace is most often regarded as an outcome or a goal instead of a behavior. When peace is viewed as an outcome or goal, the emphasis is generally on preventing violence or war. The problem with this perspective is that peace becomes the end and not the means of preventing war or violence. Viewing peace as an outcome or goal has an effect similar to holding negative perceptions about conflict: Such a view hinders the pursuit of behaviors that would help resolve disputes before violence ensues. Viewing peace as a behavior shifts the emphasis toward the actions of peacemaking.

PERCEPTIONS OF PEACE

Perceptions of peace are diverse. When asked to list words or phrases associated with peace, most adults and children respond by defining peace in the negative, as the absence of something—commotion, stress, hostility, war. The conventional wisdom seems to be that peace is the absence of conflict. It follows logically, under this viewpoint, that if conflict is in fact an inevitable part of everyday existence, as detailed in Section 2, peace is forever unattainable. Positive interpretations of peace tend to evoke elusive rather than concrete images—serenity, calm, contentment—and are articulated more as inspiration than as practice. Peace is often viewed, especially by children, as something that is weak, passive, dull, or boring. It is little wonder that most people do not perceive peace as something that they make because peace is not first understood as something concrete or practical. People who make peace perceive it simply as the practice of honoring self, one another, and the environment. Peacemakers view themselves as responsible for the health, survival, and integrity of the world—whether that world is the classroom, school, community, or earth.

To peacebreakers the notion of justice is at best compensatory and at worst retaliatory. Peacebreakers seek retribution from those who

113

threaten or harm them. They react negatively and often aggressively toward those who challenge their notion of what is "right" or "should be," even when those with other points of view express those views in nonthreatening, reasonable ways. Peacebreakers see limited potential in others and in relationships. Peacebreakers hold themselves in reserve from others, their problems, and their possibilities. Peacebreakers do not own problems; problems are someone else's fault, and someone else is responsible for solving them. Peacebreakers see themselves as disconnected from the world and its people.

On the other hand, peacemakers perceive themselves as connected to the world and its people. Peacemakers are reflective thinkers and listeners who understand personal, social, and global realities. Peacemakers see themselves as responsible for finding resolutions to problems and for taking risks to create new possibilities. Peacemakers even attempt, to the best of their abilities, to reconcile conflicts within themselves—they strive to balance their own needs.

PEACEMAKING BEHAVIOR

Peace is not static. Peace is dynamic—a present and future behavior, originated and sustained by individuals being peacemakers. Peacemaking is behaving in harmony with a larger wholeness, a harmony that begins within each individual and is connected to and part of a social integrity that sanctions one to live without violating the rights of others. The challenge is to understand what really constitutes peace, to know the behaviors of peacemaking, and to educate children to live in peace.

In the peaceable school, students learn about peacemaking in a social context that is real to them—the classroom and the school. As stated in the introduction, peace is that state in which, in any specific context, each individual fully exercises his or her responsibilities to ensure that all individuals fully enjoy all the rights accorded to any one individual in that context. Peace is that state in which every individual is able to survive and thrive without being hampered by conflict, prejudice, hatred, antagonism, or injustice. Once students have had ample opportunity to practice the behaviors of peacemaking in the relatively safe environment of the school, they develop the capacity to generalize that learning to the larger contexts of life.

How does one make peace or behave as a peacemaker? First, peace is made day by day, moment by moment, within and by each of us. Second, peace is a total behavior with simultaneous doing, thinking, and feeling components. It is easy to understand the behavior of peace by contrasting peacemaker behaviors with peacebreaker behaviors, as illustrated in Table 8.

Are withdrawing, forcing, rejecting, angering, hating, and so on going to create opportunities for honoring self and others? For pursuing fairness and justice without violence? For protecting and promoting human rights? For maintaining fulfilling human relationships? Are communicating, supporting, respecting, reflecting, calming, and the

TABLE 8   Peacemaker Versus Peacebreaker Behaviors

	Peacemaker	Peacebreaker
Doing	Risking	Reserving
	Expanding	Withdrawing
	Persuading	Forcing
	Communicating	Coercing
	Inventing	Diminishing
	Supporting	Punishing
Thinking	Concerning	Repulsing
	Creating	Positioning
	Imagining	Blocking
	Respecting	Rejecting
	Reflecting	Blaming
Feeling	Caring	Hating
	Calming	Angering
	Stimulating	Fearing
	Harmonizing	Frustrating

like going to create opportunities for honoring self and others? For pursuing fairness and justice without violence? For protecting and promoting human rights? For maintaining fulfilling human relationships?

The doing, thinking, and feeling behaviors of the peacemaker are also the behaviors of mediators, negotiators, and group problem solvers. A clear understanding of conflict resolution principles is central to all peacemaking efforts. Animosity and violence occur because conflict resolution methods are either unknown or not practiced. Adults and children can incorporate peacemaking into their daily lives by learning and practicing the principles of conflict resolution.

PRINCIPLES OF CONFLICT RESOLUTION

Much of the credit for the development of the conflict resolution profession and principles goes to the Harvard Negotiation Project, founded by Roger Fisher and William Ury. The ideas in the book *Getting to Yes* (Fisher, Ury, & Patton, 1991) have gained acceptance from a broad audience and are frequently cited. The remainder of this overview summarizes these principles, illustrating how they might be applied in the peaceable school.

Separate the People From the Problem

This first principle concerns people's strong emotions, differing perceptions, and difficulty communicating. When dealing with a problem, it is common for people to misunderstand one another, to get upset, and to take things personally. Every problem has both substantive and relationship issues. Unfortunately, the relationship of the parties tends to become involved in the substance of the problem. Fisher et al. (1991) assert that "before working on the substantive problem, the 'people problem' should be disentangled from it and dealt with separately. Figuratively if not literally, the participants should come to see themselves as working side by side, attacking the problem, not each other" (p. 11).

People problems fall into three categories: perception, emotion, and communication. These problems must be dealt with directly; they cannot be resolved indirectly with substantive concessions. Fisher et al. (1991) maintain, "Where perceptions are inaccurate, you can look for ways to educate. If emotions run high, you can find ways for each person involved to let off steam. Where misunderstanding exists, you can work to improve communication" (p. 21).

Dealing With Problems of Perception

When dealing with problems of perception, it is important to remember that conflict does not lie in objective reality but in how people perceive that reality. As Fisher et al. (1991) point out, "Truth is simply one more argument—perhaps a good one, perhaps not—for dealing with the difference. The difference itself exists because it exists in [disputants'] thinking. Facts, even if established, may do nothing to solve the problem" (p. 22). For example, two children may agree that one lost a library book and that the other found it but still disagree on who should get to read it first. Two children involved in a fight may agree on which one hit first but may never agree on who started the fight. Two children who are angry with each other may not agree on the reason for their anger. It is ultimately each child's perception that constitutes the problem—understanding each other's perceptions opens the way to resolution.

As discussed in Fisher et al.'s *Getting to Yes,* some tactics for dealing with problems of perception are as follows.*

Put yourself in their shoes. People tend to see what they want to see, focusing on facts that confirm their points of view and disregarding or misinterpreting those that do not. Being able to see the situation as the other side sees it is an important skill for dealing with problems of perception. To do this, people need to withhold judgment and attempt to understand what it feels like to be the other person. *(The behavior is empathizing.)*

---

*In the following pages, the material set in two columns has been adapted from *Getting to Yes: Negotiating Agreement Without Giving In* (2nd ed.) by Roger Fisher, William Ury, and Bruce Patton. Copyright © 1981, 1991 by Roger Fisher and William Ury. Reprinted by permission of Houghton Mifflin Co. All rights reserved.

Evaluate assumptions based on fear.	People make assumptions based on their fears, assuming that whatever they fear is the intended action of the other side. Every idea advanced by the other side is viewed suspiciously. Getting in touch with fears and assumptions about the other side's intentions allows opportunity for new directions and for new ideas to unfold. *(The behaviors are reflecting and self-evaluating.)*
Do not blame.	Viewing the other side as responsible for the problem is a common perception, and blaming is a common block to conflict resolution. Even if blaming is justified, it is counterproductive. The other side perceives blaming as an attack, becoming defensive and resistive. *(The behaviors are holding blameless and focusing on the problem, not the person, and the future, not the past.)*
Discuss each other's perceptions.	Discussing perceptions and making the differences in them explicit provide opportunity for understanding each other's concerns and interests. *(The behaviors are actively listening and openly expressing concerns.)*
Save face.	Saving face involves preserving self-respect and self-image. People need to be able to reconcile their positions and their proposals with past words, actions, and values. Often people will refuse to come to an agreement not because the proposed solutions are unacceptable but because they wish to avoid the feeling or appearance of backing down. When this happens, solutions must be conceptualized or phrased differently so that the outcome is perceived to be fair. *(The behavior is reframing.)*

Dealing With Problems of Emotion

When dealing with problems of emotion, it is important to remember that the parties may be more ready to fight it out than to work together cooperatively to solve the problem. As Fisher et al. (1991) state, "People often come to a negotiation realizing that the stakes are high and feeling threatened. Emotions on one side will generate emotions on the other. Fear may breed anger; and anger, fear. Emotions may quickly bring a negotiation to an impasse or an end" (p. 29). Some strategies for dealing with problems of emotion are as follows.

Be aware of emotions and find the cause.

Having people identify their own emotions and then the emotions of the other side opens understanding. Finding the source of the emotions is sometimes helpful: Why is the person angry? Is the person responding to past conflicts and wanting to retaliate? Are personal problems at home interfering with problems at school? *(The behaviors are self-evaluating and reflecting.)*

Make emotions explicit and acknowledge them as legitimate.

Making the feelings of each party a clear focus of discussion frees people from the burden of unexpressed emotions. When the emotions of each side are known to both, that knowledge enhances the ability of the parties to work on the problem without emotional reaction. *(The behavior is reflecting feelings.)*

Let off steam.

Venting anger, frustration, and other negative emotions helps release those feelings. Every strong statement contains some underlying interest or concern that prompted the statement. The job of conflict resolvers is to listen to other people's toxic, positional, threatening statements and translate them into problem statements that can be responded to productively. *(The behavior is reframing.)*

Do not react to emotional outbursts.

The best strategy to adopt while one side lets off steam is to listen without responding to attacks and to encourage the speaker to speak until there is little or no emotion left to erupt. Adopting the rule that only one person can express anger at a time makes it legitimate not to respond to an angry outburst while at the same time making the ventilation of anger and strong feelings legitimate. This rule helps people control their emotions. *(The behaviors are accepting and supporting.)*

Use symbolic gestures.

Simple acts such as a note of sympathy, a statement of regret, shaking hands, eating together, and so forth can have a constructive emotional impact. Sometimes a sincere apology can defuse emotions effectively. Statements such as "I am sorry we have this problem, and I am sorry you are hurt" can easily improve a hostile emotional situation. This use of apology, which will usually not include an admission of personal responsibility for the problem or intention to harm, is a valid strategy for defusing emotions in a conflict situation. This sort of apology is different from the sort often prescribed by adults for children as the strategy to conclude a conflict: "Now apologize for hurting." This latter type of apology, often coerced, is at best a soft resolution of conflict; at worst, no resolution at all. *(The behaviors are accepting and empathizing.)*

Dealing With Problems of Communication

Given the diversity of background and values among individuals, poor communication is not surprising. As Fisher et al. (1991) point out, "Communication is never an easy thing even between people who have an enormous background of shared values and experience. . . . Whatever you say, you should expect that the other side will almost always hear something different" (p. 32).

There are four basic problems in communication: (a) people may not be talking to each other; (b) even if they are talking to each other, they may not be hearing each other; (c) what one intends to communicate is almost never exactly what one communicates; and (d) people misunderstand or misinterpret the content communicated. Some skills to alleviate these communication problems are as follows.

Listen actively and acknowledge what is being said.

Listening requires total attention to and concentration on the speaker. Too often, we are too busy thinking of our response to what is being said to pay close attention to what the speaker is telling us. Active listening, or listening for understanding, enables people to understand others' perceptions and emotions. It also lets other people know that they have been heard and understood. *(The behaviors include attending with your body, summarizing or paraphrasing facts and feelings, and clarifying what was heard.)*

Speak to be understood.

Instead of talking with the intent to debate or impress, it is more productive for disputants to talk with the intent to be understood. To de-escalate the conflict, one must work hard to state one's issues or the problem in a clear, direct way that can evoke a receptive, constructive response. Talking with the intent to be understood helps both sides recognize that they see the situation differently, increasing the probability that they will become joint problem solvers. It is also important to avoid using toxic or value-laden language and to avoid presenting the problem in a positional, either/or way or as a demand. *(The behaviors are relating and reframing.)*

Speak about yourself.

Instead of trying to explain and condemn the motivations and intentions of the other side, it is more persuasive to describe a problem in terms of its impact on you. Avoid the inclination to complain about what the other party did or what you think the reason is for that behavior. A statement about how you feel is difficult to challenge; at the same time it conveys information without provoking a defensive reaction that prevents understanding. It is best to describe the situation in behavioral or operational terms, neither using global terms that give little definition to the problem nor being so specific that possible resolutions are restricted. *(The behavior is making "I" statements.)*

Speak for a purpose.

Before speaking, know what you want the other person to understand or what you want to find out and know what purpose the information will serve. Be especially alert to your assumptions and make them explicit. Also be alert to the use of contextual language when the other party is not familiar with the context. Some thoughts or disclosures, especially if they do not serve a productive purpose, are best left unsaid. *(The behavior is self-evaluating.)*

Adjust for differences in personality, gender, and culture between yourself and those with whom you are speaking.

Be sensitive to the values, perceptions, concerns, norms of behavior, and mood of those with whom you wish to communicate. Do not assume that the other person will act or react as you would. Do not ascribe your assumptions to the other person. Do not act as if the other person should adjust to your style. There are cultural and gender differences in communication style and substance. A variety of factors may influence what is said and heard. These include pacing (fast or slow), formality (high or low), physical proximity (close or distant), bluntness of speech (direct or indirect), time frame (short or long term), and relationship scope (business only or all encompassing), as well as nonverbal behaviors such as eye contact and posture. Differences exist within every human identity. Being aware of potential differences and then tempering those perceived differences by listening carefully to the message—its style and its substance—is the only strategy proven to enhance the potential for effective communication between individuals. *(The behaviors are listening and self-evaluating.)*

These techniques for dealing with the problems of perception, emotion, and communication work because the behaviors associated with separating the relationship from the problem change people from adversaries in a personal face-to-face confrontation to partners in a side-by-side search for a fair agreement advantageous to each.

Focus on Interests, Not Positions

The second principle holds that the focus of conflict resolution should not be on the positions held by the people in dispute but on what the people really want—in other words, their interests. The objective of conflict resolution is to satisfy the underlying interests of all parties. Understanding the difference between positions and interests is crucial because interests, not positions, define problems. Positions are something that people decide they want; interests are what cause people to decide. Fisher et al. (1991) note that "compromising between positions is not likely to produce an agreement which will effectively take care of the human needs that led people to adopt those positions" (p. 11). Reconciling interests rather than compromising between positions works because for every interest there are generally several possible satisfactory solutions. Furthermore, reconciling interests works because behind opposing positions lie more shared and compatible interests than conflicting ones.

For example, look at some of the shared interests of a student and teacher. Both want the student to succeed in learning, both want the class to be a cooperative group that treats members with care, both want to be liked by the other, both want to be respected, and both want school to be enjoyable. They may also have interests that differ but that may not necessarily conflict—that is, they have compatible interests. For example, the teacher may be interested in promoting cooperation and eliminating competition in a learning group, whereas the student may be interested in being recognized for individual contributions. To serve both interests, the teacher could recognize the quality work of the group, stating that this outcome is possible only because of the specific contributions of each individual group member. Or perhaps the teacher wants each student to interact with several members of the class to develop a sense of community, whereas the student wants to associate only with one or two close friends. In response, the teacher could ask the various cliques in the class to talk about what makes them special and what the group contributes to the class as a whole. The teacher could then reframe this information as the strengths and resources represented by group members and suggest that each class member try to learn more about at least one of the other groups.

Positions are usually concrete and clearly expressed. But the interests underlying the positions are less tangible and often unexpressed. Identifying the interests of both parties is done by asking the following questions:

> Why? (to determine the reasons people take particular positions and to uncover interests)

> Why not? (to encourage people to think about the choices or decisions they want made and ask why these have not been made)

In almost every conflict, multiple interests exist. Only by talking about and acknowledging interests explicitly can people uncover mutual interests and resolve conflicting interests. In searching for the interests behind people's positions, it is important to look for the basic psychological needs that motivate all people: belonging, power, freedom, and fun. If these basic needs are identified as shared or compatible interests, options can be developed to address them. For example, students nearly always want to be friends, or at least they want not to be enemies (belonging). They want to be respected for who they are and what they do (power). They also want to have options from which to choose (freedom) and to have situations be enjoyable and not painful (fun). When common or compatible interests are discovered, a foundation for cooperation is established upon which students can build to resolve their conflicting interests fairly.

To reiterate, unless interests are identified, people in conflict will not be able to make a wise agreement. Temporary agreements may be reached, but such agreements typically do not last because the real interests have not been addressed. Shared and compatible interests are the building blocks for a wise agreement.

Invent Options for Mutual Gain

The third principle allows parties the opportunity to design potential solutions without the pressure of deciding. Before trying to reach agreement, the parties brainstorm a wide range of possible options that advance shared interests and creatively reconcile differing interests. Fisher et al. (1991) say, "In most negotiations there are four major obstacles that inhibit the inventing of an abundance of options: (1) premature judgment, (2) searching for the single answer, (3) the assumptions of a fixed pie, and (4) thinking that 'solving their problem is their problem'" (p. 57).

The problem with premature judgment is that such judgment hinders the process of creating options by limiting imagination. When searching for a single answer, people see their job as narrowing the gap between positions, not broadening the options available. Looking from the outset for the single best answer impedes the wiser decision-making process in which people select from a large number of possible answers. When people make the assumption that resources are finite (i.e., a "fixed pie"), they see the situation as essentially either/or—one person or the other gets what is in dispute, or at least a bigger portion of what is in dispute. Thinking that solving the problem is the problem presents an obstacle to inventing options because each side's concern is only with its own immediate interests. If options are obvious, why bother to invent them? This shortsighted self-concern leads people to develop only partisan positions, partisan arguments, and one-sided solutions.

Ways to eliminate the obstacles to inventing options for mutual gain exist. Fisher et al. (1991) identify the following guidelines for generating options:

1. Separate the act of inventing options from the act of judging them.

2. Broaden the options on the table rather than looking for a single answer.

3. Search for mutual gains.

4. Invent ways of making decisions easy.

Brainstorming is used to separate inventing from deciding. The key ground rule in brainstorming is to postpone criticism and evaluation of ideas. To broaden options, participants think about the problem in different ways and use ideas to generate other ideas. Inventing options for mutual gain is done by developing notions that address the shared and compatible interests of the parties in dispute. The final choice of a solution is made easier when options that appeal to the interests of both parties exist.

Insist on Using Objective Criteria

This principle ensures that the agreement reflects some fair standard instead of the arbitrary will of either side. Using objective criteria means that neither party needs to give in to the other; rather, they can defer to a fair solution.

Objective criteria are developed on the basis of fair standards and fair procedures. Objective criteria are independent of will, legitimate, and practical. Theoretically, they can be applied to both sides. The example of the age-old way to divide a piece of cake between two children illustrates the use of fair standards and procedures: One cuts and the other chooses. Neither complains about an unfair division.

It is important to remember to frame each issue as a joint search for objective criteria; to reason and be open to reason as to which standards are most appropriate and how they should be applied; and to yield only to principle, not pressure of will. Pressure of will can take the form of bribes, threats, manipulative appeals to trust, or simple refusal to budge.

One standard of justification does not exclude the existence of others. When what one side believes to be fair is not what the other believes to be fair, this does not automatically exclude fairness as a criterion or mean that one notion of fairness must be accepted over the other. It does require both parties to explain what the criteria mean to them and to respond to reasons for applying another standard or for applying a standard differently.

When people advance different standards, the key is to look for an objective basis for deciding between them, such as which standard has been used by the parties in the past or which standard is more widely applied. The principled response is to invite the parties to state their reasoning, to suggest objective criteria that apply, and to refuse to yield except on the basis of these principles. Plainly, a refusal to yield except in response to sound reasons is an easier position to defend—publicly and privately—than is a refusal to yield combined with a refusal to advance sound reasons. One who insists that problem solving be based on merits can bring others around to adopting that tactic once it becomes clear that to do so is the only way to advance substantive interests.

QUESTIONS FOR CLASS MEETINGS

The following questions and statements, given in no particular order, may be used in class meetings to promote understanding of the content of this section.

1. What is peace?

2. Give examples of occasions when you felt you exhibited peacemaking behavior.

3. Can you give an example of a situation in which someone else behaved in a manner you thought was an example of peacemaking behavior?

4. How do you get to know another person's point of view?

5. How can you listen to someone you are afraid of or to someone you don't trust?

6. How do you feel when you are blamed for a problem?

7. What happens when you back down?

8. When you feel threatened, what can you do to feel safer?

9. What are all the ways you can let another person know how you feel? Which of these ways will usually not make the other person become more upset?

10. How do you deal with your own anger? With other people's anger?

11. What are ways you can make another person feel accepted and valued?

12. What are some ways you can put yourself in another person's shoes?

13. How would this class be better if we were all more alike? If we were all more different?

14. What are the common interests that we have because we are all members of this class?

15. What standards can be used to determine whether a solution is a good one for our class?

Suggested Readings

Beckman, S., & Holmes, J. (1993). *Battles, hassles, tantrums, and tears: Practical strategies for coping with conflict and managing peace at home.* New York: Hearst.

Carter, J. (1993). *Talking peace.* New York: Dutton.

Fisher, R., & Brown, S. (1988). *Getting together: Building relationships as we negotiate.* New York: Penguin.

Fisher, R., Ury, W., & Patton, B. (1991). *Getting to yes: Negotiating agreement without giving in* (2nd ed.). Boston: Houghton Mifflin.

Johnson, D. W., & Johnson, R. T. (1991). *Teaching students to be peace makers.* Edina, MN: Interaction.

Kreidler, W. J. (1990). *Elementary perspectives 1: Teaching concepts of peace and conflict.* Cambridge, MA: Educators for Social Responsibility.

Lantieri, L., & Patti, J. (1996). *Waging peace in our schools.* Boston: Beacon.

Ury, W. (1993). *Getting past no.* New York: Bantam.

A CTIVITY

1   Peace Is . . .

PURPOSE   To increase understanding of peace

MATERIALS   Student Manuals
Newsprint
Markers
Tape

FORMAT OPTIONS   Whole class discussion/participation
Class meeting

NOTE   Before beginning, prepare four sheets of newsprint by writing one of the following headings at the top of each:

> Peace at school
>
> Peace at home
>
> Peace in the world
>
> Peace in our community

PROCEDURE
1. Refer the group to "What Peace Means to Me," on page 41 in their Student Manuals. Say the word *peace*. Ask students to think of words or pictures that come to mind when they think of peace. Typical responses include the following: *calm, harmony, cooperation, quiet, no war, no violence.* Give students time to write or draw their ideas in their Student Manuals.

2. Discuss expressions students have heard associated with the word *peace,* such as the following:

> Peace on earth
>
> Peace and quiet
>
> Make peace, not war
>
> Peace of mind
>
> Peace from within
>
> Peace-loving people

3. Ask students to think of symbols of peace. For example:

   Peace pipe

   Olive branch

   Dove

   Peace treaty

   Peace sign

4. Give each group of five to seven students one of the prepared sheets of newsprint and a marker. Encourage groups to compile a list or draw pictures of peace for their assigned topic.

5. Invite each group to share their work, then post the sheets around the room. As examples are shared, ask one or two members of the group to talk in more detail about some of the words or pictures on their sheet.

6. Refer students to page 42, "Definitions of Peace," in their Student Manuals, and discuss.* The following questions may help:

   How is peace different in these definitions?

   How is peace the same in these definitions?

   What words can you think of for ideas that are important to peace (for example: *justice, honesty, love*)?

---

*The first two definitions of peace are quoted from, respectively, "Gifts, Not Stars" (p. 553), by George E. Lyon, in *Horn Book, September–October,* 1992, and *Peace Begins With You* (p. 33), by Katherine Scholes, 1990, San Francisco: Little, Brown. The last two are from the introduction to the present volume.

Student Manual
page 41

What Peace Means to Me

INSTRUCTIONS: In the boxes, write words or draw pictures that come
to mind when you think of peace.

PEACE

41

Student Manual
page 42

Definitions of Peace

PEACE is a process of responding to diversity and conflict with tolerance, imagination, and flexibility; war is a product of our intent to stamp out diversity and conflict when we give up on the process of peace. — *George E. Lyon*

PEACE is not a gap between times of fighting, or a space where nothing is happening. Peace is something that lives, spreads, and needs to be looked after. — *Katherine Scholes*

PEACE is that state when each individual fully exercises his or her responsibilities to ensure that all individuals fully enjoy all rights.

PEACE is that state when every individual is able to survive and thrive without being hampered by conflict, prejudice, hatred, antagonism, or injustice.

42

A CTIVITY

2 Peace Collage

PURPOSE To explore the concept of peace in more detail

MATERIALS Student Manuals
A story on the theme of peace
Magazines
Newspapers
Scissors
Glue
Butcher paper

FORMAT OPTIONS Whole class discussion/participation
Learning center
Cooperative learning

PROCEDURE
1. Read a story where peace is the theme. Discuss peace and how it was made in the story. Some good ones to try are "The Tree House," by Lois Lowry, and "The Birds' Peace," by Jean Craighead, from *The Big Book for Peace,* edited by Ann Durrell and Marilyn Sachs (Dutton, 1990). Other books for children are listed in Appendix B.

2. Give students magazines and newspapers and encourage them to cut out headlines and pictures representing peace. Have students glue their cutouts to the butcher paper to create peace collages.

3. Share and discuss the collages.

4. Read or have a volunteer read "A Blessing for Peace" from page 43 of the Student Manual. Give learners the opportunity to write their own poem or blessing about peace in the circle provided.

Student Manual
page 43

A Blessing for Peace

One dream: Understand

One hope: Harmony

One prayer: Peace

INSTRUCTIONS: Write your own poem or blessing about peace.

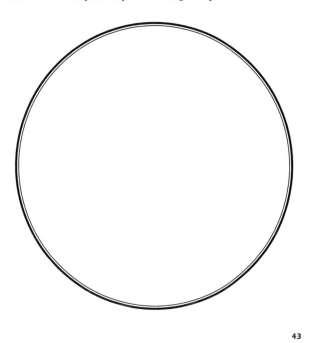

43

3 Peacemaking and Peacebreaking

PURPOSE To learn that peacemaking and peacebreaking behavior is made up of doing, thinking, and feeling components

MATERIALS Student Manuals
Markers

FORMAT OPTIONS Whole class discussion/participation
Class meeting

PROCEDURE 1. Refer the group to "Peacemakers," on page 44 in their Student Manuals, and discuss. Ask the following questions:

How do you make peace?

How does a peacemaker behave?

Stress the idea that peace is made day by day, moment by moment, within each of us and by each of us.

2. Read or have student volunteers read the "Makers and Breakers" story on pages 45–46 of the Student Manual aloud.

3. Refer the group to page 47 in their Student Manuals, "Maker and Breaker Behaviors." Ask students to list or draw the behaviors of the Makers and Breakers in the boxes provided for doing, thinking, and feeling. (The sample on page 140 shows how behaviors might be categorized.)

4. Invite students to share their responses, then discuss the following questions:

Did Makers honor themselves and others? How?

Did Breakers honor themselves and others? What did they do?

Did Makers exercise their responsibilities to ensure that everyone was able to enjoy his or her rights? How?

Did Breakers exercise their responsibilities to ensure that everyone was able to enjoy his or her rights? What did they do?

Did Makers build friendships and fulfilling relationships? How?

Did Breakers build friendships and fulfilling relationships? What did they do?

Did Makers make peace? How?

Did Breakers make peace? What did they make?

5. Refer students to page 48 in their Student Manuals, "Peacemaking and Peacebreaking: What I See Around Me." Instruct students to list or draw examples of peacemaking and peacebreaking they see at school, at home, and on television, then discuss these examples.

6. Refer students to page 49 in their Student Manuals, "Peacemaking and Peacebreaking: My Behavior." Invite students to think about a typical day and to list or draw their own peacemaking and peacebreaking behavior during this typical day, then discuss students' responses.

7. Summarize the main point that we make peace by actively choosing to behave in certain ways.

Student Manual
page 44

Peacemakers

♦ Peacemakers perceive peace simply as the practice of honoring self, one another, and the environment.

♦ Peacemakers view themselves as responsible for the health, survival, and integrity of the world, whether that world is the classroom, the school, the community, or the earth.

How do you make peace? Peace is made day by day, moment by moment, within each of us and by each of us.

44

Student Manual
page 45

Makers and Breakers

Once upon a time, in a park on a planet far away from Earth, there were beings called Makers and other beings called Breakers. As is often the way in fairy tales, Makers and Breakers were as different as night and day. In fact, Makers played in the park by night, and Breakers played in the park by day. That was the way things were done on this planet. There were daytime beings, and there were nighttime beings. Makers never saw Breakers, and Breakers never saw Makers.

One day, more beings arrived at the planet by spaceship. Silently hovering over the park in their spaceship, they observed both day and night. In the light of day, the space beings watched and listened to the Breakers. They heard raging Breakers yell at one another: *"You can't play! I hate you!" "It's your fault!"* and *"Give me your hat, or I won't play with you!"*

Some of the Breakers wrote hateful messages about other Breakers on the fence that surrounded the park. They tormented one another about being fat, ugly, or stupid. Play fights always ended in vicious real fights. There were Breakers tied to trees being punished for fighting.

Breakers were frenzied. They cut down a tree and blocked the entrance to the park. They hit and kicked one another to get their way. Their games had no rules. Breakers reveled in winning, and they taunted the losers. Many Breakers were alone and hungry—they did not laugh and play with others.

When dusk drew near, Breakers pushed and knocked one another over the tree that blocked the way out of the park. Some of the Breakers were hiding under the bushes. They were the last ones to flee the park when it became dark.

Soon after dark, the Makers arrived. It took all of their combined strength to move the huge tree away from the entrance to the park. They cheered loudly to celebrate their feat.

The Makers were kind. They cared about one another, and they cared about the park. They discussed the jobs to be done, and they negotiated to solve disagreements about what would be done and who would do what. Some Makers painted the fence to cover the hateful statements. Other Makers planted trees, bushes, and flowers. Several Makers picked up trash and repaired the broken park benches, swings, and merry-go-round.

45

When their work was finished, they played. As they played, the space beings heard them say things like *"Thanks for helping me." "That was a great effort you made! Please keep trying!"* and *"I have a new ball. Will you play with me?"*

There were many games. Everyone followed the rules and helped one another learn new games. Makers encouraged one another, urged one another to try, and praised one another's accomplishments. The Makers painted glow-in-the-dark pictures, danced in the moonlight, and listened to tales about magical fireflies. They shared snacks from their picnic baskets and planned to build a playhouse from the tree that was cut down.

Makers respected one another. They were safe in the park and so was their property—the picnic baskets, jackets, and toys they brought from home.

The space beings were disturbed by what they observed. They had been sent on a mission to live with the Makers and the Breakers. There was not enough room for all of the space beings to play in the nighttime park. The truth was, after watching, no one from the spaceship really wanted to play with the Breakers in the daytime.

The space beings pondered the problem:

"During the night the park is filled with peacemakers. They are joyous, creative, and loving. They honor one another and their environment. They know how to resolve conflicts. We witnessed these creatures communicating, inventing, imagining, reflecting, supporting, harmonizing, and calming.

"Peacebreakers dwell in the park in the daytime. They are unhappy, afraid, and hateful. They do not respect one another or their environment. They do not know how to resolve conflicts. We watched these creatures blaming, accusing, frustrating, angering, rejecting, punishing, and withdrawing.

"Each day, peace is broken, and each night, peace is made."

The space beings had learned much about peace by watching the daytime and nighttime park. One morning, the spaceship landed in the park. The space beings had realized what their true mission was. They had been sent to this planet to teach the Breakers how to make peace.

Today and tonight, as it has been ever since the space beings became peacemakers and taught peacemaking behaviors, the park is *peaceable*.

46

Student Manual
page 47

Maker and Breaker Behaviors

INSTRUCTIONS: Write or draw examples of the different kinds of Maker and Breaker behaviors shown in the story.

	PEACEMAKER BEHAVIORS	PEACEBREAKER BEHAVIORS
Doing		
Thinking		
Feeling		

47

Student Manual
page 48

Peacemaking and Peacebreaking: What I See Around Me

INSTRUCTIONS: Write or draw examples of the different kinds of peacemaking and peacebreaking behaviors you see around you.

	PEACEMAKER BEHAVIORS	PEACEBREAKER BEHAVIORS
Doing		
Thinking		
Feeling		

48

Student Manual
page 49

Peacemaking and Peacebreaking: My Behavior

INSTRUCTIONS: Write or draw examples of the different kinds of peacemaking and peacebreaking behaviors you see in yourself.

	PEACEMAKER BEHAVIORS	**PEACEBREAKER BEHAVIORS**
Doing		
Thinking		
Feeling		

49

Sample Responses: Maker and Breaker Behaviors

INSTRUCTIONS: Write or draw examples of the different kinds of peacemaking and peacebreaking behaviors you see around you.

	PEACEMAKER BEHAVIORS	PEACEBREAKER BEHAVIORS
Doing	*Negotiating* *Sharing* *Praising*	*Fighting* *Yelling* *Punishing*
Thinking	*Imagining* *Respecting* *Planning*	*Blaming* *Rejecting*
Feeling	*Caring* *Loving* *Calming*	*Hating* *Angering* *Fearing*

A CTIVITY

4 Making Peace

PURPOSE To introduce the principles of conflict resolution

MATERIALS Student Manuals

FORMAT OPTION Whole class discussion/participation

PROCEDURE
1. Refer group members to page 50 of their Student Manuals, "Principles of Conflict Resolution," and discuss.*

2. Tell students that they will now hear a story that shows how these principles work. Read or have student volunteers read the "Making Peace" story on pages 51–52 of the Student Manual.

3. Discuss the following questions:

   Why did Leah and Elizabeth not make peace in the beginning? (They did not know how to make peace.)

   What did they do? (They did not listen, they misunderstood, they got upset and hurt each other, and so on.)

   How did they change? (They learned the principles of conflict resolution and how to make principled responses.)

   What was the first conflict resolution principle they learned? (To separate the people from the problem.)

   What was the second principle they learned? (To focus on interests, not positions.)

   What did they do to focus on interests and not positions?

   What was the third principle they learned? (To invent win-win options to help them both.)

   What was the fourth principle? (To use fair criteria.)

4. Explain that students will have the opportunity to learn to make principled responses to conflict using the four principles of conflict resolution.

---

*These principles are derived from the work of R. Fisher, W. Ury, and B. Patton, 1991, *Getting to Yes: Negotiating Agreement Without Giving In* (2nd ed.), Boston: Houghton Mifflin.

Student Manual
page 50

Principles of Conflict Resolution

♦ Separate the people from the problem
   (perceptions, emotions, communication).

♦ Focus on interests, not positions.

♦ Invent options for mutual gain
   (**win-win** options).

♦ Use fair criteria.

Making Peace

Leah and Elizabeth were neighbors in a high-rise apartment building. Their apartments were next door to each other, and they shared the same balcony. Each day, Leah and Elizabeth would walk to school together, play hopscotch in the park after school, and make peanut butter sandwiches when they got home. They were best friends.

It was Saturday afternoon when Leah decided to have a pretend camping trip on the balcony. She used chairs and blankets to make a tent and her grandmother's quilts to make sleeping bags. Leah knocked on Elizabeth's balcony door and invited her "camping." The girls pretended to fish off the balcony and watched for birds through binoculars, and Leah's mother prepared a campfire in their grill so they could roast hot dogs and marshmallows. The girls thought that this was a wonderful camping trip.

When it was time for bed, Elizabeth ran inside to get her pillow. She came out with her pillow and her kitten. She snuggled into her sleeping bag with her kitten and pillow while Leah was inside brushing her teeth. When Leah returned to the balcony and began to snuggle into her own sleeping bag, the kitten began to meow. Leah yelled, *"Get your kitten out of my tent!"*

Elizabeth said, *"I always sleep with my kitten, and this is my balcony, too!"*

Leah cried, *"Camping was my idea, and I didn't invite your kitten into the tent."*

Elizabeth could see that Leah was really mad, so she closed her eyes and pretended to be asleep. Leah yelled, *"You are not going to be my friend anymore! You're a wimp if you have to sleep with a kitten!"*

Elizabeth stood up and threw the blankets over the balcony. She cried, *"I'm not camping with you if my kitten is not welcome. I'm not going to be your friend. You are too bossy!"*

When Elizabeth started to throw the pillows over the balcony, Leah grabbed her and shoved her down. Elizabeth hit Leah in the face, and they had a terrible fight. Leah and Elizabeth were both crying hysterically, so they barely noticed a dove landing on the rail of the balcony. They were startled when the dove began to speak: *"My, but you girls are certainly disturbing the peace. I am the dove of peace. I am here to teach you the principles of conflict resolution."*

Leah and Elizabeth stared open-mouthed at the dove but quietly listened as the dove continued to speak: *"There are four principles of conflict resolution. If you learn to use these principles, you can make peace.*

51

Student Manual
page 52

"The first principle is to **separate the people from the problem.** Leah, you think Elizabeth is the problem, and, Elizabeth, you think Leah is the problem. The problem is really about the kitten. You each have a different point of view about the kitten's being in the tent. You are angry with each other, and you each probably misunderstand the other. Leah and Elizabeth, if you communicate and understand each other's perceptions and feelings, you will be able to work out the problem about the kitten.

"The second principle," continued the dove, "is to **focus on interests, not positions.** Leah, your position is that the kitten will not sleep in the tent. Elizabeth, your position is that the kitten will sleep in the tent with you."

Then the dove asked Leah, "Leah, why don't you want the kitten to sleep in the tent?"

"Because I'm allergic to cats," Leah said, "and my mother said not to get near any cats."

Then the dove asked Elizabeth, "Elizabeth, why do you want the kitten to sleep in the tent?"

To this Elizabeth replied, "Because my kitten keeps my feet warm, and it's cold out here on the balcony."

So the dove said, "Leah's interest is not getting sick because of her allergy to cats, and Elizabeth's interest is keeping warm. If you focus on interests, then you will find a solution.

"The third principle," the dove went on, "is to **invent options for mutual gain.** These are called win-win options. Can you think of possible options that will help both of you?"

Elizabeth said, "I could put my kitten inside and put on more socks."

Then Leah chimed in, "I have some battery-powered warming socks that you can wear, and I have lots of stuffed animals that I can bring out to keep us warm."

"Those are win-win options," said the dove, "because they help both of you. They satisfy Elizabeth's interests and Leah's interests.

"The fourth principle," stated the dove, "is to **use fair criteria.** Would it be fair if the solution to the problem made Leah sick? Would it be fair if the solution allowed Elizabeth to be cold? A solution that is fair doesn't allow one to get sick or one to be cold.

"Use these principles to solve your problems, and you will be peacemakers." With those words the dove flew away.

Elizabeth put the kitten to bed inside, and Leah got her battery-operated warming socks and stuffed animals. They retrieved the blankets from underneath the balcony, fixed their tent, and slept peacefully the rest of the night.

52

ACTIVITY

5 Perceptions

PURPOSE To understand and deal with problems of perceptions

MATERIALS Student Manuals

FORMAT OPTIONS Whole class discussion/participation
Class meeting
Cooperative learning

NOTE In addition to the classic story retold here, another good illustration of different perceptions is *The True Story of the Three Little Pigs,* by J. Scieszka (Viking, 1989).

PROCEDURE 1. Tell students the following story:

> Once upon a time, there were six wise people who lived in the same town. All six of them were blind. One day, an elephant was brought to the town. The six wise people wanted to know what the elephant looked like. So, being blind, they each went to the elephant and began touching it. The first person touched the elephant's big, flat ear. He felt it move slowly back and forth. "The elephant is like a fan," he cried. The second person felt the elephant's leg. "The elephant is like a tree," she cried. The third person felt the elephant's tail. "You are both wrong," she exclaimed, "the elephant is like a rope." The fourth person held the elephant's trunk. "You are all wrong," he shouted, "the elephant is like a snake." The fifth person touched one of the elephant's tusks. "The elephant is like a spear!" he yelled. "No, no," the sixth person cried, "you're all stupid! The elephant is like a high wall!" She had felt the elephant's side. "Fan!" "Tree!" "Rope!" "Snake!" "Spear!" "Wall!" The six wise people shouted at each other for an hour. And they never did agree on what an elephant looked like.

2. Discuss the following questions:

> Who was right?
>
> Who told the truth?
>
> Who was wrong?
>
> Who lied?
>
> What is the problem?
>
> What assumptions did the wise people make?
>
> Did the wise people understand one another's points of view?
>
> What could they have done to understand one another better?
>
> Did blaming, name-calling, or arguing help?

3. Summarize the idea that being able to put yourself in another's shoes and see a situation as another sees it is a way of dealing with problems of perception. Stress that we must be careful not to assume that others' viewpoints are the same as ours or that others are wrong or lying if their viewpoints are different.

4. Divide the class into groups of six. Instruct each group to prepare a skit where the six wise people work together to understand one another's perceptions in order to create a peaceable end to the story.

5. Invite each group to present their skit. After each skit, ask the following questions:

> What did the wise people do to understand one another's perceptions?
>
> What peacemaking behaviors—doing, thinking, behaving—did you observe?

6. Ask students, "What can you do to deal with problems of perception?"

7. Refer the group to page 53 in their Student Manuals, "Perceptions," and discuss. Emphasize what can be done to deal with problems of perception and the importance of understanding that different people will have different viewpoints.

Student Manual
page 53

Perceptions

**People have problems with perception.
They might say:**

- ♦ *"You lied . . . it didn't happen that way."*

- ♦ *"I thought of it first."*

- ♦ *"You're wrong."*

To deal with problems of perception:

- ♦ Put yourself in the other person's shoes.

- ♦ Do not blame.

- ♦ Try to understand what it feels like
  to be the other person.

- ♦ Try not to make assumptions.

- ♦ Discuss perceptions.

> We must be careful not to assume that others are
> wrong or lying if their viewpoints are different.

53

A CTIVITY

6　Emotions

PURPOSE　To understand and deal with problems of emotion, especially anger, in a conflict situation

MATERIALS　Student Manuals

FORMAT OPTIONS　Whole class discussion/participation
Class meeting

PROCEDURE　1. Refer the group to "Emotions," on page 54 of their Student Manuals, and discuss. Emphasize the idea that to make peace we must understand and be able to deal with problems of emotion.

2. Refer the group to page 55 in their Student Manuals, "Words to Describe Some Emotions." Discuss the words and elicit examples of situations in which students have experienced these feelings.

3. Next discuss page 56 in the Student Manual, "Emotional Situations." Read each situation and ask the students to identify and record the emotions and the possible causes of the emotions. Remind them to think about basic needs (power, belonging, freedom, fun) when they are thinking about causes. (The sample on page 155 shows how a completed form might look; students' responses may differ.)

4. Summarize that being aware of your own emotions and learning about the other person's emotions opens the door to understanding. Explain that we all get angry at times and that there is nothing wrong with feeling angry. The challenge is to express anger in words so that you can work on the problem in a productive way.

5. Refer the group to page 57 in their Student Manuals, "My Anger Situation." Have students follow the instructions to describe a recent situation in which they became angry.

6. Refer the group to page 58 in their Student Manuals, "Rule for Expressing Anger," and discuss.

7. Divide students into pairs, then have the pairs sit face-to-face. Explain that each student will have the opportunity to express anger while his or her partner pretends to be the person in the anger situation. Stress that students must follow the rule for expressing anger.

8. Have students conduct the exercise, then reverse roles.

9. After each student has had the opportunity to practice both roles, ask:

> How did you feel after venting your anger?
>
> How did you feel after your partner said he or she understood you were angry?
>
> How did you feel not reacting to your partner's anger?
>
> Did taking deep breaths help?

10. Tell students that a sincere apology or statement of regret can help people focus on the problem, not their emotions. Sometimes simple acts of kindness like sending a sympathy note, shaking hands, or eating together can also help. Ask students:

> How would you feel if someone said to you, "I'm sorry we have this problem" or "I'm sorry your feelings are hurt"?
>
> Do these statements mean that you or the other person is right or wrong?
>
> Would you be able to accept this kind of apology and then begin to work on the problem?

11. Restate the idea that, when emotions are known to both sides, the people in conflict are better able to focus on solving their problem.

*Student Manual
page 54*

Emotions

People have problems with emotions:

- ♦ People in conflict often have strong emotions.

- ♦ One person's emotions can provoke another person's emotions.

- ♦ Emotions may interfere with problem solving if they are not acknowledged and understood.

> To make peace, we must understand and be able to deal with problems of emotions.

54

Words to Describe Some Emotions

Happy   Hurt   Excited

Lonely   Annoyed   Anxious

Powerless

Festive   Angry   Frustrated

Embarrassed   Comfortable   Tense

Peaceful   Sad

Courageous   Confused

Furious

Scared   Secure

Terrified

Afraid   Proud   Joyous

55

Student Manual
page 56

Emotional Situations

INSTRUCTIONS: Write the emotions and the possible causes for them in the following situations. *Clue:* Basic needs for *belonging, power, freedom,* and *fun* are often involved in emotional situations.

SITUATION	EMOTION	WHY?
Your aunt just called to say your favorite cousin is coming to spend the weekend.		
You are angry with your best friend because he or she did something with a classmate, and you were not asked to join them.		
Your teacher is punishing you for something you believe is not your fault.		
You have just learned that your best friend's father has accepted a job in another state, and the family is moving very soon.		
You have just been notified that your poster was selected to be your school's single entry in the state contest for Earth Day.		

56

Student Manual
page 57

My Anger Situation

INSTRUCTIONS: Think about a recent situation in which you became angry, then fill in the following information.

I was angry with:

_____

What happened:

_____

_____

_____

The other person wanted:

_____

_____

_____

I wanted:

_____

_____

_____

I was angry because:

_____

_____

_____

57

Student Manual
page 58

Rule for Expressing Anger

THE RULE IS . . .

Only one person can express anger at a time.

While the other person vents:

- ◆ Listen.

- ◆ Take deep breaths.

After the other person vents:

- ◆ Say, "I understand you are angry."

When emotions are known to both sides,
the people in a conflict are better able to
focus on solving their problem.

Sample Responses: Emotional Situations

INSTRUCTIONS: Write the emotions and the possible causes for them in the following situations. *Clue:* Basic needs for *belonging, power, freedom,* and *fun* are often involved in emotional situations.

SITUATION	EMOTION	WHY?
Your aunt just called to say your favorite cousin is coming to spend the weekend.	*Joy Happiness Anticipation*	*Belonging and fun needs are likely to be satisfied.*
You are angry with your best friend because he or she did something with a classmate, and you were not asked to join them.	*Anger Disappointment Frustration Confusion*	*Belonging need, power need, fun need are likely unsatisfied.*
Your teacher is punishing you for something you believe is not your fault.	*Anger Embarrassment Confusion Offended Frustration*	*Freedom need, power need, and fun need are likely not satisfied.*
You have just learned that your best friend's father has accepted a job in another state, and the family is moving very soon.	*Sad Melancholy Lonely Anxious*	*Belonging need and fun need are likely unsatisfied.*
You have just been notified that your poster was selected to be your school's single entry in the state contest for Earth Day.	*Joy Pride Excitement Eagerness*	*Power need is satisfied.*

7 Communication: Active Listening

PURPOSE To learn what active listening is and to practice its components: attending, summarizing, and clarifying

MATERIALS Student Manuals
Easel pad
Marker

FORMAT OPTIONS Whole class discussion/participation
Cooperative learning

PROCEDURE

1. Briefly discuss "Communication Problems," on page 59 of the Student Manual.

2. Group the class into pairs and instruct each pair to find a space in the room to sit face-to-face. Each pair should decide who is the speaker and who is the listener. Explain that in this activity students will have an opportunity to practice some behaviors called *active listening.*

3. Ask the question "How can you show someone you are listening without saying anything?" List students' responses on the easel pad. Elicit the following:

    Eye contact

    Smiles or other facial expressions

    Nods or gestures

    Body position and posture (leaning forward)

    Ignoring distractions

4. Refer the group to page 60 in their Student Manuals, "Active Listening: Attending," and discuss. Summarize that *attending* means both hearing and understanding, and that people know you are attending by your "body talk."

5. Tell the class the speaker in each pair is to think about the perfect weekend. Then the speaker will tell about the perfect weekend. By attending, the listener will encourage the speaker to talk. However, the listener may not speak.

6. Allow the speaker in each pair to talk for a minute. After the minute is up, call time. Ask the speakers:

   Did you think you were listened to?

   What did the listeners do to show you that they were listening and interested?

   How did it feel to be listened to?

   Ask the listeners:

   Did a minute seem like a long time to listen?

   Did you have the urge to interrupt or ask a question?

7. Have the pairs reverse speaker and listener roles and repeat the activity. Follow up with the same questions as before.

8. Discuss the idea that there is no absolutely right or wrong way to show that you are attending to a speaker: Some of what one culture thinks is attending may be thought of very differently in another culture. For example, eye contact in some cultures is considered disrespectful. Smiling and nodding mean agreement to some but do not mean agreement to others. Being too close physically may cause a speaker to be uncomfortable. However, being interested in the speaker and what is being said and not allowing yourself to be distracted is a good listening skill in all cultures. Paying close attention to the speaker and watching to see how the speaker reacts to your behavior will help you to be a good listener.

9. Refer students to page 61 in their Student Manuals, "Active Listening: Summarizing," and discuss. Explain that *summarizing* means you state the facts and reflect the feelings in a situation.

10. Tell students that next the listeners will use the verbal behavior of summarizing (in addition to the attending behaviors) to let the speakers know they have been heard. Before students begin, point out that summarizing does not mean repeating word for word. A summary should be a statement of what was said and the feelings involved but without all the details, especially negative labels (name-calling and the like).

    Example: "She is a cold, uncaring, bossy creep who wouldn't let me go to the movie, and I hate her."

    Summary: "Your mother told you that you could not go to the movie, and that made you angry."

11. Instruct the speaker in each pair to think of a problem (conflict) with someone else and then tell the listener about that problem. In describing the problem, the speaker should answer the following questions:

    What was the problem?

    Whom was it with?

How did you feel?

What did you want?

Why did you want that?

The listener attends to what the speaker is saying, then after a minute summarizes what was said. (Allow the listener in each pair 30 seconds to summarize.)

12. Ask the speakers whether their partners used attending behaviors and whether the listeners' summaries showed they understood what was said. Ask the listeners what was difficult about this exercise, if they paid better attention because they knew they had to summarize, and if they recognized the feelings expressed by the speakers.

13. Change roles in the pairs and repeat.

14. Refer group members to page 62 in their Student Manuals, "Active Listening: Clarifying," and discuss. Explain that, in addition to attending and summarizing, the listener can also encourage the speaker to continue by asking for more information, or *clarifying*.

15. Instruct the speaker in each pair to continue to talk about the problem originally presented. When time is called, the listener is to summarize what the speaker communicated and then seek additional information. Allow speakers a minute to talk; allow listeners a minute to summarize and clarify. Tell the speakers that they may respond to the listeners' requests for more information.

16. Ask the speaker in each pair whether the listener used attending behaviors, understood what was said, and recognized feelings. Ask the listener what was difficult about this, if he or she asked for clarification, and what type of response the questioning generated. Encourage the listener in each pair to give you some specific examples of the questions asked.

17. Change roles in the pairs and repeat.

18. Summarize the idea that active listening is needed to understand a problem and is made up of attending, summarizing, and clarifying behaviors.

Student Manual
page 59

Communication Problems

People have problems with communication:

♦ They may not be talking to each other.

♦ They may not be hearing what the other is saying.

♦ They may not be saying what they mean to say.

♦ They may be misunderstanding or misinterpreting what they hear.

To help prevent communication problems:

♦ Listen actively (attend, summarize, clarify).

♦ Send clear messages.

♦ Speak to be understood.

♦ Speak about yourself.

♦ Speak for a purpose.

♦ Speak with consideration for the listener.

*Student Manual
page 60*

Active Listening: Attending

**Attending means hearing and understanding.
People know you are listening by your "body talk":**

♦ Facial expression

♦ Posture

♦ Eye contact

♦ Gestures

Leaning forward, nodding your head,
and ignoring distractions are ways to show
you are attending.

60

ACTIVITY 7   161

Student Manual
page 61

Active Listening: Summarizing

Summarizing means you state the facts and reflect the feelings. To summarize, you might say:

♦ *"Your Walkman broke when you and Sam collided on the playground. You are mad."*

♦ *"You were sad when you learned that your best friend was moving to a city far away."*

61

Active Listening: Clarifying

Clarifying means getting additional information to make sure you understand. To clarify, you ask questions:

- ◆ *"Can you tell more more about _____?"*

- ◆ *"What happened next?"*

- ◆ *"Is there anything you want to add?"*

- ◆ *"How would you like this to turn out?"*

- ◆ *"How would you feel if you were the other person?"*

8 Communication: Active Listening Practice

PURPOSE   To apply active listening skills to communication situations

MATERIALS   Student Manuals
Index cards

FORMAT OPTION   Whole class

NOTE   Before beginning, prepare the index cards as directed in Step 6.

PROCEDURE

1. Review the active listening behaviors by asking students to explain what they have learned about attending, summarizing, and clarifying. Point out that in real conversations, the three behaviors of attending, summarizing, and clarifying blend together.

2. Have the students form pairs and tell them that, following a demonstration, they will have a conversation to practice the skills of active listening. During this practice conversation, before the listener can make a statement, he or she must summarize, or summarize and clarify, the speaker's statement.

3. Demonstrate this process with a student volunteer and a topic you have chosen. Some good topics include school, vacation, sports, movies, and music.

4. Have the pairs choose any topic and allow them 3 minutes to have the conversation. The pairs then reverse roles and have another 3-minute conversation.

5. Following the conversations, discuss the following questions:

   What worked well in your conversations?

   What was difficult?

   What would make your conversations more clear?

6. Next ask for six volunteers to sit in a circle in the middle of the room. Tell this group that they are to practice communicating by planning the next class party, including games, activities, and refreshments. Explain that you will give each member of the group

a card with additional instructions that are special for that member and known only to him or her. The text of the cards is as follows:

Card 1: Act as the leader. Keep the meeting going; give everyone a chance to talk.

Card 2: Try to be funny. Joke around, laugh at others and their ideas.

Card 3: Interrupt others. Try to talk often. Say, "I'm sorry to interrupt, but _____," then go ahead and talk.

Card 4: Change the subject. Pretend not to listen to the others. Start talking about something different from what was just said.

Card 5: Criticize the ideas of others. Offer others advice about how they should act or tell them what you think they should do.

Card 6: You can't sit still. Be easily distracted. Don't pay attention. Try to get someone next to you not to pay attention, too.

7. Distribute the role cards and ask students to try to follow the instructions on them. Allow students a little time to think about their roles (they may ask you questions privately if they want to). Instruct the person with the "leader" card to start the meeting. Allow 5 minutes for the meeting.

8. To discuss the meeting, stand behind each member of the group in turn and ask the class:

   What behaviors did you observe in this member during the meeting?

   How did these behaviors affect the group?

9. Refer students to page 63 in their Student Manuals, "Communication Inhibitors," and discuss. Stress the idea that these behaviors often occur in conversations between two people or in groups of people. These behaviors usually inhibit or stop communication because they shift the focus away from the speaker. To resolve conflicts, we need to encourage communication.

10. Ask the class what could have helped make the meeting more productive. Draw out ideas about active listening: attending, summarizing, and clarifying.

Student Manual
page 63

Communication Inhibitors

Interrupting

Judging

Criticizing

Changing the subject

Joking around

Offering advice

Laughing at others

Bringing up your
own experiences

63

9 Communication: Sending Clear Messages

PURPOSE To learn effective speaking skills

MATERIALS Student Manuals
Newsprint
Markers
Masking tape

NOTE Before beginning, prepare sheets of newsprint as instructed in Step 2.

PROCEDURE
1. Refer students to page 64 in their Student Manuals, "Sending Clear Messages," and discuss. Explain that active listening is crucial to effective communication. Also important in communication is the skill of clearly telling the other person what you want that person to hear. Even a very good listener, one who uses active listening skills, can hear only what is actually said. Therefore, the speaker needs to *speak to be understood*.

2. Prepare six sheets of newsprint, each with one of the following questions printed at the top:

    What would you say to someone who cuts in front of you in line?

    What would you say to someone who does not let you join a game on the playground?

    What would you say to someone who ignores you when you ask a question?

    What would you say to someone who makes a nasty comment about one of your family members?

    What would you say to someone who makes fun of something you are wearing?

    What would you say to someone who is spreading a rumor about you?

3. Give each group of four to six students one of the sheets and a marker. Instruct the group to appoint a recorder to write down all the responses the group can think of.

4. Invite each group to share their work; post the completed sheets around the room.

5. Stress that in conflict situations, instead of speaking with the intent to debate or impress, it is better to work hard to state your issues or the problem in a clear, direct way. This usually results in a receptive, constructive response. When speaking to be understood, you need to avoid name-calling, criticism, sarcasm, and demands.

6. Encourage students to examine the sheets posted around the room and find statements that are good examples of speaking to be understood. Find a few examples that could be made better and ask the class to revise them to communicate more clearly.

7. Explain that in conflict situations, instead of focusing on the motivations and intentions of the other person, it is better to *speak about yourself.* Don't complain about the other person. Don't use statements that begin with "you," such as "You make me mad when you do that." Describe the situation in terms of yourself by using statements that begin with "I." For example:

   I feel _____ because _____.

   I think _____ because _____.

   I want _____ because _____.

   Both parts of these sentences should focus on you and not on the other person.

8. Find examples of good "I" statements in the lists generated earlier, then have the class reframe a few of the less effective statements so that they are better "I" statements.

9. Explain that sending clear messages also means you *speak for a purpose.* This means you think about what you want the other person to understand and what purpose the information will serve. It is important not to assume that the other person knows what you know or sees the problem the same way you do. Some information we possess will not help in resolving the conflict and is best left unsaid.

10. Finally, point out that it is important to *speak with consideration for the listener.* This means being sensitive to the other person. You want him or her to listen to you, so be aware of how he or she is acting while you speak. If the person is not using attending behaviors, find out why. Maybe you are talking too fast or too loud, or maybe you are too close or too far away. Maybe you are too friendly or not friendly enough. If the person you are talking to is not attending, ask what you can do to make your message clearer.

11. Have the class form groups of three. Tell students they will use the six situations presented in Step 2 to practice sending a clear

message. One student will be the speaker, one will be the person who created the conflict, and the third will be an observer:

> Instruct the speaker to send a clear message to the person who created the conflict.

> Instruct the person who created the conflict to use attending behaviors to listen to the message without interrupting.

> Instruct the observer to think about the rules presented on the "Sending Clear Messages" page and tell the speaker how he or she did in terms of each of the skills listed.

12. Have each student take the role of speaker for two of the situations. After two situations, rotate the roles: Each speaker becomes an observer, and each observer then becomes a listener. After another two situations, the roles rotate again so that each student has a chance to perform in each role for two situations.

13. To summarize, ask the class to discuss whether the speakers followed the rules for sending clear messages. In particular, ask whether they used "I" statements and avoided blaming.

Student Manual
page 64

Sending Clear Messages

◆ Speak to be understood.

◆ Speak about yourself.

◆ Speak for a purpose.

◆ Speak with consideration for the listener.

64

ACTIVITY

10 Focusing on Interests, Not Positions

PURPOSE   To understand the difference between interests and positions and to learn to identify interests

MATERIALS   Student Manuals
A soccer ball

FORMAT OPTIONS   Whole class discussion/participation
Cooperative learning

PROCEDURE
1. Explain that when there is a conflict people often make demands or take *positions.*

2. Have two students role-play the first dialogue on page 65 of the Student Manual, "Focusing on Interests, Not Positions."

3. Summarize the idea that both students are demanding the ball. They are each taking a position. Ask the following questions:

   What is Student A's position?

   What is Student B's position?

   If Student A gets the ball, will the problem be solved? Why not?

   If Student B gets the ball, will the problem be solved? Why not?

   Repeat the idea that Student A's position is "I want the ball now!" and Student B's position is "I want the ball now!" Point out that this problem cannot be solved if positions are the focus and that you cannot give Student A and Student B the ball at the same time.

4. Explain that if the focus is on *interests,* then it will be possible to solve this problem. Tell students that it is possible to identify interests by asking, "Why?" or "What do you really want?"

5. Have the same two students role-play the second dialogue, then ask the following questions:

   What is Student A's interest?

   What is Student B's interest?

   Are these two interests compatible?

170

Can you think of solutions to solve the problem now that you know the interests of both people?

6. Summarize the idea that, when there is a conflict, people often make demands or take positions. Problems cannot be solved if positions are the focus, but focusing on interests works because for every interest there are several possible solutions.

7. Divide students into groups of four and have them follow the instructions on pages 66–67 of their Student Manuals, "Identifying Positions and Interests." Remind students that the basic needs for belonging, power, freedom, and fun are often the interests underlying conflicts. (Some sample responses are provided on pages 175–176; students' responses may differ.)

8. When students are finished, review their responses in the larger group. Summarize the idea that interests, not demands or positions, define the real problem. Focusing on interests opens the opportunity to create a variety of solutions.

Student Manual
page 65

Focusing on Interests, Not Positions

When there is a conflict, people often make demands or take positions. For example:

> **Student A:** I want the ball!
>
> **Student B:** I want the ball!
>
> **Student A:** It's mine. I had it first!
>
> **Student B:** It's my turn!

> Problems cannot be solved if positions are the focus.

When the focus is on interests, it is possible to solve problems. For example:

> **Teacher:** Why do you want the ball?
>
> **Student A:** To practice dribbling and pass kicks for soccer.
>
> **Teacher:** Why do you want the ball?
>
> **Student B:** To play and have fun.

You can identify interests by asking, *"Why?"* and *"What do you really want?"*

> Focusing on interests works because for every interest there will be several possible solutions.

65

Student Manual
page 66

Identifying Positions and Interests

INSTRUCTIONS: Write down the positions and possible interests for each situation.
Clue: Basic needs for *belonging, power, freedom,* and *fun* are often
the interests involved in conflicts.

SITUATION	POSITIONS	INTERESTS
Maria orders Juan, *"Get away from the computer—it's my turn. You have had it a long time, and I need to get my assignment done!"* Juan responds, *"Tough! I signed up for this time, and I'm playing my favorite game. I already finished my work."* Maria goes to tell the teacher.	Maria: Juan:	Maria: Juan:
Keisha yells at LaTasha, *"If you are going to play with Sheila every recess, then you are not my best friend anymore!"* LaTasha replies, *"I want to be your friend, but I also want to play with Sheila and have her be my friend."* LaTasha goes off to play with Sheila.	Keisha: LaTasha:	Keisha: LaTasha:
Brendan is upset with Jeremy: *"Stop putting me down, or I won't ever speak to you again!"* Jeremy shouts, *"Big deal! I'm only trying to have a little fun! Lighten up— you never understand when I'm just teasing!"* Brendan stomps away.	Brendan: Jeremy:	Brendan: Jeremy:

66

Student Manual
page 67

SITUATION	POSITIONS	INTERESTS
Linda threatens her younger sister, Dorthea, *"If you ever come into this room again and borrow my stuff without asking, I'm telling Mom!"* Dorthea cries, *"I needed your stuff to make my outfit complete, and you weren't using it. You've borrowed my stuff before!"*	Linda: Dorthea:	Linda: Dorthea:
Gene yells at his friend Peter, *"You can't ride my bike to school anymore. It is never here for me when I need it."* Peter yells, *"I'm riding your bike—you broke my bike."* Peter rides off on the bike.	Gene: Peter:	Gene: Peter:
Marcus says to Tyrone, *"Either buy a lunch or bring your own. I'm tired of sharing my lunch with you!"* Tyrone says, *"You owe me some of your lunch—you ate my candy at recess."* Marcus takes his lunch and moves to another table.	Marcus: Tyrone:	Marcus: Tyrone:

67

Sample Responses: Identifying Positions and Interests

INSTRUCTIONS: Write down the positions and possible interests for each situation. *Clue:* Basic needs for *belonging, power, freedom,* and *fun* are often the interests involved in conflicts.

SITUATION	POSITIONS	INTERESTS
Maria orders Juan, *"Get away from the computer—it's my turn. You have had it a long time, and I need to get my assignment done!"* Juan responds, *"Tough! I signed up for this time, and I'm playing my favorite game. I already finished my work."* Maria goes to tell the teacher.	Maria: *I want the computer.* Juan: *I want the computer, and I have it.*	Maria: *To use the computer to do her assignment. To be successful in school. To be Juan's friend. (power, belonging)* Juan: *To play a game on the computer. To become more skilled at using the computer. To be Maria's friend. (power, belonging, fun)*
Keisha yells at LaTasha, *"If you are going to play with Sheila every recess, then you are not my best friend anymore!"* LaTasha replies, *"I want to be your friend, but I also want to play with Sheila and have her be my friend."* LaTasha goes off to play with Sheila.	Keisha: *Play with me and not with Sheila.* LaTasha: *I will play with Sheila.*	Keisha: *To be friends with LaTasha. To have someone to play with at recess. (belonging, fun)* LaTasha: *To be friends with Keisha. To have other friends. To have someone to play with at recess. (belonging, freedom, fun)*
Brendan is upset with Jeremy: *"Stop putting me down, or I won't ever speak to you again!"* Jeremy shouts, *"Big deal! I'm only trying to have a little fun! Lighten up— you never understand when I'm just teasing!"* Brendan stomps away.	Brendan: *Stop teasing me.* Jeremy: *Teasing is OK— I'm not serious.*	Brendan: *To be respected by Jeremy and others. To have Jeremy as a friend. (power, belonging, fun)* Jeremy: *To have fun. To be Brendan's friend. (belonging, fun)*

SITUATION	POSITIONS	INTERESTS
Linda threatens her younger sister, Dorthea, *"If you ever come into this room again and borrow my stuff without asking, I'm telling Mom!"* Dorthea cries, *"I needed your stuff to make my outfit complete, and you weren't using it. You've borrowed my stuff before!"*	Linda: *Don't use my stuff.* Dorthea: *I can use your stuff if you're not using it.*	Linda: *Not to have to worry about where her stuff is. To be shown respect by being asked if her sister wants to borrow something. To be friends with her sister. (power, belonging)* Dorthea: *To have neat outfits in order to be accepted by peers. To have more dress options by sharing. To be friends with Linda. (power, freedom, belonging)*
Gene yells at his friend Peter, *"You can't ride my bike to school anymore. It is never here for me when I need it."* Peter yells, *"I'm riding your bike—you broke my bike."* Peter rides off on the bike.	Gene: *Don't ride my bike.* Peter: *I will ride your bike.*	Gene: *To have transportation. To be Peter's friend. (freedom, belonging, fun)* Peter: *To have transportation. To be Gene's friend. (freedom, belonging, fun)*
Marcus says to Tyrone, *"Either buy a lunch or bring your own. I'm tired of sharing my lunch with you!"* Tyrone says, *"You owe me some of your lunch—you ate my candy at recess."* Marcus takes his lunch and moves to another table.	Marcus: *I'm not giving you any of my lunch.* Tyrone: *You owe me some of your lunch.*	Marcus: *To have lunch. To by Tyrone's friend. (power, belonging, freedom)* Tyrone: *To have lunch. To be Marcus's friend. (power, belonging, freedom)*

11 Inventing Options for Mutual Gain

PURPOSE   To learn how to invent options for mutual gain to solve a problem

MATERIALS   Student Manuals
Newsprint
Markers
Index cards

FORMAT OPTIONS   Whole class discussion/participation
Class meeting
Cooperative learning

NOTE   Before beginning this activity, prepare the conflict situation cards as specified in Step 6.

PROCEDURE
1. Refer the group to page 68 in their Student Manuals, "Inventing Options for Mutual Gain," and discuss the idea of *win-win options*.

2. Explain that *brainstorming* is a way to help people invent win-win options. In brainstorming, the people focus only on generating ideas, not on deciding whether the ideas are good or bad.

3. Amplify the "Rules for Brainstorming" as they are given on page 69 of the Student Manual:

   Say any idea that comes to mind. (This means to blurt out your ideas; don't censor your thoughts.)

   Do not judge or discuss ideas. (This means you accept all ideas, at least for the time being; don't criticize or make fun of any ideas.)

   Come up with as many ideas as possible. (Sometimes it is helpful when you run out of ideas to try making changes to ideas that have already been given.)

   Try to think of unusual ideas. (Sometimes really weird or far-out ideas will help you and others think of new possibilities.)

4. Form groups of five or six students each, then give each group a sheet of newsprint and a marker. Instruct each group to follow the rules for brainstorming to help them think of at least 20 ideas for using a bag of marshmallows.

5. Ask one group to share their list with the class. Ask the second group to share any ideas from their list that were not on the list from the first group. Do the same for the remaining groups.

6. Give each group of students an index card on which you have written a conflict situation. The text of the cards is as follows:

   Card 1: A student keeps teasing you on the school bus.

   Card 2: You lend your kick ball to another student at recess, and it is returned to you flat.

   Card 3: The student sitting behind you keeps tapping your chair and poking you.

   Card 4: The student next to you at the lunch table takes a big bite out of your cookie.

   Card 5: A student often cuts in front of you in the lunch line.

7. Give each group another piece of newsprint and instruct them to brainstorm at least five ideas that could solve the problem described on their card. Tell them to try to think of win-win options and to record their ideas in either words or pictures.

8. Ask groups, one at a time, to share their problem and their options. After each group has shared, ask the class for other possible options. Have each group record any additional ideas. (Save these lists for use in Activity 12.)

9. Discuss the process of brainstorming by asking:

   Did anyone not bring up an idea he or she had? Why not?

   Did the groups keep from talking about whether an idea was good or bad?

   Did anyone use someone else's idea to get an idea of his or her own?

10. For each problem situation, ask the class whether options or parts of options could be combined to come up with an entirely new option. Discuss which option or combination of options offers the best opportunity for mutual gain in each problem situation.

Student Manual
page 68

Inventing Options
for Mutual Gain

An option for mutual gain is a suggestion or idea
that addresses the interests of both parties.

These ideas are also called **win-win** options.

In problem solving, the ideas should help both people.

68

Student Manual
page 69

Rules for Brainstorming

♦ Say any idea that comes to mind.

♦ Do not judge or discuss ideas.

♦ Come up with as many ideas as possible.

♦ Try to think of unusual ideas.

In brainstorming, people focus only on generating ideas, not on deciding whether the ideas are good or bad.

69

ACTIVITY

12 Using Fair Criteria

PURPOSE   To understand the concept of fairness as a criterion to apply in choosing a solution to a conflict

MATERIALS   Student Manuals
Newsprint
Markers
Large, soft cookies (enough so every pair of students has one)
List of options (saved from Activity 11)

FORMAT OPTIONS   Whole class discussion/participation
Cooperative learning
Class meeting

PROCEDURE   1. Refer the group to page 70 in their Student Manuals, "Using Fair Criteria." Say the word *fairness.* Ask students to think of words or pictures that come to mind when they think of fairness. Give students time to write or draw their thoughts on this page.

2. Invite students to share their responses. Typical responses include *equal, reasonable, just, correct, right, rules, referee,* and *umpire.*

3. Form groups of five to seven students each. Give each group a sheet of newsprint and a marker. Instruct each group to draw a picture of at least five different situations they have experienced when they said or might have said, "It's not fair!"

4. Have each group share their situations with the class.

5. Divide the students into pairs. Give each pair of students a cookie. Tell them that they are to agree on a fair way to share the cookie between the two of them. The pair is only to *think* of a way to share the cookie, not actually share it. They may be creative and assume that any equipment needed is available.

6. Have each pair share their solution with the class. As they do, ask both students if they think the solution is fair. After all the pairs have shared their solutions, each pair may divide their cookie in a fair way, then eat it.

7. Explain that it is important for both people in a dispute to agree on a solution they believe is fair. One person should not yield to pressure from the other.

8. Discuss the following questions:

> Is it possible for two people in a conflict to find a solution that is fair to both?
>
> If a solution is not fair to both, what happens?
>
> If two people in a conflict cannot agree on what is fair, what can they do?

Stress that two people do not have to share exactly the same notions about fairness to find a solution both accept as fair.

9. Refer to the lists of options generated in Activity 11. Have students choose options they feel are fair.

10. Refer students once again to page 70 in their Student Manuals. To summarize, discuss the ideas that using fair criteria means to judge:

> Without self-interest, but with mutual interest
>
> Without prejudice, but with respect
>
> Without emotion, but with reason

Student Manual
page 70

Using Fair Criteria

INSTRUCTIONS: In the boxes, write words or draw pictures that come
to mind when you think of fairness.

FAIRNESS

Using fair criteria means to judge:
Without self-interest but with mutual interest
Without prejudice, but with respect
Without emotion, but with reason

ACTIVITY

13   Key Concept Review

PURPOSE   To understand the meaning of key concepts related to peace and peacemaking

MATERIALS   Butcher paper
Magazines
Comic books
Scissors
Glue
Markers

FORMAT OPTIONS   Cooperative learning
Class meeting

PROCEDURE
1. Ask students to use their own words to define the following concepts. Solicit several definitions for each. Discuss the different definitions until the group displays a common understanding of each of the concepts.

PEACE	POSITION
PEACEMAKER	INTEREST
SUMMARIZING	WIN-WIN OPTION
CLARIFYING	FAIRNESS

2. Divide the class into eight groups of equal numbers. Assign each group one of the words and instruct the group to develop a poster that displays the meaning of the concept—draw a picture, write a definition, create a collage, and so forth.

3. Display the posters in the classroom.

Mediation

OVERVIEW

Mediation is a process in which a neutral third party—a mediator—helps disputants resolve their conflicts peaceably. The role of mediator is a valid one for the teacher, the principal, and other adults in the school to assume to help students resolve their disputes. In addition, the role of mediator can often be fulfilled by peers, thus relieving adults of responsibility and, perhaps more important, clearly demonstrating to students that they have the ability to resolve their differences without adult intervention by communicating and cooperating. When both parties agree to mediate—work cooperatively to solve the problem—a peer mediator can help.

Peer mediation involves negotiating disputes and reaching resolutions that combine the needs of the parties in conflict instead of compromising those needs. It is a way for students to deal with differences without aggression or coercion. Peer mediation works well to resolve conflicts in schools because, through it, students gain power and freedom (independence from adult authority in dictating behavior). The more students become empowered to resolve their differences peaceably, the more responsible their behavior becomes.

The activities included in this section are designed to help students learn a six-step mediation process. Students of all ages can learn this mediation process. With the support of the classroom teacher, very young students can help classmates mediate conflicts in a classroom-based program. Students as young as third graders have exhibited sufficient sophistication to learn and use the mediation process in a co-mediation format, as part of a schoolwide peer mediation program.

ROLE OF THE MEDIATOR

The mediator's role throughout the process is proactive—that is, the mediator is responsible for creating and maintaining an atmosphere that fosters mutual problem solving. The mediator orchestrates the activity by following the prescribed step-by-step procedure, asking key questions, and ensuring that the disputants hear each other. To promote fairness, the mediator sits between the disputants, who face each other from opposite sides of a table. The mediator's job is to facilitate communication between the disputants to maintain a balanced exchange, not to solve the problem for the disputants. The disputants are responsible for finding their own solution.

To build trust and cooperation, the mediator works to achieve the following goals.

The mediator is impartial. The mediator must be neutral and objective and avoid taking sides. The mediator manages the process but does not participate in the actual problem solving.

The mediator listens with empathy. Often the problem is clouded by issues in the relationship—emotions run high, unfounded inferences are treated as fact, and blame focuses attention on past actions. Effective communication skills are essential in all steps of the mediation process. The mediator's use of such skills helps ensure that the disputants hear each other; acknowledging emotions and clarifying perceptions help free the disputants to understand and work on the problem.

The mediator uses the following specific active listening skills throughout the process:

> *Attending,* or using nonverbal behaviors to indicate that what the disputants are thinking and feeling is of interest and that the listener wishes to understand. These nonverbal behaviors include eye contact, facial expressions, and body language such as posture and gestures.

> *Summarizing,* or restating facts by repeating the most important points, organizing interests, and discarding extraneous information. In summarizing, the mediator also acknowledges emotions by stating the feelings each person is experiencing.

> *Clarifying,* or using open-ended questions and statements to obtain more information and ensure understanding.

The mediator is respectful. The mediator is able to treat both parties fairly and without prejudice. Being respectful means that the mediator understands disputants' emotions and beliefs. A key to respect is knowing and accepting that we are all different.

The mediator is trustworthy. If students are to value the process, the mediator must build trust and confidence in the process. Disputants must be assured, through the actions of the mediator, that the mediation is not just another contrivance to tell them what to do—they will be allowed to author their own resolution to the problem. The mediator must also exercise the integrity to uphold confidentiality by keeping information from the mediation process private. A mediator does not discuss the disputants or their problem with peers.

The mediator helps people work together. The mediator is responsible for the process, not the solution. The solution is the responsibility of the disputants. When both parties cooperate, they are able to find their own solution. The mediator encourages the disputants to "stick it out" by assisting them to cooperate through the entire process.

THE MEDIATION PROCESS

The mediation process involves the following six steps:

Step 1: Agree to Mediate

Step 2: Gather Points of View

Step 3: Focus on Interests

Step 4: Create Win-Win Options

Step 5: Evaluate Options

Step 6: Create an Agreement

These steps parallel those in negotiation (Section 5) and group problem solving (Section 6).

Step 1: Agree to Mediate

An effective opening is very important in achieving a positive outcome in mediation. The opening sets the tone for the session and establishes that the peer mediator is in charge. The mediator begins the session by making introductions and welcoming the disputants to mediation. The mediator then makes a statement defining mediation. The opening statement defining mediation conveys the fact that the mediator's role is to help the disputants reach their own solution to the problem. Next the mediator states the ground rules designed to facilitate the process:

Mediators do not take sides.

Mediation is private.

Take turns talking and listening.

Cooperate to solve the problem.

Disputants are asked individually whether they agree to abide by these ground rules and to the mediation. Mediation is an agreed-upon process, requiring consent by each party. The consent is to cooperate to solve the problem. Although rare, it is possible to cooperate and still not solve the problem. However, resolution can never take place without cooperation.

The introduction, the definition of mediation, and the statement of ground rules, presented as positive behaviors, help structure a win-win climate by establishing the goal of reaching an agreement considerate of both parties' interests. The opening also conveys the fact that the mediator's role is to help the disputants reach their own solution to the problem. The mediator may need to restate the ground rules occasionally to remind the disputants that they began the process with the desire to cooperate to reach a resolution. If at any point either of the disputants indicates a lack of desire to cooperate, the mediation is ended. To reiterate, cooperation may not yield a solution, but no solution occurs in the absence of cooperation. In other words, cooperation is an enabling and necessary condition.

Ground rules other than the ones suggested here may be appropriate. However, any rules established should be simple and stated positively. Negative ground rules (for example, "No name-calling" or "No put-downs") are probably unnecessary. Concerns about name-calling and put-downs are covered under the ground rule of cooperating to solve the problem. Likewise, "No interrupting" is positively stated in the ground rule of taking turns talking and listening. A problem may occur when ground rules reflect the assumption that disputants have not entered the process in good faith. For example, the rule "Be as honest as possible" suggests that dishonesty is the expected behavior. It is preferable to assume that the disputants will respect the process and work to the best of their ability to reach a resolution. This is almost always the case. Besides, conflict resolution is rarely about honesty or establishing truth—it is more about unifying perceptions. Therefore, mediators are trained to respond to nonproductive behaviors when and if they occur by repeating the positively stated ground rules that the disputants have agreed to follow. Mediators may need to remind disputants that they agreed to cooperate; often this reminder is needed more than once during the mediation.

Privacy is a concern in mediation. The mediator is trained not to talk about the mediation with other students and must always adhere to that condition. However, issues may surface during a school mediation that must be reported to an adult in a position of responsibility. For example, information about illegal activities or knowledge of threats to harm self or others is not covered under the privacy provision. Whenever such information is revealed during mediation, the mediator is required to share the knowledge with appropriate school personnel.

The privacy ground rule calls for disputants to respect the privacy of each other and of the mediation proceedings. This rule is not a "gag order." It is permissable, even beneficial, for disputants to tell peers that a mediation resulted in an agreement. If not so advised, others who have an interest in the conflict may advance the dispute. Talking about the mediation process has another positive effect in the sense that other students will see that conflicts can be resolved without adult intervention. Spreading the word that the conflict has been resolved may prevent retaliation or a continuation of the dispute. Privacy issues may become increasingly important as the age of the disputants increases and the issues in the dispute become more personal and sensitive. A reasonable extension of the privacy ground rule could be stated as follows: "You may share with others the fact that the problem was resolved and tell others what you agreed to do, but you may not tell about the problem or how the problem was solved, or even what the other person agreed to do."

Step 2: Gather Points of View

The purpose of this step is to ascertain each disputant's point of view about the incident or situation. The mediator gathers information by asking each disputant, "Please tell what happened." If one of the disputants requested the mediation, that disputant should be the first to describe the problem. The mediator summarizes the first disputant's point of view to be sure that the information has been accurately heard. This process helps the mediator check out his or her understanding of the problem and gives the other disputant another opportunity to hear the point of view of the teller. (The latter is perhaps the most important reason for summarizing.) The mediator then verifies the summary by asking the disputant who reported whether it is correct. The mediator next asks the other disputant to tell what happened. Again, the mediator summarizes what is said and then verifies the summary. By alternating asking for and summarizing the disputants' points of view, the mediator helps each disputant gain awareness of the other person's major issues and perceptions.

The mediator then asks each disputant, "Do you have anything to add?" continuing to ask for additional input until all the important information has been revealed. During this process, the mediator enforces the ground rules about taking turns talking and listening. The mediator makes sure that both disputants have equal opportunity to tell their version of the incident.

As needed, the mediator seeks clarification by using questions or statements such as "How did you feel when that happened?" "What were your reasons for doing that?" and "Explain more about that." Other questions that provide clarification are "What did you do and what were you thinking when you did that?" "What do you feel is the major problem?" "What have you tried to do about the problem?" "What are you doing now about the problem?" and "What do you think is keeping you from reaching agreement?" It is important that the mediator use open-ended questions rather than questions that can be answered yes or no. The purpose is to have the disputants talk about the problem in full detail.

In brief, the information-gathering step clarifies the sequence of events in the dispute and validates the concerns and feelings of each disputant. In this step, the mediator acknowledges the messages expressed from the perspective of each disputant and, by clarifying each perspective, allows the disputants to know that they have been understood, while providing for a more accurate, shared perception of the problem. This step builds trust and encourages constructive dialogue about the problem. If the disputants have trouble with subsequent steps in the process, such difficulty may indicate that the information-gathering step was incomplete. Perhaps all the pertinent information did not surface. It may be necessary to return to this step to gather additional information or to clarify information that has already been revealed.

On occasion, a disputant is reluctant to share information. If so, the mediator tries to encourage that individual to share his or her point of view without becoming overly persistent. The mediator should understand that it is possible to return to this step if the process falters later on. The opposite problem may also occur, with a disputant being overly eager to talk and taking up too much time. If one disputant is dominating the situation or the other disputant is becoming impatient or bored, the mediator may summarize what that person has said, then allow the other disputant to talk. Allowing each disputant one chance to add to his or her point of view is the recommended procedure. Once again, the mediator can return to this step later on if more information is needed to proceed.

In this step of the process, it is recommended that the discussion flow through the mediator. It is not expected that there be a dialogue between the disputants; in fact, it is preferable that such dialogue not occur. It is at this step that strong emotions, blaming and accusing comments, or other behaviors that hinder cooperation often surface. Mediators are alert for actions that are contrary to the stated and agreed-upon ground rules and assertively enforce those rules to prevent interruptions and the deterioration of cooperation. Also, it is not necessary for the disputants to agree on the details of the problem. The goal of the step is for the disputants to better understand their own and the other's point of view.

Step 3: Focus on Interests

In this most crucial step, the mediator helps the disputants identify their underlying interests. Often the disputants are locked into their respective rigid positions. The mediator asks them to look behind their opposing positions by asking, "What do you want and why do you want that?" The *what* is the position; the *why* is the interest. At this point disputants discover that they share certain interests or that their interests, even if different, are compatible. By focusing on shared or compatible interests, the mediator helps the disputants fashion a resolution that preserves these commonalities. From this base of understanding and cooperation the disputants can seek fair ways to resolve their conflicting interests.

In addition to asking what and why, the mediator may stimulate the discovery of common interests by asking questions such as "What might happen if you don't reach an agreement?" "What would you think if you were in the other person's shoes?" "If this situation happened again, how would you like it to be?" "How do you want things to change?" and "What do you have in common that you both want?"

As in Step 2, the mediator practices active listening during the process of identifying common interests—attending, summarizing, and seeking clarification as needed. The use of these skills helps the mediator ensure that each disputant has an equal opportunity to participate and that each learns the point of view of the other disputant. Also as in Step 2, it is very important for the mediator to employ open-ended questions. Common interests should be made explicit as soon as they are revealed. The mediator can then formulate these common interests as mutual goals: "Your interests are _____."

Shared and compatible interests are the building blocks for resolving the conflict. If they are not disclosed, there is little chance of reaching an agreement that both sides can keep. The mediator does not move on to the next step until common interests are found. This is often the most difficult step in the process. It may be necessary to return to the ground rules to facilitate this step ("Please remember that you agreed to work together to solve the problem"), and/or it may be necessary to gather additional information ("Is there any information about the problem that we have not heard yet that might be causing us to be stuck here?").

Most often, the common interests in a conflict are connected to the basic psychological needs for belonging, power, freedom, and fun. The mediator looks for basic needs to identify common interests. For example, students who appear very upset with each other may still want to be friends—or at least not be enemies if being enemies will continue to get them into trouble. Similarly, very few individuals would reject an opportunity to gain acknowledgment or respect from another person.

Step 4: Create Win-Win Options

Creating options involves a brainstorming process. This step, designed to produce as many ideas as possible, helps individuals solve problems creatively—one idea usually stimulates another. Because evaluation hinders creativity, the process of generating options is separate from the process of evaluating options and from creating an agreement.

At this stage, the disputants are not attempting to determine the best solution. Instead, they are inventing options upon which they can build and from which they can jointly choose in the next steps of the mediation process. A good agreement addresses the interests of both parties in the dispute, fairly resolves those issues in conflict, and has the potential to last. Such an agreement is more likely to be found when a variety of options exist.

To begin the process, the mediator explains that the purpose is to generate ideas and that to do so it is helpful to follow specific brainstorming rules:

> Say any idea that comes to mind.
>
> Do not judge or discuss ideas.
>
> Come up with as many ideas as possible.
>
> Try to think of unusual ideas.

The mediator then asks disputants to generate as many ideas as possible: "Please suggest ideas that address the interests of both of you." When the ideas do not flow, the mediator keeps the process moving by asking additional questions—for example, "Can you think of more possibilities that will help both of you?" and "In the future, what could you do differently?" The mediator remembers the ideas as the disputants generate them. This step continues until several ideas have been advanced.

The mediator may need to remind the disputants of the common interests identified in Step 3 by saying, "You both agreed that you want [common interest]. What ideas would help that to happen?" For example, "You both agreed that you want to improve your relationship. What are some things you could do to build the relationship?" The mediator also helps the disputants follow the brainstorming rules and not judge ideas, recording the ideas as the disputants generate them. Recording ideas in a way disputants may see them (on an easel pad or on a brainstorming worksheet, for example) can help stimulate other ideas and promote cooperative problem solving. The disputants may also need to be reminded that they agreed to the ground rule to cooperate to solve the problem. When the ideas are mostly suggestions for what the other person should do, mediators ask, "What are you willing to do?"

Step 5: Evaluate Options

In this step, the mediator asks the disputants to choose, from the list of options generated in Step 4, the ideas or parts of ideas they think are fair and have the best possibility of working. The mediator circles the ideas each disputant suggests.

The disputants' task at this stage is to act as side-by-side problem solvers, evaluating and improving the circled options. The mediator may ask the following types of questions: "Is this option fair?" "Can you do it?" "Do you think it will work?" "What are the consequences of deciding to do this?" and "Does this option address the interests of everyone involved?" Also, the mediator can help the disputants look for compatible ideas by asking, "Are there options on the list that could be paired so that if one of you agreed to do one thing, the other could do the other?"

Step 6: Create an Agreement

Once the disputants have discussed the various options, the mediator asks both of them to make a plan of action describing what they will do. This plan is specific and answers the questions who, what, when, where, and how. The mediator asks each disputant to summarize the plan. If the disputants do not accurately state the agreement, the mediator clarifies: "I thought I heard you agree to _____."

After both disputants state the agreement, the mediator asks, "Is the problem solved?" Upon receiving an affirmative response from each disputant, the mediator finalizes the commitment. The commitment could be a handshake between the disputants, a written agreement, or both.

When an agreement is written, the mediator reads it aloud and asks if it expresses the intent of both students. The disputants and the mediator then sign the agreement. To close the session, the mediator shakes hands with both parties, thanks them for bringing their dispute to mediation, congratulates them for working to reach an agreement, and invites them to return to mediation if any problems develop in carrying out the agreement or if they have other conflicts, either between themselves or with others. The mediator may invite the disputants to shake hands with each other.

CO-MEDIATION

In co-mediation, two mediators work as a team to facilitate the mediation process. Co-mediators act as a single mediator, managing the process while supporting each other. In the co-mediation model, the team members have two responsibilities:

> One member of the team actively facilitates the six-step mediation process.

> The other member of the team observes the process and supports the teammate.

Supporting a teammate involves monitoring the mediation in progress to help make sure the mediator is remaining neutral, that he or she is summarizing the statements of the disputants, that the ground rules are being followed, and so on. It also involves paying close attention to what is happening and being prepared at all times to help the teammate if he or she seems stuck. Often someone who is observing can more easily think of a question that might help move the mediation toward a resolution because that person is not thinking about what has to be done in the particular step of the process.

Co-mediation works best when the two team members equally share the two responsibilities. One way of doing this is to have one member of the team facilitate Steps 1, 3, and 5 while the other mediator observes and supports. For Steps 2, 4, and 6, the mediators reverse roles.

It is important to stress during training that in co-mediation the two mediators must decide in advance how to work together. Minimally, co-mediators should answer the following questions:

> Who will facilitate Steps 1, 3, and 5, and who will facilitate Steps 2, 4, and 6?

> How will the observer help the facilitator? (How will he or she tell the facilitator he or she forgot to do something important, how will he or she offer suggestions, and so forth?)

Suggested Readings

Cohen, R. (1995). *Peer mediation in schools: Students resolving conflict.* Glenview, IL: GoodYearBooks, Scott Foresman.

Moore, C. W. (1987). *The mediation process: Practical strategies for resolving conflicts.* San Francisco: Jossey-Bass.

Schrumpf, F., Crawford, D. K., & Bodine, R. J. (1997). *Peer mediation: Conflict resolution in schools* (Rev. ed.). Champaign, IL: Research Press.

ACTIVITY

1   Mediation Is . . .

PURPOSE   To learn that mediation is a process in which a third party helps people work together to resolve conflicts peaceably

MATERIALS   Student Manuals
Newsprint
Markers

FORMAT OPTIONS   Whole class discussion/participation
Cooperative learning

PROCEDURE

1. Explain that there are times when people who are in conflict need help to solve their problems and that mediation is a way to assist them.

2. Refer group members to page 73 of their Student Manuals, "Mediation," and discuss the ideas presented there.

3. Explain that both adults and children can learn to be mediators. Tell students that peer mediation is when a student mediates a dispute between other students.

4. Give each group of four or five learners a sheet of newsprint. Ask groups to discuss why peer mediation would be helpful in assisting students to resolve conflicts. Typical responses include the following:

   Kids understand what is important to other kids.

   Kids know how it feels to be a kid in conflict.

   It would be a good feeling to solve a problem without adult involvement.

   Kids will listen to other kids.

5. Invite groups to share their lists; post these around the room.

6. Summarize by stressing the idea that it takes cooperation and understanding to resolve conflicts. Mediators, both children and adults, are peacemakers.

Student Manual
page 73

Mediation

Mediation is a communication process in which a third party helps people work together to resolve conflicts peaceably.

THE MEDIATOR HELPS THOSE IN CONFLICT . . .

♦ Focus on the problem and not blame the other person.

♦ Understand and respect different views.

♦ Communicate wants and feelings.

♦ Cooperate in solving a problem.

Mediators are peacemakers.

73

ACTIVITY

2 Role of the Mediator

PURPOSE To understand the role of the mediator in helping people resolve disputes

MATERIALS Student Manuals
A yardstick

FORMAT OPTIONS Whole class discussion/participation
Class meeting

PROCEDURE
1. Refer the group to page 74 in their Student Manuals, "Role of the Mediator."

2. Discuss each of the qualities of the mediator with the class, one at a time.

The Mediator Is Impartial (Does Not Take Sides)

Take a yardstick and balance it on your finger. Explain how a mediator is *impartial* and stays in the middle, just like your finger on the yardstick. Ask students what will happen if your finger is slightly off center.

The Mediator Listens With Empathy

Explain that the mediator uses *active listening* to try to understand the thoughts and feelings of each person. Demonstrate this idea by having a volunteer talk to you about a problem. During the demonstration, look away or otherwise act distracted. Repeat with another volunteer, this time using active listening. Ask the class what they saw. Ask the volunteers how they felt during each demonstration.

The Mediator Is Respectful

Explain that the mediator tries to understand both views of the situation without judgment: Because we all have our own views about things, this is not always easy. Being a mediator means showing everyone respect, no matter how they dress or what their shape, color, size, age, and so forth.

The Mediator Is Trustworthy

Explain that the mediator tells both people that what is discussed in the mediation will stay in the room. The mediator will not discuss the mediation with other students, nor will he or she try to get the people to accept the mediator's idea for a solution.

The Mediator Helps People Work Together

Explain that helping people work together involves developing trust and teamwork between them. Demonstrate this idea by having two students sit back-to-back on the floor, link arms, and try to stand, keeping their arms linked. Select another student to direct the activity. After they stand, bring a third student into the group and have all three link arms and try to stand. Try four, five, or six. Each time, have a student encourage and coach, showing how to help the people work together.

3. Conclude by stating that the main role of the mediator is to build trust and cooperation, which in turn makes mutual problem solving possible.

Student Manual
page 74

Role of the Mediator

THE MEDIATOR . . .

◆ Is impartial (does not take sides).

◆ Listens with empathy.

◆ Is respectful.

◆ Is trustworthy.

◆ Helps people work together.

> Mediators build trust and cooperation,
> making mutual problem solving possible.

74

ACTIVITY

3 Overview of the Mediation Process

PURPOSE   To learn what is involved in the six-step mediation process

MATERIALS   Student Manuals

FORMAT OPTIONS   Whole class discussion/participation
Class meeting

PROCEDURE   1. Refer the group to page 75 in their Student Manuals, "Steps in the Mediation Process," and briefly explain what goes on in each step.

2. Have four student volunteers perform the sample mediation on pages 76–80 of the Student Manual. Encourage the other students to follow along and see if they can identify the various steps in the process as the example unfolds.

3. After the demonstration is over, have students evaluate what they saw:

   What steps did you notice?

   What was the role of the mediator?

   Was the outcome a solution that met both people's needs?

4. Explain that in upcoming activities everyone will have the opportunity to learn and practice the mediation steps.

Student Manual
page 75

Steps in the Mediation Process

♦ **Step 1:** Agree to Mediate

♦ **Step 2:** Gather Points of View

♦ **Step 3:** Focus on Interests

♦ **Step 4:** Create Win-Win Options

♦ **Step 5:** Evaluate Options

♦ **Step 6:** Create an Agreement

75

*Student Manual
page 76*

Sample Mediation

STEP 1: AGREE TO MEDIATE

Hannah: *Welcome to mediation. My name is Hannah.*

Drake: *My name is Drake. We are your mediators. What are your names?*

Antonio: My name is Antonio.

Joe: My name is Joe.

Hannah: *Mediation is neutral third parties, the mediators, helping those with the problem to talk and listen and cooperate to develop a plan to solve their problem peaceably. The rules of mediation are: Mediators do not take sides, mediation is private, take turns talking and listening—so don't interrupt each other—and cooperate to solve the problem. Are you willing to follow these rules?*

Joe: OK.

Antonio: Yes!

STEP 2: GATHER POINTS OF VIEW

Drake: *Antonio, please tell what happened.*

Antonio: Well, I was getting the basketball out of the ball bin. I got there first. While I was asking some friends to play with me, Joe came along and tried to take the ball. He said he should get to play with the ball because he always does.

Drake: *You were getting the last basketball to play with some friends, and Joe tried to take the ball. He wanted to play with the ball like he always does.*

Antonio: Yeah . . . that's what he did.

Drake: *Joe, please tell your point of view.*

Joe: Well, it was my ball because I always play with it. That is all I wanted to say.

Drake: *Joe, you believe the ball was yours because you always play with it. Antonio, how did you feel when that happened?*

Student Manual
page 77

Antonio:	I was mad. He was being a bully. That's why we got into a fight.
Drake:	*You were mad and got into a fight with Joe. Do you have anything to add?*
Antonio:	No.
Drake:	*Joe, do you have anything to add?*
Joe:	I wanted the ball, and I fought Antonio for it. He never lets me play on his team.
Drake:	*You never get to play on Antonio's team, and you fought Antonio for the last ball.*

STEP 3: FOCUS ON INTERESTS

Hannah:	*Antonio, what do you want?*
Antonio:	I want to play basketball with my friends.
Hannah:	*Joe, what do you want?*
Joe:	If there is only one ball left, I want it.
Hannah:	*Why do you want the ball?*
Joe:	I want to play basketball.
Hannah:	*Well, you both want the same thing. You want to play basketball.*
Antonio:	Yes.
Joe:	Yes.
Hannah:	*So what's going to happen if you don't reach an agreement?*
Antonio:	Well, I think we'll be rushing out early to try to get the ball from each other and end up in the principal's office again for fighting.
Hannah:	*So you're saying if you don't solve the problem, you're both going to be rushing out to get the ball and probably fight again.*
Antonio:	Yes.

Hannah: *Joe, do you have anything to say about that?*

Joe: Well, I think if we don't find an agreement we'll just always be arguing about who gets the ball and never get to play.

Hannah: *How would you feel if you were the other person?*

Antonio: I might feel left out. I didn't know Joe wanted to play on my team.

Joe: I would be happy to play on a team with my friends.

Hannah: *Both of you seem to want to reach an agreement so you don't fight over the ball. Both of you want to play basketball and be on a team with friends.*

STEP 4: CREATE WIN-WIN OPTIONS

Drake: *Now it's time to create win-win options. We use brainstorming rules to create options. You may say any idea that comes to mind, but do not judge or discuss ideas at this time. Try to come up with as many ideas as possible, and try to think of unusual ideas. OK, suggest ideas that will help both of you.*

Antonio: Well, if we took turns—like one time he could get it, and then one time I could get it. We could keep going like that.

Joe: Well, I think that if there is only one ball left, we should just share it and play ball together.

Drake: *Remember to think of unusual ideas.*

Antonio: We could organize a team sign-up sheet.

Joe: We could have a tournament.

Antonio: We could ask the principal to buy more basketballs.

Joe: We could play indoor soccer. More people can play soccer.

Drake: *Can you think of anything else to do?*

Joe: Not right now.

Antonio: Me, either.

Student Manual
page 79

STEP 5: EVALUATE OPTIONS

Hannah: *OK, let's think about all the options. Do you think any of these will work?*

Antonio: I don't think the principal is going to buy more balls.

Joe: I don't think so either. I think it would be hard keeping track of taking turns and remembering who had the ball last.

Antonio: Yeah, we might fight over whose turn it was to play with the ball. It would work to play basketball together.

Hannah: *Can you combine options?*

Joe: We could combine the team sign-up with the tournament.

Antonio: We probably need to ask the principal if that would be all right.

Hannah: *Is playing basketball together and asking the principal about team sign-up and a tournament a fair solution?*

Antonio: It's fair.

Joe: Yes, I think so.

STEP 6: CREATE AN AGREEMENT

Drake: *How will you do it?*

Antonio: We could play basketball together tomorrow.

Drake: *When?*

Antonio: We could play at lunchtime.

Drake: *What is your plan for the sign-up and tournament?*

Joe: We can talk to the principal after school today. If he says yes, we can make the sign-up sheets for the teams and put together the tournament.

Drake: *Antonio, what have you agreed to do?*

Student Manual
page 80

Antonio: I have agreed to play basketball with Joe tomorrow at lunchtime and to go with Joe to talk with the principal about the team sign-up and the tournament.

Drake: *Joe, what have you agreed to do?*

Joe: I will play basketball with Antonio tomorrow at lunch and go with him to talk to the principal, and make the team sign-up and put the tournament together if it's OK.

Antonio: I'll help with sign-up and tournament, too!

(Hannah and Drake shake hands with Antonio and Joe.)

Drake: *Thank you for coming to mediation and working hard to get an agreement. If this agreement doesn't work or you have other problems, please feel welcome to come back to mediation.*

(Antonio and Joe shake hands.)

Activity

4   Step 1: Agree to Mediate

PURPOSE   To learn what physical arrangements are best for mediation and to understand the ground rules for the mediation process

MATERIALS   Student Manuals

FORMAT OPTION   Whole class discussion/participation

PROCEDURE

1. Discuss the physical arrangements for mediation: The best arrangement is for the people who are having the problem to sit face-to-face at a table, with the mediator (or co-mediators) in the middle. It is important that the arrangement appear fair to everyone.

2. Refer the group to page 81 in their Student Manuals, "Step 1: Agree to Mediate." Explain that the ground rules for mediation help make the process as fair as possible for everyone. To begin the process, both people must state that they agree to these rules.

3. Form groups of four in which two students play the co-mediators and the other two play the disputants. Have the co-mediators sit between the disputants. Each co-mediator should practice Step 1.

4. Have the students switch roles so that everyone has a chance to practice being a co-mediator and leading Step 1.

5. A common question about Step 1 is "What do you do if the rules are broken?" Explain that if this happens, the mediator reviews the rules and asks again for cooperation. For example:

    Do you want to solve the problem?

    Are you willing to cooperate and follow the rules?

Student Manual
page 81

Step 1: Agree to Mediate

◆ **Welcome both people and introduce yourselves as the mediators.**

◆ **Define mediation:**

Mediation is neutral third parties helping those with the problem to talk and listen and cooperate to develop a plan to solve their problem peaceably.

◆ **Explain the ground rules:**

Mediators do not take sides.

Mediation is private.

Take turns talking and listening.

Cooperate to solve the problem.

◆ **Ask each person:**

"Are you willing to follow these rules?"

The mediation rules help make the process fair.

81

5   Step 2: Gather Points of View

PURPOSE   To learn how to gather both people's points of view in order to understand the problem

MATERIALS   Student Manuals
Simulations 1 and 2 (from Appendix C—one copy of each simulation for every four students)

FORMAT OPTION   Whole class discussion/participation

NOTE   Teachers or student volunteers will need to prepare in advance to act out the script illustrating this step.

PROCEDURE   1.   Have teachers or student volunteers act out "Red Riding Hood and the Wolf," on pages 82–84 of the Student Manual.*

2.   Explain that in every conflict each person has a *point of view:* These views are not right or wrong—just two different ways of seeing a situation. The purpose of Step 2 in the mediation process is to let each person hear the other's point of view.

3.   Discuss the Red Riding Hood demonstration by asking the following questions:

What is Red Riding Hood's point of view?

What is the Wolf's point of view?

What did the mediators do to gather both points of view?

4.   Refer students to page 85 in their Student Manuals, "Step 2: Gather Points of View," and discuss. Stress that in Step 2 the mediator needs to use the active listening skills of attending, summarizing, and clarifying to understand how each person sees the problem. (Review these skills from Section 3 as necessary.)

---

*This adaptation of the classic Red Riding Hood story is based on a retelling in *Individual Development: Creativity* by Leif Fearn, 1974, San Diego: Education Improvement Associates.

5. Explain that students will next practice Steps 1 and 2 in the mediation process. Have students form the same groups they did in Activity 4. Give the students playing the co-mediators a copy of the first page of Simulation 1. Give each of the two disputants half of the second page—one is Student A, the other is Student B.

6. Have students conduct the simulation.

7. Have the students who played the co-mediators trade places with the students who played the disputants and conduct Simulation 2 in the same way.

8. After each simulation, process the activity by asking the students who acted as mediators the following questions:

   What did you do well?

   What could you do differently?

9. Summarize the main point of this activity: Step 2 helps the mediator understand the problem and allows the disputants to hear how each perceives the problem.

Student Manual
page 82

Red Riding Hood and the Wolf

Tasha: *Hello, I am Tasha and this is Shawn. We are your mediators. What is your name?*

Red: I'm Red Riding Hood. They used to call me Little Red Riding Hood, but they don't anymore. You see, the Wolf and I have had this problem a long time, and I grew up.

Tasha: *What is your name?*

Wolf: I'm the Wolf.

Tasha: *Welcome to mediation. I'm sorry it took you so long to find us. Mediation is neutral third parties, the mediators, helping those with the problem, the two of you, to talk and listen and cooperate to develop a plan to solve their problem peaceably. The rules that make mediation work are as follows: Mediators do not take sides. Mediation is private, so what is said here stays in this room. You take turns talking and listening. You cooperate to solve the problem. Red Riding Hood, do you agree to the rules?*

Red: Yes.

Tasha: *Wolf, do you agree to the rules?*

Wolf: Yes, I do.

Shawn: *Red Riding Hood, please tell what happened.*

Red: Well, you see, I was taking a loaf of fresh bread and some cakes to my granny's cottage on the other side of the woods. Granny wasn't well, so I thought I would pick some flowers for her along the way.

I was picking the flowers when the Wolf jumped out from behind a tree and started asking me a bunch of questions. He wanted to know what I was doing and where I was going, and he kept grinning this wicked grin and smacking his lips together.

He was being so gross and rude. Then he ran away.

Shawn: *You were taking some food to your grandmother on the other side of the woods, and the Wolf appeared from behind a tree and frightened you.*

Red: Yes, that's what happened.

82

Student Manual
page 83

Shawn: *Wolf, please tell what happened.*

Wolf: The forest is my home. I care about it and try to keep it clean. One day, when I was cleaning up some garbage that people had left behind, I heard footsteps. I leaped behind a tree and saw a girl coming down the trail carrying a basket.

I was suspicious because she was dressed in this strange red cape with her head covered up as if she didn't want anyone to know who she was. She started picking my flowers and stepping on my new little pine trees.

Naturally, I stopped to ask her what she was doing and all that. She gave me this song and dance about going to her granny's house with a basket of goodies.

Shawn: *You were concerned when you saw this girl dressed in red picking your flowers. You stopped her and asked her what she was doing.*

Wolf: That's right.

Shawn: *Red Riding Hood, is there anything you want to add?*

Red: Yes. When I got to my granny's house, the Wolf was disguised in my granny's nightgown. He tried to eat me with those big ugly teeth. I'd be dead today if it hadn't been for a woodsman who came in and saved me. The Wolf scared my granny. I found her hiding under the bed.

Shawn: *You are saying the Wolf put on your granny's nightgown so you would think he was your granny and that he tried to hurt you?*

Red: I said he tried to *eat* me.

Shawn: *So you felt he was trying to eat you. Wolf, do you have anything to add?*

Wolf: Of course I do. I know this girl's granny. I thought we should teach Red Riding Hood a lesson for prancing on my pine trees in that get-up and for picking my flowers. I let her go on her way, but I ran ahead to her granny's cottage.

When I saw Granny I explained what happened, and she agreed her granddaughter needed to learn a lesson. Granny hid under the bed, and I dressed up in her nightgown.

83

Student Manual
page 84

When Red Riding Hood came into the bedroom, she saw me in the bed and said something nasty about my big ears. I've been told my ears are big before, so I tried to make the best of it by saying my big ears help me hear her better.

Then she made an insulting crack about my bulging eyes. This one was really hard to blow off because she sounded so nasty. Still, I make it a policy to turn the other cheek, so I told her my big eyes help me see her better.

Her next insult about my big teeth really got to me. You see, I'm quite sensitive about them. I know when she made fun of my teeth I should have had better control, but I leaped from the bed and growled that my teeth would help me to eat her.

Shawn: *So you and Granny tried to play a trick on Red Riding Hood to teach her a lesson. Explain more about the eating part.*

Wolf: Now, let's face it. Everyone knows no wolf could ever eat a girl, but crazy Red Riding Hood started screaming and running around the house. I tried to catch her to calm her down.

All of a sudden the door came crashing open, and a big woodsman stood there with his ax. I knew I was in trouble . . . there was an open window behind me, so out I went.

I've been hiding ever since. There are terrible rumors going around the forest about me. Red Riding Hood is calling me the Big Bad Wolf. I'd like to say I've gotten over feeling bad, but the truth is I haven't lived happily ever after.

I don't understand why Granny never told my side of the story.

Shawn: *You're upset about the rumors and have been afraid to show your face in the forest. You're also confused about why Granny hasn't set things straight and has let the situation go on for this long.*

Wolf: It just isn't fair. I'm miserable and lonely.

Shawn: *Red Riding Hood, would you tell us more about Granny?*

Red: Well, Granny has been sick—and she's been very tired lately. When I asked her how she came to be under the bed, she said she couldn't remember a thing that had happened.

Shawn: *You're saying Granny doesn't really remember what happened that day.*

84

Student Manual
page 85

Step 2: Gather Points of View

♦ **Say:**

"Please tell what happened."

♦ **Listen, summarize, clarify. To clarify, ask:**

"How did you feel when that happened?"

"Do you have anything to add?"

> In this step, the disputants hear each other's perceptions and emotions.

85

ACTIVITY

6   Step 3: Focus on Interests

PURPOSE   To learn to find shared and compatible interests

MATERIALS   Student Manuals
An orange
A knife
Simulations 3 and 4 (from Appendix C—one copy of each simulation for every four students)

FORMAT OPTION   Whole class discussion/participation

NOTE   The groups formed in this activity will continue to work together in Activities 7–9, with co-mediator pairs remaining the same and Student A and Student B taking their same roles. Simulations 3 and 4, used in this activity, will be used again in the next three activities.

PROCEDURE   1. Hold up the orange and tell the following story:

> Sam and Ben are twins who usually get along fine. One day, however, they got into a terrible fight about who would have the last orange in the bag. Finally, they went to their mother for help in solving their problem. Being a fair mother, she cut the orange in half and gave one half to Sam and the other half to Ben. *(Cut the orange in half to illustrate.)* The children began to argue again, each demanding the other's half of the orange. The mother could not figure out why. She thought cutting the orange in half was a good compromise.

Stop and explain that, in a conflict situation, each person has a *position*. A position is *what* a person wants. Ask the students the following questions:

What is Ben's position? (Ben wants the orange.)

What is Sam's position? (Sam wants the orange.)

2. Continue with the story:

> When the mother finally realized that she had made a mistake, she asked Ben what was wrong. Ben sobbed that half an orange was not enough to make orange juice. Then Sam cried

that there was not enough peel in half an orange to use in the orange rolls he had planned to bake.

Stop and explain that, in a conflict situation, each person also has *interests*. A person's interests are *why* that person wants what he or she wants. Ask the following questions:

What is Ben's interest? (He wants to make orange juice.)

What is Sam's interest? (He wants to bake orange rolls.)

What interests do Ben and Sam share? (Neither of them wants to be mad at the other or fight—they both have a need for belonging.)

Why does the mother's solution of dividing the orange not solve the problem? (Ben's and Sam's real interests are not addressed.)

How could the problem be solved so that both Ben's and Sam's interests would be considered? (Ben could have the inside of the orange; Sam could have the outside.)

3. Discuss why it is difficult to find a solution by focusing only on positions: A temporary agreement may be reached, but such agreements typically do not last because the people's real interests have not been addressed. For lasting solutions, the mediator must get the people to focus on the interests they have in common, not their positions. Remind students that most common interests are associated with the basic needs for belonging, power, freedom, and fun. (Review these concepts from Section 2 as necessary.)

4. Refer the group to page 86 of their Student Manuals, "Step 3: Focus on Interests," and discuss. Explain that in Step 3, the mediator searches for shared and compatible interests that join the disputants: Such interests serve as the building blocks for an agreement. Unless interests are disclosed, there is little chance of reaching an agreement that both sides can keep.

5. Explain that students will next practice Steps 1, 2, and 3 in the mediation process. Have students form groups of four, different from those in the previous two activities. Give the two students playing the co-mediators a copy of the first page of Simulation 3. Give each of the two disputants half of the second page—one is Student A, the other is Student B.

6. Have students conduct the simulation.

7. Have the students who played the co-mediators trade places with the students who played disputants and conduct Simulation 4 in the same way.

8. After each simulation, ask the co-mediators the following questions to help process the activity:

What did you do well?

What could you do differently?

What questions seemed to help you understand the people's interests?

9. Summarize the main point of this activity by restating that interests are the building blocks of the resolution. The mediator does not move on to Step 4 until common interests are found.

Student Manual
page 86

Step 3: Focus on Interests

♦ **Ask:**

"What do you want?"

"Why?"

♦ **Listen, summarize, clarify. To clarify, ask:**

"What might happen if you don't reach an agreement?"

"How do you want things to change?"

"How will that help?"

"What would you think if you were in the other person's shoes?"

♦ **Summarize the interests. Say:**

"Your interests are _____ ."

> Shared and compatible interests are the building blocks of the resolution. Most common interests are associated with the basic needs for belonging, power, freedom, and fun.

86

7

Step 4: Create Win-Win Options

PURPOSE To learn to help disputants brainstorm to create options that address the interests of both of them

FORMAT OPTION Whole class discussion/participation

MATERIALS Student Manuals
Paper and pencils
Simulations 3 and 4 (saved from Activity 6)

PROCEDURE
1. Refer students to page 87 of their Student Manuals, "Step 4: Create Win-Win Options," and discuss. Tell students that in Step 4 the mediator begins by helping the students use *brainstorming* to come up with a number of *win-win options,* or options that will help both of them.

2. Expand on the brainstorming rules as they are given in the Student Manual to be sure students understand:

   Say any idea that comes to mind. (This means to blurt out your ideas; don't censor your thoughts.)

   Do not judge or discuss ideas. (This means you accept all ideas, at least for the time being; don't criticize or make fun of any ideas.)

   Come up with as many ideas as possible. (Sometimes it is helpful when you run out of ideas to try making changes to ideas that have already been given.)

   Try to think of unusual ideas. (Sometimes really weird or far-out ideas will help you and others think of new possibilities.)

3. Tell students that after explaining the brainstorming rules the mediator then asks the disputants to suggest ideas that address the interests of both of them. The mediator keeps the process moving by asking additional questions when the ideas do not flow. Some useful questions are:

   Can you think of more possibilities that will help both of you?

   In the future, what could you do differently?

4. Explain that the mediator remembers the ideas generated by the disputants. The brainstorming process continues until several options have been suggested.

5. Explain that students will next practice Step 4 in the mediation process. Have them get into the same groups of four as before, with co-mediator pairs remaining the same. The two students playing the co-mediators will continue to use the situation presented on the first page of Simulation 3. The students playing the two disputants will resume their roles as Student A or Student B, as specified on the second page of the simulation.

6. Have students conduct the simulation.

7. Have the students who played the co-mediators trade places with the students who played disputants, and conduct Simulation 4 in the same way.

8. After each simulation, ask the co-mediators the following questions to help process the activity:

   What did you do well?

   What could you do differently?

   What questions seemed to help the people generate lots of options?

9. After both simulations, ask co-mediators to share the options generated by their disputants.

10. Summarize by stating that in Step 4 disputants come up with as many options as they can to help both of them.

Student Manual
page 87

Step 4: Create Win-Win Options

♦ **Explain the brainstorming rules:**

Say any idea that comes to mind.

Do not judge or discuss ideas.

Come up with as many ideas
as possible.

Try to think of unusual ideas.

♦ **Say:**

*"Please suggest ideas that address
the interests of both of you."*

*"Can you think of more possibilities
that will help both of you?"*

The mediators record all the ideas presented
by the disputants.

87

8 Step 5: Evaluate Options

PURPOSE To learn to help disputants evaluate the options previously generated in terms of fairness and workability

MATERIALS Student Manuals
Simulations 3 and 4 (saved from Activity 6)

FORMAT OPTION Whole class discussion/participation

PROCEDURE 1. Refer students to page 88 in their Student Manuals, "Step 5: Evaluate Options," and discuss. Explain that in Step 5 the mediator asks questions to help disputants decide which options are fair and which will work—that is, to choose from among the options generated in the previous step the ideas or parts of ideas that they think have the best chance of resolving the conflict.

2. Explain that students will next practice Step 5 in the mediation process. Have them get into the same groups of four as before, with co-mediator pairs remaining the same. The two students playing the co-mediators will continue to use the situation presented on the first page of Simulation 3. The students playing the two disputants will resume their roles as Student A or Student B, as specified on the second page of the simulation.

3. Have students conduct the simulation.

4. Have the students who played the co-mediators trade places with the students who played disputants and conduct Simulation 4 in the same way.

5. After each simulation, ask the co-mediators the following questions to help process the activity:

    What did you do well?

    What could you do differently?

    What questions seemed to help the disputants evaluate options?

6. Summarize the idea that Step 5 involves the disputants in deciding which options will create a win-win solution. At this point, disputants become side-by-side problem solvers in evaluating options.

Student Manual
page 88

Step 5: Evaluate Options

♦ **Ask:**

"Which of the options on your list do you like?"

"Can you combine options or parts of options?"

"Can any two of the options be paired so each of you can take one of that pair?"

♦ **For each option, ask:**

"Is this option fair?"

"Can you do it?"

"Do you think it will work?"

In this step, the disputants become side-by-side problem solvers in evaluating options.

88

ACTIVITY

9 Step 6: Create an Agreement

PURPOSE   To learn to help disputants create a plan of action from the options they have generated

MATERIALS   Student Manuals
Simulations 3 and 4 (saved from Activity 6)

FORMAT OPTION   Whole class discussion/participation

PROCEDURE   1. Refer students to page 89 of their Student Manuals, "Step 6: Create an Agreement," and discuss. If the disputants do not accurately summarize the agreement, the mediator can say, "I thought I heard you agree to _____."

2. Explain that students will next practice Step 6 in the mediation process. Have them get into the same groups of four as before, with co-mediator pairs remaining the same. The two students playing the co-mediators will continue to use the situation presented on the first page of Simulation 3. The students playing the two disputants will resume their roles as Student A or Student B, as specified on the second page of the simulation.

3. Have students conduct the simulation.

4. Have the students who played the co-mediators trade places with the students who played the disputants and conduct Simulation 4 in the same way.

5. After each simulation, ask the co-mediators the following questions to help process the activity:

   What did you do well?

   What could you do differently?

   What questions seemed to help disputants create their agreement?

6. Summarize the idea that because the problem is between the two disputants, the agreement must be their agreement—something they both will do. The agreement is often a combination of ideas.

Step 6: Create an Agreement

♦ **Ask disputants to make a plan of action:**

"Who, what, when, where, and how?"

♦ **Ask each person to summarize the plan.**

♦ **Ask:**

"Is the problem solved?"

♦ **Shake hands with each person.**

♦ **Say:**

"Thank you for choosing to mediate and working hard on your agreement. Please think about mediation the next time you have a problem."

♦ **Ask:**

"Do you want to shake hands with each other?"

Because the problem is between the disputants, the agreement must be their agreement— something they both will do. The agreement is often a combination of ideas.

89

A CTIVITY

10 Putting It All Together

PURPOSE   To review the mediation process and practice all six steps

MATERIALS   Student Manuals
Simulations 5 and 6 (from Appendix C—one copy of each simulation for every four students)

FORMAT OPTION   Whole class discussion/participation

PROCEDURE   1. Refer students to pages 90–91 of their Student Manuals, "The Peaceable School Mediation Process," where all six steps in the mediation process are presented. Discuss and review the steps as needed.

2. Divide students into new groups of four—two co-mediators and two disputants. Explain that each group will practice all of the steps in the mediation process. Give the students playing the co-mediators a copy of the first page of Simulation 5. Give each of the two disputants half of the second page—one is Student A, the other is Student B.

3. Have students conduct the simulation.

4. Have the students who played the co-mediators trade places with the students who played the disputants and conduct Simulation 6 in the same way.

5. After each simulation, ask the co-mediators the following questions to help process the activity:

   What did you do well?

   What could you do differently?

   What step in the process is the hardest for you?

6. Give students a chance to ask and discuss any questions they might have about the mediation process as a whole.

Student Manual
page 90

The Peaceable School
Mediation Process

STEP 1: AGREE TO MEDIATE

♦ Welcome both people and introduce yourselves as the mediators.

♦ Define mediation.

♦ Explain the ground rules:

Mediators do not take sides.

Mediation is private.

Take turns talking and listening.

Cooperate to solve the problem.

♦ Ask each person: *"Are you willing to follow these rules?"*

STEP 2: GATHER POINTS OF VIEW

♦ Say: *"Please tell what happened."*

♦ Listen, summarize, clarify. To clarify, ask:

"How did you feel when that happened?"

"Do you have anything to add?"

STEP 3: FOCUS ON INTERESTS

♦ Ask:

"What do you want?"

"Why?"

♦ Listen, summarize, clarify. To clarify, ask:

"What might happen if you don't reach an agreement?"

"How do you want things to change?"

"How will that help?"

"What would you think if you were in the other person's shoes?

♦ Summarize the interests. Say: *"Your interests are _____."*

90

Student Manual
page 91

STEP 4: CREATE WIN-WIN OPTIONS

♦ Explain the brainstorming rules:

Say any idea that comes to mind.

Do not judge or discuss ideas.

Come up with as many ideas as possible.

Try to think of unusual ideas.

♦ Say:

"Please suggest ideas that address the interests of both of you."

"Can you think of more possibilities that will help both of you?"

STEP 5: EVALUATE OPTIONS

♦ Ask:

"Which of the options on your list do you like?"

"Can you combine options or parts of options?"

"Can any two of the options be paired so each of you can take one of that pair?"

♦ For each option, ask:

"Is this option fair?"

"Can you do it?"

"Do you think it will work?"

STEP 6: CREATE AN AGREEMENT

♦ Ask disputants to make a plan of action: *"Who, what, when, where, and how?"*

♦ Ask each person to summarize the plan.

♦ Ask: *"Is the problem solved?"*

♦ Shake hands with each person.

♦ Say: *"Thank you for choosing to mediate and working hard on your agreement. Please think about mediation the next time you have a problem."*

♦ Ask: *"Do you want to shake hands with each other?"*

91

Activity

11 Key Concept Review

PURPOSE To understand the meaning of key concepts related to mediation

MATERIALS Butcher paper
Magazines
Comic books
Scissors
Glue
Markers

FORMAT OPTIONS Cooperative learning
Class meeting

PROCEDURE 1. Ask students to use their own words to define the following concepts. Solicit several definitions for each. Discuss the different definitions until the group displays a common understanding of each of the concepts.

MEDIATION	TRUSTWORTHY
IMPARTIAL	WIN-WIN OPTION
RESPECTFUL	RESOLUTION
AGREEMENT	INTEREST

2. Divide the class into eight groups of equal numbers. Assign each group one of the words and instruct them to use the art materials to develop a poster that shows the meaning of the concept—draw a picture, write a definition, create a collage, and so forth.

3. Display the posters.

SECTION 5

Negotiation

OVERVIEW

Negotiation is a process in which disputing parties in a conflict communicate directly with each other to resolve the conflict peaceably. By engaging in the negotiation process, students solve their problems independently, thus gaining power and freedom. The more students become empowered to resolve their differences peacefully, the more responsibly they behave.

Negotiation is a way for students to deal with differences without coercion or aggression. Like mediation, negotiation involves exploring disputes and finding resolutions that combine the needs of the parties in conflict instead of compromising those needs. It differs from mediation, however, in that there is no intermediary. Negotiation is the simplest of the conflict resolution problem-solving processes because it involves only two people; it is the most difficult of the processes because it involves only two people. In mediation, the mediators assume the major responsibility for managing the problem-solving process, freeing the disputants to concentrate on satisfying their interests. In negotiation, the negotiators manage the problem-solving process while also focusing on satisfying their interests. To realize the vision of the peaceable school, a critical mass of the school population need the training to successfully negotiate their conflicts.

In the peaceable school, students learn the skills necessary to communicate their thoughts and feelings about the conflict and follow a step-by-step negotiation procedure designed to ensure a balanced exchange—to allow both disputants to tell their view of the conflict and to hear the viewpoint of the other party. When both parties agree to negotiate—work cooperatively to solve the problem—the negotiation process is undertaken. Students of all ages can learn the negotiation process. With the teacher's assistance and encouragement, even very young students can use the process to solve problems with classmates. More mature students can use the process without adult encouragement or prompting.

The activities included in this section are designed to help students master a six-step negotiation process that parallels the mediation process detailed in Section 4 and the group problem solving process presented in Section 6.

ROLE OF THE NEGOTIATOR

To build a relationship—perhaps even trust—and to develop the cooperation required to reach a resolution, the negotiating parties strive to achieve the following goals.

The negotiator listens with empathy. Effective communication skills are essential to successful negotiation and influence each step of the process. Often the problem is clouded by issues in the relationship—emotions run high, unfounded inferences are treated as fact, and attention is focused on past actions. Communication skills are required to acknowledge emotions and clarify perceptions, thus freeing the disputants to understand and work on the problem.

Specifically, the successful negotiator uses the following active listening skills throughout the process:

Attending, or using nonverbal behaviors to indicate that the listener finds what the other party is thinking and feeling of interest and wants to understand. These nonverbal behaviors include eye contact, facial expressions, and body language such as posture and gestures.

Summarizing, or restating facts by repeating the most important points, organizing interests, and discarding extraneous information. In summarizing, the negotiator also acknowledges emotions by stating the feelings the other person is experiencing.

Clarifying, or using open-ended questions and statements to obtain more information and ensure understanding.

The negotiator speaks to be understood. Even a very good listener, one who uses the active listening skills just detailed, hears only what is actually said. Therefore, the speaker, especially in negotiation, needs to speak clearly. To do so means the following:

Speak to be understood, or work hard to state the issues or the problem in a clear, direct way rather than talking to impress or debate. Avoid name-calling, criticism, sarcasm, and demands.

Speak about yourself, or describe the situation in terms of yourself by using statements that begin with "I" rather than "you." Avoid complaining about or blaming the other person.

Speak for a purpose, or think about what you want the other person to understand and what purpose the information will serve. Planning ahead is prudent. It is important to be concise, eliminating undo repetition. It is important not to assume that the other person knows what you know or sees the problem the same way you do. Some information will not help in resolving the conflict and is best left unsaid.

Speak with consideration for the listener, or be sensitive to the other person. Use a voice tone and volume that invite listening. Do not speak too rapidly or too slowly. If the other person is not using attending behavior, find out why.

The negotiator suspends judgment. The successful negotiator strives to remain open and objective throughout the process. The negotiator avoids justifying and arguing for a particular position (what that person wants), choosing instead to work hard to explain his or her interests (why that person wants what he or she wants).

The negotiator is respectful. Being respectful involves working to understand the other person's emotions and beliefs. A key to respect is knowing and accepting that we are all different: The successful negotiator is able to treat the other party fairly and without prejudice. The negotiator also honors the other person's privacy by not talking about the problem with others. The negotiator tells only that the problem was solved and perhaps what he or she agreed to do to solve the problem. The negotiator respects the process by accepting only agreements he or she intends to honor to the best of his or her ability.

The negotiator has a cooperative spirit. Having a cooperative spirit means the negotiator allows others to satisfy their interests whenever possible without compromising his or her interests. In a negotiation, the two parties may not gain equally, but a fair solution allows both to improve their situation and to better satisfy their needs. The successful negotiator views the negotiation process as being equal in importance to the problem's solution. When both parties cooperate, they are able to find their own solution.

THE NEGOTIATION PROCESS

The six steps in the negotiation process are as follows:

Step 1: Agree to Negotiate

Step 2: Gather Points of View

Step 3: Focus on Interests

Step 4: Create Win-Win Options

Step 5: Evaluate Options

Step 6: Create an Agreement

Step 1: Agree to Negotiate

In negotiation, the disputants view themselves as partners in trying to solve the problem. To begin the process, the disputants sit face-to-face and agree to follow three ground rules:

> Negotiation is private.
>
> Take turns talking and listening.
>
> Cooperate to solve the problem.

These three basic ground rules structure a win-win climate by ensuring that both parties will be heard and that the interests of both will be considered in any ensuing agreement. As in mediation, other ground rules may be helpful, if they are simple and stated positively. Ground rules such as "No name-calling" or "No put-downs" are sufficiently covered under the ground rule of cooperating to solve the problem. Negotiation should not be attempted if either of the disputants appears unable to control anger sufficiently to adhere to this rule. It is best if the disputants wait until their tempers have calmed before they attempt to negotiate.

Privacy is a concern in negotiation. The privacy ground rule calls for disputants to respect each other's privacy and the privacy of the negotiation proceedings. This rule is not a "gag order." It is permissable, even beneficial, for disputants to tell peers that a negotiation resulted in an agreement. If not so advised, others who have an interest in the conflict may advance the dispute. Talking about the negotiation process has another positive effect in the sense that other students will see that conflicts can be resolved without the intervention of other students or adults. Spreading the word that the conflict has been resolved may prevent retaliation or a continuation of the dispute. Privacy issues become increasingly important as the issues in the dispute become more personal and sensitive. A reasonable extension of the privacy ground rule could be stated as follows: "You may share with others the fact that the problem was resolved and tell others what you agreed to do, but you may not tell about the problem or how the problem was solved, or even what the other person agreed to do."

Step 2: Gather Points of View

The purpose of this step is to ascertain each person's point of view about the incident or situation. Because the negotiators each have a stake in the problem, sharing points of view is crucial but may also be volatile. It is not uncommon that a discussion of the problem evokes the strong emotions felt when the problem was first experienced. This can make the negotiation difficult and may even result in termination without an agreement. Especially in Step 2, it is important for each disputant to remember to speak for a purpose, planning what he or she wishes to say and saying it in a manner the other can hear.

The first disputant begins by telling his or her view of the problem. During this time, the other person listens actively. When the first disputant finishes, the other summarizes what was said. Next the disputants switch roles, with the second disputant telling what happened and the first listening actively and then summarizing. Each person next has an opportunity to add information or clarify what was said before. At this time, the negotiators may ask questions to better understand the situation. However, it is important to distinguish between questions seeking legitimate clarification and those masking an aggressive insistence that the other party justify actions or desires. There is a fine line between questions of clarification and questions that challenge. Open-ended questions are more likely to obtain additional information to clarify a point of view than to rationalize an action or position.

Completing the following sentence stems is a useful way for the negotiators to tell about the problem:

> I was _____. (Tell what you were doing.)
>
> I feel _____.

Step 3: Focus on Interests

As in the mediation process, determining underlying interests is the most critical step. The negotiators must be able to get beyond their respective positions to examine their interests. If interests are not disclosed, there is little chance of reaching an agreement that both sides can keep.

In this step, the negotiators again alternate stating what they want and why, listening to the other person, then summarizing what was heard. Throughout, they continue to practice active listening—attending, summarizing, and seeking clarification as needed. The negotiators look for shared or compatible interests and use these as the basis for working toward a resolution of the conflict.

The completion of the following sentence stems by each disputant provides the information required to identify interests:

> I want _____ because _____.
>
> I want to solve the problem because _____.
>
> If this problem does not get solved, I _____.

Step 4: Create Win-Win Options

In this step, the negotiators attempt to advance several ideas that address the interests of both of them. Together, they should invent at least three possible options. Such an expectation involves both individuals in the generation of possible solutions rather than allowing one of the negotiators to generate all possibilities independently. This may help prevent the less assertive of the two from becoming intimidated and quickly acquiescing to the other's plan of action. The negotiators must view the generation of options as a joint responsibility to suggest ideas that will help both of them. In the spirit of cooperation, negotiators strive to offer ideas about what they themselves might do to solve the problem rather than suggesting things the other person should do.

To help them generate the options, negotiators follow the rules for brainstorming:

> Say any idea that comes to mind.
>
> Do not judge or discuss ideas.
>
> Come up with as many ideas as possible.
>
> Try to think of unusual ideas.

Unusual ideas, even if impractical or silly, may open the creative insights to legitimate options.

Step 5: Evaluate Options

In this step, the negotiators work together as side-by-side problem solvers to elaborate on or combine options or parts of options to create new options. They then evaluate options by asking the following questions about each one:

> Is this option fair?
>
> Can we do it?
>
> Do we think it will work?

Often negotiation agreements are a combination of compatible ideas. The first disputant will agree to do something, and the second disputant will agree to do something different.

Step 6: Create an Agreement

In Step 6, the negotiators together develop a plan of action to put their idea into effect, specifying who, what, when, where, and how. Each one then takes a turn telling the other person what it is he or she will personally do: "I have agreed to _____." This agreement represents the resolution of the conflict. The negotiators then shake hands to seal the agreement.

Suggested Readings

Curhan, J. R. (1998). *Program for young negotiators.* Boston, MA: Great Source/Houghton Mifflin.

Faber, A., & Mazlish, E. (1987). *How to talk so kids will listen and listen so kids will talk.* New York: Avon.

Fisher, R., & Brown, S. (1988). *Getting together: Building relationships as we negotiate.* New York: Penguin.

Fisher, R., & Ertel, D. (1995). *Getting ready to negotiate: The getting to yes workbook.* New York: Penguin.

Fisher, R., Ury, W., & Patton, B. (1991). *Getting to yes: Negotiating agreement without giving in* (2nd ed.). Boston: Houghton Mifflin.

Stark, P. B. (1994). *It's negotiable: The how-to handbook of win-win tactics.* San Diego: Pfeiffer.

Ury, W. (1993). *Getting past no.* New York: Bantam.

1   Negotiation Is . . .

PURPOSE   To learn that negotiation is a process that allows people to communicate directly to resolve conflicts in a peaceable way

MATERIALS   Student Manuals
Newsprint
Markers

FORMAT OPTIONS   Whole class discussion/participation
Cooperative learning

PROCEDURE   1. Explain that conflict is natural and that people who are in conflict need ways to solve their problems.

2. Refer the group to page 95 in their Student Manuals, "Negotiation," and discuss. Explain that negotiation is when two people communicate directly with each other to solve a problem.

3. Ask students to think about arguments they have had or seen and what usually happens when an argument continues. Typical responses will include:

> Kids get mad and angry.
>
> Kids don't listen to each other.
>
> Nobody gets what he or she wants.
>
> Kids don't understand each other.
>
> Other kids get involved.
>
> Adults take over and punish.

4. Give each group of four or five students a sheet of newsprint. Ask groups to discuss what they think would be the hardest thing about negotiating with someone with whom they have a problem. Typical responses include:

> Staying calm—not yelling.
>
> Listening to the other person.
>
> Saying what you want clearly.

5. Invite groups to share their lists; post these around the room.

6. Summarize by stressing that it takes cooperation and understanding to resolve conflicts. Negotiators, both children and adults, are peacemakers.

Student Manual
page 95

Negotiation

Negotiation is a communication process allowing people to work together to resolve their conflicts peaceably.

THE NEGOTIATOR WORKS TO . . .

♦ Focus on the problem and not blame the other person.

♦ Understand and respect different points of view.

♦ Communicate wants and feelings.

♦ Cooperate in solving a problem.

Negotiators are peacemakers.

95

2   Role of the Negotiator

PURPOSE   To understand how negotiators behave

MATERIALS   Student Manuals

FORMAT OPTIONS   Whole class discussion/participation
Class meeting

PROCEDURE   1. Refer the group to page 96 of their Student Manuals, "Role of the Negotiator."

2. Discuss each of the points, one at a time.

The Negotiator Listens With Empathy

This means the negotiator uses *active listening* to try to understand the thoughts and feelings of the other person. Demonstrate by having a volunteer talk to you about a problem. During the demonstration, look away or otherwise act distracted. Repeat with another volunteer, this time using active listening. Ask the class what they saw. Ask the volunteers how they felt during each demonstration.

The Negotiator Speaks to Be Understood

This means the negotiator plans what to say and thinks about how to say it to best be heard by the other party. Demonstrate by asking two students to volunteer to act as listeners. Explain that you will try the demonstration twice, and in both cases you and the listener are locker partners. The listener will be expected to practice active listening. Ask one of them to leave the room.

For the first demonstration, deliver the following message: "I am really upset. On my way to math class, I grabbed the math book from our locker. When I got to class, I discovered that my homework was not in the book. The teacher collected homework to start the class, so I got a zero in math today because I didn't have my homework. I think you took my book with my homework from our locker." When speaking, be loud, angry, and accusing. Following your speech, ask the listener to summarize what you said.

Ask the second listener to return. Deliver the same message, only be calm, clear, and considerate of the listener's feelings. Following your speech, ask the listener to summarize what you said.

Ask the class what they observed about your delivery and about the summaries of the listeners. Ask the listeners how they felt during each demonstration.

The Negotiator Suspends Judgment

Explain that this means the negotiator strives to remain open and objective throughout the process. The negotiator avoids justifying and arguing for his or her position (*what* the person wants), choosing instead to work hard to explain his or her interests (*why* the person wants it).

The Negotiator Is Respectful

Being a negotiator means showing respect for everyone, no matter their dress, shape, color, size, age, and so on. Explain that the negotiator tries to understand the other person's views of the situation without judgment: Because we all have our own views about things, this is not always easy. The negotiator also shows respect by not talking about the other person or the other person's view of the problem to anyone else. The negotiator operates in good faith by not agreeing to do something he or she does not intend to do.

The Negotiator Has a Cooperative Spirit

Explain that the negotiator views the negotiation process as being as important as the solution to the problem. When both parties cooperate, they are able to find their own solution. A cooperative person allows others to satisfy their interests whenever possible without compromising his or her own interests.

3. Conclude by stating that the main role of the negotiator is to build trust and cooperation, which in turn makes mutual problem solving possible.

Student Manual
page 96

Role of the Negotiator

THE NEGOTIATOR . . .

♦ Listens with empathy.

♦ Speaks to be understood.

♦ Suspends judgment.

♦ Is respectful.

♦ Has a cooperative spirit.

Negotiators build trust and cooperation,
making mutual problem solving possible.

96

ACTIVITY

3 Overview of the Negotiation Process

PURPOSE To learn what is involved in the six-step negotiation process

MATERIALS Student Manuals

FORMAT OPTIONS Whole class discussion/participation
Class meeting

PROCEDURE
1. Refer the group to page 97 in their Student Manuals, "Steps in the Negotiation Process," and briefly explain what goes on in each step.

2. Have two student volunteers perform the sample negotiation on pages 98–100 of the Student Manual. Encourage the other students to follow along and look for the steps as they are demonstrated.

3. After the demonstration is over, have students evaluate what they saw:

    What steps did you notice?

    How did the negotiators behave?

    Was the outcome a solution that met both people's needs?

4. Explain that everyone will have the opportunity to learn and practice the negotiation steps. They will then be prepared to act as negotiators when the opportunity arises. Conclude by saying that we negotiate with others nearly all the time and that learning to do so peaceably will help us get what we want while allowing the other person to get what he or she wants, too.

Student Manual
page 97

Steps in the Negotiation Process

◆ **Step 1:** Agree to Negotiate

◆ **Step 2:** Gather Points of View

◆ **Step 3:** Focus on Interests

◆ **Step 4:** Create Win-Win Options

◆ **Step 5:** Evaluate Options

◆ **Step 6:** Create an Agreement

97

Student Manual
page 98

Sample Negotiation

STEP 1: AGREE TO NEGOTIATE

Ruthie: I agree to keep this discussion private, I agree to take turns talking and listening, and I agree to cooperate to solve the problem.

Cierra: I agree to keep this private, to take turns talking and listening, and to cooperate to solve this problem.

STEP 2: GATHER POINTS OF VIEW

Ruthie: OK, I shoved your books off the table. I was angry because I think you stole my colored pencils. You were using colored pencils, and I can't find mine.

Cierra: So you think I stole your colored pencils because you can't find yours. You were angry and shoved my books off the table because you thought I was using your pencils.

Ruthie: Yes.

Cierra: Well, my point of view is I was coloring with the pencils my aunt gave me for my birthday. I was mad when you shoved my books off the table, so I shoved your chair and you fell. I feel hurt when you accuse me of stealing your stuff.

Ruthie: Your point of view is that you were using colored pencils your aunt gave you. You were mad when I shoved your books, so you shoved my chair. You feel hurt when I accuse you of stealing.

Cierra: Yes, that's my point of view.

STEP 3: FOCUS ON INTERESTS

Ruthie: I want my colored pencils because I need to use them for the poster project and I like to draw with them.

Cierra: You want your colored pencils because you need them for the project and you like drawing with them.

98

Ruthie: Yes.

Cierra: I want you to stop accusing me of stealing because that hurts. I don't steal. I want to be your friend because I like you.

Ruthie: You want me to stop accusing you of stealing because it hurts. You don't steal, and you want to be my friend. I guess I don't want to have you mad at me and not like me.

STEP 4: CREATE WIN-WIN OPTIONS

Cierra: What are some options that could help us?

Ruthie: I could stop accusing you of stealing and ask if you have seen my stuff.

Cierra: I could help you find your colored pencils, or you could use mine for the poster project if we haven't found yours.

Ruthie: I could ask the teacher to help us look for them.

Cierra: We could make a lost-and-found box and put a notice on it that your pencils are lost. That way the whole class can help find them.

Ruthie: We could work together on the poster project and help each other.

Cierra: We could put signs up all over the school about your missing pencils.

STEP 5: EVALUATE OPTIONS

Ruthie: It would be fair if I stopped accusing you of stealing every time I'm missing something. I could ask you if you have seen my stuff. I can do that.

Cierra: I think that's fair.

Ruthie: We could look for my pencils together and share your pencils when we work on the poster project if we don't find mine right away.

Cierra: I think the lost-and-found box will really work.

Student Manual
page 100

Ruthie: Me, too. We can ask the teacher if that's OK. That way she won't need to help us look.

Cierra: We can do that together.

Ruthie: I never take my pencils out of class, so I don't think we need to put signs up all over the school.

Cierra: I think these options are fair. They cover both our interests.

STEP 6: CREATE AN AGREEMENT

Ruthie: Let's make a plan.

Cierra: OK. We can talk to the teacher about the lost-and-found box at recess this afternoon.

Ruthie: We can make the lost-and-found box today after school.

Cierra: We can look together for the pencils at lunchtime.

Ruthie: We could work on the poster project on Saturday morning at my house even if we do find my pencils.

Cierra: What if you forget and accuse me of stealing again?

Ruthie: You could remind me to ask you. OK?

Cierra: OK.

Ruthie: I don't think I'll forget.

Cierra: OK, if you accuse me of stealing, I have agreed to remind you to ask me. I have agreed to look for your pencils with you at lunchtime, talk with the teacher at recess, make the lost-and-found box after school, and work on the poster project with you on Saturday. We can use my pencils if we don't find yours.

Ruthie: I have agreed to stop accusing you of stealing, to look for my pencils at lunchtime, to go with you and talk with the teacher at recess, to make the lost-and-found box, and to work together on the poster project on Saturday.

[Ruthie and Cierra shake hands.]

100

ACTIVITY

4 Step 1: Agree to Negotiate

PURPOSE To learn what physical arrangements are best for negotiation and to understand the ground rules for the negotiation process

MATERIALS Student Manuals

FORMAT OPTION Whole class discussion/participation

PROCEDURE
1. Discuss the physical arrangements for negotiation: The best arrangement is for the two people who are having the problem to sit face-to-face.

2. Refer students to page 101 in their Student Manuals, "Step 1: Agree to Negotiate," and discuss. Explain that negotiation rules help make the process as fair as possible. Both parties must agree to the rules and want to negotiate—to begin the process, each person says the rules aloud.

3. Have the class form pairs and encourage them to practice Step 1 by stating the rules for negotiation.

4. A common question about Step 1 is "What if the rules are broken?" Explain that, in negotiation, both parties must follow and enforce the rules. If you think the other person is not following the rules, you could say:

   > I'm sorry, but I was not finished talking. May I continue?

   > We agreed to cooperate. Are we still trying to solve the problem?

   > I must not have explained my point of view. What I meant to say was _____. (Repeat your message.)

   Discuss times when these responses would be appropriate. Solicit other ideas from students. Discuss the possible impact of any ideas generated, especially the impact relative to speaking to be understood.

5. Have pairs practice making these kinds of statements to each other.

Student Manual
page 101

Step 1: Agree to Negotiate

♦ **Say:**

"I agree to keep the discussion private."

"I agree to take turns talking and listening."

"I agree to cooperate to solve the problem."

The negotiation rules help make the process fair.

101

ACTIVITY

5 Step 2: Gather Points of View

PURPOSE   To learn how to gather both people's points of view in order to understand the problem

MATERIALS   Student Manuals
Simulation 7 or Simulation 8 (from Appendix C—one copy of the simulation for every two students)

FORMAT OPTION   Whole class discussion/participation

NOTE   Teachers or student volunteers will need to prepare in advance to act out the script illustrating this step. If time permits, students could conduct both simulations for added practice.

PROCEDURE   1. Have teachers or student volunteers act out the script titled "Red Riding Hood and the Wolf: Gather Points of View," appearing on pages 102–104 of the Student Manual.*

2. Explain that in every conflict each person has a *point of view*. These views are not right or wrong—just two different ways of seeing a situation. The purpose of Step 2 is to let each person hear the other's point of view. In negotiation, the disputants tell what happened and how they felt when it happened or how they are feeling about the problem now.

3. Discuss the Red Riding Hood example by asking the following questions:

What is Red Riding Hood's point of view?

What is the Wolf's point of view?

What did the negotiators do to present their points of view?

How did each one feel about this problem?

4. Refer students to page 105 in their Student Manuals, "Step 2: Gather Points of View," and discuss. Stress that in Step 2 the

---

*The adaptations of the classic Red Riding Hood story appearing throughout the activities in this section are based on a retelling in *Individual Development: Creativity* by Leif Fearn, 1974, San Diego: Education Improvement Associates.

negotiators need to use the active listening skills of attending, summarizing, and clarifying to understand how each person sees the problem. (Review these skills from Section 3 as necessary.) Point out that it does not matter who talks first in a negotiation because both people will have an equal chance to tell their point of view. When the first person finishes, the second person summarizes. The second person then tells his or her point of view, then the first person summarizes. Each person then has the opportunity to add information, always followed by the listener's summary of what was said.

5. Next explain that students will have the opportunity to practice Steps 1 and 2 in the negotiation process. Have students form the same pairs as in Activity 4, then give each person half of either Simulation 7 or Simulation 8. One person plays the role of Student A; the other plays the role of Student B.

6. Have students conduct the simulation.

7. After the simulation, ask the following questions to help students process the activity:

    What did you do well?

    What could you do differently?

    Did the other person listen and summarize what you said?

8. Summarize the idea that, after this step is over, each person will have a better understanding of how the other feels and perceives the problem. Point out that, because the two people have agreed to cooperate, the exchange should not be an argument. They do not try to correct what the other says—only listen and summarize.

Red Riding Hood and the Wolf: Gather Points of View

Red: I'm Red Riding Hood. I agree to keep our discussion private, to take turns talking and listening, and to cooperate to solve the problem.

Wolf: I'm the Wolf. I agree to take turns talking and listening, and I agree to cooperate with you, Red Riding Hood, to solve this problem we have. I'll keep this private.

Red: I was taking a loaf of fresh bread and some cakes to my granny's cottage on the other side of the woods. Granny wasn't well, so I thought I would pick some flowers for her along the way.

I was picking the flowers when you, Wolf, jumped out from behind a tree and started asking me a bunch of questions. You wanted to know what I was doing and where I was going, and you kept grinning that wicked grin and smacking your lips together. You were being so gross and rude. Then you ran away. I was frightened.

Wolf: You were taking some food to your grandmother on the other side of the woods, and I appeared from behind a tree and frightened you.

Red: Yes, that's what happened.

Wolf: Well, look, Red, the forest is my home. I care about it and try to keep it clean. That day, I was cleaning up some garbage people had left behind when I heard footsteps. I leaped behind a tree and saw you coming down the trail carrying a basket.

I was suspicious because you were dressed in that strange red cape with your head covered up as if you didn't want anyone to know who you were. You started picking my flowers and stepping on my new little pine trees.

Naturally, I stopped to ask you what you were doing. You gave me this song and dance about going to your granny's house with a basket of goodies.

I wasn't very happy about the way you treated my home or me.

Student Manual
page 103

Red: You were concerned when you saw me in a red cape picking your flowers. You stopped me and asked me what I was doing.

Wolf: That's right.

Red: Well, the problem didn't stop there. When I got to my granny's house, you were disguised in my granny's nightgown. You tried to eat me with those big ugly teeth. I'd be dead today if it hadn't been for the woodsman who came in and saved me. You scared my granny. I found her hiding under the bed.

Wolf: You say I put on your granny's nightgown so you would think I was your granny, and that I tried to hurt you?

Red: I said you tried to *eat* me. I really thought you were going to eat me up. I was hysterical.

Wolf: Now wait a minute, Red. I know your granny. I thought we should teach you a lesson for prancing on my pine trees in that get-up and for picking my flowers. I let you go on your way in the woods, but I ran ahead to your granny's cottage.

When I saw Granny, I explained what happened, and she agreed that you needed to learn a lesson. Granny hid under the bed, and I dressed up in her nightgown.

When you came into the bedroom you saw me in the bed and said something nasty about my big ears. I've been told my ears are big before, so I tried to make the best of it by saying big ears help me hear you better.

Then you made an insulting crack about my bulging eyes. This one was really hard to blow off, because you sounded so nasty. Still, I make it a policy to turn the other cheek, so I told you my big eyes help me see you better.

Your next insult about my big teeth really got to me. You see, I'm quite sensitive about my teeth. I know that when you made fun of my teeth I should have had better control, but I leaped from the bed and growled that my teeth would help me to eat you.

But, come on, Red! Let's face it. Everyone knows no wolf could ever eat a girl, but you started screaming and running around the house. I tried to catch you to calm you down.

103

All of a sudden the door came crashing open, and a big woodsman stood there with his ax. I knew I was in trouble . . . there was an open window behind me, so out I went.

I've been hiding ever since. There are terrible rumors going around the forest about me. Red, you called me the Big Bad Wolf. I'd like to say I've gotten over feeling bad, but the truth is I haven't lived happily ever after.

I don't understand why Granny never told you and the others my side of the story. I'm upset about the rumors and have been afraid to show my face in the forest. Why have you and Granny let the situation go on for this long? It just isn't fair. I'm miserable and lonely.

Red: You think that I have started unfair rumors about you, and you are miserable and lonely and don't understand why Granny didn't tell your side of the story.

Well, Granny has been sick—and she's been very tired lately. When I asked her how she came to be under the bed, she said she couldn't remember a thing that had happened. Come to think of it, she didn't seem too upset . . . just confused.

Wolf: So you think it is possible that Granny just doesn't remember because she is sick.

104

Student Manual
page 105

Step 2: Gather Points of View

STUDENT A

♦ **Tell your view of the problem. Say:**

"I was _____." (Tell what you were doing.)

"I feel _____."

STUDENT B

♦ **Listen and summarize Student A's view of the problem.**

♦ **Tell your view of the problem. Say:**

"I was _____." (Tell what you were doing.)

"I feel _____."

STUDENT A

♦ **Listen and summarize Student B's view of the problem.**

♦ **Clarify by adding anything more about your point of view.**

STUDENT B

♦ **Listen and summarize what Student A adds.**

♦ **Clarify by adding anything more about your point of view.**

STUDENT A

♦ **Listen and summarize what Student B adds.**

Plan carefully what you wish to say to the other person.

6 Step 3: Focus on Interests

PURPOSE   To learn to find shared and compatible interests

MATERIALS   Student Manuals
Simulation 9 or Simulation 10 (from Appendix C—one copy of the simulation for every two students)

FORMAT OPTION   Whole class discussion/participation

NOTE   If the class has not already completed Section 4 activities on mediation, first use the story of Sam and Ben's conflict from Activity 6 in that section in order to illustrate the idea of shared and compatible interests. Teachers or student volunteers will need to prepare in advance to act out the script illustrating this step. The groups formed in this activity will continue to work together in Activities 7–9, with Student A and Student B taking their same roles. Simulations 9 and/or 10 will be used again in the next three activities. If time permits, students could conduct both simulations for added practice.

PROCEDURE   1. Have teachers or students act out the script titled "Red Riding Hood and the Wolf: Focus on Interests," on page 106 of the Student Manual.

2. Briefly explain that people often take a *position* when they have a problem: A position is *what* the person wants. It is difficult to find a solution by focusing only on positions. A temporary agreement may be reached, but such agreements typically do not last because the person's real *interests* (*why* the person wants what he or she does) have not been addressed. For lasting solutions, the negotiators must focus on their interests, not their positions.

3. Discuss the following questions:

What are Red Riding Hood's positions? What does she want?

What are the Wolf's positions? What does he want?

What are Red Riding Hood's interests?

What are the Wolf's interests?

4. Refer students to page 107 of their Student Manuals, "Step 3: Focus on Interests," and discuss. Explain that in Step 3, the negotiators

take turns telling what they want and why, trying to find interests. Shared and compatible interests serve as the building blocks for an agreement. Remind students that most common interests are associated with the basic needs for belonging, power, freedom, and fun. (Review these concepts from Section 2 as necessary.)

5. Explain that if one or both of the negotiators are uncertain about what the other person wants and why, clarification is needed. Questions to clarify interests are:

> What do you really want?
>
> Why do you want to solve this problem?
>
> If we cannot solve this problem, what will happen?
>
> What would you think if you were in my shoes?

6. Have the students form pairs different from those in Activity 5 and explain that each pair will practice Steps 1, 2, and 3 in the negotiation process. Give each negotiator half of either Simulation 9 or Simulation 10. One person plays the role of Student A; the other plays the role of Student B.

7. Have students conduct the simulation.

8. After the simulation, ask the negotiators the following questions to help process the activity:

> What did the two of you do well?
>
> What could you do differently?
>
> What seemed to help you understand each other's interests?

9. Summarize the main point of this activity by restating that shared and compatible interests are the building blocks of the resolution. The negotiators do not move on to Step 4 until interests are understood.

Red Riding Hood and the Wolf:
Focus on Interests

Red: I want to be able to take flowers to Granny when I visit her because she is lonely and flowers help cheer her up.

I want to be able to go through the forest to Granny's house because it is too far to take the road around the forest.

I want you to stop trying to scare me or threaten me in the forest because I want to feel safe. Besides, I think the forest is a fun place.

Wolf: You want to go through the forest to visit Granny, who is lonely, and you want to feel safe because you think the forest is a neat place.

Red: Yes, and I want to take flowers to Granny.

Wolf: I want you to watch where you are walking and to stop picking my flowers because I want to keep my forest home looking nice.

I want the rumors to stop because I want people to like me, and I want to be able to enjoy the forest without being afraid that someone is hunting for me.

Red: You want the forest to be pretty, you want people who visit the forest to like you and not be afraid of you, and you want to be safe in the forest.

Wolf: Right, the forest is my home. I should be free to enjoy my own home.

106

Student Manual
page 107

Step 3: Focus on Interests

♦ **Say what you want and why:**

"I want _____ because _____."

♦ **Listen, summarize, clarify. To clarify, ask:**

"What will happen if we do not solve the problem?"

"What would you think if you were in my shoes?"

> Shared and compatible interests are the building blocks of the resolution. Most interests are associated with the basic needs for belonging, power, freedom, and fun.

107

A C T I V I T Y

7

Step 4: Create Win-Win Options

PURPOSE To learn to brainstorm to create options that address both individuals' interests

MATERIALS Student Manuals
Simulation 9 or Simulation 10 (saved from Activity 6)

FORMAT OPTION Whole class discussion/participation

NOTE Teachers or student volunteers will need to prepare in advance to act out the script illustrating this step. If time permits, students could conduct both simulations for added practice.

PROCEDURE 1. Have teachers or students act out the script titled "Red Riding Hood and the Wolf: Create Win-Win Options," on page 108 of the Student Manual.

2. Refer the group to page 109 of their Student Manuals, "Step 4: Create Win-Win Options," and discuss. Explain that in Step 4, the negotiators use *brainstorming* to create *win-win options,* or options that will help both of them.

3. Expand on the brainstorming rules as they are given in the Student Manual to be sure students understand:

> Say any idea that comes to mind. (This means to blurt out your ideas; don't censor your thoughts.)

> Do not judge or discuss ideas. (This means you accept all ideas, at least for the time being; don't criticize or make fun of any ideas.)

> Come up with as many ideas as possible. (Sometimes it is helpful when you run out of ideas to try making changes to ideas that have already been given.)

> Try to think of unusual ideas. (Sometimes really weird or far-out ideas will help you and others think of new possibilities.)

Tell students that they should work together to get at least three win-win options. Stress the importance of having each person suggest some of the ideas.

4. Ask the following questions about the demonstration:

What options did Red Riding Hood suggest?

What options did the Wolf suggest?

5. Have students form the same pairs as in the previous activity. Explain that each pair will practice Step 4 in the negotiation process, using either Simulation 9 or Simulation 10. The students should continue in their roles as either Student A or Student B.

6. Have students conduct the simulation.

7. After the simulation, ask the negotiators the following questions to help process the activity:

What did you do well?

What could you do differently?

What seemed to help you generate win-win options?

What win-win options did you generate?

8. Summarize that during Step 4 the people in conflict attempt to generate as many options as they can to solve the problem.

Red Riding Hood and the Wolf: Create Win-Win Options

Red: In order to solve this problem, I could try to stay on the path when I walk through the forest.

Wolf: I could try to remember to call out when I hear you coming instead of quietly stepping out from behind a tree. I could plant some flowers over by Granny's house for you to pick.

Red: I could pick up trash I see in the forest and take it to Granny's trash can.

Wolf: I could check up on Granny to make sure she is OK on those days when you can't make it. She is my friend, you see.

Red: Granny and I can talk to the woodsman and tell him we made a mistake about you. I could tell my friends that I'm not afraid of you anymore—that you can be nice.

Wolf: I could meet your friends on the edge of the forest and show them through it.

Student Manual
page 109

Step 4: Create Win-Win Options

- ◆ **Invent at least three options to address the interests of both of you.**

- ◆ **Follow the brainstorming rules:**

   Say any idea that comes to mind.

   Do not judge or discuss ideas.

   Come up with as many ideas as possible.

   Try to think of unusual ideas.

Negotiators keep track of the options generated.

109

ACTIVITY

8   Step 5: Evaluate Options

PURPOSE   To learn to evaluate the options previously generated in terms of fairness and workability

MATERIALS   Student Manuals
Simulation 9 or Simulation 10 (saved from Activity 6)

FORMAT OPTION   Whole class discussion/participation

NOTE   Teachers or student volunteers will need to prepare in advance to act out the script illustrating this step. If time permits, students could conduct both simulations for added practice.

PROCEDURE

1. Have teachers or students act out the script titled "Red Riding Hood and the Wolf: Evaluate Options," on page 110 of the Student Manual.

2. Refer students to page 111 of their Student Manuals, "Step 5: Evaluate Options," and discuss. Explain that in this step the negotiators decide which options are fair and which will work—that is, they choose from among the options generated in the previous step the ideas or parts of ideas that they think have the best chance of resolving the conflict.

3. Ask the following questions:

   How did Red Riding Hood and the Wolf improve on the options they generated in Step 4?

   Did they discuss what would work?

4. To practice Step 5, have students form the same pairs as in the previous activity. Explain that each pair will work together to evaluate the options they have generated, continuing to use either Simulation 9 or Simulation 10. The students should resume their roles as either Student A or Student B.

5. Have students conduct the simulation.

6. After giving the students time to discuss, ask the following questions to help process the activity:

   What did you do well?

What could you do differently?

What seemed to help you evaluate options?

7. Summarize the idea that Step 5 involves the negotiators in deciding which options or parts of options will best create a win-win solution. At this point, they become side-by-side problem solvers.

Student Manual
page 110

Red Riding Hood and the Wolf: Evaluate Options

Wolf: Do you think if you tell the woodsman and your friends that you made a mistake about me and that I'm really nice, then I won't have to worry about the woodsman and his hunters catching me?

Red: I think that will work.

Wolf: Maybe I could go with you to talk to the woodsman.

Red: Yes, that would help. You could also go with me when I tell my friends I'm not afraid of you anymore. . . . I'd like to help you plant some flowers at Granny's, and I could also help you plant some in the forest. It would be nice to visit Granny together. She's pretty lonely.

Wolf: That sounds good.

Red: I agree.

Wolf: I don't think it will work for you to stay on the path all the time. I can show you where to walk so you don't harm anything.

Red: I think that's fair.

Wolf: I agree.

Red: Will it work for you to check on Granny when I can't visit her?

Wolf: Yes, if you call me early in the morning.

Red: I think it would be a good idea if I ask my friends for a donation when you give them a tour of the forest, and we could use the money to buy more trees to plant and start a recycling program for the trash we pick up.

Wolf: I think we've taken care of both of our interests.

Red: This solution will help both of us.

110

Student Manual
page 111

Step 5: Evaluate Options

♦ **Combine options or parts of options.**

♦ **For each option, work together to decide:**

"Is this option fair?"

"Can we do it?"

"Do we think it will work?"

In this step, negotiators become side-by-side
problem solvers in evaluating options.

111

9 Step 6: Create an Agreement

PURPOSE To learn to create a plan of action from the options generated

MATERIALS Student Manuals
Simulation 9 or Simulation 10 (saved from Activity 6)

FORMAT OPTION Whole class discussion/participation

NOTE Teachers or student volunteers will need to prepare in advance to act out the script illustrating this step. If time permits, students could conduct both simulations for added practice.

PROCEDURE 1. Have teachers or students act out the script titled "Red Riding Hood and the Wolf: Create an Agreement," on page 112 of the Student Manual.

2. Refer the group to page 113 in their Student Manuals, "Step 6: Create an Agreement," and discuss. Stress that in this step the negotiators work together to make a plan of action. At the end of the step, it should be clear what each one is planning to do, how it will be accomplished, and when these actions will take place.

3. Ask the following questions about the demonstration:

   Does Red know what the Wolf will do?

   Does the Wolf know what Red will do?

   Did the two of them set a time to do these things?

4. To practice Step 6, have students form the same pairs as in the previous activity. Explain that each pair will work together to create an agreement, continuing to use either Simulation 9 or Simulation 10. The students should resume their roles as either Student A or Student B.

5. Have students conduct the simulation.

6. After the negotiators have made their agreement, ask the following questions to help process the activity:

   What did you do well?

What could you do differently?

What seemed to help you create your agreement?

7. Summarize the idea that the final agreement is often a combination of ideas. Because the problem is between the two individuals, the agreement must be *their* agreement—something they both will do.

Student Manual
page 112

Red Riding Hood and the Wolf: Create an Agreement

Red: I'll arrange for Granny and myself to talk to the woodsman. I'll try to get an appointment for this afternoon, and I'll let you know when.

Wolf: I'll get some flowers to plant at Granny's. I'll have them ready to plant by Saturday. I'll draw up a possible forest tour map and give it to you.

Red: As soon as I get your tour map, I'll bring some friends over to try it out. That's when I'll introduce you and tell them you're nice.

Wolf: I'll put a donations box at the edge of the forest for our tree planting and recycling program.

Red: And I'll call you by 7 o'clock if I can't go visit Granny.

Wolf: OK. I've agreed to get flowers to plant by Saturday, to draw a tour map of the forest, to go along with you to talk with the woodsman, to meet your friends and lead a tour through the forest, to take care of the donations box, and to visit Granny when you can't do it.

Red: I've agreed to arrange for an appointment with Granny and the woodsman, to plant flowers with you, to bring my friends to tour the forest and introduce you as a nice wolf, and to call you by 7 o'clock if I can't visit Granny.

[The two shake hands.]

Student Manual
page 113

Step 6: Create an Agreement

◆ **Make a plan of action:**

  "Who, what, when, where, and how?"

◆ **Summarize what you have agreed to do. Say:**

  "I have agreed to _____."

◆ **Shake hands.**

The agreement is often a combination of ideas.
It must be something both people will do.

ACTIVITY

10 Putting It All Together

PURPOSE   To review the negotiation process and practice all six steps

MATERIALS   Student Manuals
Simulation 11 and Simulation 12 (from Appendix C—one copy of each simulation for every two students)

FORMAT OPTION   Whole class discussion/participation

PROCEDURE   1. Refer the group to pages 114–115 in their Student Manuals, "The Peaceable School Negotiation Process," where all six steps in the negotiation process are presented. Discuss and review the steps as needed.

2. Divide students into new pairs and explain that each pair will practice all six steps. Use Simulation 11, giving each of the students half of the page so that one is Student A and the other is Student B.

3. Have the students conduct the simulation.

4. Afterwards, ask the negotiators the following questions to help process the activity:

   What did you do well?

   What could you do differently?

   What step of the process is the hardest for you?

5. Pair the students differently and have them conduct Simulation 12.

6. Repeat the follow-up questions.

Student Manual
page 114

The Peaceable School
Negotiation Process

STEP 1: AGREE TO NEGOTIATE

♦ Say:

"I agree to keep the discussion private."

"I agree to take turns talking and listening."

"I agree to cooperate to solve the problem."

STEP 2: GATHER POINTS OF VIEW

STUDENT A

♦ Tell your view of the problem. Say:

"I was _____." (Tell what you were doing.)

"I feel _____."

STUDENT B

♦ Listen and summarize Student A's view of the problem.

♦ Tell your view of the problem. Say:

"I was _____." (Tell what you were doing.)

"I feel _____."

STUDENT A

♦ Listen and summarize Student B's view of the problem.

♦ Clarify by adding anything more about your point of view.

STUDENT B

♦ Listen and summarize what Student A adds.

♦ Clarify by adding anything more about your point of view.

STUDENT A

♦ Listen and summarize what Student B adds.

114

Student Manual
page 115

STEP 3: FOCUS ON INTERESTS

♦ Say what you want and why: *"I want _____ because _____."*

♦ Listen, summarize, clarify. To clarify, ask:

"What will happen if we do not solve the problem?"

"What would you think if you were in my shoes?"

STEP 4: CREATE WIN-WIN OPTIONS

♦ Invent at least three options to address the interests of both of you.

♦ Follow the brainstorming rules:

Say any idea that comes to mind.

Do not judge or discuss ideas.

Come up with as many ideas as possible.

Try to think of unusual ideas.

STEP 5: EVALUATE OPTIONS

♦ Combine options or parts of options.

♦ For each option, work together to decide:

"Is this option fair?"

"Can we do it?"

"Do we think it will work?"

STEP 6: CREATE AN AGREEMENT

♦ Make a plan of action: *"Who, what, when, where, and how?"*

♦ Summarize what you have agreed to do.
Say: *"I have agreed to _____."*

♦ Shake hands.

115

ACTIVITY

11 Key Concept Review

PURPOSE To understand the meaning of key concepts related to negotiation

MATERIALS Butcher paper
Magazines
Comic books
Scissors
Glue
Markers

FORMAT OPTIONS Cooperative learning
Class meeting

PROCEDURE 1. Ask students to use their own words to define the following concepts. Solicit several definitions for each. Discuss the different definitions until the group displays a common understanding of each of the concepts.

COOPERATIVE SPIRIT	ACTIVE LISTENING
NEGOTIATION	AGREEMENT
ANGER	RESOLUTION
INVENTING	BRAINSTORMING

2. Divide the class into eight groups of equal numbers. Assign each group one of the words and instruct them to use the art materials to develop a poster that shows the meaning of the concept—draw a picture, write a definition, create a collage, and so forth.

3. Display the posters.

Group Problem Solving

OVERVIEW

Mediation, presented in Section 4, and negotiation, presented in Section 5, are primarily strategies for resolving conflicts between two disputants. The strategy of group problem solving is employed when a conflict affects many or all members of a group, such as a classroom. In the peaceable school, group problem solving involves a step-by-step process that parallels that for mediation and negotiation. The process varies slightly in that Step 5, the step devoted to evaluating options in mediation and negotiation, is divided into two parts: The first part focuses on establishing criteria to evaluate options, and the second focuses on the actual evaluation of options.

The group problem solving process is usually facilitated by the teacher or another adult and is designed to provide for complete disclosure of the issues involved in the conflict. All problems relating to the class as a group or to any individual in the class are potential topics for discussion. Two basic principles govern the strategy:

1. The discussion is always directed toward solving the problem.

2. The solution never includes punishment or fault finding.

The vehicle for group problem solving is the class meeting, or what Glasser (1969) calls the "open-ended meeting." In the first five sections of this book, the class meeting has been used along with other teaching formats to help students acquire the specific knowledge and skills they need to be peacemakers. Because there are no preconceived correct responses, the class meeting allows a wide range of viewpoints and lends itself well to presentation of content concerning responsibility, cooperation, conflict, peacemaking, and the like. It will be helpful for readers to review the general discussion presented in the introduction on this use of the class meeting.

Glasser (1969) maintains that "the many social problems of school itself, some of which lead to discipline of the students, are best attacked through the use of each class as a problem-solving group with each teacher as the group leader" (p. 122). This use of the class meeting—as the forum for students to work together to find mutually satisfying solutions—is integral to the group problem solving strategy presented here.

In addition to familiarity with the function and process of the class meeting, an understanding of consensus decision making is central to the success of the group problem solving approach.

CONSENSUS DECISION MAKING

Consensus decision making is a procedure enabling a group to arrive at an agreement by gathering of information and viewpoints, discussion, analysis, persuasion, a combination or synthesis of proposals, and/or the development of totally new solutions acceptable to the group. Consensus means that the group reaches a collective decision that each member supports after openly and extensively considering the many diverse points of view of the problem under discussion.

Consensus does not mean unanimity—that everyone agrees with every single point of a proposal or feels equally good about the decision. Consensus does mean that, although the decision may not be the best for each group member, it is the best for the group as a whole. Consensus does not mean settling for the lowest common denominator in the ideas expressed in the group—agreeing to the little piece of common ground among the varied perspectives in the group. Rather, consensus means seeking higher ground, creating a new solution that incorporates and goes beyond individual perspectives.

The interests of all group members are addressed by a consensus decision. In consensus, each group member can acknowledge that he or she was afforded sufficient opportunity to influence the decision, each supports the decision even though it may not represent his or her first choice, and each accepts a commitment to implement the decision as if it were his or her first choice. The decision is the best the group can do at the time to solve the problem, and all members of the group agree to support the decision actively.

In the pursuit of consensus, it is counterproductive for group members to argue persistently for their own positions. It is better simply to present positions in a clear and logical fashion, including reasons in support of them (in other words, interests). Group members should work hard to satisfy their own interests as well as the interests of others in the group. Although they should not yield to positions regardless of the force with which such positions are presented, group members should also consider others' interests fully. In considering proposed options, each group member should adopt the attitude that "I could be wrong, and another could be right." This attitude permits careful examination of other points of view and helps clear the way for a group solution that is stronger than any single perspective. In short, consensus is about win-win resolutions in a group context.

ROLE OF THE TEACHER-FACILITATOR

Although mediation, negotiation, and group problem solving follow the same prescribed set of steps, group problem solving depends more heavily on the contributions of the teacher-facilitator. The facilitator orchestrates the meeting by initiating the process, monitoring progress, and intervening when necessary. The facilitator has major responsibilities for each step of the process; however, he or she must exercise these responsibilities as unobtrusively as possible. The more the problem-solving session flows without the facilitator's direct intervention, the more students will feel ownership of the process and the resulting decision.

When trained and experienced student mediators are members of the group, the teacher may elect to have those individuals co-facilitate the group problem solving. These students may co-facilitate with the teacher, or the teacher may choose to have two or more of them co-facilitate the group while he or she serves as a monitor and guardian of the process. In the latter scenario, the teacher makes sure the ground rules are followed and that the process moves through the six steps in an efficient, effective manner.

The teacher-facilitator's specific responsibilities are enumerated in the following discussion.

The teacher-facilitator prepares for the meeting. Preparations involve determining the purpose of the meeting and developing a question map (a plan for stimulating or redirecting discussion). The facilitator's first question frames the purpose of the meeting and is designed to initiate the deliberations. Additional questions anticipate potential directions the discussion may take. Ideally, students will adhere to the purpose of the meeting. However, the map also includes questions to extend discussion if it lags or focus discussion if it strays nonproductively from the original purpose.

It is especially important to have in mind questions that will facilitate the six-step problem-solving process. This process includes questions to ask in each step and questions to ask that may assist the transition from one step to the next.

The teacher-facilitator conveys the essence of consensus decision making in age-appropriate constructs. The facilitator tells the group that the task is to find solutions that address the various interests of group members and that can and will be supported by all members. The best solution possible is the goal of the meeting.

The teacher-facilitator states the purpose of the meeting. The facilitator tells the group at the outset what the purpose of the session is and states any constraints or assumptions that limit the deliberations. This lets the group know the parameters of problem solving and provides the rationale for the facilitator's redirecting the discussion if the group strays from the purpose.

One common constraint is expressed in the following way: "The group may only decide behaviors for members of the group or the group as a whole. If the group wants others not in the group to behave in a certain way, all the group can do is decide on a plan to inform those others of the group's concerns and requests."

The teacher-facilitator reviews general ground rules and states any additional ground rules needed for the specific problem being addressed. The ground rules structure a positive problem-solving atmosphere in which peaceable resolutions can be achieved through consensus decision making. Adherence to the ground rules is vital to any conflict resolution process, and the facilitator has an important role in enforcing these rules. Basic ground rules (enumerated in the following discussion of Step 1) spell out the requirements for the conduct of the class meeting. Additional ground rules can, for example, protect confidentiality or help preserve individual group members' self-esteem. Such ground rules may be needed for some but not all group problem solving meetings.

A common example of such a ground rule is phrased in this way: "To solve this problem, the group needs complete information. Please share the specific situations where the problem has occurred and what actually occurred, but do not talk about any individual's role in the problem. In other words, 'No names, please.'"

The teacher-facilitator sets a positive, optimistic tone. The facilitator conveys to the group the belief that the problem can be solved by identifying and choosing positive future actions. Perhaps most important, the facilitator conveys to the class that he or she really believes the group can make a wise decision—in other words, that "we" are smarter than "me."

The teacher-facilitator ensures that all parties disclose their needs and concerns. During the steps devoted to gathering points of view and focusing on interests, the facilitator asks key questions to stimulate discussion. The facilitator also prevents a few students from dominating the discussion and encourages quieter members to speak up.

The teacher-facilitator summarizes the proceedings as needed and lists key issues to be resolved. By summarizing and listing key issues, the facilitator refocuses the group on the stated purpose and helps the group move through the process. This behavior is especially important when shared or compatible interests surface in the group. The facilitator may summarize these by saying something like "Class, it seems that we are all concerned with safety. We want to feel safe here."

The teacher-facilitator is concerned more with process than with content. The facilitator's main role is to ensure that all the steps in the process are completed rather than to lobby for a particular outcome. If the facilitator has a preconceived notion of how the problem should be solved and is unwilling to raise other possibilities, he or she should attempt to gain students' compliance without involving them in the group process.

The following questions are useful in determining whether a process facilitative of consensus decision making has been followed:

> Did the group fully involve all members as participants in the problem-solving process?

Were all points of view listened to carefully, especially the unpopular perspectives?

Did the group seriously face the issues in the conflict and work conscientiously to resolve them?

Were differences of opinion sought out and disagreements fully examined?

Did the group thoroughly exhaust all possibilities for a quality decision by allowing ample time to work through the process?

The teacher-facilitator introduces his or her own point of view by asking questions. The facilitator may not have a preconceived idea about how the problem should be resolved but still may want the class to consider certain possibilities. In this situation, those possibilities would appear in the facilitator's question map for the problem-solving session. If the possibilities do not arise from the group during the discussion, the facilitator might ask, "Could _____ be a possibility?" or "Would you consider doing _____?" or "Has anyone thought of trying _____?"

The teacher-facilitator restates agreements as they occur. The facilitator keeps track of the progress of the group toward resolution and helps the group focus on the common interests that have been revealed as well as on any agreed-upon actions. In involved problems it is especially important that the group be reminded that they are making progress. Even small successes need to be highlighted.

The teacher-facilitator helps the class develop a plan to implement the agreement. The facilitator may need to take an active role to ascertain that a plan exists to carry out the group's decision. It should not be assumed simply because group members reach a decision that they can implement the decision. Again, through the questioning process, the facilitator helps the group plan details (who, what, when, where, how) and solicits collective and individual commitment to any proposed actions.

Group problem solving solutions are often "the best we can do for now." It may be prudent for the group to establish a timeline that includes a trial period with an agreement to revisit the problem at some future date.

The teacher-facilitator expresses appreciation for the efforts and accomplishments of the group. The facilitator knows that group problem solving is important and hard work, and that all efforts, successful or not, are worthy of praise. He or she says so and provides specific feedback to the group about things that worked particularly well so that members can continue to develop their problem-solving skills. Any feedback focuses more on the group's process than on the final decision.

ROLE OF THE GROUP PROBLEM SOLVER

To build relationships—perhaps even trust—within the group and to develop the cooperation required to reach a consensus decision, the individual group problem solver strives to achieve the following goals.

The group problem solver listens with empathy. Effective communication skills are essential to successful group problem solving. Because the problem is significant to many, if not all, members of the class, it is likely to be clouded by issues in the relationships among class members—emotions run high, unfounded inferences are treated as fact, and blaming focuses attention on past actions. Effective communication skills are essential to acknowledge emotions and clarify perceptions, thus freeing group members to understand and work on the problem.

In successful problem-solving groups, the majority of members use the following active listening skills throughout the process:

Attending, or using nonverbal behaviors to indicate that what the speaker is thinking and feeling is being heard and that understanding is desired. These nonverbal behaviors include eye contact, facial expressions, and body language such as posture and gestures.

Summarizing, or restating facts by repeating the most important points, organizing interests, and discarding extraneous information. In summarizing, the problem solver also acknowledges emotions by stating the feelings the speaker is experiencing.

Clarifying, or using open-ended questions and statements to obtain more information and ensure understanding.

The group problem solver speaks to be understood. Even a very good listener, one who uses the active listening skills just detailed, can hear only what is actually said. Therefore, the speaker needs to speak clearly. To do so means to do as follows:

Speak to be understood, or work hard to state issues or the problem in a clear, direct way rather than talking to impress or debate. Avoid name-calling, criticism, sarcasm, and demands.

Speak about yourself, or describe the situation in terms of yourself by using statements that begin with "I" rather than "you." Avoid complaining about or blaming others.

Speak for a purpose, or think about what you want the other persons to understand and what purpose the information will serve. Planning ahead is prudent. It is important to be concise, eliminating undo repetition. It is important not to assume that the others know what you know or see the problem the same way you do. Some information will not help in resolving the conflict and is best left unsaid.

Speak with consideration for the listeners, or be sensitive to the other persons. Use a voice tone and volume that invite listening. Do not speak too rapidly or too slowly. If others are not using attending behavior, find out why.

For the group to have ownership of the process, and subsequently of the solution, communication—both active listening and speaking for a purpose—should not be the sole responsibility of the facilitator. It is critical that communication skills be broadly distributed among the members of the problem-solving group.

The group problem solver suspends judgment. The group problem solver strives to remain open and objective throughout the group process. The problem solver avoids justifying and arguing for a particular position (*what* that person wants), choosing instead to work hard to make his or her interests (*why* that person wants it) known to the group and to see that those interests are addressed in the solution accepted by the group.

The group problem solver is respectful. Being respectful involves working to understand the emotions and beliefs of the other group members. A key to respect is knowing and accepting that we are all different: The successful problem solver is able to treat the other members of the group fairly and without prejudice. Being respectful also means that the group problem solver does not direct ridicule, criticism, or sarcasm toward other group members or their ideas, nor does he or she talk about the ideas or feelings expressed by other group members except during the group deliberations.

The group problem solver has a cooperative spirit. The group problem solver views the group process as being equal in importance to the problem's solution. If the group process is followed, and if each group member assumes responsibility for facilitating the process, the group has a good chance of resolving the conflict. A cooperative group member gives in whenever possible without compromising his or her own interests. The cooperative group member also helps others in the group work together. A cooperative group member does not block the group consensus for trivial reasons but does stand up for his or her interests and principles. When the group member has an objection or concern, he or she states the point of disagreement clearly and concisely. If the group member objects for a valid reason to the direction in which the group is headed, such an objection should not be viewed as a lack of cooperation.

THE GROUP PROBLEM SOLVING PROCESS

The steps of the group problem solving process parallel those of the mediation and negotiation processes except that, as already noted, the step concerning evaluation of options is divided into two parts. Specifically, the steps include the following:

Step 1: Agree to Problem Solve

Step 2: Gather Points of View

Step 3: Focus on Interests in the Group

Step 4: Create Win-Win Options

Step 5a: Establish Criteria to Evaluate Options

Step 5b: Evaluate Options

Step 6: Create an Agreement

A sample group problem solving class meeting illustrating how these steps occur is reproduced following discussion of the steps.

Step 1: Agree to Problem Solve

Anyone in the class—teacher or students—can suggest topics for a group problem solving meeting. The teacher-facilitator's role is to screen requests, select the concerns to be addressed, and arrange an appropriate time for the meeting.

Once the need for a meeting has been established, the facilitator organizes the class for the meeting and states the meeting's general purpose—for example, "Today our meeting will focus on how to deal with a bully" or "Many of you have expressed concerns about being excluded by others from an activity, so today's meeting will be a discussion about exclusion/inclusion issues and how to address those issues" or "Because of considerable damage to items displayed in our school hallways, the principal has asked all classrooms to discuss this problem and to generate ideas to preserve our school's work displays." This general statement of purpose is different from the specific problem statement arrived at during Step 2.

The facilitator next reviews the two general principles underlying the group problem solving process—that the discussion is always directed toward solving the problem and that the solution never includes punishment or fault finding. The facilitator also states and obtains agreement on the basic ground rules under which the group will operate. These rules are the same as for the more general use of the class meeting, and students should already be accustomed to following them. As is the case for the general class meeting, the rules define the operational setting for the group process and structure a climate that enables all parties to be heard and all interests in the group to be identified.

The basic ground rules are as follows:

1. Participants sit in a circle.

2. Every member of the class is responsible for communication *(listening* and *speaking).* This means that each member is responsible for sharing his or her point of view about the problem if it has not already been shared by another.

3. The "Rule of Focus" applies to all discussion. This means that whoever is speaking will be allowed to talk without being interrupted.

4. Participants show respect for others. This means no criticism or sarcasm toward group members or their ideas.

5. Each time someone in the group finishes making a statement, another group member summarizes and clarifies it before anyone else goes on to a new idea.

The first two rules establish an equality base within the group—each group member is valued, and all have similar status. The circle allows visual contact among members, which contributes to good listening and affords no single individual any special status. (The facilitator should be careful not to sit always in the same place in the circle or by the same students at every meeting.) The remaining rules ensure that group members will be heard and understood and put the focus on positive future action toward resolving the problem.

Depending on the content of a particular meeting, it may be helpful for the facilitator to suggest additional ground rules. For example, if an individual student's behavior is the focus of the meeting, a rule might be "Before group members can make a negative statement about _____'s behavior, they will say something positive about _____'s behavior." Another situation might call for a rule such as "When discussing the problem today, do not use the names of the individuals who exhibited the behavior—just talk about the behavior."

Step 2: Gather Points of View

The purpose of this step is to make certain that the group has a complete picture of the problem under consideration. Group members participate in discussion, telling both what they know and how they feel about the problem.

During this step, each speaker must be allowed to finish without interruption. When one speaker concludes, another group member summarizes and clarifies the statements made. The teacher-facilitator guarantees that this communication process is followed. It is important that another group member and not the facilitator does the summarizing and clarifying. Giving this responsibility to group members establishes the expectation that all will listen carefully to the speaker. The summarizing and clarifying process also gives the group a second opportunity to hear the speaker's message and lets the speaker know the message was heard.

The facilitator works to elicit as much information as possible by asking questions like, "Is there more to the problem?" "Can anyone tell the group any more about this situation?" or "Does anyone have anything different to say?" Having group members complete the following sentence stems can help them begin to define the problem:

I was _____. (Tell what you were doing.)

I feel _____.

The facilitator enforces the ground rules and attempts to keep the process free from unnecessary repetition by asking, "Is this different from what has already been said by someone else?" or "Can you please limit what you want to say to something we have not already heard?" It is not necessary for everyone in the group to contribute information; rather, the goal is to have all pertinent information about the problem disclosed.

When the facilitator is satisfied that all pertinent information is before the group, a statement of the problem the group is trying to resolve is generated. This problem statement helps focus discussion during the remaining steps of the process. The facilitator can frame the problem statement and seek agreement from the group or solicit the problem statement from the group and then seek agreement. The following types of statements and questions are helpful:

> Based on what I have heard so far, it seems to me that the problem we need to find a solution to is _____.

> Can someone provide us with a concise statement of the problem we are trying to solve based on what has been said so far?

> How many think that this is an accurate statement of the problem?

> What, if anything, should be added to the problem statement?

Step 3: Focus on Interests in the Group

Group members who believe they have a direct stake in the problem are no less positional in their thinking than are the disputants in a mediation or negotiation. As for mediation and negotiation, discovering interests is the most critical step. To reach an acceptable solution, group members must get beyond their respective positions and look at their interests and the interests of other group members.

When there are only two disputants, as in mediation and negotiation, shared and/or compatible interests usually exist. In a group, however, the situation is generally more complex. Some members may have shared interests, and some may have compatible interests, but it is rare that a single interest is common to all. Through the consensus process, the group attempts to address the interests of all members. Group solutions are usually more elaborate and more difficult to achieve than two-party resolutions.

In this step, the teacher-facilitator asks group members to focus on the problem statement generated in Step 2, state their wants relative to that problem, and tell why they want what they want. (Remember that the *what* is the person's position and the *why* is the person's interest.)

The following questions are helpful in uncovering the group's interests:

> Why do you think the problem isn't going away?

> What is likely to happen if we cannot agree on a solution to this problem?

Step 4: Create Win-Win Options

As for mediation and negotiation, the purpose of this step is to produce as many ideas as possible about how the problem might be solved. At this stage, the group is not attempting to evaluate options. Instead, they are inventing options upon which the group can build and from which they can choose. A good problem solution is more likely to come from a variety of possibilities.

During this step, the teacher-facilitator encourages the group to come up with ideas that address the issues of everyone and helps group members follow the brainstorming rules:

Say any idea that comes to mind.

Do not judge or discuss ideas.

Come up with as many ideas as possible.

Try to think of unusual ideas.

Unusual ideas, even if impractical or silly, may open or stimulate the creative insights of other members of the group to legitimate options. This is a good time to remind the group of the ground rules agreed to in Step 1, especially the ground rule prohibiting criticism or sarcasm toward group members or their ideas. In doing so, the facilitator helps group members focus on telling what they are willing to do rather than on what they want others to do. The facilitator keeps the process moving by making certain that the brainstorming ground rules are not violated (especially the one concerning premature evaluation of ideas) and by asking additional questions when the ideas do not flow. Three useful questions are "What other possibilities can you think of?" "In the future, what could be done differently?" and "If we didn't have to worry about being practical, how could we solve this problem?" The facilitator may also need to remind the group members of the interests they identified in Step 3 by saying, "We've agreed that we want [common interest]. What ideas would help that to happen?" For example, "We've agreed that we all want to be treated fairly and not be left out. What are some things we could do to create fairness or to involve everyone?" The facilitator records all the ideas generated by the group members. This step continues until several ideas for solving the problem or parts of the problem have been advanced.

Step 5a: Establish Criteria to Evaluate Options

In mediation and negotiation, a formal discussion of evaluation criteria is rarely necessary because only two disputants are involved. In group problem solving, however, it is more important to make evaluation criteria explicit because more people are affected by the problem and by its proposed solution. The probability that the group will be able to implement a solution is enhanced when the criteria used to select the solution are made explicit. Step 5 is therefore divided into two parts: The first involves establishing criteria for evaluating options; the second involves actual evaluation of those options.

The teacher-facilitator invites group members to think about criteria for evaluating the options they have generated. In addition to the injunction that the solution never involve punishment or fault finding, some other specific criteria are reflected in the following questions:

Does the option follow our school's rights and responsibilities?

Does the option help everyone involved?

Is the option fair?

Can the option solve the problem?

Can the group do it?

It is important not to discuss evaluation criteria until after Step 4 is complete and a number of options have been generated. If criteria are discussed before the brainstorming process, group members might tend to screen their ideas according to the criteria before voicing them. Others in the group might also be more inclined to evaluate ideas as they are first advanced.

Step 5b: Evaluate Options

In this step, the teacher-facilitator instructs the group to choose from among the options generated in Step 4 the ideas or parts of ideas that they think best satisfy the evaluation criteria. The facilitator actively directs this step by asking the group to say whether or not each of the options meets the criteria.

During this evaluation process, the facilitator also helps the group understand what they do and do not have control over. The facilitator helps the group understand any constraints that may apply to the decision. For example, the facilitator might say, "The group may only decide behaviors for members of the group or the group as a whole. If the group wants others not in the group to behave in a certain way, all the group can do is decide on a plan to inform those others of the group's concerns and requests."

If the group believes a particular option is a good solution but implementing that solution is beyond their power, the facilitator must make that fact clear. Such might be the case, for example, if the solution calls for the school principal to take some action or if it disregards some aspect of school policy. If, despite an explanation that the group does not have the authority to implement a solution, members still wish to pursue that solution, a plan can be developed to take the suggestion to the individual or the forum empowered to make the change.

Step 6: Create an Agreement

Once options have been evaluated, the teacher-facilitator guides the group in making a final agreement. Because the variety of interests in a group is greater than in a mediation or negotiation situation, agreements more commonly represent a creative combination of options or parts of options. The facilitator should be alert to such possibilities and actively work to make them known to the group.

When a solution is proposed, the facilitator restates it and asks the group for a show of support. This informal poll—not to be construed as voting to obtain a majority decision—allows the facilitator and the group members to see how close the group is to agreement. The facilitator identifies and clarifies areas of agreement and calls attention to areas of continuing disagreement. The discussion continues until all group members agree on a common solution as being the best that can be done for now—the essence of a consensus decision.

Once it is clear that the entire group supports the solution, the facilitator helps the group make a plan of action, asking the following types of questions:

What action will be taken?

Who will do what?

When will action be taken?

Where will the plan be done?

Finally, individual group members are asked to verbalize their specific responsibilities for implementing the solution.

SAMPLE GROUP PROBLEM SOLVING MEETING

The following group problem solving meeting took place in a classroom of third and fourth graders. Minimal changes have been made to the following exchange for the sake of readability, and the names of the children have been altered. Otherwise, the dialogue is presented as it actually occurred.

Step 1: Agree to Problem Solve

Facilitator: Class, today I've decided for our class meeting we should talk about a behavior that several of you have complained about to me: teasing, harassing, making fun of each other, and so forth. How many of you have experienced a problem like that? . . . I see nearly everyone's hand up. First of all, let's remind ourselves of the ground rules for class meetings.

I would like a tight circle, please. Ruthie, April, could you slide over so Antwanne can get into the circle? Thanks!

We want to get everyone's point of view, so each of you is responsible for stating yours if it hasn't been stated.

Remember that when one person is telling a point of view, the rest of us listen carefully, and we don't interrupt. When that person is finished saying what it is they want to say, someone else in the group tells the rest of the group what they heard that person say. That is, summarize what the person said before we get new information.

Be respectful by not using sarcasm or criticizing. We don't make fun of people or their ideas.

Because we'll be talking about something that usually someone else does to us, please just tell us about the problem behavior, but don't use anyone's name.

OK, any questions about the rules? . . . Ready!

Step 2: Gather Points of View

Facilitator: Who has something they want to say about today's problem?

Cathy: Well, sometimes when I play kick ball I don't run very fast, and if I get out at first base people make fun of me, like you're a slow-poke and stuff like that, and that hurts my feelings when they do that.

Facilitator: Are you going to tell us what Cathy said, Joe?

Joe: She said that since she's a slow runner, whenever she plays kick ball sometimes she gets out at first base, and the people on her team make fun of her by calling her slowpoke.

Facilitator: Did you want to add something, Nathaniel?

Nathaniel: Yeah. My speech isn't that good, and so sometimes when I talk, people like to make fun of me.

Andre: He said that sometimes his speech isn't very good, so sometimes people make fun of him because of the way he talks.

Facilitator: Do you want to add something?

Andre: Yeah. When I'm playing football sometimes people get mad at everybody else, and sometimes they make threats to other people. That's no good.

Facilitator: What kind of threats would they make, Andre?

Andre: They say, like, well, "I'm going to get you after school," or something like that.

Facilitator: Mark, can you tell us what Andre said?

Mark: Well, he was saying that at football sometimes people threaten and say that they're going to beat them up after school and stuff like that.

Facilitator: Did you have another problem you wanted to add?

Mark: Sometimes when you're playing tag and stuff, and you get tagged real hard, people start calling you slowpoke, and they call you a wimp if you complain about how hard you were tagged.

Joe: I have another thing to add about playing tag. Tag usually gets out of hand, like what he said—people push too hard. When someone gets hurt and they start to cry, then the person that pushed them says, "I barely even touched you. I just tagged you." Then it gets into a big argument or fight.

Facilitator: Problems with tag seem to be one area of concern. How many have experienced problems in tag games? . . . Lots of you, I see! So, let's say that we have established that the behavior we are concerned about today happens in tag games. What else?

Andre: Well, in class sometimes while the teacher is out of the room and there is no adult in the room, sometimes people, like, throw things around at people, and they run around and mess around until the teacher comes back.

Nathaniel: He said that when the teacher is out of the classroom sometimes the people are mean to each other because the teacher isn't around. Also, sometimes people get made fun of because of their name. People call me Kibbles and Bits because Kibbles sounds like my last name. I don't like that.

Jenny: Sometimes in PE, if you're playing a game where there's two teams and one team wins, they make fun of the other team because they didn't win and they lost.

April: I have something to add.

Facilitator: Can you tell what Jenny said first?

April: Sometimes when people are playing games with teams, the team that wins sometimes makes fun of the other team.

Facilitator: I don't want to lose Nathaniel's point. He talked about people making fun of others by using their real name and twisting it up. Sorry to interrupt you. Please go ahead, April.

April: Well, when we're playing hockey, I'm not very good at it. Someone on my team at the end of the game said that our team would have won the game if it hadn't been for me. I felt really low.

Facilitator: That made you feel pretty bad! Can you summarize what she said, Cathy?

Cathy: She said that during PE sometimes she doesn't play a game very well and that the people on her team, if they lose, say that they would have won if she was any good, but it's all her fault that they lost.

Facilitator: How many of you have had an experience like that where you sort of get blamed for the whole team situation? . . . Quite a few of you. OK, did you have something else you wanted to add, Cathy?

Cathy: Yes, there is also a problem with sex discrimination and racism, like when the girls try to play football or basketball, the boys say girls are sissies and can't do this or that. Why don't you go play jump rope and hopscotch and stuff like that? Also racist, like some of the white kids when they're playing basketball say the black kids can't play because they stink, and the black kids say the same thing about the white kids. It's not just one race always making the problem, it's just one race against the other race.

Facilitator: OK, that's an important point. Could someone summarize what Cathy said?

Shannon: She said there's a problem with sexes and race because, as she said, when the girls want to play sports with the boys, the boys make fun of them, and they call them names and tell them they can't play. Also, when white kids are playing basketball they don't want the black kids to play with them, and when the black kids are playing, they don't want the white kids to play with them.

Facilitator: Antonio, did you have something you wanted to add?

Antonio: Yeah, about my problem. Sometimes in sports I get teased about how short I am, but sometimes I have more of an advantage in other sports.

Noel: I hate it when people call me fat!

Facilitator: Marcus?

Marcus: Well, I'll just summarize what Antonio said. He said that people would make fun of him because of his height, and he would be better in other sports and stuff like that. Also, Noel says people call her fat.

Step 3: Focus on Interests in the Group

Facilitator: I want to move on to another area here. I think we've pretty well identified the problem—teasing, harassing, and making fun of other people. It seems to me that it is serious enough that it has bugged almost all of you at some time or another. Is there anyone here who has not been bugged by some of those things that have been mentioned, even though you haven't said anything yet? . . . I didn't really expect to see any hands, considering the number of complaints I have been getting lately. OK! What would we really like to have happen, and why would we like that to happen?

Cathy: Well, I think I would like it that if I have a problem with somebody I would like to be able to tell the teacher and the teacher would help me work it out and not say, "Oh, forget about it and go back to what you were doing." I'd like to have people stop making fun of people.

Andre: Well, she said she'd like for the teacher to listen to her and help her, and she also said she doesn't want people making fun of other people.

Matthew: I think if we're, like, teasing someone, we should think of what the other person will be thinking when we tease them.

Facilitator: So you would like the person to stop first and think about how it would feel if that happened to them. Why do you think that would be a good idea?

Matthew: Because then the person will kind of understand the other person's point of view, and then they might think about it and not do the slamming or teasing.

Latasha: I think you should really put yourself in the other person's shoes before you call them a name because you should think about how you feel when you get called a name—think about, have I made this mistake before?

Joe: I think people shouldn't make fun of someone when they do bad on a test but just say, "Well, you tried your hardest and try to do better next time," or something like that.

Hannah:	Well, I guess in like the sports thing, where people are calling people slowpokes, I think people should just respect the people for trying to do their best.
Facilitator:	Mark, do you have something you want to say?
Mark:	Yeah—treat people like you'd like to be treated. Treat them how you want them to treat yourself.
Andre:	To add to Joe's idea, kind of to generalize it. It's not good to tell people that they're not as smart as somebody else or, like, to tell them that they're dumb or something.
Brandy:	Well, some people are just better at things. Like, if somebody is good at sports and somebody else is good at academics, it's not their fault they're just not as good in sports. That may be a disadvantage, but they're good in academics, so people should respect that.
Facilitator:	Would it be a true statement that we would all like for teasing and harassing to go away as a problem? . . . Why would we like that?
Ramon:	Because then you wouldn't have as much problems, and you'd be happier lots of the time, and you wouldn't have to worry about things. I think sometimes people worry about other people. Like what this person is going to do to me. You're, like, afraid of them or something. People would be happier, and nobody would be mean that much, and people wouldn't be afraid.
Matthew:	I think name-calling hurts a lot more than just physical fighting because it leaves you feeling bad inside, and that really hurts for a while longer.
Jocelyn:	Sometimes when people are teased a lot in their childhood then they're always real mad and maybe picking fights, and they might grow up and not be as successful as people that aren't teased.
Joe:	Well, what Matthew said, we think that fighting isn't really good. But if you just call them a name it just hurts a lot. Like being the new kid, nobody wants to play with you because they, like, well, he's different, but I don't really know a lot about him, or something like that. Eventually the new kid would have to make the first move. I think if there is a new kid in the class, you should talk to him and try to be his friend and help him out in school.

Step 4: Create Win-Win Options

Facilitator:	OK, now let's try to think about all the ways that we can do something about this problem. We all seem to recognize that there is a problem here. What really is the problem?
Quentin:	I think it is how to respect each other. How we can eliminate teasing and harassing and other disrespectful stuff.
Mark:	Yeah, like put-downs and name-calling.
Facilitator:	What are some things that we can do about this problem? Let's do some brainstorming. Any idea is a good idea to start with. Give me your ideas quickly as they come to you and pay attention to what other people say because they might suggest an idea that you're

thinking about, and you can add to it. We will not judge any ideas just yet, and unusual ideas might help us think of more possibilities. I will write ideas on the easel pad so that we can talk more about each later. Matthew, what's an idea? What can we do?

Matthew: First, think what the other person might think when you tease them.

Facilitator: All right. Think about the other person.

Matthew: Think about things you've done. Think if you would like to be called a name or have the things you're bad at brought up all the time.

Andre: Think about how your behavior affects others.

Cathy: Think about the consequences of what's going to happen if you make fun of a person. Like if you insulted somebody, and that person's friends aren't going to think you're cool anymore because if you insult a person not everyone is going to like you, because maybe they like that person, too.

Facilitator: OK, suppose someone is teasing you. What can you do?

Joe: Well, you can just leave them alone or go somewhere else besides in that general area. Just leave them alone so they won't tease you, or if they follow you around go to someone in charge, and they'll probably do something about it.

Andre: Well, to add to Joe's idea, I think it would be best if you tried to work it out with that person who is making fun of you. You two are holding a grudge against each other. If you tell a teacher or something, then that person might just do it more because they're mad at you for trying to tell on them.

Facilitator: Does anyone else have any other ideas? Anything else we can do when we're having a problem with somebody who is teasing us or harassing us or giving us a bad time?

Ruthie: Well, first you can try to ignore them, like Joe said, and if that doesn't work, then since some of the people in school are trained as peer mediators, if you feel comfortable, try to go talk to them. Talk to your friends first, and if that still doesn't work, then go get a teacher or an adult.

Amanda: Maybe when they say something nasty to you, you could say something nice back at them.

Antwanne: Yeah, how about just smiling or laughing or making like they are just joking.

Charrise: Ask them something that causes them to think about what they just said or did. Sometimes they might change their minds or think, gee, I shouldn't say that.

Facilitator: OK. Let me summarize what I have written here:

> Think about the other person before you do something.
>
> Think about how they're going to feel.
>
> Matthew, I'm not sure I got your whole idea, but you said think about when you've done something that you weren't

particularly great at before you lay it on someone else that they're not doing the best that they can do.

Think about how your behavior affects others.

Think of the consequences not only from the other person but maybe the other person's friends.

Get away from them or try to ignore them. That idea came up a couple of times.

Get help from somebody in charge.

Andre, I think it was you who said try to work it out with the person first before you get someone else involved because it might get to be a bigger problem.

Give them an example of what it feels like.

Be nice when they are nasty.

Try not to let them know it bothers you—make like they aren't serious.

Ask them a question.

These are all ideas we might consider. How will we choose ideas we like? What criteria should we consider?

Step 5a: Establish Criteria to Evaluate Options

Sheryl: It shouldn't make the problem worse.

Nathaniel: Yeah. We could send a bad example if we try to get even. What we do should probably help us and not hurt the other person.

Marcus: We have to be willing to do it. We should think it might work.

Kristin: It can't be against the rules.

Facilitator: How about our ideas? Can we do them, and will they work?

Step 5b: Evaluate Options

Cathy: We can probably do most of them, except that I think calling them a name back wouldn't be the best solution because then it will just go on and on and get into a bigger fight, and if that person is your friend, they may not be your friend anymore.

Kristin: Besides, that's against the rule about being respectful.

Facilitator: How many agree with Cathy and Kristin? . . . We seem to agree that's probably not going to be very helpful. Does anybody want to disagree—think we should do back to them whatever they do to us? So we ought to throw that idea away? Cathy said we could try probably most anything else on here. Anybody have an idea of anything else on here that might not work?

Shannon: I think the one about trying to work it out with the other person before you go get a teacher. Sometimes that doesn't work because they wouldn't listen to you, and then they would just walk over and say blah, blah, blah or just keep going off on you.

Facilitator: OK. So do you think it does work sometimes to try to talk it out first?

Shannon: Depends on what kind of person it is.

Facilitator: Do you know beforehand how the other person is going to react?

Shannon: Yeah, usually.

Matthew: I agree, some people you would try that with and some you wouldn't.

Facilitator: How many agree with Shannon and Matthew, that you can sort of make that judgment? . . . Nearly everyone. Any other thoughts to solve our problem? Several of you said try to work it out with that person first. How many of you think that is a good idea? . . . Anybody think that is a bad idea? How about the idea of getting away from them or trying to ignore them? What do we think about that idea?

Andre: I don't think it's a very good idea 'cause if you're in a fight and someone is calling you names and things, I don't think it's very good because they'll just follow you around, and if you try to ignore them it will be worse for you because they'll keep on hurting you, and if you just try to go away from them without anybody to help you, it's not good.

Janelle: Well, I kind of think the same thing because if you just ignore them or you make a face like they're annoying you, they'll think it's good because they want to annoy you. So you should try to do something about it before it gets worse. If they know they're annoying you, then they'll just keep on doing it.

April: The problem with ignoring them is they may think what they are doing is OK. You should say something.

Facilitator: OK. That's a good point.

Cathy: Well, it depends on why the person is doing it. But sometimes the person is just doing it to show off to their friends. If you ignore it, then the friends will think, oh, God, they're not insulting them enough and they're not intimidating them enough, and their friends will just leave, and they'll have no other reason to do it. Because the person doesn't react, they lose all interest. Really depends on why the person is doing it.

Facilitator: Do you have a way of telling the difference?

Cathy: Well, it depends on if you ignore them first and they start to sound really agitated—that probably means they're getting upset because you're not mad, but if they keep on doing it and they don't give up for a long time, then they're probably insulting you for another reason and you should go get help before it gets real out of hand.

Facilitator: Did you want to rebut that? Do you want to go back at that same point?

Janelle: It's kind of like the thing we were talking about before—you can kind of tell it by the person or the personality.

Matthew: I don't think it would work because if they really are trying to annoy you, they're going to keep going after you even if you ignore them or you walk away. If they're trying to annoy you, they're going to keep after you.

Hannah: Even if they do leave you alone, things are not going to get better.

Facilitator: Oh, that's a good point. Did anyone hear what Hannah said? She said even when you ignore it, it doesn't get any better. It may not get any worse, but it doesn't get any better, right?

Andre: To add on to Cathy's thing what she said about friends, you can kind of tell if there is somebody doing something just to make it with their friends because you see lots of people that are close by, kind of all together.

Facilitator: It sounds to me like trying to ignore or trying to get away from them, most of us don't think it is a real good idea most of the time—it might work once in a while. Anything else that we can think of that is a good idea?

Kristin: First we can try to work it out, but if it doesn't work, then we can do a peer mediation.

Facilitator: OK. How many have had experience with mediation helping you solve problems? Do you think that is a good idea? That if you can't work it out by yourselves, you try mediation? How many think that is a good idea? . . . So that is something we can put down that we can try. What else do we think might be a good idea? So far I've got try to work it out with the other person first, and if that doesn't work, then try peer mediation.

Janelle: It's not anything big, but when people go to peer mediation it usually does solve the problem. I've never heard that a person had to go to the principal to solve it or something.

Andre: If the other person doesn't agree on the peer mediation, then you probably should see the principal or a teacher or somebody to solve the problem.

Facilitator: So mediation is voluntary, and if they won't go and you still have a problem, you need to get help from an adult.

Peter: I'm a peer mediator, and I think using a peer mediator is a real good idea, but I think the first thing you should always try is telling the person nicely that what they are doing or saying bothers you. Just be honest in a sort of nice way.

Step 6: Create an Agreement

Facilitator: This obviously is a serious problem, and it's a problem that's not going to go away just because we had this meeting. But maybe because we've had a chance to talk about it you can think of some things to do the next time it happens. Sounds to me like most of you think that trying to work it out with that person first is a good idea, then you think peer mediation is a pretty good idea. But if that doesn't work, if you can't get the person to go to peer mediation with you, then you need to get help from somebody who's in charge. Could we agree to do the following when these problems happen, at least in our classroom?

First, I will tell the person that I am bothered by the behavior.

Second, if the behavior continues, I will request a mediation.

Third, if the mediation doesn't work, I will find a convenient time to tell the teacher about the problem.

How many are willing to try this? . . . Good, all of you! Thanks. I think this was a good meeting. It was a good discussion, and I really liked how well you followed our rules and how carefully you listened to each other. I'll make myself a note to bring up this topic again in about a month to see how our plan worked.

Suggested Readings

Crawford, D. K., Bodine, R. J., & Hoglund, R. G. (1993). *The school for quality learning: Managing the school and classroom the Deming way.* Champaign, IL: Research Press.

Glasser, W. (1969). *Schools without failure.* New York: Harper & Row.

Johnson, D. W., & Johnson, F. P. (1975). *Joining together: Group theory and group skills.* Englewood Cliffs, NJ: Prentice Hall.

Schrumpf, F., Freiburg, S., & Skadden, D. (1993). *Life lessons for young adolescents: An advisory guide for teachers.* Champaign, IL: Research Press.

Shure, M. B. (1992). *I Can Problem Solve (ICPS): An interpersonal cognitive problem-solving program for children.* Champaign, IL: Research Press.

ACTIVITY

1 Group Cohesiveness and Cooperation

PURPOSE To build a sense of community and group cohesiveness and to experience cooperation in a group

MATERIALS Student Manuals
Other materials, as specified for each exercise

FORMAT OPTIONS Whole class participation/discussion (Exercises 1–3)
Class meeting (Exercise 4)
Cooperative learning (Exercises 5–8)

NOTE As needed, choose from among the following exercises to help students get to know one another and learn what cooperating in a group is like. As a way of introducing these exercises, explain the following ideas: Group problem solving requires a collection of people to cooperate to attack a problem. Groups usually work together better if the members know something about one another and understand how to cooperate. Cooperation in a group often means working closely with others we might not otherwise have chosen to help or to have help us.

PROCEDURE **Exercise 1: Where Do I Belong?**

1. Have all the students stand in a circle. Pick a starting point and ask them to rearrange the circle so that they are lined up in alphabetical order by their first names.

2. After the circle is complete, start with the As and have each student tell the class his or her name and favorite food.

3. Pick a student and, starting with that person, have the students line up again in the circle, this time according to the month and day of their birth—January 1 would be first; December 31 would be last.

4. After the circle is complete, have each student check with the person to the left and to the right to confirm that the order of the circle is correct.

5. Divide the students into groups according to the month of their birth (a group for January, February, and so forth). If there is only one student for any month, put him or her with the month before or after. Give each group a sheet of newsprint and a marker. Instruct the group to lists things they have in common.

6. Invite the groups to share their lists.

Exercise 2: Find Someone Who . . .

1. Refer students to page 119 of their Student Manuals, "Find Someone Who . . . " Allow students 10 minutes to circulate around the room to collect a different signature for each statement.

2. Read each statement and instruct students to raise their hands if the statement applies to them. Have students look around to see who has hands raised.

3. Discuss what group members have in common.

Exercise 3: Sentence Completions

1. Refer students to page 120 of their Student Manuals, "Sentence Completions," and give them a few minutes to complete this form.

2. Randomly assign students to groups of four and instruct the groups to share their responses.

3. After 5 or 10 minutes, ask each group to talk about what was shared in the groups. Ask the following questions:

> In what ways were the responses in your group similar?

> Were you surprised by any of the responses?

> Did you hear any responses that were also true of yourself?

Exercise 4: What About Me?

1. Organize the group into a class meeting circle.

2. Go around the circle, giving each student an opportunity to share information about the following topics. (Select topics appropriate to your group; give students the option to pass on any of the topics if they wish.)

> Things you like to do and do well

> Three positive words to describe yourself

> The last time an adult (for example, teacher or parent) gave you a compliment

> What world's record you would break if you could break any world's record (and why)

> A favorite memory or joyful experience

> One trait you would like to be remembered for

An area of knowledge or skill you could teach another person (and what you would most like to learn from another person)

This last topic could be used by students to pair up voluntarily to share and expand talents.

Exercise 5: Square Deal

1. Make a 3-foot square on the floor with masking tape. Select 10 students and tell them the object is to get all 10 people into the space. Allow the group 2 minutes to plan how they will solve the problem before they perform the task. Instruct the remaining students to observe the activity.

2. After the task is completed, ask students the following questions:

> Was there a leader in the group?
>
> Who gave the most ideas?
>
> Whose ideas were accepted?
>
> What ideas seemed to work best?

3. Select another group of 10 students and repeat the activity. Continue until all the students have had a chance to participate.

Exercise 6: Balloons Aloft

1. Divide the class into groups of five and give each group an inflated balloon. Have each group go to a different part of the room—be sure they have enough space to move around.

2. Have students face one another in a circle and keep the balloon aloft. After 30 seconds, ask students to continue to keep the balloon aloft using anything but hands or fingers. After 30 seconds more, see if they can keep the balloon aloft using only their heads. After 30 seconds more, see if they can keep the balloon aloft using just their legs and feet. Finally, have students make a very tight circle and see if they can keep the balloon in the air just by blowing on it.

3. Discuss the following questions:

> What was difficult about the task?
>
> What was easy about the task?
>
> How was cooperation involved?

Exercise 7: Together We Can

1. Divide students into groups of five. Tell the groups that you will be giving them directions for some group tasks. As they complete each task, the group should signal you to check their solution. Instruct the groups to do the following:

> Spell the word *yes* using their bodies.

Have four group members stand on a chair and keep their balance. (The fifth member helps balance the group.)

Have everyone hold hands and touch feet at the same time.

Have everyone touch something yellow.

2. Discuss the following questions:

What was difficult about the tasks?

What was easy about the tasks?

How was cooperation involved?

Exercise 8: Castles in the Air

1. Divide the class into random groups of four and give each group member 25 index cards. Have each group stand around a desk or table. Tell students to make an index card castle that will use all 100 cards and be as tall as possible. Tell groups to be creative; give them 8 to 10 minutes to complete their castles. After 5 minutes, warn them that their time is running out.

2. Ask each group to tell about their castle:

What was their plan?

What worked?

What didn't work?

3. Discuss how planning can affect a group's work.

Student Manual
page 119

Find Someone Who . . .

INSTRUCTIONS: Find someone in the group who fits each of the following statements. Have the person sign his or her name by the statement.

Is left-handed   _____

Likes rap music   _____

Is good at math   _____

Has a pierced ear   _____

Has braces or a retainer   _____

Plays a musical instrument   _____

Has a parent who was born in a foreign country   _____

Plays on a sports team   _____

Has black hair   _____

Is good at art   _____

Is a cat lover   _____

Likes to fish   _____

Has allergies   _____

Has freckles   _____

Likes to skateboard or rollerblade   _____

119

Student Manual
page 120

Sentence Completions

INSTRUCTIONS: Please finish these sentences with the first thought that comes
to your mind.

I like to:	I am best at:
One word that describes me is:	**I sometimes wish:**
I worry when:	**I am afraid of:**
I hate to hear people say:	**I get angry when:**

120

ACTIVITY

2   Consensus Decision Making

PURPOSE   To learn about consensus decision making and to practice making a decision in this way

MATERIALS   Newsprint
Markers
A large glass jar
326 M&Ms

FORMAT OPTION   Cooperative learning

PROCEDURE

1. Give every student a piece of newsprint and a marker and instruct each one to write the following lines:

    My guess: _____

    Our guess: _____

    Guess by the four of us: _____

    Guess by the eight of us: _____

    Class guess: _____

2. Hold up the jar and ask students to record privately the number of M&Ms they think are in the jar in the blank for "My guess." (Allow 30 seconds.)

3. Pair students and instruct them to work together to make one guess as to how many M&Ms there are in the jar. Have them record the number on both their sheets in the blank for "Our guess." (Allow 30 seconds.)

4. Instruct each pair to join another pair, forming a group of four. Have these groups agree on a guess for the number of M&Ms in the jar, then have them record that number on all sheets in the blank for "Guess by the four of us." (Allow 1 minute.)

5. Instruct each group of four to join another group of four to make a group of eight. Again have students agree on a group guess and record that number on all the sheets in the blank for "Guess by the eight of us." (Allow 2 minutes.)

6. Join the whole class and ask them to agree on one guess. Have everyone record this guess on all sheets in the blank for "Class guess." (Allow 5 minutes.)

7. Ask students the following questions:

> Which number do you think will be closest to the actual number of M&Ms?
>
> Which number was hardest to agree on?
>
> Would you revise your first guess now?

8. Explain that, usually, the larger the group, the harder it is to agree on one answer. A *consensus decision* is the best answer the group can find that everyone in the group can support. That answer may not be the favorite answer of each group member, but each group member thinks it is reasonable.

9. Tell the class the real number of M&Ms, then allow the students to eat the candy.

3   Group Problem Solving Is . . .

PURPOSE   To learn that group problem solving is a process to help groups of people work together to resolve conflicts in a peaceable way

MATERIALS   Student Manuals
Newsprint
Markers

FORMAT OPTION   Class meeting

PROCEDURE   1.   Begin by saying that each person in the class probably belongs to several groups, such as family, church sports team, scouts, and the like. Point out that everyone there belongs to at least one common group—the classroom.

2.   Explain that often conflicts affect many or all members of a group. For example, in the classroom there may be conflicts concerning decisions about classroom rules, schedules, activities, or materials. Other group problems concern the behaviors of a certain student or group of students, such as being excessively noisy, name-calling, teasing, cheating, not cooperating, or not sharing. Group problem solving is a way to discuss and make decisions about situations that affect a whole group of people. Both adults and children can learn to be group problem solvers.

3.   Refer students to page 121 in their Student Manuals, "Group Problem Solving," and discuss.

4.   Next give each group of four or five learners a sheet of newsprint. Ask groups to discuss why group problem solving would help the class. Typical responses include the following:

   Kids understand what is important to other kids.

   Kids know how it feels to be a kid in conflict.

   There are problems in the classroom that bother many of us.

   It would be a good feeling to solve a problem ourselves.

   Kids will listen to other kids.

   Kids could help the teacher make the classroom better.

5. Invite groups to share their lists; post these around the room.

6. Summarize that it takes cooperation and understanding to resolve conflicts. Group problem solvers, both children and adults, are peacemakers.

Student Manual
page 121

Group Problem Solving

Group problem solving is a communication process for helping people work together to resolve conflicts. Group problem solving follows two main guidelines:

♦ The discussion is always directed toward solving the problem.

♦ The solution never includes punishment or fault finding.

THE GROUP PROBLEM SOLVER WORKS TO . . .

♦ Understand and respect different points of view.

♦ Focus on the problem and not blame others.

♦ Communicate wants and feelings.

♦ Cooperate to solve the problem.

Group problem solvers are peacemakers.

121

4   Role of the Group Problem Solver

PURPOSE   To understand how the group problem solver behaves

MATERIALS   Student Manuals

FORMAT OPTION   Class meeting

PROCEDURE
1. Refer students to page 122 in their Student Manuals, "Role of the Group Problem Solver."

2. Discuss each of the following points with the class, one at a time.

The Group Problem Solver Listens With Empathy

This means the group problem solver uses active listening to try to understand the thoughts and feelings of the other person. Demonstrate by having a volunteer talk to you about a problem. During the demonstration, look away or otherwise act distracted. Repeat with another volunteer, this time using active listening and demonstrating good attending behavior. Ask the class what they saw. Ask the two volunteers how they felt during each demonstration.

The Group Problem Solver Suspends Judgment

Explain that the group problem solver strives to remain open and objective throughout the process. The group problem solver avoids justifying and arguing for his or her *position* (*what* the person wants), choosing instead to work hard to justify his or her *interests* (*why* the person wants it). The group problem solver should never tell other people in the group what they want. If necessary, review the difference between interests and positions (see Section 3, Activity 10).

The Group Problem Solver Is Respectful

Explain that being a group problem solver means showing everyone respect, no matter their dress, shape, color, size, age, and so on. The group problem solver tries to understand the other people's points of view about the situation without judgment. Because we have our own points of view about things, this is not always easy. The group problem solver also honors the privacy of others by not talking about their views of the problem except during the group deliberations.

The Group Problem Solver Has a Cooperative Spirit

Explain that the group problem solver views the group problem solving process as being as important as the solution to the problem. When all parties cooperate, they are able to find their own solution. Having a cooperative spirit means allowing others to satisfy their interests whenever possible without giving up your own interests.

3. Conclude by stating that the main role of the group problem solver is to build trust and cooperation, which in turn makes group problem solving possible.

Student Manual
page 122

Role of the Group Problem Solver

THE GROUP PROBLEM SOLVER . . .

♦ Listens with empathy.

♦ Suspends judgement.

♦ Is respectful.

♦ Has a cooperative spirit.

The group problem solver builds
trust and cooperation.

122

5 Understanding Group Problem Solving Rules

PURPOSE To learn the rules for group problem solving

MATERIALS Student Manuals

FORMAT OPTION Class meeting

NOTE The ground rules for group problem solving presented here have already been established as ground rules for the class meeting (see Section 1, Activity 1). The present activity is therefore a review of these rules as they apply specifically to the group problem solving strategy.

PROCEDURE 1. Refer the group to page 123 in their Student Manuals, "Ground Rules for Group Problem Solving." Explain that for group problem solving to work, everyone must know the ground rules and help the facilitator be sure the rules are followed. Review each of the following rules in detail.

Participants Sit in a Circle

Discuss the idea that group problem solving works best when everyone in the group strives to be an effective group problem solver. Tell students that group problem solving takes place in the circle arrangement so that group members can clearly see one another and so no one has special status—all are equal points on the circle.

Every Member of the Class Is Responsible for Communication (Listening and Speaking)

Explain that this means each group member is responsible for sharing his or her point of view about the problem if it has not already been shared by another. Each member of the class is important. For the group to find a solution that will address the interests of all members, the class needs all the information. Each person should assume that no one knows what he or she thinks or feels: If our thoughts or feelings have not been stated, we must state them. This is our responsibility to the group.

The "Rule of Focus" Applies to All Discussion

Ask a student to talk about a problem he or she has strong feelings about (for example, peer pressure to do something). Interrupt frequently, and after each interruption invite the student to continue. After two or three interruptions, stop and ask the group:

> What did I do while _____ was talking?
>
> What happened when I did that?
>
> _____, how did you feel when I interrupted?

Tell students that the "Rule of Focus" means that we listen carefully to the speaker and that no one interrupts the speaker.

Participants Show Respect for Others

Ask another student to talk about the same problem. Frequently criticize the speaker or the speaker's ideas and make sarcastic remarks about those ideas. After each interruption, say, "I'm sorry, please continue." After two or three interruptions, stop and ask:

> What did I do while _____ was talking?
>
> What happened when I did that?
>
> _____, how did you feel when I did that?
>
> What effect did my saying, "I'm sorry" have?

Explain that criticism and sarcasm show disrespect and limit the information people are willing to share. Stress that if students disagree with what a group member says, they need to state their disagreement differently: "My point of view about _____ is different. I think _____." Do not attack the other person or the other person's point of view.

Each Time Someone in the Group Finishes Making a Statement, Another Group Member Summarizes and Clarifies It Before Anyone Else Goes on to a New Idea

Ask yet another student to talk about the same problem. When that student finishes speaking, summarize what was said and clarify where possible. Check out the accuracy of your understanding with the speaker, then ask the following questions:

> What did I do when _____ talked?
>
> _____, how did you feel when I did that?

2. Explain that some problems might require additional rules. For example, if many in the class are complaining about being harassed or intimidated, the class could discuss the problem by talking about the behavior that is bothersome without naming anyone who is behaving that way. This would allow everyone to help solve the problem because no one would be identified as the cause. Another time an additional rule would be helpful would be

if the complaints that caused the meeting to be called were about a particular student. A rule might require that you say something you like about that student before you tell about a behavior you do not like. This would help the group see the person's good side as well as the problem behavior.

3. Summarize by saying that the rules for group problem solving help the group cooperate to solve the problem.

Student Manual
page 123

Ground Rules for
Group Problem Solving

◆ **Participants sit in a circle.**

◆ **Every member of the class is responsible
for communication** *(listening and speaking)*.
This means that each member is responsible for
sharing his or her point of view about the problem
if it has not already been shared by another.

◆ **The** *"Rule of Focus"* **applies to all discussion.**
This means that whoever is speaking will be
allowed to talk without being interrupted.

◆ **Participants show respect for others.**
This means no criticism or sarcasm toward
group members or their ideas.

◆ **Each time someone in the group finishes
making a statement, another group member
summarizes and clarifies it before anyone
else goes on to a new idea.**

123

ACTIVITY

6 Overview and Steps 1–3

PURPOSE To learn what is involved in the six-step group problem solving process and to practice Steps 1, 2, and 3

MATERIALS Student Manuals
Easel pad
Marker

FORMAT OPTION Class meeting

PROCEDURE 1. Refer students to page 124 in their Student Manuals, "Steps in the Group Problem Solving Process," and briefly explain what happens in each step.

2. Tell the students that they will have the opportunity to practice the first three steps by using a problem common in groups. In fact, it may be a problem that some of them have experienced. Have them get into the class meeting circle if they are not already.

Step 1: Agree to Problem Solve

3. Refer the group to page 125 in their Student Manuals, "Step 1: Agree to Problem Solve." Explain the rules for group problem solving and answer any questions students might have.

4. Tell the class that the purpose of the meeting is to deal with the problem of being teased or harassed by another person or group of persons. Tell the students that because they may have experienced this problem and can give specific examples, an additional ground rule will be that, when they are describing the problem, they may describe behaviors, situations, and feelings, but they may not use anyone's name.

Step 2: Gather Points of View

5. Refer the group to page 126 in their Student Manuals, "Step 2: Gather Points of View," and discuss. Stress the importance of not placing blame on anyone. Clarify that students should contribute *new* ideas to the discussion; if someone else has already raised an idea, that idea does not need to be repeated.

6. Ask, "Have you experienced teasing or harassing? Please tell the group what happened in your experience." Enforce the special ground rules during the discussion by interrupting immediately if a specific name is mentioned. Allow the other ground rules to be violated during the discussion, but note specific examples to discuss when you process this step. Whenever the discussion lags, ask:

Is there more to this problem?

Can anyone give an example of teasing or harassing that is really different from what we have heard so far?

Is there anything more we need to know about this problem?

7. Help students frame the problem statement. For example: "What can be done to eliminate teasing, harassing, or other disrespectful behaviors?"

8. Discuss Steps 1 and 2 by asking the following questions:

Was the "Rule of Focus" followed in our discussion?

Was each point of view summarized before another point of view was given?

What is the problem?

Did we hear many ideas about the problem?

Is there anyone who still has a point of view the group has not heard?

Step 3: Focus on Interests in the Group

9. Refer the group to page 127 in their Student Manuals, "Step 3: Focus on Interests in the Group," and discuss.

10. Begin the discussion by saying, "We have gathered points of view about the problem of teasing and harassing. Pretend this is a problem we are having in our class. What would we want and why?" If the discussion lags, ask:

Why does teasing and harassing continue?

What do you think the person doing the teasing and harassing wants? Why?

What might happen if teasing and harassing continue?

11. Discuss Step 3 by asking:

Did we follow our ground rules during this step of the process?

What examples of summarizing or clarifying did you hear during the discussion?

What interests were identified in our group?

What interests were shared by several members of the group?

12. Repeat the problem statement and the interests identified. Record both the problem statement and the interests identified on the easel pad. Save this page for use in Activity 7.

Student Manual
page 124

Steps in the
Group Problem Solving Process

- ◆ **Step 1:** Agree to Problem Solve

- ◆ **Step 2:** Gather Points of View

- ◆ **Step 3:** Focus on Interests in the Group

- ◆ **Step 4:** Create Win-Win Options

- ◆ **Step 5a:** Establish Criteria to Evaluate Options

- ◆ **Step 5b:** Evaluate Options

- ◆ **Step 6:** Create an Agreement

124

Student Manual
page 125

Step 1: Agree to Problem Solve

♦ **Listen for the purpose of the meeting.**

♦ **Follow the group problem solving rules:**

Participants sit in a circle.

Every member of the class is responsible for communication *(listening and speaking)*. This means that each member is responsible for sharing his or her point of view about the problem if it has not already been shared by another.

The *"Rule of Focus"* applies to all discussion. This means that whoever is speaking will be allowed to talk without being interrupted.

Participants show respect for others. This means no criticism or sarcasm toward group members or their ideas.

Each time someone in the group finishes making a statement, another group member summarizes and clarifies it before anyone else goes on to a new idea.

♦ **Listen for and think about any special rules for this particular meeting.**

125

Step 2: Gather Points of View

♦ **Participate in the discussion**
(listen and speak).

♦ **Tell what you know and how you feel about the problem:**

Speak to be understood.

Do not place blame.

Speak if your point of view has not already been stated by another group member.

♦ **Help the group decide on the problem statement. The problem statement tells exactly what problem you are trying to solve.**

Group members hear one another's perceptions and emotions.

126

Student Manual
page 127

Step 3: Focus on Interests in the Group

◆ **Tell what you want in the situation and why you want what you want.**

◆ **If you don't know what you want and why:**

Tell why you think the problem is not going away.

Tell what you think is likely to happen if the group cannot agree on a solution.

> Group members' shared and compatible interests are the building blocks of the resolution.

127

7 Steps 4–6

PURPOSE To learn and practice Steps 4, 5a, 5b, and 6 in the group problem solving process

MATERIALS Student Manuals
Problem statement and list of interests (saved from Activity 6)
Easel pad
Marker

FORMAT OPTION Class meeting

PROCEDURE 1. Post the page listing the problem statement and interests generated during the previous activity. Tell the class that they will continue with the problem of teasing and harassing, working through Steps 4, 5a, 5b, and 6 of the group problem solving process.

Step 4: Create Win-Win Options

2. Have the group form a class meeting circle, then refer them to page 128 in their Student Manuals, "Step 4: Create Win-Win Options." Explain that a *win-win option* is an option that will help everyone in the group.

3. Review the brainstorming rules, expanding on them as given in the Student Manual to be sure students understand:

   Say any idea that comes to mind. (This means to blurt out your ideas; don't censor your thoughts.)

   Do not judge or discuss ideas. (This means you accept all ideas, at least for the time being; don't criticize or make fun of any ideas.)

   Come up with as many ideas as possible. (Sometimes it is helpful, when you run out of ideas, to try making changes to ideas that have already been given.)

   Try to think of unusual ideas. (Sometimes really weird or far-out ideas will help you and others think of new possibilities.)

4. Encourage students to come up with as many win-win options as they can. Record all the ideas students generate on the easel pad. If the generation of ideas lags, ask the following questions:

   What other possibilities can you think of?

   In the future, what could you do differently when you are teased or harassed?

318

5. Discuss Step 4 by asking the following questions:

   Were any of the ideas evaluated in this step?

   In what ways were ideas evaluated?

   Can laughing be an evaluation?

Step 5a: Establish Criteria to Evaluate Options

6. Refer students to page 129 in their Student Manuals, "Step 5a: Establish Criteria to Evaluate Options," and discuss. Explain that in Step 5a the task is to think of criteria, or things to consider, to help decide whether or not an option is a good idea.

7. Ask which of the criteria listed on page 129 should be considered. Encourage the group to state other criteria they feel should also be considered.

Step 5b: Evaluate Options

8. Refer students to page 130 of their Student Manuals, "Step 5b: Evaluate Options." Explain that Step 5b uses criteria from Step 5a to evaluate the win-win options. Facilitate discussion by asking:

   Which options on our list do we need to eliminate because they do not satisfy one of our criteria?

   What criteria do the options to be eliminated not satisfy? (Cross these options off the list.)

   Which options do satisfy all of our criteria? (Circle these options on the list.)

9. Explain that reaching consensus means the group looks for the best solution they can find to solve the problem and that the decision can be supported by each member of the group. The best solution may not be each individual's particular favorite, but it is one that everyone thinks is OK. Remind students that punishment and faultfinding are not options that solve problems.

10. Continue the discussion by telling the group to look at the options that are left, especially those circled. Point to each option, asking group members to hold up their hands if they think an option is a good solution. If they think more than one of the options is good, they can hold up their hands as many times as they want. Record the number of group members who thought the option was good next to that option on the list.

11. Explain that a consensus decision is sometimes made by putting options or parts of options together. Invite the group to attempt to reach a consensus decision in this fashion. For example, "Think about how you would like to be treated before you do something to someone else" and "Don't laugh at someone who has trouble doing something" might be combined as "When someone has trouble doing something, praise the person for trying." Write these ideas down as well on the list of options.

12. For each option the group decides meets the evaluation criteria, ask:

> Who cannot support this idea as a solution to the problem?
>
> (If anyone cannot support the idea) Would you tell the rest of the group why you cannot support this idea?

13. Summarize the ideas that the group can support. Ask, "Is there anything about our solution that we need to change?"

Step 6: Create an Agreement

14. Refer students to page 131 in their Student Manuals, "Step 6: Create an Agreement," and discuss. Explain that in this step, the group decides exactly how the solution will be carried out. Summarize the solution the group has proposed and ask for a show of support:

> I think the class has agreed that to solve this problem we will _____.
>
> Please raise your hand if you support this agreement.
>
> Please raise your hand if you do not support this agreement.
>
> (If any hands are raised) What is it about the agreement you cannot support?
>
> If a change in the solution is suggested, again ask for support or lack of support. Continue until no member of the group indicates a lack of support for the agreement.

15. Explain that to be put to work, a solution always needs a specific plan of action. The plan tells who, what, when, where, and how. Ask the group to specify the particulars of their plan to put their solution into effect. Stress that each person must agree to do his or her best to make the solution work.

16. Congratulate everyone on working together to arrive at an agreement, then refer the group to "The Peaceable School Group Problem Solving Process," on pages 132–133 of the Student Manual, where all the steps are displayed. Encourage students to use the group problem solving strategy when problems affecting the group arise in the future.

Student Manual
page 128

Step 4: Create Win-Win Options

♦ **Suggest ideas that will address the interests of group members.**

♦ **Follow the brainstorming rules:**

Say any idea that comes to mind.

Do not judge or discuss ideas.

Come up with as many ideas as possible.

Try to think of unusual ideas.

128

Step 5a: Establish Criteria to Evaluate Options

♦ **Decide what criteria are important to consider. For example:**

Does the option follow our school's rights and responsiblities?

Does the option help everyone involved?

Is the option fair?

Can the option solve the problem?

Can the group do it?

Criteria are the standards you use to decide whether or not an option will work.

129

Student Manual
page 130

Step 5b: Evaluate Options

◆ **Discuss each option generated in Step 4.**

Does it meet the criteria you think
are important?

◆ **Combine options or parts of options.**

Does the newly created option meet
the criteria?

> Punishment and fault finding are not
> options that solve problems.

130

Step 6: Create an Agreement

♦ **Listen to understand the agreement.**

♦ **Show your support for the agreement or show you do not support the agreement.**

♦ **If you do not support the agreement, say why.**

♦ **Help the group make a plan to decide exactly how the solution will be carried out:**

"Who, what, when, where, and how?"

♦ **Agree to do your part to make the solution work.**

131

Student Manual
page 132

The Peaceable School
Group Problem Solving Process

STEP 1: AGREE TO PROBLEM SOLVE

◆ Listen for the purpose of the meeting.

◆ Follow the group problem solving rules:

Participants sit in a circle.

Every member of the class is responsible for communication *(listening and speaking)*. This means that each member is responsible for sharing his or her point of view about the problem if it has not already been shared by another.

The *"Rule of Focus"* applies to all discussion. This means that whoever is speaking will be allowed to talk without being interrupted.

Participants show respect for others. This means no criticism or sarcasm toward group members or their ideas.

Each time someone in the group finishes making a statement, another group member summarizes and clarifies it before anyone else goes on to a new idea.

◆ Listen for and think about any special rules for this particular meeting.

STEP 2: GATHER POINTS OF VIEW

◆ Participate in the discussion *(listen and speak)*.

◆ Tell what you know and how you feel about the problem:

Speak to be understood.

Do not place blame.

Speak if your point of view has not already been stated by another group member.

◆ Help the group decide on the problem statement. The problem statement tells exactly what problem you are trying to solve.

STEP 3: FOCUS ON INTERESTS IN THE GROUP

◆ Tell what you want in the situation and why you want what you want.

◆ If you don't know what you want and why:

Tell why you think the problem is not going away.

Tell what you think is likely to happen if the group cannot agree on a solution.

132

Student Manual
page 133

STEP 4: CREATE WIN-WIN OPTIONS

♦ Suggest ideas that will address the interests of group members.

♦ Follow the brainstorming rules:

Say any idea that comes to mind.

Do not judge or discuss ideas.

Come up with as many ideas as possible.

Try to think of unusual ideas.

STEP 5A: ESTABLISH CRITERIA TO EVALUATE OPTIONS

♦ Decide what criteria are important to consider. For example:

Does the option follow our school's rights and responsibilities?

Does the option help everyone involved?

Is the option fair?

Can the option solve the problem?

Can the group do it?

STEP 5B: EVALUATE OPTIONS

♦ Discuss each option generated in Step 4.

Does it meet the criteria you think are important?

♦ Combine options or parts of options.

Does the newly created option meet the criteria?

STEP 6: CREATE AN AGREEMENT

♦ Listen to understand the agreement.

♦ Show your support for the agreement or show you do not support the agreement.

♦ If you do not support the agreement, say why.

♦ Help the group make a plan to decide exactly how the solution will be carried out: *"Who, what, when, where, and how?"*

♦ Agree to do your part to make the solution work.

133

ACTIVITY

8   Key Concept Review

PURPOSE   To understand the meaning of key concepts related to group problem solving

MATERIALS   Butcher paper
Magazines
Comics
Scissors
Glue
Markers

FORMAT OPTION   Cooperative learning
Class meeting

PROCEDURE   1. Ask students to use their own words to define the following concepts. Solicit several definitions for each. Discuss the different definitions until the group displays a common understanding of each of the concepts.

CONSENSUS DECISION	TOLERANCE
CRITERIA	COMMITMENT
PLAN	CLASS MEETING
DIVERSITY	GROUP

2. Divide the class into eight groups of equal size. Assign each group one of the words and instruct them to use the art materials to develop a poster that displays the meaning of the concept—draw a picture, write a definition, create a collage, and so on.

3. Display the posters.

Program Development and Implementation

An individual teacher or a group of teachers may implement the concepts in this Program Guide and create a peaceable classroom or a peaceable unit within a school. However, this guide provides the framework for a comprehensive program for an entire school. The ideas presented here will yield the best results when applied on a schoolwide basis within a community of peacemakers.

To implement and sustain a successful conflict resolution education program, participants must embrace the belief that conflicts can be resolved peacefully. Many adults in schools are most familiar with and comfortable using conflict resolution grounded in methods such as the exercise of adult authority, reliance on school rules, disciplinary hearings, and other administrative procedures. Moving from these methods to ones that encourage people to talk about their interests and needs and to work collaboratively to create solutions requires a major paradigm shift.

It is important to realize that students' success in developing an awareness of the positive potential of conflict resolution is an outgrowth of the endeavors and commitment of the adults in the school to approach conflict in a positive way. Educators who bring positive ways of resolving conflict into their classrooms will see results that have a powerful effect on their lives and work, as well as on the lives and work of their students. It is the comprehensive nature of *Creating the Peaceable School*—directed toward students, adults, and institutions—that provides the potential to truly impact the future.

A comprehensive peaceable school program can be implemented in six developmental phases. Phase 1 involves creating and training the conflict resolution program team, conducting a needs assessment, and building consensus for staff development. Phase 2 covers designing the staff development program and timelines, conducting staff

---

Portions of the following text have been excerpted from *Developing Emotional Intelligence: A Guide to Behavior Management and Conflict Resolution in Schools,* by R. J. Bodine and D. K. Crawford (Research Press, 1998), and *Peer Mediation: Conflict Resolution in Schools* (rev. ed.), by F. Schrumpf, D. K. Crawford, and R. J. Bodine (Research Press, 1997). To learn more about the construction and implementation of a noncoercive behavior management program, see the first source; for more forms and instructions helpful in implementing a schoolwide peer mediation program, see the second.

training sessions, and building consensus for program development. Phase 3 encompasses the development and implementation of a sense-based behavior management system to facilitate construction of the peaceable climate. This includes establishing rights and responsibilities, developing school rules and consequences, formulating rules for the classroom and other school areas, and building a responsibility education program. Phase 4 focuses on conflict resolution education in the classroom, which includes establishing a conflict resolution space; teaching the understanding of conflict and of peace and peacemaking; and teaching and implementing mediation, negotiation, and group problem solving. Phase 5 concerns designing and executing a peaceable school awareness campaign, establishing a schoolwide peer mediation program, providing peaceable school orientation for parents and community, and providing peaceable school orientation and conflict resolution skill development workshops for parents. Phase 6 focuses on strengthening program quality by evaluating program progress and impact, providing ongoing staff training and support, and conducting ongoing student training, including integrating conflict resolution in curricula. These six developmental phases, enumerated in Table 9, can be adapted readily to serve the varying needs and interests of almost any school.

The remainder of this section describes these developmental phases in more detail and offers a number of sample forms useful in planning, implementing, and evaluating a peaceable school program. Necessary forms are reproduced for program use in Appendix D.

PHASE 1: PROGRAM TEAM DEVELOPMENT

Create Program Team

A peaceable school program will succeed only if it is perceived to be need fulfilling by both staff and students. Formulating a leadership group composed of administrators, classroom teachers, special educators, counselors, deans, social workers, and health educators who have an interest in developing a conflict resolution education program within the school will provide the broad-based coalition necessary to build a need-fulfilling program. The program team initiates the conflict resolution education program, builds consensus for the staff development program, and eventually will be charged with eliciting the support of the entire school staff for program development.

Train Program Team

Once the program team has been formed, the next step is building their capacity to develop a peaceable school program. To become informed decision makers, effective implementers, and strong advocates for the program, program team members require training. In training program team members, it is beneficial to use the same model and resources used for training students and other staff. Because the

TABLE 9   Peaceable School Developmental Phases

PHASE 1: PROGRAM TEAM DEVELOPMENT
- Create program team.
- Train program team.
- Conduct needs assessment.
- Build faculty consensus for staff development.

PHASE 2: STAFF DEVELOPMENT
- Plan initial peaceable school training.
- Conduct training sessions.
- Build consensus for program implementation.
- Develop timeline for program implementation.

PHASE 3: DEVELOPMENT OF THE SENSE-BASED BEHAVIOR MANAGEMENT SYSTEM
- Establish rights and responsibilities.
- Develop school rules and consequences.
- Develop classroom and special area rules.
- Build a responsibility education program.

PHASE 4: CONFLICT RESOLUTION EDUCATION
- Establish conflict resolution space.
- Teach understanding of conflict.
- Teach understanding of peace and peacemaking.
- Teach and implement mediation.
- Teach and implement negotiation.
- Teach and implement group problem solving.

PHASE 5: SUPPORT INITIATIVES
- Design and execute peaceable school awareness campaign.
- Establish peer mediation program.
- Provide peaceable school orientation for parents and community.
- Provide conflict resolution skill development workshops for parents.

PHASE 6: QUALITY IMPROVEMENT
- Evaluate program progress and impact.
- Provide ongoing staff training and technical assistance.
- Provide ongoing student training and integration of curricula.

---

program team may be responsible for training faculty, they need training in both content areas (such as the principles of conflict resolution and the conflict resolution processes) and in techniques or methods for conflict resolution training.

Basic training typically ranges from 2 to 4 days. Such training covers the following content:

Understanding conflict

Understanding peace and peacemaking

Principles of conflict resolution

Social and cultural diversity and conflict resolution

Mediation, negotiation, and group problem solving processes and skills

Quality behavior management

Program organization and implementation

Rationale for establishing the peaceable school program

It is important for those training students to have actual conflict resolution process experience, preferably in mediation and/or negotiation. Mediation and negotiation processes cannot be learned by reading a book or following a curriculum guide. Skilled mediators and negotiators make a number of astute and consequential decisions during the course of the mediation or negotiation process, based on their ability to apply the principles of conflict resolution. Unskilled mediators and negotiators follow the six-step process without much discretion. Becoming a skilled mediator or negotiator requires simulated and real mediation and negotiation experiences with the guided feedback of skilled trainers. Therefore, it is important for the team to be involved in mediation and negotiation training and to continue to seek opportunities to increase their skill levels.

Conduct Needs Assessment

To move beyond the individual efforts of staff members toward school-community support for a conflict resolution education program, a needs assessment is helpful. Such an assessment can determine the specific nature of the need for conflict resolution education in the school and identify the resources already available to the school to address those needs.

Support for any new school program depends to a large extent on (a) the degree to which school staff recognize that the new program addresses current needs and/or (b) the degree to which the new program draws upon existing efforts, extending or embellishing the school mission. A well-designed needs assessment can elicit information relative to these two points.

General areas to assess in planning and designing a peaceable school program are detailed in Table 10. Some of these probes may not be applicable to a specific school, and not all are required of any school. The probes are provided to help the program team think about information to gather that might assist them in designing and planning a conflict resolution education program for the school. In addition to general assessment in these areas, a more specific needs assessment can help gather information from potential program "consumers." Table 11 shows a sample conflict resolution in schools needs assessment.

TABLE 10   General Assessment Areas for Program Design

1. To what extent are conflicts interfering with the teaching and learning processes within the school?

2. What percentage of these conflicts are attributable to these factors:

    Competitive atmosphere of the school or classroom

    Intolerant atmosphere in the school or classroom

    Poor communication

    Inappropriate expression of emotion

    Lack of conflict resolution skills

    Adult misuse of power in the school or classroom

3. To what extent are diversity issues manifested as conflicts in the school community?

4. To what extent is representation (or lack of it) in decision making an issue manifested in the conflicts observed in the school?

5. What percentage of the conflicts arising in the school is between the following groups:

    Students

    Teachers and students

    Teachers

    Students and school expectations, rules, or policies

    Teachers and administrators

    School staff and parents

    Various other combinations specific to the school

6. What procedures are followed when conflicts cause disruption of the teaching-learning processes?

7. Who administers which procedures? Who are the sources of referrals to these procedures?

8. Regarding the effectiveness of these procedures, what are the perceptions of students? Parents? Teachers? Administrators? Others?

9. What attitudes or behaviors exist that will facilitate the implementation of a conflict resolution education program in the school? Who exhibits these?

10. What attitudes or behaviors exist that will impede the implementation of a conflict resolution education program in the school? Who exhibits these?

11. Which foundation skills for conflict resolution are now included in the school curriculum, when are they developed, who provides training in the skills, and which students receive the training?

12. To what extent have staff members received training in conflict resolution?

13. What staff development opportunities in conflict resolution are available? What opportunities are desired?

14. What present/future monetary resources are available to support implementation of a conflict resolution education program?

15. What conflict resolution processes currently exist within the school? Within the school-community?

16. What community resources exist to assist the school in designing and implementing a conflict resolution education program in the school?

Note. From *The Handbook of Conflict Resolution Education: A Guide to Building Quality Programs in Schools* (pp. 136–137), by R. J. Bodine and D. K. Crawford, 1998, San Francisco: Jossey-Bass. Copyright © 1998 by John Wiley & Sons, Inc. Reprinted by permission.

TABLE 11 Sample Conflict Resolution in Schools Needs Assessment

Answer each question by providing the response that most accurately reflects your personal view of your school.

1. I am a: ❏ student ❏ staff member ❏ parent ❏ other
2. Conflicts interfere with the teaching and learning process: ❏ often ❏ sometimes ❏ rarely
3. Problems between people at this school are caused by:

	often	sometimes	rarely
Expectation to be competitive	❏	❏	❏
Intolerance between adults and students	❏	❏	❏
Intolerance between students	❏	❏	❏
Poor communication	❏	❏	❏
Anger and/or frustration	❏	❏	❏
Rumors	❏	❏	❏
Problems brought to school from somewhere else	❏	❏	❏

4. Without exceeding 100 percent as the total, what percentage of the problems referred for disciplinary action are problems:

Between students	_____ percent
Between student and classroom teacher	_____ percent
Between student and other staff members	_____ percent
Between student and school rules	_____ percent
Other _____	_____ percent
	Total: 100 percent

5. Indicate the types and frequency of conflicts experienced by students in this school:

	often	sometimes	rarely
Put-downs/insults/teasing	❏	❏	❏
Threats	❏	❏	❏
Intolerance of differences	❏	❏	❏
Loss of property	❏	❏	❏
Access to groups	❏	❏	❏
Rumors	❏	❏	❏
Physical fighting	❏	❏	❏
Verbal fighting	❏	❏	❏
Schoolwork	❏	❏	❏
Other_____	❏	❏	❏

6. Indicate the effectiveness of each of the following actions in causing a student to *change* a problem behavior:

	very effective	somewhat effective	not effective
Time-out	❏	❏	❏
Detention	❏	❏	❏
Conference with an adult	❏	❏	❏
Suspension	❏	❏	❏
Contacting parent(s)	❏	❏	❏
Expulsion	❏	❏	❏

Note. From *The Handbook of Conflict Resolution Education: A Guide to Building Quality Programs in Schools* (pp. 138–140), by R. J. Bodine and D. K. Crawford, 1998, San Francisco: Jossey-Bass. Copyright © 1998 by John Wiley & Sons, Inc. Reprinted by permission.

7. Without exceeding 100 percent as the total, what percentage of influence do the following groups have in the way the school operates?

Students _____ percent

Teachers _____ percent

Parents _____ percent

School building administration _____ percent

School district administration _____ percent

Board of education _____ percent

Other _____ _____ percent

Total: 100 percent

8. In this school, I am generally:

	most of the time	about half the time	not very often
Treated fairly	❏	❏	❏
Treated with respect	❏	❏	❏
Given equal opportunity	❏	❏	❏
Treated with compassion	❏	❏	❏
Accepted	❏	❏	❏

9. I am allowed to solve problems that affect me: ❏ nearly always ❏ sometimes ❏ hardly ever

10. This school should do a better job teaching students to:

	definitely yes	maybe	definitely no
Tell another person how you feel	❏	❏	❏
Disagree without making the other person angry	❏	❏	❏
Respect authority	❏	❏	❏
Control anger	❏	❏	❏
Ignore someone who is bothering you	❏	❏	❏
Solve problems with other students	❏	❏	❏

11. When I need help, I usually ask for it: ❏ nearly always ❏ sometimes ❏ almost never

12. If I needed help, I think I could get it from:

	definitely yes	maybe	definitely no
A parent	❏	❏	❏
A brother or sister	❏	❏	❏
Another family member	❏	❏	❏
A teacher	❏	❏	❏
A counselor	❏	❏	❏
Another school staff member	❏	❏	❏
Another adult	❏	❏	❏
Another student	❏	❏	❏

Build Faculty Consensus for Staff Development

The program team conducts a meeting to build faculty consensus for staff development. Showing segments of the *Creating the Peaceable School* video to open this session provides the anticipatory set, presenting the faculty with a vision of the peaceable school.

The following *Creating the Peaceable School* video segments (approximately the first 20 minutes and the last 5 minutes) are recommended viewing:*

1. Introduction

2. Understanding Conflict

3. Understanding Peace and Peacemaking

4. Conflict Resolution Strategies (only the segment demonstrating the six steps)

5. Building the Peaceable Climate

The program team then presents the results of the needs assessment, distributes written information regarding results of research on conflict resolution education programs (see Appendix A), and shares personal experiences and outcomes from participating in the peaceable school workshop.

After sharing information and experiences, the program team polls the faculty as to whether they support the idea of participating in a staff development program designed to learn how to create a peaceable school. Faculty involvement is essential to go forward. It is not required that each faculty member commit, but a critical mass of the staff must agree to participate in staff development to learn more about peaceable school program implementation. What actually constitutes a critical mass varies from school to school, but a minimum is probably 75 percent of those who have instructional responsibility for student learning.

PHASE 2: STAFF DEVELOPMENT

Plan Initial Peaceable School Training

The initial peaceable school workshop requires a minimum of 12 hours. A 2-day workshop may be conducted with two 6-hour sessions, divided into six 2-hour sessions, or presented as a combination of a 6-hour day and three 2-hour sessions. With this flexibility in mind, the program team will be able to design the staff development program in accordance with their school district's inservice schedule and their school's faculty meeting schedule. The staff development program is

---

*The *Creating the Peaceable School* video (1995) is available from Research Press at the address given on the title page of this guide.

designed to equip staff members with the experience and information needed to provide conflict resolution education to students.

Conduct Training Sessions

The program team may conduct the workshops, arrange for a consultant to conduct the workshops, or facilitate the workshops in collaboration with a consultant. A sample 2-day staff workshop agenda is shown in Table 12. Handouts for use in the workshop appear at the end of this section. The lesson plans for teaching conflict resolution to staff are the same lesson plans that staff will use to teach conflict resolution to students in the classroom. (These lesson plans are located in Sections 1 through 6 of this guide.) In order for staff to internalize conflict resolution skills, they need experience in negotiating and mediating conflicts. Conflict simulations are provided in Appendix C. Adults are asked to role-play students in conflict. The simulated practice and the discussions generated from that practice should focus on the conflict resolution process, not on the content of the problem.

Each person participating in the training who will have direct instructional responsibilities in delivering the program to students should have a copy of this Program Guide to use during and after the training. A copy of the Student Manual is useful but optional. Staff participating in the training who will help support the program but who are not expected to teach conflict resolution—for example, secretaries, custodians, aides, and lunch supervisors—will need to work with a staff member who has a copy of the Program Guide.

Build Consensus for Program Implementation

The program team may then utilize the following definitions and examples of belief statements and statement of program goals to facilitate the development of a shared vision and consensus for program development among faculty.

Belief Statements

Belief statements are a comprehensive collection of statements expressing fundamental convictions and tenets. As related to conflict and conflict resolution, belief statements provide a basis for achieving consensus within the school community regarding a conflict resolution education program in the school. The beliefs are the basis for obtaining a commitment to specific goals for such a program.

Belief statements are simply stated and easily understood. Sample belief statements include the following:

1. Conflict is a natural part of everyday life.

2. Conflict is an opportunity to grow and learn.

3. Neither avoidance nor violence are healthy responses to conflict.

TABLE 12   Creating the Peaceable School Staff Workshop Agenda

Note: Handouts mentioned appear at the end of this section (see pp. 370–376).

Day 1

8:30 A.M.   Boundary breaker: "Find Someone Who . . . " (Handout 1)

8:50 A.M.   Workshop overview (Handout 2)

9:00 A.M.   **Section 2: Understanding Conflict**

Teach the following activities:

"Conflict Is . . . " (Activity 1, procedures 1 and 7)

"Basic Needs" (Activity 3, procedures 1–6, 8)

"Enough Is Not Enough" (limited resources; Activity 4, procedures 1 and 5)

"Different Values" (diversity issues; Activity 5, procedures 1–3 and 8).
Emphasize that even though values may be based on biases and prejudices,
they are still values because the individual chooses behaviors based on
those beliefs and attitudes.

"What's My Response?" (Activity 7, procedures 1–3; procedures 4 and 5 as
a whole-group activity)

10:15 A.M.   BREAK

10:30 A.M.   **Section 2: Understanding Conflict (continued)**

1. Continue with these activities:

"Soft, Hard, or Principled Responses" (Activity 8, procedures 1–7;
procedure 8 as a whole-group activity)

"Getting to Win-Win" (Activity 9, procedures 1 and 4)

2. Summarize by referring participants to Table 7 in this guide, "Conflict Myths
and Conflict Realities" (p. 72). Emphasize that a central purpose of Section 2
training activities is to change orientation abilities to the reality side of this
chart. Another is to see behavior as a choice over which one has control at all
times.

11:00 A.M.   **Section 3: Understanding Peace and Peacemaking**

1. Randomly assign participants to work in pairs. Distribute Negotiation
Simulation 1, "Pease Middle School" (Handout 3) by giving the first page to one
member of the pair and the second page to the other. Explain that "the two of
you are staff members in the same building and you disagree on an important
issue. You have agreed to talk. Read your information sheet and try to become
that person. Talk to each other, but do not read your information to the other
person." Allow the negotiation to proceed for 5 to 8 minutes. Process the experience by asking for a show of hands in response to the following questions:

Do you think you and your partner were making progress toward solving
the problem between you?

338

Do you think you and your partner were making no real progress toward a solution, or do you think you were even making the problem worse?

Ask, "Reflecting on what happened in this simulation (or on other times you remember being in a situation like this one and you were not making progress or you were making the problem worse), tell how you were behaving toward each other." Record the responses on an easel pad or chalkboard.

Ask, "Reflecting on what happened in this simulation or on other times you remember being in a situation like this one and you were making progress, tell how you were behaving toward each other." Record these responses, too. Compare the two lists. Emphasize that conflict resolution processes are designed to maximize the use of helping behaviors and minimize blocking behaviors.

2. Work through these activities:

"Making Peace" (Activity 4, all procedures)

"Perceptions" (Activity 5, procedures 1–3 and 7)

"Emotions" (Activity 6, procedures 1, 4, 6, and 11)

12:00 P.M.   LUNCH

1:00 P.M.   **Section 3: Understanding Peace and Peacemaking (continued)**

Continue with "Communication" (active listening; Activity 7, procedures 1–18). This exercise can be shortened by having one member of the pair practice each active listening behavior (i.e., delete procedures 7, 13, and 17).

1:30 P.M.   **Section 4: Mediation**

1. Reference Table 1 in this guide, "Prevalent Practice Versus Conflict Resolution" (p. 14). Discuss the differences and emphasize that the three conflict resolution processes are designed to help in planning for future behavior.

2. Conduct the following activities:

"Mediation Is . . ." (Activity 1, procedures 1 and 2)

"Role of the Mediator" (Activity 2, procedures 1–3)

"Overview of the Mediation Process" (Activity 3, procedure 1). Show the 6-minute mediation segment of the *Creating the Peaceable School* video or role-play the sample mediation from pages 202–206 of this guide (pp. 76–80 in the Student Manual). Discuss the following questions:

How did the mediators display or not display the qualities discussed in Activity 2?

Was the outcome of the mediation a solution that met both people's needs?

Do the disputants have a behavior plan that appears to be better than the behaviors that brought them to mediation?

3. Conclude with "Overview of the Mediation Process" (Activity 3, procedure 4).

TABLE 12 (continued)

2:15 P.M   BREAK

2:30 P.M.   **Section 4: Mediation (Steps 1 and 2)**

Combine Activities 4 and 5 as follows:

1. Have four volunteers act out the Red Riding Hood and the Wolf mediation, which appears on pages 211–214 of this guide (pp. 82–84 in the Student Manual). Two of the volunteers will be the mediators; the other two will be Red and the Wolf.

   Explain co-mediation before beginning the role play:

   > In co-mediation, two mediators work as a team to facilitate the mediation process. The mediation team has two responsibilities: One member of the team actively facilitates, and one member of the team observes, monitors, and supports the facilitator. Co-mediators model cooperation. Co-mediation works best when the two team members equally share these two responsibilities. The co-mediators must decide in advance how they will work together—in other words, who will facilitate Steps 1, 3, and 5 and who will facilitate Steps 2, 4, and 6. They must also decide how the observer will help the facilitator (offer suggestions, remind the facilitator of something omitted, etc.).

2. After the volunteers have acted out the mediation, process by asking, "Did Red Riding Hood and the Wolf solve their problem?"

3. Explain that the demonstration involved only Steps 1 and 2 of a six-step process. Steps 1 and 2 cover the first principle of conflict resolution—separate the people from the problem—by establishing rules for cooperating (including constructively dealing with emotions) and for sharing points of view.

4. Form groups of four and have the groups conduct "Step 1: Agree to Mediate" (Activity 4, procedures 1 and 4).

5. Have the groups continue with "Step 2: Gather Points of View" (Activity 5, procedures 2–5. Use Simulations 15 and 16, from Appendix C.)

3:15 P.M.   **Section 4: Mediation (Step 3)**

Conduct the following activities:

1. Tell the "orange story" from Section 4 (Activity 6, procedure 1).

2. Conduct "Focus on Interests, Not Positions" from Section 3 (Activity 10, procedures 1–7). Do the first scenario as a demonstration in the large group; assign participants to pairs and do the remaining scenarios as cooperative learning activities. Conduct procedure 8.

3. Form new groups of four. Conduct procedures 1–7 (from Section 3, Activity 10) again. Use Simulations 13 and 14, from Appendix C.

4:00 P.M.   CLOSE

Give the following reading assignment from the Program Guide:

> Introduction, "Origins of Conflict" (pp. 5–9)
>
> Section 2, "Overview" (pp. 65–73)

Section 3, "Overview" (pp. 113–125)

Section 4, "Overview" (pp. 185–194)

Day 2

8:30 A.M. **Review of Day 1**

8:45 A.M. **Section 4: Mediation (Steps 4–6)**

Teach the following activities:

"Step 4: Create Win-Win Options" (Activity 7, procedures 1, 2, 4, and 8)

"Step 5: "Evaluate Options" (Activity 8, procedures 1–3 and 7)

"Step 6: "Create an Agreement" (Activity 9, procedures 1–3 and 7)

"Putting It All Together" (Activity 10, procedures 1 and 2). Use Simulations 17 and 18, from Appendix C.

9:45 A.M. **Section 5: Negotiation**

Teach the following activities:

"Negotiation Is . . . " (Activity 1, procedures 1 and 2). Compare definition of negotiation with that of mediation (on p. 196 of this guide, p. 73 of the Student Manual).

"Role of the Negotiator" (Activity 2, procedures 1–3)

"Overview of the Negotiation Process" (Activity 3, procedure 1). Refer participants to the Steps in the Negotiation Process (on p. 242 of this guide; p. 97 in the Student Manual).

10:15 A.M. BREAK

10:30 A.M. **Section 5: Negotiation (continued)**

Show the negotiation segment of the *Creating the Peaceable School* video (5 minutes), or role-play the sample negotiation on pages 243–245 of this guide (pp. 98–100 in the Student Manual). Process by asking, "How did negotiators exhibit the qualities of a negotiator discussed in Activity 2? Do the disputants have a plan to behave differently from this point forward?"

Conduct "Putting It All Together" (Activity 10, procedures 1–3). Use Negotiation Simulation 2, "Parent-Teacher Conflict" (Handout 4).

12:00 P.M. LUNCH

1:00 P.M. **Section 6: Group Problem Solving**

1. Conduct the following activities:

"Group Problem Solving Is . . . " (Activity 3, procedures 3 and 6)

"Role of the Group Problem Solver" (Activity 4, procedures 1–3). Point out that the qualities that allow one to negotiate successfully are the same ones needed for effective group problem solving.

2. Show the group problem solving segment of the *Creating the Peaceable School* video (7 minutes), or role-play the sample group problem solving meeting on pages 285–294 of the Program Guide.

TABLE 12   (continued)

3. In the large group, brainstorm conflicts that would be suitable topics for group problem solving.

4. Highlight and discuss the section titled "Role of the Teacher-Facilitator" from pages 274–277 of this guide.

1:45 P.M.   **Section 1: Building a Peaceable Climate**

Lead a general discussion of the information provided in the overview of Section 1 of this guide under the heading "Managing Behavior Without Coercion" (pp. 23–40).

2:15 P.M.   BREAK

2:30 P.M.   **Section 1: Building a Peaceable Climate (continued)**

Teach the following activities from Section 1:

"Rights and Responsibilities" (Activity 4, all procedures)

"Rules" (Activity 5, all procedures)

3:30 P.M.   CLOSE

Give the following reading assignment:

Section 1, "Overview" (pp. 21–42)

Section 5, "Overview" (pp. 229–235)

Section 6, "Overview" (pp. 273–294)

---

4. Through awareness of cultural differences, we grow to respect others and to value diversity.

5. Everyone deserves respect; the school environment should allow everyone to live together with respect for differences (racial, cultural, social, and behavioral).

6. All people have basic needs (belonging, power, freedom, fun), and each wants his or her needs met.

7. Discipline is a learning process for developing responsible behavior.

8. Adults provide powerful behavioral models for students; this is especially true in dealing with conflict.

9. Individuals—students and adults—can learn to solve problems peaceably through conflict resolution education.

10. Students can learn to resolve many of their conflicts without adult involvement.

Provide faculty the opportunity to brainstorm their own list of belief statements; use a few examples from the preceding list only as a guide to introduce the activity. Beliefs establish moral and ethical priorities that guide all policies and activities of the school. As such, there must be consensus (i.e., everyone in the group must support the statements). There are two phases in the process of developing belief statements: The first involves generating the list of beliefs (brainstorming); the second involves selecting from the list. It is important to separate these two parts of the process.

Statement of Program Goals

Goals are expressions of the desired outcomes of a conflict resolution education program in the school. The goals guide the setting of priorities and the allocation of resources and provide the framework for program evaluation. Goals are aspirations and intentions. Sample goals include the following:

1. To enable students to take responsibility for peacefully resolving disputes without the intervention of staff

2. To provide all individuals in the school with the problem-solving skills of conflict resolution—negotiation, mediation, and group problem solving

3. To increase the ability of students to deal effectively with issues of cultural and social diversity

4. To prevent disputes from escalating into incidents requiring disciplinary actions

5. To design a behavior management plan with reasonable and clear behavioral expectations that is consistent with and promotes the conflict resolution education program and that is accepted as fair and effective by all constituencies of the school

6. To create a school climate characterized by cooperation and collaboration

Faculty should develop statements of program goals, with a few of the preceding examples as guides. A strategy for generating goals might be to organize into job-alike groups (e.g., administrators, support staff, core-subject teachers, teachers of elective courses) and have each group come up with three or four goals. The total faculty would then cluster, modify, and adapt these goals to build a consensus list.

After goal statements have been clarified, it is important to poll faculty as to whether they support the idea of developing a peaceable schools program. Faculty support is required to go forward with implementation. It is not required that each faculty member commit to direct involvement in the program, but nearly all must agree to support the program at least minimally. Minimal support means the staff member agrees to implement rights and responsibilities.

Shared Vision Statement

The program team, using the beliefs and goals generated by the staff, develops a vision statement for the peaceable school program that builds upon the vision statement in the introduction of this guide (see p. 1).

> Shared vision is a verbal representation of what is observable within the school when a critical mass of the adults and students are using conflict resolution to live day to day in the school environment. Shared vision paints a picture of how the school will look and feel when the mission is operational. Following is a sample shared vision statement:
>
> We see our school as:
>
> > A learning environment exemplified by happy, friendly, busy, caring individuals who are sharing, communicating, creating, helping, and encouraging.
> >
> > A friendly, orderly, inviting, and comfortable place characterized by mutual respect, acceptance of differences, and cooperation.
> >
> > A peaceable, harmonious community with a welcoming, inviting environment that is educationally enriching and challenging, where all students are reaching their potential.
>
> We see each person taking ownership for his or her learning and developing a sense of belonging to, and pride in, our school community. (Bodine & Crawford, 1998, p. 163)

Along with the belief statement, the shared vision provides a relatively clear way to communicate to all school constituencies. This is an important consideration in Phase 5, "Support Initiatives." Whereas the goals statement often uses language specific to educators, the belief statement and the shared vision statement communicate in a more general fashion and may be more meaningful to students and to those not directly involved in the management of the day-to-day functioning of the school.

Develop Timeline for Program Implementation

Implementing a successful peaceable school program requires further planning. After reaching consensus for program development, the next responsibility for the program team is to develop a timeline for program implementation in collaboration with school staff. It is not essential to implement Phase 3, "Development of the Sense-Based Behavior Management System," before implementing Phase 4, "Conflict Resolution Education." Doing Phase 4 first may better meet faculty interests, whereas Phase 3 can be very controversial and thus very time-consuming. Furthermore, success in Phase 4 may well stimulate the desire to develop the sense-based behavior system when adults actually observe that students can learn and use conflict resolution processes. This is a decision the program team can make with the input of staff. To fully realize the impact of the peaceable school concept, all phases must be addressed eventually. The sample program implementation timeline shown in Table 13 will help the program team guide the staff through the crucial steps.

PHASE 3: DEVELOPMENT OF THE SENSE-BASED BEHAVIOR MANAGEMENT SYSTEM

Each individual, student and adult, must fully understand the behavioral expectations of the school and the classroom. Such understanding is simplified when those expectations make sense; this is especially critical for students. Expectations make sense when there is a logical, age-appropriate explanation for their existence; when rules are few and simple; when expectations are predictable and can be applied to new situations; and when the consequences for inappropriate behavior are known, nonpunitive, and consistently applied. The rights and responsibilities concept is understandable to students because it is based on a logical system of thought—a system that also happens to be fundamental to our democratic traditions. Rules within such a framework simply serve to let everyone know his or her responsibilities and safeguard the rights of all: In other words, rules make explicit the relationship between responsibilities and rights. Such a logical and fundamentally simple notion provides students with a framework they can use even without adult intervention to determine what is and what is not acceptable behavior. This type of independent assessment is crucial to the development of responsible behavior. In brief, the sense-based system for determining acceptable and unacceptable behavior reduces rule confusion and concerns regarding the uniform enforcement of rules.

Establish Rights and Responsibilities

Rights and responsibilities provide the foundation for expectations of quality behavior and for the elimination of coercion in the management process, the principal element in building the peaceable climate. School faculty, lead by the program team, work together to develop the rights and responsibilities statement for the school. Because a total commitment to the rights and responsibilities is critical to building a peaceable climate, total staff involvement in establishing the school rights and responsibilities is required.

One strategy, likely the most expeditious, is to start with the Rights and Responsibilities prototype (see Section 1, Table 2). The group decides which rights to delete from the prototype and/or which rights to add. If a right is deleted, so is the related responsibility; if a right is added, the related responsibility must also be stated. Important questions are as follows: Do these rights and responsibilities, in a general way, encompass what the staff members believe are the necessary rules for behavior? (In other words, are there rules in the present system that do not fit the rights and responsibilities format?) If yes, are those rules necessary in a noncoercive system? If yes, what justification for those rules will make sense to students?

TABLE 13   Sample Program Implementation Timeline

Goal	Date

1. Build the peaceable climate

Establish rights and responsibilities. _____

Develop school rules and consequences. _____

Implement the responsibility education program. _____

Implement the sense-based behavior management program. _____

2. Conduct conflict resolution education

Establish conflict resolution space. _____

Teach understanding of conflict. _____

Teach understanding of peace and peacemaking. _____

Teach and implement mediation. _____

Teach and implement negotiation. _____

Teach and implement group problem solving. _____

3. Develop program support initiatives

Design and execute peaceable school awareness campaign. _____

Establish peer mediation program. _____

Provide peaceable school orientation for parents
and community. _____

Provide conflict resolution skill development workshops
for parents. _____

4. Execute quality improvement

Evaluate program progress and impact. _____

Provide ongoing staff training and technical assistance. _____

Provide ongoing student training and integration of curricula. _____

Another strategy is to approach the task as a step-by-step creative process from an unencumbered perspective. The group begins by brainstorming two lists (remember, the brainstorming process should be free of evaluation), following these steps:

1. List all the privileges or freedoms that you believe individuals should be able to experience.

2. List all the responsibilities—a way one is always expected to behave, something one is always expected to do—that individuals are expected to perform.

3. Combine the two lists by matching any related rights and responsibilities, using the two-column format exhibited for the prototype (see Table 2).

4. List any leftover rights in the left column, and generate a responsibility statement for each.

5. List any leftover responsibilities in the right column, and generate a rights statement for each.

6. Eliminate any rights or responsibilities that would not apply to everyone.

7. Combine statements where appropriate.

A third strategy, likely the most cumbersome, is to approach the task as a step-by-step process of reconstruction. The group examines the school's present discipline policy and behavioral expectations and constructs two lists from what is gleaned from the examination—one list written as rights, the other as responsibilities. These two lists are used to complete Steps 3 through 7, as just described for the second strategy. If any part of the present discipline policy cannot be reconstructed as rights and responsibilities, that part of the present policy requires further consideration. What remains of the present policy may be specific rules not easily reconstituted as rights and responsibilities.

The goal is to have a relatively small number of general statements with broad application. For example, rights and responsibilities for a school apply to the youngest students as well as to the oldest students, to adults as well as to students. The goal is not to cover every conceivable circumstance but to generally define expectations for all conceivable circumstances. Rights and responsibilities are not rules but a framework under which specific rules could fit. Rights and responsibilities are designed to imply behavioral expectations, not to make all behavioral expectations explicit.

Develop School Rules and Consequences

In addition to the general school constitution—rights and responsibilities—it is prudent to develop staff consensus on the most undesirable behaviors, those the school would target to extinguish. These select few behaviors, whether presently exhibited or not, would have a profoundly negative impact on the school climate. Although these behaviors may differ from school to school, most schools probably could focus on some or all of the following objectionable behaviors: (a) fighting or attacking, (b) stealing and property defacement or destruction, (c) intimidation or extortion, (d) harassment, and (e) aggressive acts toward school employees. The school should have a plan involving all available resources to deal with the selected behaviors consistently and at every occurrence. The plan for doing so should be clearly communicated to all learners and all other constituents.

Targeting highly undesirable behaviors will likely give rise to some specific all-school rules to govern behavior. A rule is a statement that attempts either to clarify the relationship between a right and a responsibility or to emphasize the importance of a particular responsibility. To be consistent with the management plan advocated here, rules generated must meet the "rules for rules" (see Section 1, pp. 33–34)

Breaking a rule results in a consequence. In a noncoercive management system, the logical consequence that is always applicable in all circumstances for each individual is the requirement to choose another behavior that is acceptable within the social context—in other words, a responsible behavior. If it is deemed, through the consensus process of constructing the management system, that additional consequences are appropriate, those consequences must not be punitive or coercive. They also must be logical consequences. The characteristics of logical consequences are as follows:

1. They are known in advance.

2. They do not cause physical pain and do not involve public humiliation.

3. They are related to the problem behavior.

Two strategies exist for identifying problem behaviors and generating the rules needed to communicate the importance of behaving appropriately in these areas. The creative process from the unencumbered perspective is to brainstorm problem behaviors and then to prioritize the four or five targeted. The reconstruction strategy might involve examining that part of the present discipline policy that does not fit into the rights and responsibilities framework. Is the leftover part necessary? If yes, what is the justification? Does the leftover policy focus on behaviors to target? Are these the four or five most important behaviors to target?

It is important to acknowledge that schools are a part of a larger community and society. That which is clearly illegal in the larger community and society is also illegal in school; therefore, schools do not need their own rules about possession of illegal substances or drugs or weapons. Legal consequences exist for such behaviors; schools should involve community resources and authorities whenever these behaviors are manifested in the school. Examples of these behaviors and their consequences are listed in Table 14.

A consensus agreement among the staff is also required regarding what constitutes acceptable learner behavior and what strategies to employ to help learners display acceptable behavior. This consensus is built upon the notion that each learner is doing the best the learner knows how to do to meet his or her basic psychological needs for belonging, power, freedom, and fun. If, in the judgment of the adults in the school, the learner's behavior is unacceptable, the adults are responsible for assisting the learner, through a self-evaluation/planning process, to choose an acceptable behavior. (See discussion in Section 1 of class meetings, life rules, CARE time, time-out, and STAR plans).

TABLE 14   Consequences for Targeted Inappropriate Behaviors

Targeted Inappropriate Behavior	Consequence
Fighting or attacking	Parents or guardians will be notified. Fighter or attacker will be assigned to in-school suspension. Student will meet with designated staff member to develop a plan to behave constructively and appropriately under similar future circumstances. Repeat of the behavior in the near future may result in out-of-school suspension.
Stealing or property damage	Parents or guardians will be notified. Student will replace or pay for the replacement of the missing or damaged items. If unable to pay, student will provide community service to the school in lieu of payment. Student will meet with designated staff member to develop a plan to behave constructively and appropriately under similar future circumstances.
Harassment	Parents or guardians will be notified. Perpetrator will be assigned to in-school suspension. Student will meet with designated staff member to develop a plan to behave constructively and appropriately under similar future circumstances. Perpetrator/victim mediation may be considered. Repeat of the behavior in the near future may result in out-of-school suspension.
Aggression toward staff	Parents or guardians will be notified. Aggressor will be assigned to in-school suspension. Student will meet with designated staff member to develop a plan to behave constructively and appropriately under similar future circumstances. Repeat of the behavior in the near future may result in out-of-school suspension.

The school rights and responsibilities, consensus about unacceptable behaviors, consensus about acceptable behaviors, and the strategies to use to help learners display acceptable behaviors provide a framework for the behavior management system. Everyone is unified by these behavioral expectations at all times. Once the basic framework is agreed upon, strategies must be developed to inform all school clients (students, parents, guardians, staff, etc.) about the rights and responsibilities, school rules, expectations, and consequences for inappropriate behavior.

Develop Classroom and Special Area Rules

Again following the rules for rules, special-circumstance rules are generated. These rules, unlike the school rules, may apply only in some circumstances and not in others. The rules may be different for the cafeteria than for the gymnasium, for the science laboratory than for the library, for the kindergarten classroom than for the fifth-grade classroom, and so forth. All these rules, justified by the rights and responsibilities, define what behaviors are emphasized in that particular setting. Some examples are shown in Table 15.

There should be staff consensus on how many rules are appropriate and how these rules are to be developed, discussed, and implemented. However, these rules are best developed by the individuals responsible for the space. It is recommended that student input be utilized in constructing these rules.

Build a Responsibility Education Program

It is insufficient merely to inform students about rights and responsibilities, rules and consequences. Developing an effective behavior management program that is in concert with the philosophy and the principles of conflict resolution involves more than the creation of rights and responsibilities and sense-based rules. The program also provides a plan to educate students about expectations and about the processes available for choosing appropriate behaviors. These instructional activities for responsibility education—especially group discussions in the format of the class meeting—are scheduled regularly and constitute the most important element of the social and emotional education program of the school and classroom. The discussions are designed to help learners gain understanding about their behavior and about the effect that behavior has on others. Learners are also exposed to alternative behaviors. Failure of the entire school to devote adequate time to the process of social education will result in a school characterized by disciplinary concerns. Behavior problems will largely be the result of individuals attempting to do the best they know how to do in situations where they are either uncertain as to what is expected or where they believe the expectations to be unreasonable and capricious. Individuals will follow a rule if it is known and if it is seen as in their best interest—that is, it is need satisfying.

The activities of Section 1 are the basis for teaching the concepts of rights and responsibilities, rules and consequences.

Section 1: Training Activities
for Building a Peaceable Climate

1. Introduction

2. Responsibility Is . . .

3. What Is a Right?

4. Rights and Responsibilities

5. Rules

6. Cooperation Is . . .

7. What's in the Box?

8. Key Concept Review

TABLE 15   Special-Circumstance Rules and Consequences

Location	Rule	Consequence (for failing to follow the rule)
Cafeteria	When in line, stay within your own space.	You will be placed at the end of the line.
Cafeteria	Clean up after yourself in the space you use.	You will be required to return and clean up your area plus at least one other area.
Gym	Include all willing participants; encourage others.	You will be excluded from participation until you have a plan to follow the rule.
Library	Return all materials you use to the circulation desk.	You will be denied unsupervised library privileges until you have a plan to comply with the rule.
Classroom	During class discussions, the person talking will have the undivided attention of everyone in the class.	You will be asked to make a plan immediately to attend or go to time-out until you have such a plan.

The questions for class meetings in the overview of Section 1 suggest topics for discussion to educate learners about the important climate issues of the peaceable school.

PHASE 4: CONFLICT RESOLUTION EDUCATION

The knowledge base presented in Section 2 ("Understanding Conflict") and Section 3 ("Understanding Peace and Peacemaking") is prerequisite to the successful use of the three conflict resolution strategies presented in Sections 4, 5, and 6. Students must understand conflict and peace to become fully effective mediators, negotiators, or group problem solvers.

Once a sufficient knowledge base has been established, the conflict resolution strategies of mediation, negotiation, and group problem solving may be presented in any order. Because the steps in the three strategies are parallel, training in one strategy will likely make training in another that much easier. However, special instruction for each approach is required regardless of proficiency in a previously learned approach.

Although the strategies may be taught in any order, it may be easier for students to focus on the basic steps of the conflict resolution process if they are first trained as mediators. The process of training in any of the conflict resolution strategies involves immersing learners in conflict situations and allowing them to work to resolve the conflict. The purpose of training is to develop facility with the resolution process. Therefore, the goal is to focus learners' attention on the process and away from the actual problem. Mediators are neutral third parties in a dispute; human nature allows one to be more objective when not emotionally involved in a situation. If students experience difficulty with the negotiation or group problem solving strategy, it may be because they are too involved in the conflict to focus effectively on the process.

Once the goals of the peaceable school have been fully realized, the problem-solving strategies maintain the peaceable climate. Group problem solving will become the forum for resolving conflicts among groups of students, and negotiation will become the strategy of choice for resolving disputes between individual students. Mediation will become a backup strategy for use when disputants have difficulty solving their problems without assistance. Regardless of the approach students choose, the goal of the peaceable school remains the same—to empower students to resolve conflicts on their own.

Establish Conflict Resolution Space

Designate a place in the classroom for "peace talks." This space not only provides a location for mediations and negotiations to take place, it also sends a message that conflicts are a natural part of life in the classroom and that positive ways exist to deal with them. A "peace center" or "peace corner" within the classroom allows disputants to sit face-to-face to conduct mediations and negotiations while other classroom activities proceed.

Teach Understanding of Conflict

Lesson plans for activities designed to develop a shared understanding of the nature and causes of conflict and the range of responses and respective outcomes of those responses are presented in Section 2. The basic needs activities enable the individual to understand his or her behavior as choices over which he or she has control. In conflict situations, every individual can choose to behave differently.

Section 2: Training Activities for Understanding Conflict

1. Conflict Is . . .

2. Conflict Collage

3. Basic Needs

4. Enough Is Not Enough

5. Different Values

6. Origins of Conflict

7. What's My Response?

8. Soft, Hard, or Principled Responses

9. Getting to Win-Win

10. Conflict Review

11. Negative-Positive

12. Key Concept Review

Teach Understanding of Peace and Peacemaking

Lesson plans for activities designed to help students learn about peace, peacemaking, and the principles of conflict resolution are presented in Section 3. Nearly all of the foundation abilities described in this guide's introduction are taught through the activities in Section 3.

Section 3: Training Activities for Understanding Peace and Peacemaking

1. Peace Is . . .

2. Peace Collage

3. Peacemaking and Peacebreaking

4. Making Peace

5. Perceptions

6. Emotions

7. Communication: Active Listening

8. Communication: Active Listening Practice

9. Communication: Sending Clear Messages

10. Focusing on Interests, Not Positions

11. Inventing Options for Mutual Gain

12. Using Fair Criteria

13. Key Concept Review

Teach and Implement Mediation

In the classroom mediation program, everyone is trained in mediation. Students as young as third grade have shown the ability and sophistication to serve as co-mediators in the classroom; younger students, from kindergarten through second grade, are able to participate in mediations led by the teacher. Lesson plans for mediation training are provided in Section 4.

Section 4: Training Activities for Mediation

1. Mediation Is . . .

2. Role of the Mediator

3. Overview of the Mediation Process

4. Step 1: Agree to Mediate

5. Step 2: Gather Points of View

6. Step 3: Focus on Interests

7. Step 4: Create Win-Win Options

8. Step 5: Evaluate Options

9. Step 6: Create an Agreement

10. Putting It All Together

11. Key Concept Review

Mediation is voluntary. Students may request mediation when they are involved in a dispute, or teachers and administrators may refer them. The teacher coordinates mediation in the classroom, and a committee of students may be appointed to assist. Sample forms for the mediation program appear in Appendix D; these may be adapted according to the needs of the particular classroom.

When conducting actual mediations, mediators should have access to a page listing the steps in the process (see p. 201 in this guide; p. 75 in the Student Manual). The steps in the process can also be listed on a poster prominently displayed in the peace center. Mediators thus do not need to memorize the steps or the questions involved in each step; the poster also helps focus the attention of the disputants.

Because the mediation process is difficult, the use of co-mediators is highly recommended for all ages (see Section 4 for detailed discussion). Co-mediation is a must at the elementary level.

The teacher or an adult should be physically present in the room during all mediations conducted at the elementary level. For older students, it may be sufficient for the adult to be available to help if mediators feel it is necessary.

Teach and Implement Negotiation

As noted earlier, it may be easier for students to be successful in the unassisted conflict resolution strategy of negotiation if they have first been trained as mediators. Having experienced a parallel conflict resolution process as a disinterested third party can help students be more objective when the conflict concerns themselves. Lesson plans for negotiation training are provided in Section 5.

Section 5: Training Activities for Negotiation

1. Negotiation Is . . .

2. Role of the Negotiator

3. Overview of the Negotiation Process

4. Step 1: Agree to Negotiate

5. Step 2: Gather Points of View

6. Step 3: Focus on Interests

7. Step 4: Create Win-Win Options

8. Step 5: Evaluate Options

9. Step 6: Create an Agreement

10. Putting It All Together

11. Key Concept Review

Negotiation can be a powerful tool, especially within a classroom when all of the students have been trained in the process and related skills. Likewise, the greater the number of students in a school familiar with negotiation, the more effective the approach and the greater the impact on the overall school climate.

Once students are familiar with the negotiation process, when a dispute erupts in the classroom, they may proceed to negotiate at that moment or agree to meet later. A negotiation center or peace center within the classroom allows disputants to sit face-to-face to conduct the negotiation while other classroom activities proceed. Those who wish to negotiate disputes on the playground, in the lunchroom, in the halls, or elsewhere would simply find a place to talk.

Like mediation, negotiation is voluntary. A student may request negotiation with another student when a dispute arises by making a specific request:

> I'm having a problem with what you are doing. Could we talk about it now?

> I'm really upset with you. Can I tell you about it?

> I believe we have a problem. Can we try to work it out?

> I think you're mad at me. Can we talk?

Negotiation may also be suggested to disputing students by teachers, administrators, parents, or other students. When suggested by others, the person making the suggestion is responsible for checking out whether the disputants wish to negotiate and can do so at the moment or whether they need to wait until they are in better control of their emotions.

While negotiating, students should have access to a page listing the steps in the process (see p. 242 in this guide; p. 97 in the Student Manual). The steps in the process can also be listed on a poster displayed prominently in the peace center.

As mentioned, in the school in which students have been trained in both negotiation and mediation, it is likely that negotiation will be the first strategy students employ to resolve problems. Although the unassisted negotiation strategy is most consistent with the peaceable school's goal for students to resolve conflicts independently, it is important to note that students may choose mediation instead of negotiation in their attempt to resolve conflicts. If students are unsuccessful at solving a problem with negotiation, mediation is the next logical choice. The choice of strategy is an individual one, with the primary goal being for disputants to resolve conflicts peaceably. As students become increasingly familiar with and skilled in the negotiation strategy, the more comfortable they will be attempting to solve their difficulties without outside help, either by adults or peers.

Although forms are probably not necessary for all negotiations, a negotiation agreement form like the sample in Appendix D may be useful in a classroom peace center.

Teach and Implement Group Problem Solving

Group problem solving is the most complex of the conflict resolution strategies because of the dynamics created by the number of individuals involved. However, because the teacher normally orchestrates the strategy, it is perhaps the easiest to implement. For this reason, this strategy may be implemented before mediation or negotiation. To get started, a class should experience all of the activities in Section 6.

Section 6: Training Activities for Group Problem Solving

1. Group Cohesiveness and Cooperation

2. Consensus Decision Making

3. Group Problem Solving Is . . .

4. Role of the Group Problem Solver

5. Understanding Group Problem Solving Rules

6. Overview and Steps 1–3

7. Steps 4–6

8. Key Concept Review

In addition to familiarity with the group problem solving approach and basic communication skills, students also must have a clear understanding of the ground rules for the group problem solving meeting. In the group, each student has, at minimum, the responsibility to tell the group his or her view of the problem under consideration. It is useful for each group member to view himself or herself in partnership with the other members in trying to solve the problem. Successful group problem solving meetings are conducted in a tight circle seating arrangement—all members can make eye contact with all other members, and no physical obstructions exist within the circle.

Once these basics are established, the teacher will be able to conduct successful group problem solving meetings. When training is complete, students will require less guidance. Successful participation in group problem solving and regular use of the strategy will help strengthen students' skills.

Group problem solving provides a forum for considering and resolving specific issues in the classroom. In addition, regular use of the strategy sends the message that the teacher believes students' problems exist and that their ideas about those problems are important to the class. Allowing students to help determine which problems will be selected for discussion further underscores the message that students can use their minds to solve the problems of living in their school world. The placement of a problem jar or box in the room, in which anyone can place a topic for consideration, is a good way for the teacher to learn about students' concerns. The teacher can then determine the topics for group problem solving meetings by reviewing the contents of the jar or box, by listening to concerns students express verbally, and by observing student behavior.

As students learn more about conflict and the process of peace and peacemaking, and as they gain an appreciation for the relationship between rights and responsibilities, they will become better group problem solvers.

PHASE 5: SUPPORT INITIATIVES

Design and Execute Peaceable School Awareness Campaign

Advertising and promotional campaigns help increase youth and faculty support for the peaceable school initiatives. Such efforts are fun for students and can help establish the expectation that conflicts can be resolved peaceably. Signs, posters, buttons, banners, pencils, T-shirts, and the like with reminders to use mediation, negotiation, and group problem solving help establish a peaceable school climate. Banners, signs, and posters are particularly useful in those areas of the school where the potential for conflict is high—lunchroom, playground, halls, rest rooms, gym, and so on. Some possible messages include the following:

Caution—Work-It-Out Zone

Win-Win With "N" and "M"

Think Peace—Negotiate!

Have You Made Peace Today?

Talk It Out—Shift Happens

Got a Problem? ME-D-8!

PEACE Power

T-shirts or buttons proclaiming, "I'm a Peacemaker" may be given to students in recognition of their peacemaking efforts. A different student could be recognized in each classroom as "Peacemaker of the Week." School public address announcements promoting the peaceable school program can also raise awareness and give the program legitimacy. The options are endless.

Establish Peer Mediation Program

The implementation of a schoolwide peer mediation program provides an ongoing strategy to sustain the peaceable school. Mediation in the context of a schoolwide program is available to all students for conflicts that may occur outside of the classroom setting. Sample program forms are shown in Appendix D; these may be adapted according to the needs of the particular school.

A schoolwide peer mediation program employs a limited number of students to provide mediation services outside the classroom. Before selecting mediators, it is essential to introduce the student body to the opportunities mediation presents. Student orientation provides an overview of the program, generates student interest and support, describes the schoolwide role of peer mediators, and helps recruit peer mediators through student nominations and applications. Following the orientation, Mediator Application and Mediator Student Nomination Forms are distributed (see Appendix D for samples). Any interested student may apply or make nominations.

Selecting Mediators

When selecting the cadre of peer mediators, it is important that the group represent the diversity of the student population in terms of race, gender, school achievement, behavior, extracurricular interests, group membership, and residential neighborhood. If only those with exemplary school behavior and high academic achievement are selected, many students will not see the program as representing their peer group and therefore will not choose to participate in mediation. Personal qualifications of student mediators include the following:

> Respect of peers
>
> Skill in communication
>
> Leadership ability
>
> Sense of responsibility
>
> Trustworthiness and fairness
>
> Empathy

Staff members may nominate peer mediators by completing the Mediator Staff Nomination form (Appendix D). Particular faculty—such as social workers, counselors, and disciplinarians—can be especially helpful in focusing their nominations to ensure a representative cross section of students.

The value of student input in the selection of mediators is twofold: First, students feel ownership of the program from the outset. Second, it is likely that peers will name some students who would not otherwise be identified. Students who are nominated by their peers or by faculty are encouraged to complete an application form if they have not done so prior to their nomination. Obviously, participation is voluntary.

Once application forms are complete, student mediators are selected. One of the more effective selection processes is a lottery. The advantage of selection by lottery is mainly that students typically perceive the lottery process as an opportunity and not a personal risk. More students will chance applying to become mediators if the selection criteria are random than if judges make the selection in a criterion-driven process. If the first experience a student has with the peer mediation program is one of rejection, the student may avoid participation in the mediation process. This rejection can potentially spread from individuals to groups of peers who refuse to participate in mediation.

For the lottery process to work appropriately, it must include a system to ensure proper representation of the diversity of the school. This system is a "controlled lottery," or actually several lotteries. For example:

1. To generate gender balance, separate the candidates into male and female groups and draw an equal number.

2. To reflect the school's racial composition, first draw from the minority pool the minimum number of candidates to guarantee a representative group.

3. Place all remaining minority candidates in the general pool and continue to draw until the total number of mediators is determined.

If desired, the pool may be separated by grade level or other criteria to ensure other types of diversity.

Selection may also be done by the program team or the program team in conjunction with others. With these methods, the nomination and application forms are reviewed and evaluated. Prospective mediators may also be interviewed by the program team or program coordinator(s) before being finally selected.

Depending on the size of the school, it is recommended that between 20 and 40 students be selected to be peer mediators. The goal is to have enough mediators so that it will not be a burden for them to miss class and other school activities but not to have so many that trainees only infrequently mediate, thus reducing their opportunities to gain skill through practice. Twenty to 40 mediators can handle several hundred mediation requests per school year.

After the schoolwide mediators have been selected, the principal may officially notify and congratulate them. The program coordinator(s) then notify the students' parents or guardians and obtain parental permission for their participation. Either before beginning training or at the first training session, mediators are expected to sign a Mediator Application Form (see Appendix D), which spells out the terms of mediators' training and service. A sample Parent/Guardian Permission Letter is also presented in this appendix.

Basic Training Activities for Peer Mediators

Following selection, the prospective mediators participate in training. Basic peer mediation training requires approximately 12 hours. It is recommended that the training for elementary students be scheduled in four half-day sessions, with those days either scheduled consecutively or at least within a 2-week period. For middle school and older students, the training can be accomplished in two consecutive full days.

Because the students selected for training may not all be well acquainted and because they will work together closely during training, each training session should start with an activity designed to create interaction, allow participants to learn about one another, and promote group cohesiveness. Appropriate activities are described in Section 6, Activity 1: "Where Do I Belong?" (Exercise 1) and "Find Someone Who . . ." (Exercise 2).

Initial training activities and the appropriate sequence for training are detailed here. Unless otherwise indicated, you should conduct the entire activity. If time is short, you may abbreviate certain activities by conducting only the steps listed. (These numbered steps appear under the "Procedure" heading for each activity.)

Section 2: Understanding Conflict

Conflict Is . . . (Activity 1)

Basic Needs (Activity 3)

Enough Is Not Enough (Activity 4)

Different Values (Activity 5; Steps 1–3 and 6–8)

What's My Response? (Activity 7; Steps 1, 3, and 5)

Soft, Hard, or Principled Responses (Activity 8)

Getting to Win-Win (Activity 9)

Negative-Positive (Activity 11; Steps 6 and 7)

Section 3: Understanding Peace and Peacemaking

Peace Is . . . (Activity 1; Steps 1 and 4–6)

Peacemaking and Peacebreaking (Activity 3; Steps 2–7)

Making Peace (Activity 4)

Perceptions (Activity 5; Steps 1–3 and 7)

Communication: Active Listening (Activity 7)

Communication: Active Listening Practice (Activity 8; Steps 1–5 and 9)

Focusing on Interests, Not Positions (Activity 10)

Inventing Options for Mutual Gain (Activity 11)

Using Fair Criteria (Activity 12)

Section 4: Mediation

Mediation Is . . . (Activity 1)

Role of the Mediator (Activity 2)

Overview of the Mediation Process (Activity 3)

Step 1: Agree to Mediate (Activity 4)

Step 2: Gather Points of View (Activity 5)

Step 3: Focus on Interests (Activity 6)

Step 4: Create Win-Win Options (Activity 7)

Step 5: Evaluate Options (Activity 8)

Step 6: Create an Agreement (Activity 9)

Putting It All Together (Activity 10)

This training outline assumes that the participants have no prior conflict resolution education experience. If the program has already been implemented in the classrooms and the future mediators have already been exposed to Sections 2, 3, and 4, the training may be reduced to one day. Following a brief review of Section 2 and Section 3, the day would be devoted to mediation training through simulated conflicts.

Provide Peaceable School Orientation for Parents and Community

Parent and community involvement is a necessary and important part of program development. A parent group, community organization, service club, or police department may form a partnership with the school to sponsor peaceable school activities. An evening and/or lunch meeting can provide these supporters with an overview of the program and an opportunity to discuss the benefits of peaceful problem solving. Parents and other community members often want to learn more about the conflict resolution processes after such an informational meeting. Offering an educational series for interested community members broadens program support and encourages volunteers who might help with the training and other program activities. Trained students can play an integral part in these orientation efforts by demonstrating their skills in conflict resolution simulations.

Provide Conflict Resolution Skill Development Workshops for Parents

Workshops for parents interested in conflict resolution training support the potential for students to apply conflict resolution strategies in the home. A 4-hour workshop may be conducted in one session or divided into two 2-hour sessions. The purpose of the parent workshop is to help parents develop a common understanding of conflict, understand the principles of conflict resolution, and learn how to apply the principles of conflict resolution in the home. Students can assist in such training, and their participation may help ensure parental involvement.

The agenda for parent workshops includes the following subjects:

Understanding conflict

Responses to conflict

Origins of conflict

Principles of conflict resolution

Conflict resolution strategies in the home

PHASE 6: QUALITY IMPROVEMENT

Evaluate Program Progress and Impact

Evaluation provides the information needed to plan for continual improvement in program quality. In addition, evaluation can build substantive evidence of program efficacy. Evaluation of the peaceable school program may involve an uncomplicated design that the program team assimilate into their responsibilities, or there may be a more complex experimental design carried out by researchers. Because schools typically do not have the financial or human resources to conduct an elaborate program evaluation, a simple plan for program evaluation is described here.

With the assistance of students and teachers, the program team monitors the number of mediations, negotiations, and group problem solving sessions; types of conflicts; source of requests; location where conflicts materialized; attributes of disputants; and outcomes of conflict resolution strategy. The Conflict Resolution Record Form (see Appendix D) is an efficient form for gathering information.

The primary goal of the peaceable school program is to bring about changes in students' and educators' attitudes and behavior concerning conflict and approaches to resolution. The program team conducts preassessments and postassessments to determine whether or not changes are taking place. The Preprogram Student Assessment, Preprogram Staff Assessment, Postprogram Student Assessment, and Postprogram Staff Assessment instruments are designed to assess the impact of the peaceable school program. (Copies of all these instruments appear in Appendix D.) All staff and students should complete the preassessments at the same time the needs assessment is being conducted (i.e., during Phase 1 of program development). The postassessments should be conducted at least 6 months after the program has been in place. For staff, forms could be distributed during a staff meeting. It will take staff approximately 5 minutes to complete each form. For students, forms could be distributed, completed, and collected during a class period in which every student in the school will be present. It will take students approximately 10 minutes to complete each form.

Provide Ongoing Staff Training and Technical Assistance

It is recommended that staff meet regularly as a group with the program team. Ideally, meetings are held twice monthly for about 1 hour each. A portion of that time may be used for the staff to share experiences and take turns presenting conflicts that illustrate particular challenges and issues. The remaining time may be used to extend the staff training. This training may involve a review of aspects of the basic training and/or provide more advanced training.

Developing Emotional Intelligence: A Guide to Behavior Management and Conflict Resolution in Schools (Bodine & Crawford, 1999) extends and amplifies the concepts introduced in Section 1 of this program guide.

Provide Ongoing Student Training and Integration of Curricula

Ongoing developmentally appropriate learning experiences and integration of conflict resolution concepts, skills, and processes into the curricula are practical strategies for ensuring that all students in a school will learn how to manage conflicts constructively.

The activities presented in Sections 1, 2, and 3 of this guide may be conducted more than once to reinforce the basic principles underlying conflict resolution. Each time and/or each year that students experience these activities it will be at a new level of understanding and experience.

The developmental sequence shown in Table 16 provides guideposts for learning about and developing proficiency in conflict resolution. The sequence is not intended to be an all-inclusive representation of conflict resolution education. The crucial consideration is not the age but the developmental stage of the student. If the student has not developed the proficiencies expected for someone younger, the development of those proficiencies must be addressed through age-appropriate learning experiences.

Literature, social studies, and thematic units of instruction at all grade levels include numerous examples of unresolved conflict and provide abundant opportunity to integrate conflict resolution into academic curricula. Integrating conflict resolution training into academic subject matter involves identifying examples of conflicts and applying group problem solving, negotiation, and mediation procedures to resolve the conflict; focusing on concepts such as perceptions or basic needs to understand the conflict; or practicing communication skills when discussing the issues. The integration and learning opportunities are numerous. When integrating conflict resolution into the curriculum, keep in mind that learning must go beyond thinking and talking about conflicts, causes, and solutions. Cumulative practice resolving conflicts also must occur. Academic curricula may provide the substance for students to engage in such practice.

Table 16   Conflict Resolution Developmental Sequence

	EARLY CHILDHOOD–GRADE 2	GRADES 3–5	GRADES 6–8	GRADES 9–12
Orientation Abilities	Understands that having conflicts is natural; knows that involvement in conflicts is all right.	Understands that conflict is inevitable and that it can be a positive force for growth.	Recognizes that the sources of conflict and the problem-solving processes of conflict resolution are applicable to all types of conflicts: interpersonal, intergroup, and international.	Maintains a variety of good working relationships with parents, family, siblings, boyfriends, girlfriends, teachers, acquaintances, bosses, and so on.
	Knows conflicts can be solved through cooperation.	Understands that conflicts can become better or worse, depending upon the chosen response.		Analyzes conflict in the context of a present relationship and uses an appropriate problem-solving strategy.
	Differentiates between prejudice and dislike.	Understands and recognizes soft, hard, and principled responses to conflicts.	Diagnoses conflicts appropriately and selects conflict resolution strategies for conflicts in various settings (school, home, neighborhood, etc.).	Recognizes patterns in his or her responses to conflict and strives for positive growth and change in those patterns.
	Views peace as a desired condition and can identify several peacemaking and peacebreaking behaviors.	Participates in cooperative endeavors.		
		Recognizes prejudice in self and in the actions of others.	Exhibits effective responses to another who, in a shared conflict, chooses a soft or hard response.	Understands that conflict resolution skills are life skills.
		Understands own behavior in terms of the need for belonging, power, freedom, and fun.	Takes action to inform when prejudice is displayed.	Confronts prejudice effectively in self and others and in the school as an institution.
		Understands peace as a personal action; differentiates between peacemaking and peacebreaking behaviors in self and others.	Suggests a peacemaking action as an alternative to a displayed peacebreaking action.	Promotes equal access and opportunity on many fronts.
				Seeks diverse and multicultural experiences and relationships.
				Works actively to promote peace in the school and in the community.

Perception Abilities	Accepts that he or she is not always "right." Accepts that others may see things differently. Describes a conflict from own perspective and from the point of view of others. Withholds blame.	Identifies and checks own assumptions about a situation. Understands how others perceive words and actions. Empathizes and accepts the feelings and perceptions of others. Analyzes a conflict from the perspective of unmet basic psychological needs. Understands friendships and good working relationships and strives to build and maintain them. Understands the effects of blaming and accusing behaviors; chooses not to act in that manner.	Recognizes the limitations of own perceptions and understands selective filters that affect seeing and hearing. Identifies and checks assumptions that self and others make about a situation. Possesses a rudimentary understanding of how problem-solving strategies can be influenced. Recognizes the prevalence and glamorization of violence in society. Recognizes that conflict can escalate into violence.	Critically analyzes own perceptions and modifies understanding as new information emerges. Articulates how own words, actions, and emotions are perceived by others. Analyzes how perceptions of others relate to probable intent or purpose. Understands how problem-solving strategies can be influenced, and regularly chooses to exercise positive influence. Prevents escalation of conflicts, even with adults. Helps others recognize the potential for violence and for nonviolent conflict resolution.
Emotion Abilities	Knows that feeling anger, frustration, and fear is all right. Controls anger. Expresses feelings in language that expands beyond happy, sad, glad, or mad. Hears and acknowledges the feelings of others. Does not react to emotional outbursts of others by elevating own emotional response.	Understands own emotions. Understands that others have emotional responses and that those responses may be different from his or her own. Expresses emotions effectively and appropriately. Disagrees without being disagreeable.	Takes responsibility for emotions. Accepts and validates emotions and perceptions of others. Possesses effective strategies for "cooldown" and uses them at appropriate times.	Remains calm and focused on problem solving when confronted by a strong emotional display from another person, including an adult. Prevents conflict escalation and violence effectively by using communication-based conflict resolution strategies.

Note. From *The Handbook of Conflict Resolution Education: A Guide to Building Quality Programs in Schools* (pp. 122–128), by R. J. Bodine & D. K. Crawford, 1998, San Francisco: Jossey-Bass. Copyright © 1998 by John Wiley & Sons. Adapted by permission.

Table 16 (continued)

	EARLY CHILDHOOD–GRADE 2	GRADES 3–5	GRADES 6–8	GRADES 9–12
Communication Abilities	Listens without interruption while another describes an incident or defines the problem, and summarizes what that person has said.	Summarizes the facts and feelings in another person's point of view.	Uses summarizing and clarifying to defuse anger and otherwise de-escalate conflict.	Summarizes positions and interests of others in conflict situations efficiently and accurately.
	Tells what happened by speaking to be understood, using "I" language.	Asks specific clarifying questions to gather more information.	Withholds judgment and is open to persuasion.	Acknowledges the validity of emotions and perspectives of others.
	Uses questions like "How did that make you feel?" and "What happened next?"	Uses appropriate problem-solving phraseology (e.g., using *and* rather than *but* and *we* instead of *I* or *you*).	Is productively persuasive.	Reframes statements of others, removing biased or inflammatory messages to capture the underlying meaning.
	Answers questions about a conflict.	Makes "I" statements rather than "you" statements in expressing points of view.	Tests understanding, listens to understand, and speaks to be understood.	Expresses interests explicitly.
	Uses a conflict resolution vocabulary (e.g., *interests, options, brainstorm, negotiate, point of view,* etc.).	Shows awareness of nonverbal communication by self and by others, especially related to feelings.	Reframes own statements using unbiased and non-inflammatory language.	Uses clarifying questions to uncover "hidden" interests of others.
		Communicates desire for cooperative working relationships.		Possesses a conflict resolution vocabulary (e.g., *position, interests, options, alternatives, consensus, commitment, legitimacy, brainstorm,* etc.) and uses it appropriately.

366

Creative Thinking Abilities			
Describes what is wanted and why it is wanted.	Distinguishes between positions and interests.	Understands that underlying interests, not positions, define the problem in conflict situations.	Evaluates and reconciles positions and interests of self and others in most situations.
Generates ideas for solving a problem.	Identifies interests beyond own position in any situation.	Understands that there are often multiple, unclear, or conflicting interests.	Prioritizes interests and develops a strategy for working toward agreement, focusing on easier issues first (those of mutual concern) and most difficult issues last (those of conflicting concern).
Improves a simple idea.	Separates inventing options from making decisions.	Understands and begins to use analytical tools to diagnose problems.	Articulates mutual interests and reconciles conflicting interests.
	Identifies mutual and compatible interests and creates behavioral options to satisfy those interests.	Uses problem solving for conflicting as well as common or compatible interests.	Switches perspectives to generate new options.
			Manages brainstorming effectively, separating inventing from deciding, and focuses on and advocates for options for mutual gain.
			Brainstorms multiple options in any situation—improving, refining, embellishing, and expanding on existing options.
			Uses various analytical tools to diagnose problems, formulate new approaches, and evaluate the likely effectiveness of those approaches.

Table 16 (continued)

	EARLY CHILDHOOD–GRADE 2	GRADES 3–5	GRADES 6–8	GRADES 9–12
Critical Thinking Abilities	Chooses from multiple ideas.	Evaluates realistically the risks and consequences of "flight or fight" in conflict.	Challenges assumptions about what is possible.	Uses problem-solving processes when engaging in difficult conversations.
	Understands when something is fair to self and fair to another person.	Identifies best self-help alternative in a conflict situation.	Thinks about both short- and long-term consequences of proposed options.	Speculates best alternatives to negotiated agreement for self and others.
	Explains why something is not fair.	Chooses to work toward mutual fairness in resolving a dispute rather than to accomplish self-imposed will.	Negotiates without giving in.	Analyzes ways to improve best alternatives to negotiated agreement.
	Expresses a realistic and workable plan for resolving a conflict.	Evaluates interests of self and others according to fairness standards.	Identifies outside standards and criteria for fairness (e.g., legal standards or school rules) when evaluating interests and solutions.	Analyzes willingness and ability of self and other person to honor a plan of action in any situation.
	Understands what it means to commit to a plan and be trustworthy.	Crafts win-win resolutions.	Recognizes the efficacy of committing only to solutions that are fair, realistic, and workable.	Identifies uncontrollable factors that might affect the ability of the parties to fulfill an agreement.
		Specifies clear agreement by stating who, what, when, where, and how.	Endeavors to fulfill commitments.	Identifies external standards of fairness and uses them in resolving conflicts.
				Honors commitments and encourages others to do the same.

Negotiation Abilities	Participates unassisted with a peer in simplified problem solving: each cools off, tells what happened, imagines ways to solve problem, chooses one of the ways. Participates in a negotiation session when coached by an adult or older child.	Manages the negotiation process without assistance.	Performs principled negotiation with peers and adults. Involves a peer who has little or no conflict resolution training in the negotiation of a conflict. Understands that nearly every interaction is a negotiation. Teaches younger students the negotiation process.	Negotiates with difficult parties effectively. Teaches negotiation process to peers and adults. Enjoys negotiation process.
Mediation Abilities	Participates in mediation facilitated by an adult or older student mediator.	Participates in the mediation process facilitated by other student(s) or an adult. Serves as a peer mediator in a classroom or schoolwide program.	Mediates disputes among peers. Co-mediates disputes between peers and adults. Coaches younger students and peers as they learn to mediate.	Mediates a wide assortment of disputes involving various disputants. Trains others in the mediation process.
Consensus Decision Making Abilities	Engages in group problem solving discussions and processes facilitated by a teacher or other adult.	Participates in classroom sessions endeavoring to resolve group conflicts and problems.	Manages consensus problem-solving sessions for classroom groups of younger students. Manages consensus decision making in a small group of peers (e.g., classroom work group or student council committee).	Manages consensus problem solving in various groups. Facilitates consensus decision making as a member of a group.

Directions: Find someone in the group for whom each of the following statements is true. Ask that person to sign her or his name by the statement. A person may sign your sheet only once.

1. Was born in another state _____

2. Likes classical music _____

3. Cries at movies or TV shows _____

4. Refuses to walk under a ladder _____

5. Lived in a home with an outhouse _____

6. Finished reading a book last week _____

7. Plays a musical instrument _____

8. Speaks more than one language _____

9. Plays on a sports team _____

10. Is the youngest in the family _____

11. Likes to cook _____

12. Has more than three pets _____

13. Has a parent who was not born in the USA _____

14. Likes to play tennis _____

15. Has a family of more than five _____

16. Likes to dance _____

17. Was born on a holiday _____

18. Likes to roller skate or rollerblade _____

19. Has an allergy _____

20. Has been at current school less than a year _____

Creating the Peaceable School (2nd ed.) © 2002 by R. L. Bodine, D. K. Crawford, and F. Schrumpf. Research Press (800) 519-2707.

Day 1

Opening: Boundary Breaker

Workshop overview

Understanding Conflict

1. Conflict Is . . .

2. Basic Needs

3. Enough Is Not Enough (limited resources)

4. Different Values (diversity issues)

5. What's My Response

6. Soft, Hard, or Principled Responses

7. Getting to Win-Win

Understanding Peace and Peacemaking

1. Making Peace

2. Perceptions

3. Emotions

4. Communication (active listening)

Mediation

1. Mediation Is . . .

2. Role of the Mediator

3. Learn and practice Steps 1 and 2

4. Learn and practice Step 3

5. Overview of the Mediation Process

Closing

> Reading assignment from the Program Guide:
>
> Introduction, "Origins of Conflict" (pp. 5–9)
>
> Section 2, "Overview" (pp. 65–73)
>
> Section 3, "Overview" (pp. 113–125)
>
> Section 4, "Overview" (pp. 185–194)

Day 2

Review of Day 1

Mediation, continued

1. Learn Steps 4–6

2. Practice Steps 1–6

Negotiation

1. Negotiation Is . . .

2. Role of the Negotiator

3. Overview of the Negotiation Process

4. Learn and practice negotiation

Group Problem Solving

1. Group Problem Solving Is . . .

2. Role of the Group Problem Solver

3. Sample group problem solving meeting

4. Topics for group problem solving

5. Role of the teacher-facilitator in group problem solving

Building a Peaceable Climate

1. Managing Behavior Without Coercion

2. Rights and Responsibilities

3. Rules

Closing

Reading assignment from the Program Guide:

       Section 1, "Overview" (pp. 21–42)

       Section 5, "Overview" (pp. 229–235)

       Section 6, "Overview" (pp. 273–294)

Creating the Peaceable School (2nd ed.) © 2002 by R. L. Bodine, D. K. Crawford, and F. Schrumpf. Research Press (800) 519-2707.

Disputant A

Situation

Pease High School, where you work, is experiencing serious problems with student behavior. These behavior problems seem to be at an all-time high. It feels as though the students (or their parents) are running the school—things are out of control. Discipline is the number one common concern among Pease staff. However, there is no consensus within the staff concerning how to deal with discipline problems. You have volunteered to serve on a discipline committee with other staff members to develop a school discipline policy that will, you hope, straighten out the current mess. After several meetings, the committee appears deadlocked. You have agreed to meet with a committee member who holds opposing views, and who has been very vocal expressing those views to the committee, to see if it is possible to negotiate beyond the deadlock.

Your Position

Our current problems with discipline started when "they" brought this humanist stuff into the schools several years ago. Schools need to get back to the basic 3 Rs, plus respect. School is a privilege, not a right that can be abused. Mostly, we need kids here who want to learn and to behave—kids who are respectful. The professionals need to regain control of the school. We should throw out the biggest problem students and enact swift, strong punishment for other miscreants. Kids, and their parents, will get the message—either "shape up or ship out." Without student compliance to firm rules, learning and teaching are impossible.

Background

You have a 23-year tenure at Pease, and you have seen it all come and go—mostly you have seen discipline erode. You come from the school of thought that "sparing the rod spoils the child." You are not advocating paddling—it is forbidden by the school code—but you do think that high expectations, backed up by consistent use of punishment and rewards, are the only answer these kids, and their parents, understand.

Creating the Peaceable School (2nd ed.) © 2002 by R. L. Bodine, D. K. Crawford, and F. Schrumpf. Research Press (800) 519-2707.

Disputant B

Situation

Pease High School, where you work, is experiencing serious problems with student behavior. These behavior problems seem to be at an all-time high. It feels as though the students (or their parents) are running the school—things are out of control. Discipline is the number one common concern among Pease staff. However, there is no consensus within the staff concerning how to deal with discipline problems. You have volunteered to serve on a discipline committee with other staff members to develop a school discipline policy that will, you hope, straighten out the current mess. After several meetings, the committee appears deadlocked. You have agreed to meet with a committee member who holds opposing views, and who has been very vocal expressing those views to the committee, to see if it is possible to negotiate beyond the deadlock.

Your Position

We need to work to develop our students into responsible citizens. Kids learn and behave in healthy, humane environments, not in prisonlike settings. Controlling others begets resentment; respect begets respect. We need a student rights and responsibilities policy at school that gives a basis for a discipline program that encourages mutual respect and self-control strategies rather than a program of other-control through punishment or rewards. We need thinking, responsible citizens, not compliant automatons.

Background

You have been teaching for 6 years, all at Pease. You feel you give and get a lot of respect to and from kids, and your hope is to get other staff to offer kids the same treatment. Your hope is that a recommendation for a humane approach to discipline will come from this committee. You grew up in a family and attended a school where fear of punishment was the main motivation for "acting good." Following a stormy adolescence in which you rejected this approach, both at home and at school, you entered teaching vowing to "do unto others as you would have them do unto you" (in other words, be respectful). You follow this path in your personal life and in your teaching, and it works for you.

Creating the Peaceable School (2nd ed.) © 2002 by R. L. Bodine, D. K. Crawford, and F. Schrumpf. Research Press (800) 519-2707.

Disputant A: Terry's Parent

Situation

Terry is a fourth-grade student at Clearview Elementary School. You have requested a conference with Terry's teacher because you are concerned about the curriculum. Terry complains about being bored much of the time and about the behavior of the class. He/she talks about frequent class meetings in which behavior is discussed and complains about rarely having class discussions about what is being taught. Terry says that most of the kids in the class do not work during work time and rarely finish their homework. You have examined Terry's homework and think it is too little and too easy. You are also concerned because you have not seen evidence of work in science. You have visited the classroom and believe the teacher has a difficult class. You were also impressed with the teacher's energy and the caring manner in which he/she interacted with individual children. From previous conferences, you believe the teacher likes Terry, and Terry seems to like the teacher.

Your Position

You want the teacher to tighten up the curricular requirements and spend less class time on socialization programs and more time on content—especially science.

Background

Terry has always been a good student and has never been a behavior problem. He/she has always liked school, is interested in a variety of topics, and has always been excited when learning new and challenging things. You have been an involved parent, volunteering to share your expertise as a chemist, even when to do so required you to take time off from your job at a local pharmacy, and serving as a parent representative on the school council. Terry is your third child to attend Clearview. You believe that the school has been gradually moving away from the rigorous requirement that first attracted your family to build a home in the district.

Page 2 of 2

Disputant B: Terry's Teacher

Situation

You are a fourth-grade teacher at Clearview Elementary School. The parent of Terry, one of your students, has requested a conference to talk about the curriculum. Terry is one of your "bright spots" this year. He/she is a very capable learner and is never a behavior problem. Terry always completes the assignments. Although there are others in the class you believe to be equally capable, Terry is your most consistent high achiever. The class, as a whole, has been difficult this year. You believe in developing a cooperative atmosphere in the classroom where there is a "sense of family," and to do so this year has required a number of class meetings on rights and responsibilities, communication, and self-esteem. Although class management still requires more of your time than you would like, you feel the class has come a long way in their ability and willingness to work together and to stick to a task. This climate is essential to your classroom design because you believe in developing self-directed learners who will challenge themselves to learn and to do quality work. You try to deemphasize homework and encourage students to choose to go beyond the minimum.

Your Position

You believe that learning to cooperate and the development of good citizenship are as important as any of the standard curricular concepts and, for this age level, are first priority. To operate an individualized classroom program, it is necessary first to establish an environment of cooperation and sharing.

Background

The school faculty feel that the school student population is changing rapidly and that an increasing percentage of the students do not possess proper school behavior and seem less motivated to learn. It has been decided that the whole school should make a concerted effort in responsibility education. You are very supportive of this effort because you have always emphasized students' accepting responsibility for their behavior and their learning. You feel you are an excellent elementary teacher with real strengths in relating to students and in providing challenging learning activities on a variety of learning levels. The areas in which you feel least well prepared are math and science. You work extra hard to provide activities in these areas, but you still feel less comfortable in these areas than in the other areas of the curriculum.

Creating the Peaceable School (2nd ed.) © 2002 by R. L. Bodine, D. K. Crawford, and F. Schrumpf. Research Press (800) 519-2707.

Implementation Results for Creating the Peaceable School and Other Conflict Resolution Education Programs

CONFLICT RESOLUTION IN CONTEXT

> Conflict resolution as a field has emerged out of several disciplines—sociology, social psychology, anthropology, law, criminal justice, political science, economics, education, communication and even the biological sciences. Theories and research on interpersonal dynamics, group dynamics, culture and conflict, legal ethics, the role of our legal system, the cost of litigation, violence in the schools, and the psychology of anger have all contributed to our growing understanding of conflict and conflict resolution, including the costs associated with resolving conflicts and the effectiveness of various conflict resolution methods. (Girard & Koch, 1996, p. xxii)

Early research on conflict reflects the impact of social psychology and anthropology on conflict resolution. Mary Parker Follett, a pioneer in conflict study, was the first to forward ideas about truly integrative solutions to conflict. Her thinking led beyond compromise to true collaboration to find solutions that meet underlying interests. The social psychologist Morton Deutsch, a major contributor to the development of conflict resolution theory, initiated his work in 1949 with the theoretical analysis and experimental study of the effects of cooperation and competition on group processes. This landmark work served as a springboard for the cooperative learning movement. Deutsch and colleagues at the International Center for Cooperation and Conflict Resolution have also conducted extensive research and developed theory in the areas of conflict and controversy. Deutsch's book *The Resolution of Conflict: Constructive and Restrictive Processes* (1973) remains one of the standard texts for the field. The notion of a cooperative context as a necessary condition (see Section 1 of this guide) is based on the work of Deutsch and others in the cooperative learning movement.

Roger Fisher and William Ury, writing from a legal perspective with the Harvard Negotiation Project, provided another seminal work in conflict resolution: *Getting to Yes: Negotiating Agreement without Giving In.* First published in 1981 and revised a decade later (Fisher, Ury, & Patton, 1991), this book is considered the primer on negotiation. The principles of conflict resolution described in Section 3 of this guide are drawn from this research.

Also integral to the *Creating the Peaceable School* program is the understanding of behavior—in general and specifically with regard to conflict—from the psychological perspective of internal motivation, as espoused in control theory or choice theory (see the introduction and Section 2 of this guide). Thus *Creating the Peaceable School* is rooted in practice that has been proved effective and in classic research on conflict resolution and psychology.

Conflict resolution in the schools emerged out of concerns for social justice during the late 1960s and early 1970s. Conflict resolution education (CRE) is a relatively new phenomenon in schools. In 1984, approximately 50 school-based conflict resolution programs existed throughout the country. Programs have grown exponentially in recent years. In 1998, the Conflict Resolution Education Network (CREnet) of the National Institute for Dispute Resolution (NIDR) estimated that at least 8,500 conflict resolution programs existed in schools; this meant that about 10 percent of the public schools had some type of program (Bodine & Crawford, 1998). The number of programs and the quality of existing programs continue to grow, with perhaps 15 percent of public and private schools currently offering some type of CRE program to at least some of their students.

ISSUES IN EVALUATING CONFLICT RESOLUTION PROGRAMS

Hundreds of studies have evaluated the impact of CRE on students' knowledge, attitudes, and behavior. The results of these studies have been positive far more often than not, providing an extensive literature of support for more constructive conflict resolution behavior brought about by CRE programs. However, few of these studies constitute rigorous research, and weak methodology—coupled with sketchy descriptions of research variables, procedures, and assessment instruments—has contributed to questioning of the efficacy of CRE in improving conflict behavior.

Several factors weigh in on the interpretation of the results of CRE evaluation studies. First, major obstacles exist to institutionalizing conflict resolution education programs. These obstacles are often overlooked in studies purporting to evaluate the effectiveness of programs. One obstacle is premature judgments. CRE programs are a relatively recent phenomenon and, as such, have not realized their potential—it may take as many as 10 years to fully realize the vision of the peaceable school. If CRE programs are seen as a "quick fix" for classroom and school problems, they will surely fail.

Second, public schools are remarkably resistant to change. Decades of research on schools, as well as the experience of school personnel, confirm that new programs are frequently initiated and then neglected as new problems gain attention. Programs not seen by school personnel as integral to the school curriculum—so-called add-on or stand-alone programs—are especially likely to be discontinued or ignored after other issues engage the attention of staff. Unfortunately, CRE programs may be implemented quickly in schools, with varying degrees of quality, and proclaimed by their proponents as panaceas, especially in response to the perceived increase in school violence. In a relatively short time, however, people will say, "We tried conflict resolution and it failed!" (Lindsey, 1998, p. 86). CRE programs that are implemented by mandate and that do not include careful planning concerning how to grow and sustain the initial effort will likely sputter and fade away.

Third, whereas some programs emphasize identifying the destructive aspects of conflict and focus on immediate crisis intervention techniques, quality CRE programs, especially the peaceable school approach, is broad based in focusing on the constructive aspects of conflict and in teaching long-term positive methods such as negotiation, mediation, and/or group problem solving. Research on the impact of the Teaching Students to Be Peacemakers program (Johnson & Johnson, 1994; see discussion later in this appendix) showed that students can learn conflict resolution concepts and negotiation and mediation strategies and can apply them to conflicts at school and at home. Moreover, conflict resolution training can enhance learning of academic material. This research is especially significant because the authors of the various studies empirically tested a model for conflict resolution based on social-psychological theory, using random assignment of students to experimental and control groups.

Fourth, the evaluation criteria applied may not be fully compatible with the intended goals of the CRE program. Most CRE professionals identify the goal of CRE as life skills education and training to develop responsible citizens, empowered to engage in constructive relationships within a diverse population. This complex, long-term goal extends beyond the immediate setting of the school. CRE programs are often evaluated by short-term standards for violence prevention in the immediate setting by studies examining whether there are declines in fighting incidents, suspensions or expulsions, and other serious discipline referrals. The evaluations may focus nearly exclusively on physical victimization, whereas CRE programs endeavor to reduce psychological as well as physical victimization.

Fifth, CRE programs are based on a set of assumptions incongruent with the culture of many schools. Simply put, CRE programs emphasize cooperation, whereas the culture of schools emphasizes competition. Most adults in schools have little training in or encouragement for managing conflicts cooperatively. The norm is to avoid conflict, and the adults use authoritarian methods to gain compliance. In this competitive context, staff members figure out ways to control their students and to maintain some degree of order. CRE programs assume more open, trusting, democratic relationships—relationships in which there is conflict, but the conflict is handled in more constructive ways. CRE programs in settings incongruent with the principles of constructive conflict resolution will have little effect. They may involve student instruction, but opportunities for students to use their learning will be insignificant.

Sixth, it is difficult to isolate the impact of CRE programs. Program effects are always intertwined with the effects of other factors, such as management style of administrators, varying classroom management practices of teachers, presence of related programs such as character education and social skills development training, and changing composition of student population. Measuring the effectiveness of conflict resolution education programs through cognitive gains is thus problematic. Researchers tend to discredit other data that could provide valid measures of success, either because those measures are difficult to obtain or the results are difficult to quantify into easily reported statistics. Other measures that could be available include the effect on classroom and school climate, reduced reliance on adults to solve problems, reduction in number and nature of disputes, and transfer of conflict resolution skills outside of the school setting.

Seventh, negative views of CRE programs are likely to result from unrealistic or uninformed expectations held by many of the adults who respond to assessment measures. Salient among these expectations are those concerning the duration and intensity of the program. Adults may expect significant behavior change from minimal or infrequent training. Also salient is misunderstanding about or lack of appreciation for the role of conflict in children's development. The general view of adults is that conflict can and should be avoided. Further, researchers and evaluators may not acknowledge the difference in abilities of elementary versus secondary school students that practitioners of conflict resolution education recognize. Practitioners, for example, have different expectations for younger students engaged in CRE than for older, more experienced students and therefore produce developmentally appropriate materials for different grade levels. The ultimate goal of any CRE program is to give youth the ability to constructively talk out problems without the help of others.

Eighth, the pervasive view that only children, not adults, require CRE training greatly influences the extent to which school personnel understand and are invested in CRE programming, a critical factor in the success or failure of student training efforts. Student outcomes are dependent upon adult competence and orientation. It is rare that all school staff receive comparable training. Regardless of the level of training, some staff will believe strongly in the program; others will be skeptical. Those who value the program will infuse their students with that view; it is unlikely that such infusion will occur for students when adults are uncommitted or lack enthusiasm. CRE programs that begin without a common vision and commitment to that vision among the adult population likely will achieve, at best, sporadic results.

Finally, in considering the implementation results for the *Creating the Peaceable School* program, it is important to bear in mind the notion advanced in Section 7 of this guide that this program presents a comprehensive training strategy necessary for the realization of the vision of the peaceable school, but that the peaceable school itself is a concept, not a program. Many elements are involved in implementing the program, and how those are enacted will vary in form and even in importance from location to location.

PEACEABLE SCHOOL EVALUATIONS

Beginning in 1992, the authors have been active in providing training based on the peaceable schools model, later codified in the first edition of *Creating the Peaceable School* (Bodine, Crawford, & Schrumpf, 1994) to well over 10,000 educators who have attended our national, regional, or on-site workshops. These workshops were first sponsored by the Illinois Institute for Dispute Resolution (IIDR). IIDR quickly gained national recognition for providing quality professional development programs. In 1997, IIDR evolved into the National Center for Conflict Resolution Education (NCCRE) and Conflict Resolution Education, Inc. (CRE, Inc.). The authors were instrumental founders of IIDR, NCCRE and CRE, Inc.

The authors have also, to a limited degree, provided technical assistance to schools and districts for their program implementation efforts. However, the mission and funding of IIDR, NCCRE, and CRE, Inc., focus on providing professional development workshops and resources for conflict resolution education. Conducting systematic evaluation of implementation efforts was not and is not part of the function and design of these entities. Nonetheless, state departments of education, local school districts, and individual educators have attempted to collect data to support the efficacy of their peaceable school programs.

What follows next is a description of efforts to evaluate programs based on the *Creating the Peaceable School* model, ranging from a statewide evaluation to individual school endeavors. Whenever possible, we have referenced published materials relating to these programs. In general, however, participating schools generated unpublished, in-house reports. Program descriptions based on these unpublished materials reflect our own synthesis and interpretation of information gathered from a questionnaire we circulated, followed up by on-site or telephone interviews.

Peaceable Schools Tennessee

Why did I get involved in Peaceable Schools? Bullying, gossiping, physical fighting, verbal attacks, lack of respect for anything, property damage; repeat offenses over and over; I pretty much did disciplining kids and putting out fires all year long. (Middle school principal)

I think that peer mediation is great and that it helps other students to solve their problems peacefully without getting out of control. I know that some students need someone to talk to when solving problems and that is why we are here to help them. (Elementary-level Peaceable School peer mediator)

I see [the Peaceable Schools initiative] will be the cohesive thing that helps tie it all together. It will work in well with the other things we have to do. (Middle school teacher)

Since Peaceable Schools started, we only had one suspension in 3 years! (Middle school principal)

Excellent—the process [noncoercive discipline approach] has worked well, with the kids quickly responding to the process. (Advanced Peaceable School Training Institute participant)

It [noncoercive discipline approach] has changed my whole approach to discipline, and I find students respond to that method. (Advanced Peaceable School Training Institute participant)

Peaceable Schools Tennessee (PST) is a significant peaceable school implementation effort that has been under way since 1996. The PST initiative is designed as a training curriculum and structure for a "train the trainer" model of putting into practice conflict resolution skills within schools across the state of Tennessee. This initiative is supported through a collaborative arrangement among the Tennessee Department of Education's Safe and Drug Free Schools Program, the Tennessee School Safety Center, the Tennessee Legal Community Foundation, and the Tennessee legal and mediation communities. Funding support comes from the Tennessee Department of Education's Safe and Drug Free Schools budget, and the Tennessee Legal Community Foundation (TLCF) has been responsible for the design and implementation of this initiative. TLCF is the nonprofit arm of the Tennessee Bar Association.

The Director of the Tennessee Department of Education's School Safety Center and the Director of Law Related Education of TLCF saw a need to move toward institutionalization of conflict resolution in Tennessee schools, kindergarten through grade 12. These project developers conducted a needs assessment among selected and representative teachers, counselors, and administrators. Results indicated that Tennessee schools needed and wanted to address conflict in a positive way and that they desired guidance in doing so. Based on assessment feedback, available research, and the Tennessee Department of Education's expectations, the major goals of the initiative were set forth:

1. Decrease the number of disciplinary office referrals.

2. Enhance students' critical thinking skills.

3. Provide a safe school environment that is not authoritarian.

4. Build school-community partnerships.

The PST initiative is a broad-based conflict resolution program offered through 3-day professional development institutes. Teams of school personnel—including teachers, counselors, administrators, school resource officers, and other related personnel—attend the institute to learn to teach conflict resolution skills. The strategies of group problem solving, mediation, and negotiation are included. The 3-day institutes provide the school team with classroom strategies, a team planning structure, a forum for questions and answers, and opportunities to practice conflict resolution skills through role-play. The primary text is the first edition of *Creating the Peaceable School* (Bodine et al., 1994). The design and implementation of the training program have involved a partnership with the authors through the NCCRE. The 3-day institute is followed up with on-site technical assistance by PST. Also, advanced training institutes are provided by NCCRE. Most of the peaceable school trainers are teachers and school administrators, an added benefit because these people bring the program to their own schools and provide expert guidance locally.

The Training Institute

Because the designers wanted a broad-based approach firmly grounded in learning theory, they selected the *Creating the Peaceable School* program. The PST institutes offer an experiential learning environment. The participants are able to try out this different view of conflict, some for the first time, in a format that allows them to begin to see that they can establish classrooms and schools where conflict is normalized and discipline is not coercive.

The PST initiative began in late 1996 with construction of a basic framework that included identifying the organization that was to provide the training and coordination services and appointing an initiative director. A pilot training institute was conducted in May of 1997. Fifteen teams of middle school administrators, teachers, and counselors from Tennessee schools participated in the pilot training. After refining the institute training format, beginning in July 1997, PST conducted regional, 3-day institutes across the state that took place mostly, but not entirely, during the summer months. PST trainers have also conducted institutes for whole school districts.

Further, as PST expanded the number of summer institutes, it was necessary to recruit and train additional trainers. This training was in collaboration with NCCRE. Additionally, starting during the 1998–1999 school year, PST, in partnership with NCCRE, has offered advanced peaceable schools training to over 70 school teams.

To date, PST has provided basic peaceable school training to nearly 2,000 educators on 495 peaceable school teams from 441 different schools—78 percent of the total number of schools in Tennessee. Seven school districts have sent teams from each of their schools, and 48 schools have sent more than one team. Approximately one-half of the schools that participated in PST workshops have received in-school technical assistance by a PST trainer and/or have attended an advanced training institute.

Assessments

The effort in Tennessee is largely a training effort, and no implementation constraints from the state were placed on the participating school teams, except that after the teams attended the workshops they were to go back to their schools and share the knowledge they had gained. As a result, the project did not have the resources to capture or track outcomes of the programs that developed following the PST training institutes. A thorough evaluation of the training content and process showed the training to be well received and effective in that the trainees learned what the organizers expected. This evaluation enabled PST to refine and improve its training protocol.

The outcome evaluation of the Tennessee effort is based on data that all the schools in the state were required to report. The data mostly focused on student suspension rates. The data have shown the following:

1. Overall suspension rates decreased in Tennessee schools from 1997–2000 by an average of 14 percent. Suspension rates in school districts that sent 50 percent or more of their schools to a training institute decreased on average 39 percent in that same period.

2. Of the school districts that received technical assistance and also showed a decrease in suspension rates, over half experienced at least a 20 percent decrease in their suspension rates. These rates were as high as an 83 percent decline in suspension rate, with an average of a 39 percent decrease in the 3-year period.

3. Four of the school districts that made major commitments to the program are among the schools with the greatest decrease in suspension rates for the state; all showed a decline in suspension rates above 60 percent. Major program commitments included one or more of the following: sending representatives from at least 50 percent of schools to the institutes, having one or more strong program advocates who worked hard to move the program in their district and/or specific schools, and receiving technical assistance and/or attending an advanced institute.

In addition to the data from the required state reports, PST has recently begun to collect school-by-school data to ascertain whether other program goals are being realized.

1. Of the schools surveyed, information from principals indicates that disciplinary referrals are down in peaceable classrooms as compared with other classrooms in the same school. The data are showing fewer disciplinary infractions overall for the schools. Every school reporting to date has cited a decrease in office referral rates, ranging from 10 to 80 percent.

2. Another program goal is to improve critical thinking skills. Peaceable school teachers surveyed report that, following training, students are better able to brainstorm possible solutions (analysis), create a best solution (synthesis), and evaluate the solution (evaluation). Additionally, students are better able to communicate with adults and peers and to work cooperatively.

3. Pretests and posttests were administered to a number of students to ascertain gains in knowledge and skills. Analysis of the resulting data showed conflict resolution knowledge increases of 10 to 50 percent. Students' analysis of an open-ended conflict scenario indicated increased ability to provide multiple solutions and select one or more they believe to be viable. These data back up the anecdotes reported by teachers.

4. Teachers and counselors who have responded to recent PST surveys indicate that the students who learn peaceable skills have exhibited improved cooperation and communication skills. These teachers and counselors have also seen improved problem-solving skills and overall academic performance through enhanced critical thinking skills.

5. For a school to be more peaceable, students must be able to resolve conflicts through cooperation, not confrontation. Data from the open-ended scenario solutions showed significant decreases in confrontational solutions and major increases in cooperative, negotiated solutions. This information fits with the principals' and counselors' reported anecdotes.

District of Columbia Peaceable Schools

The District of Columbia Public Schools will implement a "Peaceable Schools Model" in order to create an environment that supports the teaching and learning process and the development of social and civic responsibility. The successful implementation of the "Model" will be assessed during the school appraisal process each school year. Minimally, to start, all schools will conduct a student driven, school-wide activity or project that promotes the peaceable school concept and within two years all schools will have a peer mediation program in place. (Directive from the Office of the Superintendent of Schools, District of Columbia)

The Peaceable Schools Initiative (PSI) is a systematic effort instituted in the District of Columbia Public Schools (DCPS) to reduce violence and create safe, secure, drug-free schools. The primary training vehicle of the PSI is the summer institute. Since the summer of 1998, basic and advanced peaceable school training and peer mediation training have been conducted, all based on *Creating the Peaceable School*. These training programs, each of 2 days' duration, have been provided in partnership with the authors through the NCCRE. All PSI staff members have participated in the programs: Some now serve as in-house trainers for related summer institute offerings.

The PSI offers district teachers and administrators the opportunity to earn university credit and inservice training hours for participation in the summer institute and in subsequent practicum activities within their respective schools. Practicum activities may include turnkey training of other staff and of student peer mediators within the trainees' respective schools. Staff members are also given opportunities to implement best practices within their classrooms and to seek consultation and support from PSI staff on maintaining and generalizing strategies and lessons learned into their instructional practices.

PSI is a broad-based effort that addresses, in addition to conflict resolution education but under the umbrella of the peaceable school, other overarching issues facing the school system. These include the following:

1. Lowering the number of daily absences

2. Promoting character development

3. Creating a school climate that supports achieving academic excellence

4. Increasing parental involvement

The intent of the PSI is to reduce fragmentation by building the capacity of local schools to reduce risk factors that compromise students' ability to achieve to their fullest potential. The capacity-building approach promotes institutionalization of best practices within local schools to build resilience and provide students with viable alternatives to engaging in risky behaviors. The major components of this initiative are these:

1. Attendance intervention

2. Conflict resolution, anger management, and peer mediation training

3. Ongoing support for local training of peer mediation coordinators and adult facilitators of alternatives-to-violence programs

4. Parent-centered support programs

5. Citywide school capacity-building activities, including Peace Month activities

6. Safe Schools, Safe Streets learning modules that emphasize communication, problem solving, critical thinking, conflict resolution, and decision-making skills that support alternatives to unsafe behaviors

7. Internships for local university students to assist in infusing conflict resolution skills into the classroom curricula

8. Problem-solving focus groups and intervention assistance to local schools

9. Substance abuse prevention education

Focusing on "big-picture issues," the PSI evaluation concentrates on assessing change, both systemwide and in individual schools. In the latter situation, the "unit of analysis" is the school building; however, change is analyzed and discussed within the context of the three different school levels—elementary schools, middle and junior high schools, and senior high schools.

The process data analyzed included (a) end-of-course evaluation data collected for six courses offered at the district's summer institute for 2000; (b) a follow-up survey of institute participants from both the 1999 and 2000 programs; and (c) surveys and focus group data from parents, student peer mediators, peer mediation coordinators, and the district's Parent Centered Prevention Program staff.

Data Sources for Assessing Program Impact

The PSI has available a variety of data sources for assessing program impact. Most of this information results from annual data collection systems that DCPS implemented at various times throughout the 1990s. The sources and instruments for outcome data include the following.

Youth Risk Behavior Survey (YRBS). The YRBS was developed by the Centers for Disease Control and Prevention and is used to monitor priority health-risk behaviors that contribute to the leading social problems among youth in the United States. DCPS began collecting YRBS data in 1989. High school students in grades 9, 10, 11, and 12 are asked safety-related questions on a variety of topics such as carrying a weapon, physical fighting and drinking, or using drugs. The survey data are collected in schools during regularly scheduled classroom times.

D.C. School Satisfaction Survey. This survey provides the results of a set of school satisfaction surveys that includes all schools within the District of Columbia. Since 1998, four separate groups of people have been surveyed each June: principals and vice principals; teachers and counselors; students in grades 5, 8, 10, and 12; and parents. The staff and student surveys are collected in schools, whereas the parent survey is administered through the mail. Like the YRBS, these surveys asked a variety of safety-related questions.

D.C. School Incident Data. The DCPS Security Office collects comprehensive incident data from all school buildings in the District of Columbia. DCPS has 3 consecutive years of incident data collected from 1998, 1999, and 2000. These data include actual counts of assaults, drug and alcohol violations, thefts, and other crimes committed in schools.

In addition to the preceding sources, the PSI collected data for evaluation purposes from a variety of other sources during the 1999–2000 school year. These sources included (a) focus groups of students, mediation coordinators, and parents; (b) surveys of school-based peer mediators; and (c) individual school ratings of all school-based conflict resolution education programs. These ratings were derived through actual site visits performed by PSI program staff.

Initial components of the PSI, including the first summer institute in 1998, were first implemented in DCPS during the 1998–1999 and 1999–2000 school years. For evaluation and comparative purposes, the 1997–1998 school year was designated as the base year preceding formal program implementation.

Generally, all data analysis reported here took place during the fall of 2000. YRBS data are collected in accordance with the national schedule for that survey during the spring of odd-numbered years. Spring of 1993 was therefore used as the baseline for comparison with the 1997 and 1999 data. The YRBS evaluation effort focused on two key topics: violence-related behaviors and substance-abuse behaviors. YRBS addressed these behaviors by asking questions like the following:

1. During the past 30 days, on how many days did you carry a gun?

2. During the past 12 months, how many times were you in a physical fight?

3. During the past 30 days, on how many days did you have at least one drink of alcohol?

4. During your life, how many times have you used marijuana?

For the school satisfaction survey—conducted in May of 1998, 1999, and 2000—teachers, students, and parents were asked how favorably they rated various aspects of school safety and discipline issues. Typical survey statements, with which respondents were asked to agree or disagree, are these:

1. My school is a safe place. (Teacher)

2. My things are safe in this school. (Student)

3. My child's school is a drug-free school. (Parent)

The certification of levels of the schools' conflict mediation programs was conducted during the spring of 2000. Mediation programs were placed into four categories: Emerging Program 1, Emerging Program 2, Proficient Program, and Distinguished Program. Placement in one of the categories was derived from a "site visitation rubric" developed by DCPS personnel. The rubric rated programs on twenty-six distinct characteristics. These characteristics included an examination of issues such as the following:

1. Training of core school staff (Are the staff trained?)

2. Presence of a mediation program coordinator (Does one exist?)

3. Parent awareness of the mediation program (Do parents know of the program's existence?)

4. Does the program have a core group of peer mediators?

The schools' incident data are collected incrementally, as the incidents occur during each school year, from September 1 through the following August, then are tallied for the 12-month period. Twelve-month data for the 1997–1998, 1998–1999, and 1999–2000 school years were analyzed for this evaluation. For evaluation purposes, school incident data were grouped into seven major categories: alarms (e.g., a pulled fire alarm); assaults (e.g., fighting); drugs and alcohol (e.g., drug possession); serious crimes (e.g., rape); theft (e.g., stealing school property); weapons (e.g., gun possession); and all others (e.g., indecent exposure).

Questions Addressed by the Evaluation

Overall, how have substance abuse and violence-related behavior trends changed for DCPS students? With data available both prior to and after the initiation of the PSI, it is possible to address this trend question with YRBS data. These data show the following:

1. *Drinking alcohol.* The percentage of DCPS students who had at least one drink of alcohol on one or more days during their life declined significantly from 1993 to 1999. In 1993, the percentage of high school (grades 9 through 12) students who had at least one drink of alcohol on one or more days during their life stood at 74 percent. In 1999, this figure dropped to 67 percent.

2. *Using marijuana.* The percentage of DCPS students using marijuana increased significantly from 1993 to 1999. In 1993, the percentage of high school students who used marijuana one or more times during their life stood at 29 percent. In 1999, this figure climbed to 45 percent. The percentage using marijuana the past 30 days and the percentage trying it before age 13 also increased.

3. *Carrying weapons and guns.* The percentage of DCPS students carrying a weapon or gun on one or more of the past 30 days declined significantly from 1993 to 1999. For example, in 1993, the percentage of high school students who carried a gun on one or more of the past 30 days stood at 14 percent. In 1999, this figure dropped to 7 percent. The percentage of students who carried a weapon dropped from 34 percent in 1993 to 21 percent in 1999. The percentage of students who carried a weapon on school property also dropped from 16 percent in 1993 to 9 percent in 1999.

4. *Fighting in the past 12 months.* The percentage of DCPS students who were in a physical fight one or more times in the past 12 months declined significantly from 1993 to 1999. In 1993, the

percentage of high school students who were in a physical fight during one or more of the past 12 months stood at 46 percent. In 1999, this percentage had dropped to 37 percent.

It is difficult to associate these specific YRBS outcomes and changes in trends with certain program aspects of the PSI. Nonetheless, YRBS trends reveal that in some respects schools in the District of Columbia are safer (e.g., fewer high school students carry weapons on school property). In addition, fewer high school students drink alcohol; however, the use of marijuana by high school students has increased significantly. Some of this increase is perhaps associated with a reported increase in the availability of illegal drugs on school property. In 1993, the percentage of high school students who had someone offer to sell or give them an illegal drug on school property during the past 12 months stood at 16 percent. In 1999, this figure had climbed to 25 percent.

Are school incident declines associated with the presence of peer mediation programs? Overall, the mean number of reported incidents in schools in the District of Columbia declined both years from the baseline school year, 1997–1998. In 1997–1998, the mean number of incidents reported for all schools stood at 17.1 incidents per school. In 1998–1999, the mean dropped to 16.8 incidents per school, and in 1999–2000, the mean dropped further to 16.0 incidents per school. At the elementary and high school levels, schools with the highest rated mediation programs (Distinguished) had larger declines in reported incidents than did schools with the lowest rated mediation programs (Emerging 1 and Emerging 2). The data in Table 17 show that the two senior high schools with Distinguished programs had a larger 2-year decline than did senior high schools in the other three categories: 32 percent fewer incidents compared to 12, 11 and 1 percent fewer in the other categories.

It also is worth pointing out that the Distinguished senior high schools ended up reporting far fewer incidents than did high schools in the other three categories. For example, in 1997–1998, Emerging 2 and Distinguished senior high schools had about the same mean number of incidents—51 mean incidents and 49 mean incidents, respectively. By the end of the 1999–2000 fiscal year, mean incidents at the two Distinguished senior high schools had dropped by 32 incidents, as compared with a drop of 11 incidents in Emerging 2 senior high schools.

How does the PSI impact student, teacher, and parent satisfaction levels? Perhaps overlooked as a key initiative of the PSI is the investment in school-based security technology, both closed circuit television (CCTV) for monitoring isolated school building locations and X-ray machines for scanning students and their bags. An analysis of the school satisfaction data reveals that the presence of both technologies is not necessarily associated with higher levels of student, teacher, and parent satisfaction levels; however, the levels of change in the sat-

TABLE 17   *Second-Year Incident Changes in Senior High Schools*

Level of Certification	No. of Schools	1997–1998 Mean No. of Incidents	1999–2000 Mean No. of Incidents	Second Year Mean Change
Emerging 1	3	36.33	23.33	−13.00
Emerging 2	7	50.71	39.42	−11.29
Proficient	5	32.20	31.40	−0.80
Distinguished	2	48.50	16.50	−32.00

isfaction levels are greater in the schools with both technologies. The data in Table 18, taken from senior high schools only, show this relationship.

Senior high schools with equipment are not as highly rated as senior high schools without equipment. For example, 63 percent of the students in high schools without equipment agreed with the statement "I feel safe at school," compared with 48 percent of the students in high schools with equipment. Nevertheless, satisfaction levels have increased more in the high schools with equipment than those without equipment (11 percent versus 4 percent). Both of these sets of numbers make sense. It is likely that the neediest high schools received the CCTV and X-ray technologies first and that the presence of the equipment might have caused higher numbers of students to begin agreeing that they subsequently felt safer in school.

Conclusions

As the District of Columbia public school system continues to implement the PSI, anecdotal evidence suggests that students, parents, and teachers view mediation as one of the effective strategies that schools can institute to model alternatives to violence. The broad range of conflict resolution strategies offered in the district has most recently been infused into the curriculum content standards for health and physical education and social studies. The PSI addresses the relationship among alcohol, tobacco, and other drugs as risk factors that often lead to violence. As a result, training to infuse the Safe Schools, Safe Streets curriculum into the core curriculum is currently being conducted.

The PSI continues to focus on empowering students to make choices and on allowing adults to facilitate learning that supports prosocial choices and decision making by children and youth. By providing developmentally appropriate and culturally congruent learning opportunities, students are joining adults in taking joint ownership and responsibility for creating safe and drug-free learning environments. The initiative continues to address the systemwide infusion of the peaceable school approach by incorporating process curriculum, mediation, and peaceable

TABLE 18   Percentage of Respondents Agreeing That School Is Safe (High Schools Only)

	No. of Schools	Student %	3-year % Change	Teacher %	3-year % Change	Parent %	3-year % Change
Schools with CCTV and X-ray	8	48	11	66	8	60	12
Schools without equipment	10	63	4	72	4	68	4

classroom approaches. To allow schools to be reflective on their work as they strengthen the school climate and to recognize that work, criteria will be established to facilitate school certification at the levels of Peacekeeping, Peacemaking, and Peace Building. The district is using the preliminary research findings to refine future efforts to increase safety and reduce substance abuse in schools.

Lessons learned reflect that students are safer in schools but that the environment around the school poses significant challenges that may have an impact on the school as a community. As a result, the DCPS continues to strengthen community-based collaboration and engage in ongoing prevention activities with multiple agencies to reduce external risk and insulate students within the schools' safe learning environment. These ongoing community-based collaborations include engaging the private, nonpublic, parochial, and charter schools in broad-range efforts to build peaceable learning environments within the district. This strategy also offers continual opportunities for resource sharing across multiple governmental agencies, universities, private agencies, and faith-based communities within the District of Columbia. Creating such multiple linkages and partnerships through community outreach has provided schools with additional supports to reduce risk.

William Fremd High School Peer Mediation

> Peer mediation is very important . . . because you are helping people out. One of the main things in my life is out-reaching and trying to make a positive difference. That is what peer mediation is all about. (Fremd student mediator)

> Peer mediation gives me the chance to help people in a way that I haven't been able to do before, and it gives me a sense of accomplishment that is unmatched by anything else. (Fremd student mediator)

Since 1993, William Fremd High School has had a peer mediation program based on the mediation program first described in *Peer Mediation: Conflict Resolution in Schools* (Schrumpf, Crawford, & Usadel, 1991) and later included as a key component of the *Creating the Peaceable School* program. Fremd is a large suburban high school outside of Chicago that has approximately 2,600 students in grades 9 through 12. The school has a 17 percent minority population. The students are from the full range of socioeconomic levels, with the majority of the students from what would be considered middle-class families. The Student Supportive Services Office, which also provides student counseling and guidance services, sponsors the peer mediation program.

Approximately 30 students are chosen as peer mediators at Fremd annually. Each year, the program replaces the graduating senior mediators (generally a third of the mediators). Peer mediators are selected through a nomination process, including self-nominations. The nominees then go through an interview process, and program sponsors make a conscious effort to select students representative of the student body. At the high school there is a mediation center, which is a dedicated conference room for conflict resolution activities. At a minimum, each of the peer mediators reports to the mediation center biweekly during his or her free periods. This allows peer mediators to be available throughout the day.

Conflicts between students can end up at mediation in many ways. A student experiencing conflict with another student or group of students can ask for a mediation session. Administrators, teachers, other staff members, fellow students, and even parents who recognize a potentially serious conflict may also refer disputants to peer mediation.

The initial four-dimensional evaluation of the peer mediation program concluded in 1996. This evaluation included the discipline statistics from the school. These statistics are collected annually by the principal and reported to the state department of education. The evaluation focused on suspensions that were a result of specific conflict-related types of behavior, including (a) battery, (b) dangerous behavior, (c) fighting, and (d) harassment.

To ascertain the amount of administrative support and the impact that might have on the success of the program, the evaluator designed a measure of administrative support that was given to the program sponsors. The Supportive Administrative Behavioral Checklist (SABC) included six questions regarding building level administrators' support for the peer mediation program:

1. How many building level administrators are officially assigned to your peer mediation program?

2. How many building level administrators have received formal training in peer mediation?

3. Does your building level administrator:

    Help select peer mediators?

    Help train peer mediators?

    Observe mediation sessions?

    Attend mediator meetings?

4. In which of your official school documents is peer mediation described?

    Discipline policy

    Student handbook

    Teacher handbook

    Principal's newsletter

    Informal fliers/pamphlets

5. Approximately what percentage of the faculty at your school has received peer mediation training through an inservice or otherwise?

6. Answer from strongly agree (1) to strongly disagree (5):

    As a program sponsor I feel that I have administrative support.

    There is a lack of administrative financial support for peer mediation.

    Administration provides for the physical needs of the mediation program.

The effect of peer mediation on the escalation and/or continuance of conflict was measured through records of interviews conducted with mediation disputants. This simple four-question survey was used:

1. Have you had any more problems with the other student since mediation?

2. What did you like about mediation?

3. What would you change about the mediation process?

4. Would you refer a friend to mediation?

Is peer mediation effective in reducing the number of suspensions related to student-to-student conflict? The proportion of students involved in conflict-related suspensions and the total school enrollment in the year prior to the introduction of the peer mediation program was compared with the same proportion during subsequent years when the peer mediation program was operating. At a level of .05, a significant drop in suspensions occurred in the first year of the program's existence. In the initial year of the program the suspension rate decreased from 3.5 percent to 2.5 percent of the student body. That means that some 70 students were not suspended who might have been without the peer mediation program. The analysis of suspension rates from 1994 to 2000 shows the lower level of suspensions has been maintained.

Do students involved as peer mediators believe they have gained skills? Not only is the suspension rate positively affected, perhaps more important, many students involved as peer mediators believe they have gained skills that can help them throughout their lives. The answers of mediators to the question "What do you get from being a peer mediator?" illustrate this belief:

> I like meeting people from different schools. See where other people are coming from. Even if you don't agree with them I can still respect them.

> It is now easier for me to meet other people.

> We do so much for other people: teaching and outreach.

> I am more outgoing and not afraid of talking.

> I am not going to judge people. I listen to them.

> With my brother we don't fight as much. I talk to him more instead of punching him. We are really close in age and it has been difficult in the past.

> It keeps me accountable. Yeah, I have the skills and when I don't use them, it's good that my siblings rub it in my face and keep me accountable.

> It has deepened my level of friendship with people.

> It has also helped my dad. He grew up in a really harsh environment with prejudice, and the only way he knew how to deal with conflict was to fight. His philosophy used to be if ever someone is bothering you just go beat them up. Through the program what I learned about conflict resolution I had to pass it on to him. I overheard a conversation with him and my little brother, who was complaining about a bully who was picking on him. My dad told my brother to talk to the other kid about it. It was a really big change for him.

Is administrative support an essential component of the effective peer mediation program? The study found that the amount of administrative support had an impact on the program's success. When the responses of two similar high schools on the SABC were compared, the evaluator found that the level of administrative support had a great impact on the success of the program. Fremd had an 88.4 percent rating in administrative support and showed a decrease in conflict-related suspensions, whereas the other school had a 15.7 percent administrative support rating and showed an increase in conflict-related suspensions.

In the view of disputants, does peer mediation resolve conflicts and prevent them from escalating and continuing? The study found that disputants believed the process helped keep them from further altercations and that they liked the process. From their perspective, peer mediation was an overwhelming success. Ninety percent of the disputants surveyed reported that they did not have any further problems with the other disputant after mediation. All of the disputants surveyed avoided suspension related to the incident that was mediated. Forty-seven percent of the respondents reported that the ability to talk out the problem and avoid the suspension was the component of peer mediation that they most liked. Three percent of the respondents did not like having a silent adult monitor and would have liked the mediation better if that person had not been present. Eighty-nine percent reported that they would indeed refer a friend for mediation if the friend needed it.

Since obtaining these initial positive evaluation findings for the Fremd peer mediation program, program sponsors have sought ways to expand and enhance the work of mediators. Over the last 2 or 3 years, the focus of the peer mediation program has shifted from doing mediations only to using peer mediators as conflict resolution mentors and instructors. Currently, 25 percent of the mediators' time is used in formal mediation sessions, whereas 75 percent of their time is used for other related activities, including (a) conflict resolution workshops for elementary and middle school students, (b) staff development presentations, (c) training newly selected mediators, (d) consultation to schools building new programs, (e) co-facilitation of student support groups, and (f) facilitation of small discussion groups.

In an attempt to explore the impact of integration of conflict resolution models beyond formal peer mediation sessions, mediators took part in a focus group. Some of those participating served in the program both when mediators were used exclusively for mediation and when mediators took on a more expanded role. Youth who participated were in grades 11 and 12; the data gathered will be used to help Fremd develop an evaluation model to begin to identify differences between students exposed to conflict resolution education at earlier and later ages. The following quotes are from focus group members.

How have the changes in the structure and the role of the mediator impacted you and the other students?

> We were much more focused on mediation; now we are doing so much more outreach and teaching younger kids the basics of conflict resolution.

> I don't think it will necessarily decrease the number of conflicts because when we teach them we aren't teaching them how to avoid conflict. We are teaching them when they have conflict there are ways to deal with it that can build you up and be positive. We teach them that conflict can be lose-lose or win-win.

You can teach a man to fish in a day, but if you teach a man to fish he will eat for a lifetime. . . . [We] taught the younger kids how to deal with their problems early. I think it would have helped me a lot going through sixth, seventh, and eighth grade, which are some of the toughest years for a lot of people.

I am amazed how the younger kids in elementary school are so into it and so interested in learning. I was honored to teach them. They actually listened.

The earlier we start the better. Walking cold into a seventh- or eighth-grade class can be brutal. It is hard to get them to listen. The younger kids really get into it.

We did a freshman orientation program and went to that and taught them. Some of the people there ended up being mediators. We did the skills training. We are going to start seeing a difference over time. We have seen these kids for multiple years. We are going to start talking with incoming students about respect and what it is like to come to high school. They are going to get to hear from kids who had a horrible transition to high school and kids who had a good transition.

The kids are coming from all different schools into the high school, so we try and do things to build relationships. I think it is very important to have the mediators integrated. They take these skills with them into whatever they do throughout the school. I think this expanded job idea keeps the mediation program alive at Fremd.

How has the mediation program affected overall school climate?

We have a lot of cliques. The peer mediators are very diverse, and we can be examples. We have jocks, skaters, and smart kids—all types of people. We all get along. We pull the strengths from all types of people.

There are so many opportunities for us to talk, especially with the staff. We get to give our input.

[We try] to get people to respect each other.

The Vikings ROCS is a movement; every room has the poster and has these concepts for everyone to live by. We want you to be friends with your friends and not be mean to everyone else. We want the level of respect to be the same.

The Vikings ROCS (Reaching Out in Community Service) is an undertaking by the Fremd mediators to bring respect and understanding of others to all members of the Fremd community. The text of a poster that hangs throughout the high school is as follows:

> Within the Fremd High School community, we choose to . . .
>
> Communicate in an understanding, empathic, and appropriate manner
>
> Model pride, integrity, and fairness while taking responsibility for our actions
>
> Recognize and appreciate each individual's uniqueness
>
> Value the development of positive and caring everyday relationships
>
> Demonstrate respect for ourselves, others, and to our school

Fremd High School is integrating the theory and practice of conflict resolution education throughout the school, and it is continuing to extend its efforts into the rest of the district. The students involved are excited and motivated. The sponsors have used the data to continue to change the support and function of the peer mediators to provide the school with the best conflict resolution education program that they know how to provide.

East Prairie School District Peaceable School

> Discipline and classroom management had become the focus of many classrooms with attention being taken away from academics. Any discipline policies that were used were used inconsistently. We felt that by giving youth the tools necessary to relate positively and resolve conflicts without violence, we were enabling them to develop lifelong skills. We wanted a program that was consistent and fair to all involved. We wanted students to have an opportunity to be listened to and involved. At the same time, we wanted teachers to be able to get back to teaching. . . . Our program teaches lifelong skills that can be implemented and integrated into all areas of our life. . . . Once the language is learned it becomes natural and easy to use. This program fosters respect and responsibility for all. It proves that if you treat people with respect you get it in return. . . . For teachers it is not an extra thing to teach but rather something that can be modeled and integrated successfully into the already existing curriculum. . . . It works! (East Prairie Safe Schools coordinator/conflict resolution specialist)

East Prairie School District believes that a successful peaceable school program is built on the understanding that all members of a school, from the staff to the students, can improve the school climate through the use of conflict resolution skills. The East Prairie School District is a one-school, suburban district that serves students from kindergarten through the eighth grade. Located in suburban Skokie, Illinois, the school serves a diverse student population, including those of Asian, Hispanic, Syrian, European, and African descent. When walking its halls, you can expect to hear any of over 50 different languages being spoken.

East Prairie developed its current peaceable school program over a 4-year period. The school used the *Creating the Peaceable School* curriculum. A safe school coordinator/conflict resolution specialist was hired who had previous training in and experience with the program. A program team, the Safe School Committee, was formed, and the members attended a peaceable school training. The school members responsible for implementing the program after the initial training included East Prairie's principal, the superintendent of schools, and members of the Safe School Committee. The committee consisted of representatives from the board of education, PTA, school administration and staff, police and fire departments, park district, mental health associations, and, more recently, students. In the fall of 2000, all school staff, including all administrators, joined with members of the Safe School Committee to participate in a 2-day training, conducted by one of the authors (Bodine).

The East Prairie peaceable school program has three major components: student and staff training, the peer mediation program, and the rights and responsibilities section of the school discipline policy.

School staff members and students are trained each year. Returning staff members receive a refresher workshop at the beginning of each academic year. New staff members receive basic training for 1 or 2 days at the beginning of the year. In addition, the conflict resolution specialist provides ongoing support and training for all staff when necessary. Once trained, East Prairie's teachers make all students familiar with conflict resolution strategies and skills through classroom work. Because students learn not only from what they are taught but also from the behaviors of the school's staff, staff members have the additional responsibility of modeling the skills as much as possible.

East Prairie lays a foundation for the peaceable school program through its discipline policy based on rights and responsibilities. The entire staff participated in a 2-day training workshop with author Bodine, during which they finalized their school plan for creating a peaceable climate, incorporating the concepts described in Section 1 of this guide.

The peaceable school program conflict resolution strategies are used frequently at East Prairie. On average, there are 15 negotiations, 10 mediations facilitated by the conflict resolution specialist, 5 peer mediations, and 5 group problem solving sessions held formally each week.

Before the peaceable school program was implemented, the most common types of disputes at East Prairie involved disrespect, physical and verbal fighting, not taking responsibility for actions, and being unprepared for class. Although these conflicts still exist, they are no longer managed through detentions and visits to the principal. Students and school staff members resolve these disputes and develop plans of action through negotiation, mediation, and group problem solving.

The peaceable school program has improved the school climate in many ways over the past 4 years:

1. Detentions and suspensions have decreased.

2. Repeat detentions (for the same offense by the same individual) have decreased.

3. Mediations have increased, both those conducted by an adult and by peers.

4. More students are referring themselves to mediation.

5. More parents are suggesting to their children that they seek out the assistance of the conflict resolution specialist when faced with a conflict.

6. Less time is spent on managing behavior, leaving more time for learning.

7. Students receive more individualized attention in managing their disputes.

On a personal level, staff and students who regularly use conflict resolution skills and strategies tend to be more respectful and more willing to listen to the perspectives of other people. The students take responsibility for their actions and are willing to come up with solutions to resolve disputes. Ultimately, the students are being given more responsibility and power to help manage conflicts.

Ingram Sowell Elementary Peaceable School

> Before implementing the peaceable schools program, we were unable to place paper towels and soap in our student restrooms. [Since we implemented] our PS program, children have shown more respect and pride in their school building. As a matter of fact, students, faculty, and parents have noticed a change in our school's climate. . . . Words such as *rights, responsibilities, trust, honesty*, etc., are not only said more often but practiced regularly by many of the students. (Ingram Sowell counselor/teacher)

Ingram Sowell Elementary School is a kindergarten through sixth-grade school, located in rural Lawrenceburg, Tennessee, which has spent the past 3 years developing a peaceable school program with a goal of providing "a peaceable setting for student success." The school's enrollment is approximately 500 students, of which 89 percent are Caucasian, 9 percent are African American, and 2 percent are of Asian or

Hispanic/Latino descent. The majority of Ingram Sowell's students come from families with incomes below the poverty line, resulting in 75 percent of the student population's being eligible for free or reduced-price meals. There are approximately 77 staff members at Ingram Sowell.

Ingram's decision to create a peaceable school program resulted from circumstances that caused all members of the school's community to need a more peaceful environment. Originally two Lawrenceburg schools, Ingram and Sowell consolidated in 1997, causing the number of students and staff members to almost double. As the lead educator of the school's peaceable school team explained, the school was greatly affected by the consolidation and subsequent growth:

> Our school spirit dropped tremendously. Misbehavior and poor student discipline coupled with new expectations for students and a lower economic background of students made for a really rough year. Many parents withdrew their children and moved them to other schools in the county. This exodus of "good families" hurt our image in the community. We decided to try the peaceable school program to help turn our image around and send a message to faculty, students, parents, and the community.

Once they decided a peaceable school program would improve the school's image in the community, five Ingram staff members attended a 3-day workshop facilitated by the staff of the Peaceable Schools Tennessee program. Upon returning from the training, the Ingram staff members established a peaceable school committee to help tailor the program to meet the needs and talents of Ingram Sowell Elementary. The committee is composed of the school's principal, guidance counselor, librarian, and regular and special education teachers.

The Ingram Sowell program teaches and celebrates its peacemakers both inside and outside of the classroom. Ingram starts each year by supporting the peaceable school philosophy through a peaceable school theme week. During this period, teachers dedicate the majority of their time to teaching the rights and responsibilities program, plus the rules of the school under that program. Additionally, the school designates one day during that week as "CAPS Day." Ingram Sowell staff members and students wear caps during the day in support of various principles of the peaceable school: *C*ool off, *A*gree to work it out, express and understand *P*oints of view, and generate mutually beneficial *S*olutions.

Students have the opportunity to learn and practice conflict resolution skills throughout the year through peaceable school lessons integrated into each classroom's academic curriculum. In addition, students participate in group problem solving during weekly class meetings to discuss issues that involve the entire class. Ingram Sowell's guidance counselor also makes biweekly visits to classrooms to conduct peaceable school lessons.

Ingram Sowell has established a system for acknowledging and celebrating those students who demonstrate positive peaceable school behaviors. Each week, Ingram Sowell classrooms nominate a Peacemaker of the Week, a student who has exhibited that week's targeted peaceable behavior. Once a Peacemaker of the Week is selected, that student's name is read over the intercom, and an announcement is posted in the lobby and outside the student's classroom with a description of the behavior that resulted in his or her selection.

To recognize those students who receive the honor of Peacemaker of the Week multiple times, Ingram Sowell maintains a Practicing Peacemaker display in its lobby. After a student is chosen as the Peacemaker of the Week twice, his or her name is placed on the Practicing Peacemaker bulletin board. Successive selections result in a star's being placed by the student's name. If a student is chosen as Peacemaker of the Week three times during a year, a book is dedicated to Ingram Sowell's library in the student's honor. During the 2000–2001 academic year, Ingram Sowell honored over 200 different Practicing Peacemakers.

In an effort to provide even more support for the peaceable school program and to encourage students and staff to participate in school-wide activities, Ingram Sowell hosts two events that involve all members of the school community. The school holds a peaceable school pep rally each fall, during which each grade level performs a chant, cheer, song, or skit that addresses an aspect of a peaceable school. Ingram also organizes a peaceable school parade each spring, during which students make posters, banners, and wagon floats, all with a peaceable school theme. All Ingram Sowell students and staff march around the school accompanied by a police car and fire truck escort as school board members, community members, and parents watch.

The peaceable school committee at Ingram Sowell actively promotes the program to untrained staff and parents. Five staff members are selected to attend Peaceable Schools Tennessee training each year. Additionally, all staff members attend inservice meetings about the program conducted by the committee. These meetings, typically lasting from over 1 hour to a full day, are facilitated by teachers who have attended Peaceable Schools Tennessee training. Parents also learn of the program through the Ingram Sowell parent/student handbook, PTO meetings, newspaper articles about peaceable school events, and certificates given to students.

The peaceable school program has had a great impact on the Ingram Sowell school community. Before the program was implemented, as the school and community struggled with the difficulties of consolidation, Ingram Sowell was rife with frustration, anger, and negative feelings about the school and its population. This attitude was pervasive among students, who generally resorted to fighting, name-calling, and arguing to resolve their disputes. The program at Ingram has helped improve the school's climate by giving students the opportunity and skills to de-escalate problems by talking them out. As a result, students are more accepting of differences, show staff members more respect, and have more school spirit and pride. Fewer punitive measures have been taken to change students' behaviors, and academic gains have continued at Ingram Sowell. In brief, the school has created an atmosphere of caring for its students, staff, and surrounding community. As the school continues its efforts to maintain a respectful and peaceful environment, the consensus of all constituents is that the school is molding very successful students who have a definitive understanding of conflict resolution.

Cleveland Middle School Peaceable School

> This training has certainly made a difference in our lives at home. We can now have a conversation within our family. It is nice that through the training offered at Cleveland Middle School, both to parents and students, we can speak the same language and deal with our conflicts. My two sons have received the conflict resolution training and are constantly trying to decide what is the origin of the conflict and how would be the best means to handle it so that both feel it is a win-win situation. (Parent of two Cleveland Middle School students)

Cleveland Middle School (CMS) of Cleveland, Tennessee, houses approximately 1,000 sixth-, seventh-, and eighth-grade students, served by approximately 70 staff members. CMS seeks to develop responsible citizens who will set the standards for excellence in a global society. To help develop such citizens, the school emphasizes the teaching and practice of conflict resolution skills through its peaceable school program. Through this program, educators at CMS build leadership skills in their students and members of the community.

The peaceable school program began 4 years ago at CMS, following a mediation training of students and staff members. The peaceable school planning committee, responsible for developing and maintaining the program at CMS, consists of the school's principal, two assistant principals, a parent, a local police officer, and a teacher who also is a member of the Peaceable School Tennessee's trainer cadre. Recognizing that a peaceable school can be achieved only through the hard work of all members of the CMS community, the committee helps students, parents, and staff members develop a number of conflict resolution skills, including an understanding of the nature and origins of conflict and the essence of peacemaking. Additionally, the committee focuses on student rights, responsibilities, and cooperation; classroom constitutions; and noncoercive discipline as tools of classroom management. Upon this foundation, the committee has built several processes to manage disputes. The school conducts class meetings, using the group problem solving model, for disputes and issues that arise in the classroom and maintains a peer mediation program to resolve more intimate disputes between students.

To help build and maintain the program, CMS receives additional training and program development opportunities through a partnership with Peaceable Schools Tennessee. Initially, five CMS teachers attended a 3-day Peaceable Schools Tennessee training. Two of those teachers attended an additional Peaceable Schools Tennessee training session to learn how to train other educators in the *Creating the Peaceable School* model.

Students and staff of CMS have many opportunities to learn and practice conflict resolution skills. Peaceable school lessons are integrated into the traditional CMS academic program, allowing students to experience conflict resolution lessons taught by educators in the classrooms. Students have the opportunity to use these skills through negotiation and group problem solving sessions held in classrooms. CMS educators are also encouraged to include in their classrooms a peace corner, a safe area where two students can go to work out their problems peaceably or where one person can choose to go for a time-out to cool off. The school holds approximately 30 negotiation sessions, 20 group problem solving sessions, and 25 visits to the peace corner per day.

In addition to the peace corner in classrooms, CMS also maintains a schoolwide peaceful area called the "Chill Room." Students use this room to calm down after they have been sent to the office due to a conflict with other students. To help the students manage the conflict and change the behaviors that helped create it, teachers and administrators use a written plan. This plan helps students think of the needs they are trying to fulfill and the positive behaviors that might help them meet these needs while also resolving the conflict.

CMS has also developed a conflict resolution course for its students to learn and practice their skills. The teen leadership class lasts for 6 weeks and is repeated throughout the year. In this class, students practice negotiation, mediation, and group problem solving skills by applying these methods to issues affecting their own lives. In the teen leadership class, students previously trained help the peaceable school teacher/trainer to train current students in peaceable school concepts.

In addition, the CMS peaceable school committee has developed a peer mediation program, in which both teachers and students select the individuals to participate in peer mediation training. There are approximately 20 mediations held per week at CMS.

With so many opportunities to learn and practice the peaceable school philosophy, members of the CMS community recognize the importance of promoting and celebrating their successes. CMS promotes the program through an in-house television and radio station. In addition, students, staff members, and parents and guardians are able to watch a video production of a peaceable school training to learn more about conflict resolution skills and processes. Parents and guardians also learn of the program through the newsletter "Parent Link."

To keep the conflict resolution skills and processes fresh in the minds of current students, and to bring newly admitted and transfer students up to speed, CMS conducts follow-up training sessions whenever necessary. The teen leadership class is repeated every 6 weeks, allowing students entering the school during the year to have the opportunity for in-depth study of conflict resolution and peaceable school topics. Peer mediators also participate in a 2-day training whenever necessary to replenish the cadre of mediators.

CMS staff members also have the opportunity to participate in refresher training provided by two Peaceable Schools Tennessee trainers who are members of the CMS staff. These trainers conduct an in-depth 2½-day training for faculty.

CMS has been extremely gratified by the growth of its peaceable school program and its effect on both students and staff members. Before the program was implemented, the school officially handled approximately 75 fights during the year, mostly involving threats and bullying behaviors. After the program was in place, the number of fights decreased to approximately 35 per year, and students began replacing fighting with requests for peer mediators or visits to the peace corner and Chill Room if they needed assistance calming down or resolving disputes. Students dealing with conflicts outside the school have since sought help from the school's resource officer to deal with those conflicts in more productive ways.

The peaceable school program has also helped the students and staff members relate to each other differently. Students have developed a common conflict resolution language that makes resolving their disputes easier. Additionally, the responses to conflicts between students have changed since the program was implemented. Conflicts before the program often became physical in nature, whereas disputes between students now are more likely to be discussed instead of handled in a physical way.

In addition to the changes in student behaviors, CMS administrators also have altered the ways they respond to student conflicts, moving away from coercive discipline to a system that encourages students to discover unmet basic needs and develop a plan to meet those needs and resolve their conflicts.

CMS has developed a number of other complementary programs and partnerships to bring services to its students. The school maintains a "We the People . . . the Citizen and the Constitution" program and also serves as an after-school site, providing learning opportunities for youth and families until 6:30 P.M. each evening through its ROCKETS (Responsibility, Opportunity, Citizenship, Knowledge, Empowerment, Teamwork, and Service) program. CMS also partners with the local police department, the county juvenile court, local attorneys and banks, and the civic education center to bring programs to its youth.

Finally, the impact of the CMS peaceable school program has not been limited to school grounds. The skills these students learn are applicable in many areas of life, including managing disputes with family. With the guidance of strong leadership from the peaceable school committee, CMS is that much closer to reaching its goal of developing responsible citizens who will set new standards for excellence in society.

OTHER CONFLICT RESOLUTION EDUCATION EVALUATIONS

The studies described next have shown support for the efficacy of models of CRE other than the *Creating the Peaceable Schools* approach. This sampling is not intended to be exhaustive but rather to highlight findings about aspects of the comprehensive peaceable school program: mediation, negotiation, group problem solving, curriculum infusion, peacemaking, and peaceable classrooms.

Teaching Students to Be Peacemakers

David Johnson and Roger Johnson and colleagues, of the Cooperative Learning Center at the University of Minnesota, have reported the results of a series of landmark studies they conducted over a 5-year period. As described in *Teaching Students to Be Peacemakers: Results of Five Years of Research* (Johnson & Johnson, 1994), these studies were designed to examine students' ability to manage conflict before and after conflict resolution training. The program had as its basis the theories of integrative bargaining (Pruitt, 1981), perspective reversal (Johnson, 1971), and constructive conflict (Deutsch, 1973). Student training focused on the negotiation and/or mediation process and lasted from 9 to 15 hours for the various studies; students involved were in first through ninth grades. The studies were conducted in both suburban and urban settings. Five studies used control groups, three studies randomly selected classrooms and/or controls from the school, one study randomly assigned students to conditions, and four studies rotated teachers across conditions.

Johnson and Johnson's (1994) research is highly significant because their program is based on the theoretical literature on conflicts of interests, integrative bargaining, perspective reversal, and third-party intervention. These same theories pervade most conflict resolution programs in operation within schools today. Results of these studies provide educators and conflict resolution experts with valuable information about the need for conflict resolution programs and the impact of conflict management training programs on students' ability to manage their conflicts constructively. The program studied is a peaceable classroom/peaceable school approach. The following discussion summarizes results of Johnson and Johnson's research and suggests implications for the development of subsequent conflict resolution programs.

Need for Conflict Resolution Programs

Before conflict resolution training, most students were found to be involved in conflicts daily, indicating that conflicts are pervasive within classrooms and schools. The conflicts reported most frequently involved put-downs and teasing, playground problems, access or possession, physical aggression and fights, academic work, and turn taking. Before training, students referred the majority of their conflicts to the teacher, used destructive strategies that tended to escalate the conflict rather than resolve it, and lacked knowledge of how to negotiate. If they did not bring their conflict to a teacher, students typically used destructive strategies (such as repeating their request and trying to force the other person to give in) that would escalate the conflict and increase the likelihood that the teacher would have to intervene. Untrained students never indicated that they would negotiate a solution to a conflict. Students had no idea how to negotiate an agreement satisfactory to both. The finding that students were not being taught negotiation procedures and skills in the home or community at large suggested, therefore, that all students could benefit from training in how to manage conflicts constructively.

Impact of Conflict Resolution Training

Johnson and Johnson (1994) established some parameters to judge the effectiveness of conflict resolution training. Specifically, they determined that conflict resolution training works if it results in (a) reduction in student-student conflicts referred to teachers and the principal, (b) students' mastery of the negotiation and mediation procedures and skills taught, and (c) students' use of these procedures and skills in settings other than the classroom.

Their research indicated that after negotiation and mediation training, the student-student conflicts that did occur were by and large managed by the students themselves without the involvement of adults. The frequency of student-student conflicts that teachers had to manage dropped 80 percent after the training, and the number of conflicts referred to the principal was reduced to zero. Such a dramatic reduction of referrals of conflicts to adult authorities changed the discipline program from arbitrating conflicts to maintaining and supporting the peer mediation process. At the end of the academic year, months after students received training in negotiation and mediation, almost all the students who had been trained still knew all the negotiation and mediation steps. This knowledge was assessed by giving students conflict scenarios to respond to in written, interview, and videotaped simulation formats. The high rate of retention was attributed to the fact that students were using the procedures to manage their day-to-day conflicts with classmates and peers. Students who received training also could apply the procedures to actual conflict situations. Trained students were carefully observed, and information was gathered from teachers, principals, and parents to find out whether or not the negotiation and mediation skills transferred to nonclassroom and nonschool settings. Results indicated that students did use the negotiation and mediation procedures in playground, neighborhood, and family settings. A number of parents volunteered to teachers that students used negotiation and mediation procedures and skills with their brothers and sisters, neighborhood friends, and grandparents.

Academic Achievement

Johnson and Johnson's (1994) findings indicated that learning the negotiation procedure affects students' academic achievement. The peacemaker training was integrated into a 2-week high school English literature unit. Students were randomly assigned to experimental or control groups. Students in the experimental group studied a novel, learned the negotiation procedure, and role-played each of the major conflicts in the novel using the integrative negotiation procedure. Students in the control group spent all their time studying the novel. Students in both conditions took an achievement test the last day of the instructional unit. Students in the experimental condition scored significantly higher on the achievement test than did students in the control condition. This finding suggests that, even though it takes time to teach the negotiation procedure, learning of academic material can be substantially improved.

As reported by Stevahn, Johnson, Johnson, Laginski, and O'Coin (1996), the high school students actually learned and retained the conflict resolution procedures taught in class. Before the 2-week unit, the majority of both groups of students tried to resolve a simulated conflict by using force or by telling the teacher. After the unit, half the students trained in conflict resolution used the negotiation process, whereas the majority of the untrained students still resorted to force or telling the teacher. None of the untrained students used the negotiation process.

Trained students were also found more likely to master and retain the negotiation process. Immediately after training, 76 percent of those trained demonstrated an understanding of the negotiation process. Thirteen weeks after training, 62 percent still used all the steps, and 19 percent still used five of the six steps of the negotiation process.

The study also investigated whether students' attitudes toward conflict are affected by the integration of conflict resolution theory into an English curriculum. Before training, all students viewed conflict as a negative experience. After training, the majority still saw conflict as negative, but there was a significant increase in the number of positive words associated with conflict among trained students.

Link Between Peer Mediation Training and Negotiation Research

Two different approaches to peer mediation exist: school cadre and total student body. The school cadre approach is based on the assumption that a few specially trained students can constructively defuse and resolve the interpersonal conflicts taking place among members of the student body. A small number of students are trained to serve as peer mediators, usually during a 1- or 2-day workshop or a semester-long class. The total student body approach emphasizes training every student in the school in ways to manage conflicts constructively.

Investigating how students would manage conflicts in which they could use a win-lose strategy or win-win (integrative negotiation) strategy, Johnson and Johnson (1994) found that all untrained students used the win-lose strategy. Students who had undergone training primarily used the integrative negotiation strategy. This finding provides an important link between peer mediation training and the research on negotiation. If mediation is to succeed, disputants must be taught how conflicts are managed. This means that if previous training has not taken place, disputants will need to be trained in integrative negotiation as part of the process of mediation. It may well be that destructive conflict management techniques are the result of ignorance of conflict resolution procedures. If so, this would validate the importance of the total student body approach to peer mediation.

Adult Perceptions

Johnson and Johnson (1994) found adult perceptions of the peer mediation program helpful in their assessment of program effectiveness. Interviews indicated that teachers, principals, and parents believed the program reduced the incidence of destructively managed conflicts and resulted in a more positive classroom climate. When students regulate their own behavior, the need for teachers and administrators to monitor and control student actions declines. Discipline improves, while teachers are freed to devote their energies to teaching. By training the teachers to train the students, both the faculty and the student body learn the same procedures for managing conflict. Schoolwide norms and procedures are thus established for everyone in the school.

Summary

The Johnson and Johnson (1994) research demonstrated that even young children can be taught how to negotiate and mediate. This finding has relevance for professionals who work with families, youth programs, or schools. Knowing how to negotiate and mediate conflicts is important for a number of reasons. First, it empowers students to regulate their own behavior. Self-regulation is the ability to act in socially approved ways in the absence of monitoring by others. It is a central and significant hallmark of cognitive and social development. Frequently, adults act as referees and judges in the lives of children. When they take on these roles, adults place children in a dependent position and deprive them of opportunities to learn valuable social skills. Second, children who are able to negotiate and mediate have a developmental advantage over children who do not know how to do so. It may be hypothesized that using one's own competencies to resolve conflicts with others constructively increases children's strength and ability to cope with stress and adversity and their ability to build and maintain high-quality relationships with peers.

Comprehensive Peer Mediation Evaluation Project

This landmark 2-year research project clearly establishes the efficacy of peer mediation training and peer mediation programs, an important keystone of the *Creating the Peaceable School* program. Twenty-seven schools in Philadelphia, Laredo (Texas), and Denver participated in the project. These schools included elementary, middle, and high schools. As described by Jones (1998), the general findings are as follows.

Peer mediation programs provide significant benefit in developing constructive social and conflict behavior in children at all educational levels. Students who are direct recipients of program training are most greatly affected; however, students without direct training also benefit. In other words, youth trained as peer mediators are able to enact and utilize the behavioral skills taught in training in real-life situations as well as in formal mediation settings.

Peer mediation programs have a significant and sustained impact on teacher and staff perceptions of school climate. Elements of school climate most notably affected are the development of a productive learning environment, maintenance of high standards, creation of a supportive and friendly environment, and development of a positive overall climate.

Peer mediation, when used, is very effective at handling disputes. There is a very high rate of agreement that peer mediation is effective, along with high mediator and disputant satisfaction. However, the number of cases documented suggests that mediation may be underutilized in comparison to its potential benefits.

The policy implication of these results is clear. The promotion and specific training in mediation-related skills should be a priority for the development of social and conflict competence in young people at all ages.

This study also attempted to compare the effectiveness of peer mediation cadre programs versus peer mediation whole-school programs. In cadre programs, a select number of students were trained as mediators, whereas in the whole-school programs, a select number of students were trained as mediators and all students were exposed to conflict resolution training through curriculum infusion.

Students exposed to conflict resolution under both the cadre and whole-school approaches reduced their personal conflicts; increased their prosocial values, perspective-taking skills, and conflict competence skills; and experienced a decrease in aggressiveness.

Staff members at all levels found that both approaches positively affected the school climate by helping develop a productive learning environment. There was no significant effect on student's perceptions of climate, nor was there evidence that either approach affected overall incidents of suspension or violence.

The effect of both approaches on handling disputes was also examined. Under both approaches, 92 percent of cases ended in an agreement in middle and high school programs. There were also high rates of mediator and disputant satisfaction under both approaches. High school mediators and disputants were more satisfied than those in middle school with mediator performance. Finally, students involved in the whole-school approach were more satisfied with mediator performance than were those in peer mediation cadre programs.

The cadre approach had a stronger effect on students' conflict attitudes and behaviors. It was also more effective at increasing perspective-taking and conflict competence skills in both the peer mediators and other students. The whole-school approach had a stronger positive impact on climate in middle and high schools. Both were equally effective in usage, agreement and satisfaction rates, and staff perceptions of climate. The whole-school approach, however, was more effective in positively impacting students' perceptions of climate.

The study results for peer mediation for both the cadre and whole-school approach are clear. However, the results are less clear for the comparison of the two approaches. Curriculum infusion training in the whole-school approach was generally limited to lessons of about 45 minutes, delivered once a week for one semester only. Such limited exposure would hardly qualify as a comprehensive, quality, sustained CRE program.

Ohio School Conflict Management Project

The Ohio Committee on Dispute Resolution and Conflict Management (OCDRCM) and the Ohio Department of Education formed a partnership to help implement conflict resolution programs in Ohio elementary schools (Ohio Commission on Dispute Resolution and Conflict Management & Ohio Department of Education, 1997). The following summarizes the effect of the partnership on 12 elementary schools over a 3-year period.

Teams of school staff participated in training at OCDRCM regional centers. They returned to their schools and trained students and other staff members. OCDRCM trainers supported the schools during the first year of program implementation. Schools used a variety of methods to teach conflict resolution skills to all members of the school community:

1. Special all-school assembly programs

2. Whole-group instruction in classrooms provided by special teachers

3. Curriculum infusion activities by regular classroom teachers into classes, including language arts, social studies, and health

4. Peer mediation training for a small cadre of students

5. All-school celebrations such as "Peace Day"

6. Special all-school activities recognizing days without fighting and suspensions

7. Reward programs for students who use positive social skills

8. Older students teaching younger students conflict resolution skills

9. Workshops for support staff and parents to learn conflict resolution skills

As a result of the partnership participation:

1. Suspension rates significantly decreased. (One school had its total days of suspension drop from approximately 275 in the year before the conflict management program was implemented to approximately 75 in the second year of the program.)

2. The number of fights, put-downs, and other disputes decreased. (The number of fights in one school decreased from 99 in the year before the conflict management program was implemented to 4 in the third year of the program.)

3. The number of acts of kindness and good sportsmanship increased. Less time was spent by staff on conflict, and more time was spent on learning. (Emergency removals of students in one school decreased by 77 percent.)

4. The number of students on the honor roll and with perfect attendance increased.

5. Use of conflict resolution language among staff and students increased.

Also, the Ohio partnership awarded 2-year grants of $3,000 to 50 high schools to support the introduction of CRE programs (Tschannen-Moran, 1991). Forty-three of the schools received follow-up grants of $1,450. School approaches to implementation varied but fit into one of three categories: peer mediation, curriculum infusion, or special events. Three years after the initial grants were made, a survey of the degree and effect of implementation of the conflict management program in schools, taken by 452 teachers in 14 schools, indicated the far-reaching impact these grants have had: Almost 90 percent of teachers surveyed said that the school was safer to some degree as a result of implementation of the conflict management program. In addition, more than 80 percent said the degree of physical fighting had decreased in their school to some degree since the start of the program.

Given the typically poor track records of programs continuing past the end of funding and the small size of the initial grants, these are remarkable results. Not only were schools safer as a result of the implementation of these conflict management programs, teachers saw benefits extend to their classrooms. Seventy percent said the conflict resolution program had reduced the amount of time they spent resolving student disputes. Eighty-seven percent said they had used, to some extent, conflict management techniques for dealing with classroom management and discipline.

Teachers also witnessed changes in their students as a result of conflict management instruction: Eighty-seven percent saw an increase in students' willingness to cooperate with each other, and the same percentage reported that students had begun to use the skills taught when they observed students use negotiation skills to deal with interpersonal problems; in addition, 86 percent reported having seen students take responsibility for solving their own problems without asking for adult help.

Resolving Conflict Creatively Program

The Resolving Conflict Creatively Program (RCCP) is a peaceable schools approach to conflict resolution education that begins in kindergarten and extends through grade 12. RCCP originated in New York City schools and has gradually extended to other school districts, particularly large, urban settings. An early evaluation of the impact of RCCP (Metis Associates, Inc., 1990) in four multiracial, multiethnic school districts in New York City showed that 84 percent of teachers surveyed reported positive changes in classroom climate. A total of 71 percent of teachers in the RCCP evaluation reported moderate or great decreases in physical violence in the classroom, and 66 percent observed less name-calling and fewer verbal put-downs. Similar percentages observed that students were showing better perspective-taking skills, greater willingness to cooperate, and more caring behavior. In addition, over 98 percent of respondents said that the mediation component gave children an important tool for dealing with conflicts. Other changes reported by teachers and administrators in the evaluation included children's spontaneously using conflict resolution skills, increased self-esteem and sense of empowerment, increased awareness and verbalization of feelings, and greater acceptance of differences.

Another evaluation of RCCP was conducted by the National Center for Children in Poverty (NCCP) and focused on RCCP as a violence prevention program (Aber, Jones, Brown, Chaudry, & Samples, 1998). The evaluation was planned so that it could assess the impact of the RCCP on the social-cognitive processes that lead to the development of aggressive behavior and violence, as well as on aggressive behavior itself. This rigorous, 2-year study included approximately 5,000 second- through sixth-grade children in 15 New York City public schools. RCCP's three main components are the training and coaching of teachers implementing a conflict resolution curriculum, classroom instruction of children in the curriculum, and training and supervision of peer mediators. The researchers analyzed the impact of the curriculum on several developmental processes known to lead to violence and antisocial behavior. They also examined the influence classroom beliefs about aggression (classroom climate) and violent/poor neighborhoods (neighborhood climate) had on the effectiveness of the RCCP program.

Over the 2-year study, it was found that developmental processes that place children at risk of violence increase as children age. Independent of their participation in RCCP, children's aggressive thoughts and behaviors increased over time. Children reported significantly higher levels of aggressive negotiation strategies, aggressive fantasies, and conduct problems and significantly lower levels of competent negotiation strategies as they aged. Evaluation results take this general tendency of youth development into account.

Overall, NCCP's evaluation found RCCP had a significantly positive impact when teachers taught a high number of lessons from the curriculum (on average, 25 lessons over the school year). Children taught these lessons showed a slower growth in self-reported hostile attributions, aggressive fantasies, and aggressive problem-solving strategies, as well as in teacher-reported aggressive behavior, as compared with those children receiving few or no lessons. Children in the high-lessons group also received significantly increased ratings from their teachers on positive social behaviors and emotional control and showed greater improvement on standardized academic achievement tests when compared with the other two groups. Importantly, children receiving a low number of lessons did somewhat more poorly than children receiving no lessons on a number of these outcomes.

Other results, reported by Aber, Jones, Brown, Samples, and Chaudry (1996), indicated that the RCCP benefits all children regardless of gender, grade, or risk status, although the evidence suggests slightly reduced benefits for boys, younger children, and children in high-risk classrooms and neighborhoods. Classrooms in which the use of aggression was allowed and neighborhoods with high poverty and homicide rates reduced, but did not totally negate, the effectiveness of exposure to many conflict resolution lessons. Children in these classrooms and neighborhoods reported significantly higher levels of aggressive negotiation strategies, aggressive fantasies, and conduct problems and significantly lower levels of competent negotiation strategies.

The NCCP evaluators report the following lessons learned from the RCCP study:

1. Teachers, administration, the school board, and parents must voluntarily join the program for it to be successful.

2. Teachers should examine their own behaviors as they teach a conflict resolution curriculum to students. Conflict resolution should be presented to children as a way of life, not a set of skills.

3. Staff and students must be allowed to celebrate their program accomplishments, publicly and collectively.

4. The whole-school approach provides schools with better conflict resolution programs.

5. Teachers must receive ongoing training and technical assistance for the program to succeed.

6. The school principals and program staff must work together throughout all stages of implementation, including planning.

7. Conflict resolution education must be combined with other efforts that improve education (e.g., smaller schools and classrooms) to help change levels of violence.

Peer Mediation Youthful Frames of Power and Influence

A study by Hessler, Hollis, and Crowe (1998) investigated and compared school staff's and students' views of status and motivation of peer mediators, conflict and violence, and role of mediators in the school. Of the three midwestern elementary schools examined, two implemented peer mediation programs, whereas the third infused conflict resolution theory and skills into its curriculum.

The study noted that two views of mediation emerged: School staff thought mediation empowered students and elevated the status of those trained. The peer mediators were more idealistic and thought of mediation as an intellectually challenging opportunity to help others. Specific findings included the following.

Status and motivation of peer mediators. Staff gave peer mediators a higher status than other students. They thought the student mediators would internalize this status and think of themselves as higher in status than other students. Students trained minimized their selection as mediators. Most became mediators to help others. Only one mentioned higher status as a motivation for becoming a mediator.

Perceptions of conflict and violence. Some staff saw conflict as necessary for social change. Most thought mediators couldn't manage violence because it involves many factors, including economic conditions, alienation from school, parental abuse, behavior disorders, and racism. Student mediators saw conflict and violence as a range of behaviors from verbal to physical disputes. Unlike staff, students believed that mediation could be used to manage violence.

Role of mediators. Adults saw mediation as a means to prevent violent behavior and to help find solutions to conflict. Students who had experienced dispute mediation thought of peer mediators as socially and academically above other students but attributed no additional power to the mediators. Student mediators believed it was their role to help others, the school, and society by stopping conflicts before they escalate into physical disputes.

Peer Mediation and Transfer of Knowledge

In a study conducted by Gentry and Benenson (1992), researchers worked with an Illinois elementary school to help examine the effect conflict resolution training had on students' working to manage conflicts with siblings. Teachers integrated conflict resolution awareness exercises into their curriculum for a 4-week period. Twenty-seven students attending the fourth through sixth grades received 6 hours of peer mediation training. The peer mediators were then allowed to mediate playground disputes for 10 weeks to practice their conflict resolution skills. Trained students and their parents were then questioned about sibling interactions at home.

The students reported that it was difficult for them to use conflict resolution skills with untrained siblings. However, the trained students also expressed a significant decline in the frequency and intensity of conflicts with siblings. Parents noted an improved use of productive communication skills by trained students during conflicts and a significant decline in parental intervention in conflicts at home.

The Mountain Home Project

The Mountain Home Project of Idaho, a small pilot project, examined how teaching conflict resolution skills affects students' skills and knowledge, mediators' self-concepts, and number of conflicts on the playground. As reported by Roush and Hall (1993), approximately 100 elementary students and 8 junior high school students were taught conflict resolution skills during the 1990–1991 academic school year. The project consisted of six conflict resolution lessons taught to students in the fourth through the sixth grades (for approximately 12 hours of instruction), an elective conflict resolution course at the junior high school level (for 90 hours of instruction), and peer mediation training for use on the elementary school playground.

The elementary school students demonstrated a significant increase in knowledge of conflict resolution theory. The researchers also found that a student's self-concept was affected by the amount of time that she or he was trained and allowed to interact with the instructor and other students: Although junior high school students' self-concept was affected in a positive way after 90 hours of training, there was no effect on elementary student's self-concept after 12 hours of training. Eight of the elementary students were selected because they were "playground bullies." Half of these students showed a positive change in self-concept.

Finally, the number of conflicts on the elementary playground decreased when mediators were used to settle disputes. Misconduct notices decreased by 40 percent. Misconduct notices specifically for fighting dropped from seven before the mediators were on the playground to zero after mediators were used to resolve playground disputes.

Peace Education Foundation

In 1991, the Peace Education Foundation (PEF) initiated conflict resolution and peer mediation programs throughout Dade County, Florida, Region II Public Schools (Hanson, 1994). Training for school staff was provided in order to establish both classroom-based and schoolwide student mediation programs and to infuse school curricula with conflict resolution instruction. A review of mediator reports showed that 86 percent of conflicts mediated were resolved. A system of incident reporting showed a statistically significant reduction in the rate of referrals for general disruptive behavior in the elementary schools that had the highest levels of implementation. Conflict resolution affected student attitudes toward resolving conflicts positively. Results from student surveys indicated that those who received training were more willing to respond to conflict situations with actions other than threats and violence.

In 1994, staff teams from seven alternative and two middle schools with a high percentage of at-risk students received training in the peace education conflict resolution model. Postintervention surveys showed the following:

1. Student attitudes toward conflict changed significantly after learning the model.

2. Students were more inclined to explain, reason, compromise, or share in order to resolve their conflicts.

3. Students were less likely to appeal to authority figures or to use aggression and threats when in conflict.

4. Teachers felt more respected and less frustrated as a result of implementing the model.

Evaluations of the Palm Beach County Schools initiative revealed a considerable reduction in student disciplinary referrals and suspensions. For example, the number of referrals at one elementary school dropped to 5 between September and December of 1994 from 124 during the same period in 1992. One Palm Beach high school trained all teachers using the PEF model in 1996. In 1997 and 1998, the years the study reported here concluded, all students were taught the PEF model during a specific period. The school reported a reduction in the number of fights and disciplinary referrals each year from 1996 until 1998. There was a reduction in the number of disciplinary events and in the number and percentage of students with out-of-school suspensions from 1997 until 1998.

Parents who attended a "Fighting Fair for Families" workshop also reported favorable results. According to 2-month follow-up surveys from 163 participants, 79 percent saw improvement in the way conflicts were handled at home, 76 percent reported improvement in the way feelings were treated at home, 70 percent reported improvement in the way people listened to each other at home, and 80 percent reported that their "Rules for Fighting Fair" program poster was still displayed in their homes.

CONCLUSION

A significant, although not exhaustive, body of outcome data support the need for and viability of conflict resolution education. Quality comprehensive programs like *Creating the Peaceable School* have been shown clearly to impact school climate and provide young people with skills and processes that they do, in fact, retain and use in their immediate life contexts, especially in school. What is largely lacking from the current body of research on CRE programs is information on long-term effects relating to how those trained in school utilize their learning in their adult life contexts.

Research supports and legitimizes the contention that effective conflict resolution programs must be based on proven negotiation theory. Such theory must be operationalized as instructional procedures that educators can be trained to use and that students can use to resolve their own conflicts. Use of the demonstrated theoretical base and pragmatic delivery system is the critical benchmark of a quality CRE program. Outcome data show that a little quality instruction, even one-dimensional approaches such as peer mediation, is superior to none. However, a comprehensive, sustained approach is required to overcome the natural social influences working against peaceful, constructive conflict resolution. The peaceable school approach, based on demonstrated principles and implemented throughout the school system, is the only approach likely to have sustained impact on the culture—not just an immediate impact in the school, but also a long-term impact on society in general.

If we can train a whole generation of young people to be peacemakers by constructively resolving conflicts, the future can be very different from what we now reasonably foresee it to be. As Dr. Tricia S. Jones, lead researcher of the Comprehensive Peer Mediation Project, states in an unpublished brief, "these CRE programs should be seen as a vaccination for, and not a cure to, the disease of violence."

APPENDIX B

Annotated Bibliography

ADDITIONAL CONFLICT RESOLUTION EDUCATION RESOURCES

The training activities in Sections 2 and 3 of Creating the Peaceable School *are comprehensive in that they address all of the foundation abilities for conflict resolution described in this guide's introduction. The training activities may be repeated from time to time because the thinking promoted and the responses and reactions generated will change with changing circumstances, especially as young people age. The activities, however, are not exhaustive, and educators may seek other materials to promote understanding of conflict and peace. Following are some suggested resources for additional or alternative activities.*

Bennett, B., Rolheiser, C., & Stevahn, L. (1991) *Cooperative learning: Where heart meets mind.* Toronto: Educational Connections.

> This resource book makes cooperative learning an ongoing reality in schools. It involves educators in critical inquiry, personal reflection, and supportive discussion about the concepts underlying cooperative strategies and effective classroom applications. The three main sections deal with cooperative learning as a strategy within a framework of other effective classroom practices and student interaction patterns. Practical ideas, sample lessons, and activities are presented in the text. Each chapter within the sections includes questions and activity sheets, making this book a resource to be used interactively among colleagues.

Johnson, D. W., & Johnson, R. T. (1992). *Creative controversy: Intellectual challenge in the classroom.* Edina, MN: Interaction.

> A comprehensive treatment of ways to structure intellectual/academic conflicts within cooperative learning groups. Intellectual conflicts are created to promote higher level reasoning, critical thinking, creative problem solving, and long-term retention. Plus, they are fun and energizing. Controversies may be structured in any subject area and at any grade level. Lesson plans and lesson structures are included.

Kreidler, W. J. (1984). *Creative conflict resolution: More than 200 activities for keeping peace in the classroom.* Glenview, IL: Scott, Foresman.

> This definitive manual provides elementary school educators with thoughtful, effective activities for responding to everyday

classroom conflicts. It contains over 200 classroom-tested activities and games and over 20 different teaching techniques with examples. It offers ways to turn conflict into productive opportunity by helping students deal nonviolently and constructively with anger, fear, aggression, and prejudice.

Kreidler, W. J. (1990). *Elementary perspectives: Teaching concepts of peace and conflict.* Cambridge, MA: Educators for Social Responsibility.

This teacher's guide offers more than 80 activities particularly suitable for middle and upper elementary grades. The activities help teachers and students define peace, explore justice, and learn the value of conflict and its resolution. Students read, write, draw, role-play, sing, and discuss their way through a process that helps them acquire the concrete cooperative and conflict resolution skills they need to become caring and socially responsible citizens.

Kreidler, W. J. (1994). *Teaching conflict resolution through children's literature.* New York: Scholastic.

An important challenge for all who choose to teach conflict resolution is the integration of conflict resolution education into existing school curricula. This "how to" guide presents ideas for using children's books to teach conflict resolution foundation abilities and other social skills. Giving at least three titles for each area, the author details how to use children's books to teach the nature of conflict, how conflict escalates, how conflict can be resolved, understanding other points of view, the role of feelings in conflict, and appreciation of diversity. The titles presented are generally for primary ages, but the techniques are easily adapted for older learners.

Kreidler, W. J. (1997). *Conflict resolution in the middle school.* Cambridge, MA: Educators for Social Responsibility.

This guide features 28 skill-building sections to help students address the conflicts that come with adolescence. It also provides ideas for implementing programs at the middle school level and offers ideas for curriculum infusion, including math and science.

Kreidler, W. J., & Furlong, L. (1996). *Adventures in peacemaking: A conflict resolution guide for school-age programs.* Cambridge, MA: Educators for Social Responsibility.

Designed to meet the unique needs of after-school programs, camps, and recreation centers, this guide contains hundreds of hands-on, engaging activities to teach basic conflict resolution concepts through cooperative challenges, drama, crafts, music, and cooking. These activities are adaptable to the classroom by any teacher looking for unusual, active projects. This book blends conflict resolution curricula with Project Adventure's activity-based programming.

Lieber, C. M. (1998). *Conflict resolution in the high school.* Cambridge, MA: Educators for Social Responsibility.

This comprehensive, sequenced curriculum will help secondary educators address conflict resolution and problem solving, build community and create a peaceable classroom, encourage diversity and intergroup relations, and promote social and emotional development. It includes a section on infusion of conflict resolution throughout a standard curriculum.

Porro, B. (1996). *Talk it out: Conflict resolution in the elementary classroom.* Alexandria, VA: Association for Supervision and Curriculum Development.

Talk It Out focuses on resolving real-life problems that occur in most classrooms—teasing, put-downs, pushing, hitting, cheating, gossiping, and refusing to share. It provides practical tips, lesson plans, step-by-step scripts, and other materials to help the primary classroom teacher introduce conflict resolution skills and help students internalize those skills as a four-step prenegotiation model.

Schrumpf, F., Freiberg, S., & Skadden, D. (1993). *Life lessons for young adolescents: An advisory guide for teachers.* Champaign, IL: Research Press

This book provides 94 group activities, many related directly to the abilities necessary for constructive conflict resolution. These activities are interesting, enjoyable, and—most important—relevant to students' social and personal development. Activities are short and simple, require minimal materials, and can be completed during homeroom or advisory periods. The book also provides helpful guidelines on group facilitation skills and on handling common group problems.

CHILDREN'S LITERATURE

Primary

Baker, B. (1969). *The pig war.* New York: Harper & Row.

American farmers and British troops fight for possession of an island both call their own. They reach a fair but funny solution.

Baker, B. (1988). *Digby and Kate.* New York: Dutton.

Digby the dog and Kate the cat enjoy each other's company even when they have their differences.

Blame, M. (1975). *The terrible thing that happened at our house.* New York: Parents Magazine Press.

> A youngster relates the terrible problems that occurred after her mother went to work and how the family solved them.

Blos, J. W. (1987). *Old Henry.* New York: William Morrow.

> Henry's neighbors are upset that he ignores them and lets his property get run down. However, after they drive him away, they begin to realize how much they miss him.

Bonsall, C. (1964). *It's mine.* New York: Harper and Row.

> Mabel Ann and Patrick are good friends until the subject of sharing comes up. Each wants all the toys, but they finally learn the benefits of sharing.

Bronin, A. (1979). *Gus and Buster work things out.* New York: Putnam.

> Two animal brothers have many squabbles and differences but manage to work things out.

Brown, M. (1978). *Moose and Goose.* New York: Dutton.

> Moose lives upstairs and likes to tap dance. Goose lives downstairs and likes to sleep. Their noisy dilemma is creatively resolved.

Caseley, J. (1989). *Ada Potato.* New York: Greenwillow.

> Ada stops playing her violin after some older children make fun of her, but Mama helps her find a way to handle their teasing.

Delton, J. (1974). *Two good friends.* New York: Crown.

> Bear and Duck resolve their differences by sharing their talents.

dePaola, T. (1989). *The knight and the dragon.* New York: Putnam.

> A young knight and dragon prepare to fight each other. After they engage in battle, they decide to work together to open an outdoor barbecue.

Durrell, A., & Sachs, M. (1990). *The big book for peace.* New York: Dutton.

> The wisdom of peace and the absurdity of fighting are demonstrated in 17 stories and poems by outstanding contemporary authors.

Erickson, E. (1985). *Jealousy.* Minneapolis: Carolrhoda.

> While Rosalie has the mumps, her best friend, Victory, starts playing with another girl, which incites Rosalie's jealousy.

Hoban, R. (1970). *A bargain for Frances.* New York: Harper and Row.

> Frances is tricked into buying her friend Thelma's plastic tea set instead of the china set she's been saving for. The two friends eventually resolve their conflict.

Kellogg, S. (1971). *The mystery beast of Ostergeest.* New York: Dial.

> A short story about six wise blind men and an elephant. Each perceives the same elephant to be something totally different.

Kellogg, S. (1976). *The island of the Skog.* New York: Dial.

> A short book that tells a story about how assumptions and perceptions affect our behaviors.

King, L. (1988). *Because of Lozo Brown.* New York: Viking.

> A little boy is afraid to meet his new neighbor, Lozo Brown, until they begin to play and become friends.

Leaf, M. (1936). *The story of Ferdinand.* New York: Viking.

> A young bull in Spain refuses to fight. Instead, he sits and smells the flowers—until he sits on a bee.

Lucas, E. (1991). *Peace on the playground.* Chicago: Franklin Watts.

> A nonfiction book for children about how to get along on the playground.

McNulty, F. (1980). *The elephant who couldn't forget.* New York: Harper and Row.

> Congo could not forget that his brother had treated him unkindly.

Naylor, P. (1991). *King of the playground.* New York: Atheneum.

> Kevin loves to go to the playground but not when Sammy the bully is there. If he catches Kevin there, Sammy says he will do awful, terrible things to him. Kevin tells his dad what Sammy says and they talk it over.

Scholes, K. (1992). *Peace begins with you.* Boston: Little, Brown.

> Explains in simple terms the concept of peace, why conflicts occur, how they can be resolved in positive ways, and how to practice peace.

Scieszka, J. (1989). *The true story of the three little pigs.* New York: Viking.

> A very short story telling this traditional tale from the wolf's perspective and showing there are two sides to a story.

Seuss, Dr. (1961). *The Sneetches.* New York: Random House.

> A short story that deals with the issues of prejudice and discrimination.

Seuss, Dr. (1971). *The Lorax.* New York: Random House.

> A story with implications about the environment and the long-term consequences of business decisions.

Seuss, Dr. (1984). *The butter battle book.* New York: Random House.

> Engaged in a long-running battle, the Yooks and Zooks develop more and more sophisticated weapons as they attempt to outdo each other.

Weiss, N. (1986). *Princess Pearl.* New York: Greenwillow.

> Rosemary taunts and dominates her younger sister, Pearl. She becomes Pearl's ally when she sees her younger sister victimized by an outsider.

Winthrop, E. (1983). *Katherine's doll.* New York: Dutton.

> Katherine and Molly learn to appreciate their friendship after resolving a conflict over Katherine's new doll.

Winthrop, E. (1989). *Best friends' club.* New York: Lothrop, Lee and Shepard.

> Lizzie and Harold form a select club, only to discover that it is a bad idea.

Ziefert, H. (1987). *Mike and Tony: Best friends.* New York: Puffin.

> Mike and Tony enjoy being best friends until the Friday night they have a big fight.

Zolotow, C. (1963). *The quarreling book.* New York: Harper and Row.

> A family suffers through a disagreeable rainy day, but all ends well when Father returns home happy.

Middle Elementary

Baker, B. (1989). *Third grade is terrible.* New York: Dutton.

> Moved to the strictest teacher's class and separated from her best friend, Liza is sure that school will be dreadful until she makes a truce with Mrs. Rumford and meets a new friend.

Bograd, L. (1989). *The fourth grade dinosaur club.* New York: Delacorte.

> Fourth grader Billy Gelford feels that everything in his life is wrong, especially regarding the bullies at school and his spoiled friendship with his best friend, Juan.

Havill, J. (1989). *It always happens to Leona.* New York: Crown.

Feeling left out between her older sister and younger brother, Leona decides to run away with Uncle Rosco, a motorcycle racer.

Singer, M. (1990). *Twenty ways to lose your best friend.* New York: Harper and Row.

Emma loses her best friend when she votes for another girl to get the lead role in the class play.

Upper Elementary and Middle School

Barrie, B. (1990). *Lone star.* New York: Delacorte.

Moving from Chicago to Corpus Christi, Texas, in 1944, a young Jewish girl copes with her parents' problems and adopts a new lifestyle that alienates her grandfather.

Cooper, I. (1988). *Queen of the sixth grade.* New York: Morrow.

After helping her supposed best friend, Veronica, found a sixth-grade secret club, Robin accidentally gets on her wrong side and discovers how bossy and cruel Veronica really is.

Cooper, I. (1990). *Choosing sides.* New York: William Morrow.

Jonathan doesn't want his father to think he's a quitter, but middle school basketball under the lash of a gung-ho coach is turning out to be anything but fun.

Cooper, I. (1991). *Mean streak.* New York: William Morrow.

Having alienated her best friend, Robert, 11-year-old Veronica has no one to turn to for sympathy and support when it appears her divorced father might remarry.

Fenner, C. (1991). *Randall's wall.* New York: Macmillan.

Artistically talented but socially underprivileged, fifth grader Randall has built a wall of defense to protect himself from the pain of human relationships—a wall that begins to crumble when a dynamic and compassionate classmate decides to interfere in his life.

Ferguson, A. (1991). *The practical joke war.* New York: Bradbury.

The Dillon children's practical jokes on each other grow and increase to a breaking point where they are finally drawn together in friendship.

Fine, A. (1989). *My war with Goggle Eyes.* Boston: Little, Brown.

> Kitty is not pleased with her mother's boyfriend, especially his views on the antinuclear issue, until unexpected events prompt her to help him find his place in the family.

Gilson, J. (1991). *Sticks and stones and skeleton bones.* New York: Lothrop, Lee and Shepard.

> Fifth grader Hoobie has a disagreement with his best friend, Nick, that escalates into a big fight as the day continues. The conflict is resolved by mediation in the school's conflict resolution program.

Hermes, P. (1988). *Heads I win.* Orlando, FL: Harcourt Brace Jovanovich.

> Bailey runs for class president, hoping that popularity will secure her place in her current foster home. Bailey also wants to win to impress Janie and the other girls, who treat her as the "new kid."

Jukes, M. (1988). *Getting even.* New York: Knopf.

> Maggie has to decide whether to get even with Corky Newton, an obnoxious classmate who has played a mean trick on her.

Roberts, W. D. (1986). *The magic book.* New York: Atheneum.

> The spell for eliminating bullies goes awry, but by acting bravely, Alex manages to stand up to a bully without magical help.

Smith, D. B. (1991). *The pennywhistle tree.* New York: Putnam.

> Jonathan tries to ignore the belligerent new boy, Sanders, who moves into the corner house with his poor family. But Sanders won't let Jonathan alone.

Windsor, P. (1986). *How a weirdo and a ghost can change your entire life.* New York: Delacorte.

> Two friends learn what the friendship they have is all about.

Mediation and Negotiation Simulations

This appendix includes 20 simulations. Although any of the situations depicted in the simulations may be either mediated or negotiated, the simulations are set forth here in three categories: Simulations 1 though 6 allow students to experience the mediation process, as explained in Section 4 of this program guide. Simulations 7 through 12 are intended for negotiation practice, as discussed in Section 5. Supplemental simulations, numbered 13 through 20, may be mediated or negotiated to provide additional practice with these processes. The supplemental simulations may be more typical of student conflicts for some schools; if so, they may be used in place of any of the first 12 situations.

SIMULATIONS 1–6: MEDIATION

1. When using a mediation simulation, give mediator(s) a copy of the Request for Mediation. Instruct the mediator(s) to fill in the date and the grade levels of each of the disputants.

2. Copy and cut the disputant information sheet in half, and give each disputant the Student A half or the Student B half. Instruct each disputant to study the information to provide a convincing portrayal instead of simply reading the information during the mediation.

    If you wish, you may assign training assistants to coach the group of Student A role-players and Student B role-players, respectively. (Coaches could be staff or experienced students.) Coaching consists of making certain disputants understand the conflict and helping them to develop a strategy for presenting their disputant's point of view. Such coaching is helpful in either mediation or negotiation practice.

3. Start the simulation. If desired, have assistant trainers provide coaching during the simulation. Coaching can be very helpful, but the coaches must allow the mediator(s) to experience the process. Coaches intervene only if the mediator(s) get stuck or are otherwise struggling.

4. End the simulation, and have the mediation group discuss the results among themselves. The following types of questions will be helpful.

To mediators

What did you do well in the simulation?

What was the hardest part of the process?

What could you do differently?

To disputants

What did the mediator(s) do well?

Do you think the agreement will hold?

What might you have done differently if you were mediating the conflict?

5. Process the simulations with the larger group by asking several groups to report the common interests they found. The focus of this discussion should be on the problem-solving process, not on the specific problem. You may ask for a few examples of the agreements formulated, asking if the agreement is "a better plan than the disputants seemed to be following before they chose to problem solve."

SIMULATIONS 7–12: NEGOTIATION

Written requests for negotiation are not required. Instead, disputants and others in the school verbally request the negotiation. Copy and cut the disputant information sheet in half, and give each disputant the Student A half or the Student B half. Conduct and process the negotiation simulations in the same way as for the mediation simulations.

SIMULATIONS 13–20: MEDIATION OR NEGOTIATION

When using a supplemental situation for peer mediation practice, copy and prepare a Request for Mediation (see Appendix D, p. 471) by writing the problem situation information for the simulation chosen. Table 19 (on pp. 447–448) gives this information for each supplemental simulation. Again, no request forms are required for negotiation. Conduct and process the simulations as explained.

SIMULATION 1

REQUEST FOR MEDIATION

Your name ___*Teacher*_____ Date _____

Names of students in conflict (first name and last name of each):

___*Student A*_____

___*Student B*_____

Where conflict occurred (check one):

☐ Bus   ☐ Classroom   ☐ Rest room   ☐ Outside grounds   ☐ Lunchroom

☐ Hall   ☒ Other (specify) _*Library*_____

Briefly describe the problem:

___*Students A and B were scuffling near the computer in the library, and the librarian made*___

___*them leave and return to the classroom.*_____

_____

_____

Creating the Peaceable School (2nd ed.) © 2002 by R. L. Bodine, D. K. Crawford, and F. Schrumpf. Research Press (800) 519-2707.

SIMULATION 1   STUDENT A

Situation

You and Student B have been sent back to class for disrupting the library. Your classroom teacher has requested a mediation for you both.

Your Point of View

You and Student B had permission to go to the library to check out a book. You needed to find a book for a class project. You were using the library computer to help you find the book you needed when Student B yelled at you to hurry up and then pushed you out of the chair. You pushed Student B back. You are upset with Student B because you have been sent out of the library without getting to check out the book you needed, and now you cannot do your work.

Background Information

You are not very good with the computer. It takes you a long time to find anything on it, and you get frustrated easily. You don't like to ask for help because you want others to see you as being able to do things well.

SIMULATION 1   STUDENT B

Situation

You and Student A have been sent back to class for disrupting the library. Your classroom teacher has requested a mediation for you both.

Your Point of View

You and Student A had permission to go to the library to check out a book. You wanted a good book to read during free time. You wanted to use the computer to look for a title by your favorite author. You waited a long time for a turn at the computer but got impatient because your free time was about over. You told Student A that you needed the computer, but when Student A didn't move, you pushed him/her out of the chair. You are upset with Student A because you both got sent out of the library and you don't have a book to read. You think the problem is Student A's fault for being so slow.

Background Information

You love to read and read every chance you get. You are very skilled in using the library computer and sometimes help the librarian by teaching other students how to use it.

SIMULATION 2

REQUEST FOR MEDIATION

Your name ___*Teacher*___ Date _____

Names of students in conflict (first name and last name of each):

___*Student A*___

___*Student B*___

Where conflict occurred (check one):

☐ Bus   ☒ Classroom   ☐ Rest room   ☐ Outside grounds   ☐ Lunchroom

☐ Hall   ☐ Other (specify) _____

Briefly describe the problem:

___*Student A and Student B were disrupting the class by arguing loudly. They were sent to*___

___*time-out. Student A and Student B seem to dislike each other and often get into loud*___

___*disagreements in class.*___

Creating the Peaceable School (2nd ed.) © 2002 by R. L. Bodine, D. K. Crawford, and F. Schrumpf. Research Press (800) 519-2707.

SIMULATION 2 — STUDENT A

Situation

You and Student B had a loud disagreement in the classroom, then got sent to time-out. Your teacher has requested the mediation.

Your Point of View

Student B is always bugging you in your math group. Today Student B looked at you, kicked your chair, and pushed your materials on the floor. You are ready to fight.

Background Information

Math is hard for you, and you feel the other students in the group are putting you down.

SIMULATION 2 — STUDENT B

Situation

You and Student A had a loud disagreement in the classroom, then got sent to time-out. Your teacher has requested the mediation.

Your Point of View

You think Student A asks dumb questions that disrupt the math group. The whole group has to wait around while Student A asks questions.

Background Information

You think Student A should be in another math group. You are not very patient with people you think are stupid.

Simulation 3

REQUEST FOR MEDIATION

Your name _____*Student A*_____ Date _____

Names of students in conflict (first name and last name of each):

____*Student A*_____

____*Student B*_____

Where conflict occurred (check one):

☐ Bus ☐ Classroom ☐ Rest room ☒ Outside grounds ☐ Lunchroom

☐ Hall ☐ Other (specify) _____

Briefly describe the problem:

____*There was only one ball left in the basket, and Student B and I both wanted it so we*____

____*could play a game with friends. We were fighting over the ball, and the playground*____

____*supervisor took it and wouldn't let either of us have it.*____

SIMULATION 3

STUDENT A

Situation

There was only one ball left in the basket, and you and Student B both wanted it. You were fighting over the ball when the playground supervisor took it and would not let either of you have it. You have requested the mediation.

Your Point of View

You got to the basket before Student B and had the ball first. You were going to ask your friends to play a game with the ball.

Background Information

You don't have many friends and don't get invited to play with others as much as you would like. Some of the other students play with you when you ask them to. Student B is not nice to you most of the time and does not seem to like anyone who will play with you.

SIMULATION 3

STUDENT B

Situation

There was only one ball left in the basket, and Student A and you both wanted it. You were fighting over the ball when the playground supervisor took it and would not let either of you have it. Student A has requested the mediation.

Your Point of View

You and your friends always play ball at recess, and it was your turn to get the ball. Student A took the ball just before you got there. Student A does not like to play ball games and chooses not to join you and your friends in your activities. The playground supervisor knows you always play ball, and you think she should have let you have the ball and told Student A to find something else to do.

Background Information

You have a special group of friends who like to play active games, and you are all good players. You are looked up to by several members of your group of friends because you are often the best player in the game.

SIMULATION 4

REQUEST FOR MEDIATION

Your name ___*Student A*___ Date _____

Names of students in conflict (first name and last name of each):

___*Student A*___

___*Student B*___

Where conflict occurred (check one):

☐ Bus   ☐ Classroom   ☐ Rest room   ☐ Outside grounds   ☒ Lunchroom

☐ Hall   ☐ Other (specify) _____

Briefly describe the problem:

___*Student B keeps bugging me and talking about me. Student B throws food at me in the*___

___*lunchroom all the time.*___

_____

_____

SIMULATION 4   STUDENT A

Situation

You accidentally dropped a piece of pizza in Student B's lap today in the cafeteria, and Student B was ready to fight you. You have requested the mediation.

Your Point of View

Student B sits two tables away from you in the lunchroom and keeps making faces and whispering to friends about you. Student B even throws food at you when the teacher is not looking.

Background Information

You were friends with Student B last school year, but the friendship broke off when the new school year began. You are not sure why the relationship changed.

SIMULATION 4   STUDENT B

Situation

Student A dropped a piece of pizza in your lap in the cafeteria today. You were ready to fight. Student A has requested the mediation.

Your Point of View

Student A was your friend until this year. You believe Student A acts superior to everyone else and is always putting other people down. You know it was no accident that the slice of pizza dropped in your lap. You want your pants dry-cleaned at Student A's expense.

Background Information

You think Student A is acting this way because Student A is in a "gifted" classroom and is trying to make you feel dumb.

SIMULATION 5

REQUEST FOR MEDIATION

Your name ___*Student A*_____ Date _____

Names of students in conflict (first name and last name of each):

_____*Student A*_____

_____*Student B*_____

Where conflict occurred (check one):

[X] Bus   [ ] Classroom   [ ] Rest room   [ ] Outside grounds   [ ] Lunchroom

[ ] Hall   [ ] Other (specify) _____

Briefly describe the problem:

_____*Student B has been telling everyone on the bus something that is none of his/her*_____

_____*business. Student B better shut up or else!*_____

_____

_____

SIMULATION 5 — STUDENT A

Situation

You are upset because Student B is spreading the rumor that your parents are divorcing. You have requested the mediation.

Your Point of View

It is true that your parents are divorcing, but you don't think it is anyone else's business.

Background Information

You think Student B has a big mouth and loves to gossip.

SIMULATION 5 — STUDENT B

Situation

Student A is upset because you told someone his/her parents are divorcing. Student A has requested the mediation.

Your Point of View

You have told only one person that Student A's parents are divorcing, and you told because that person asked about it. You heard the rumor from other people.

Background Information

You know Student A's family and think of them as friends. You think that Student A doesn't need to be so sensitive about the situation because a lot of people get divorced.

Simulation 6

REQUEST FOR MEDIATION

Your name _____*Student A*_____ Date _____

Names of students in conflict (first name and last name of each):

_____*Student A*_____

_____*Student B*_____

Where conflict occurred (check one):

☐ Bus   ☐ Classroom   ☐ Rest room   ☒ Outside grounds   ☐ Lunchroom

☐ Hall   ☐ Other (specify) _____

Briefly describe the problem:

_____*I told the teacher that Student B was cheating on a spelling test, and the teacher took*_____

_____*away Student B's spelling workbook. Student B threatened me and pushed me down.*_____

_____*Now I'm afraid of Student B.*_____

SIMULATION 6   STUDENT A

Situation

You told the teacher that Student B was cheating on a spelling test. The teacher took away Student B's spelling materials, so Student B couldn't finish the test. Student B threatened you and pushed you down. You have requested the mediation.

Your Point of View

You believe that no one should cheat on tests and that it is each student's responsibility to report anyone who does cheat. You think Student B is lazy and looks for shortcuts instead of working hard. Student B gets by with things because everyone is afraid of him/her.

Background Information

You are a good student who nearly always gets the best scores on tests. You think that Student B is a bully, and you are afraid of Student B.

SIMULATION 6   STUDENT B

Situation

Student A tells the teacher that you were cheating on a spelling test. The teacher took your spelling materials away, so now you can't finish the test. You got a little rough with Student A, but he/she was asking for it. Student A has requested the mediation.

Your Point of View

You think Student A should keep out of your business. You have a hard time with spelling and think spelling tests are unfair, but you are not dumb. School stuff is easy for Student A, who puts you down when you have trouble.

Background Information

Most schoolwork is hard for you, but your parents expect you to do well. They get upset with you when you don't score well on tests. Other kids think you are tough, and you don't want to lose face by asking the teacher for help.

Situation

You and Student B are arguing about things missing from the locker you share.

Your Point of View

Yesterday you opened your locker, and your lunch money and math book with your completed homework in it were missing. You had to stay after school to redo the homework, and when you asked Student B about it Student B would not say anything.

Background Information

You are a messy person, and Student B is very neat. You and Student B were friends in the past.

Situation

You and Student A are arguing about things missing from the locker you share.

Your Point of View

Last week some of your pictures inside the locker were gone, as well as your math book. The locker is always a mess, and you just take the first book you see. You admit to taking the book and the money from Student A because you were not sure whose they were.

Background Information

You are a neat person and have given up on trying to keep the locker clean because Student A is so messy.

SIMULATION 8   STUDENT A

Situation

You and Student B are threatening each other and ready to fight. The teacher has suggested a negotiation.

Your Point of View

You are a new student in school. For the past month, Student B has been saying junk about you and giving you dirty looks. Yesterday, Student B bumped into you in the hallway and then wanted to fight.

Background Information

You miss your old friends and want to make some new friends in this school.

SIMULATION 8   STUDENT B

Situation

You and Student A are threatening each other and ready to fight. The teacher has suggested a negotiation.

Your Point of View

You are angry at Student A because Student A came into the school as a new student and put down all your friends. If that is going to be Student A's attitude, there is going to be trouble.

Background Information

You are the informal leader of a large group of students in the class. You have the influence to have the new student accepted or rejected by classmates.

SIMULATION 9

STUDENT A

Situation

You and Student B were playing basketball outside when you began hitting and pushing each other. The supervisor made you both sit in time-out.

Your Point of View

You were in the act of shooting a basket when Student B fouled you and caused you to miss the shot. Student B denied fouling you. You got mad and threw the ball at Student B. When Student B came back toward you, you pushed Student B.

Background Information

You and Student B play a lot of basketball together. You are a good basketball player, and the team looks to you to score. You do not like to lose, so you play hard and with a lot of feeling.

SIMULATION 9

STUDENT B

Situation

You and Student A were playing basketball outside when you began hitting and pushing each other. The supervisor made you sit in time-out.

Your Point of View

You blocked Student A's shot, and Student A had no reason to throw the ball at you. You ran at him/her when you got hit with the ball. The supervisor should have sat Student A out for starting the fight.

Background Information

You and Student A play a lot of basketball together. You like to play rough in games, and you often make up for lack of skill with lots of hustle. You think Student A is a good shooter but is too wimpy and always cries "foul."

SIMULATION 10

STUDENT A

Situation

You and Student B were in the hall threatening each other and calling each other names. You were both sent to the office. The principal has asked you if you want to work the problem out on your own.

Your Point of View

You think Student B can be a goody-goody and tries to show you up on purpose. You think Student B sucks up to the teacher, so you called him/her "teacher's pet." Student B called you a cow.

Background Information

You don't much like school, and the work is not interesting. You goof around a lot and try to avoid schoolwork.

Creating the Peaceable School (2nd ed.) © 2002 by R. L. Bodine, D. K. Crawford, and F. Schrumpf. Research Press (800) 519-2707.

SIMULATION 10

STUDENT B

Situation

You and Student A were in the hall threatening each other and calling each other names. You were both sent to the office. The principal has asked you if you want to work the problem out on your own.

Your Point of View

You think Student A is jealous of you because you are a good student and the teachers often praise your work. You don't like to be called names, and you want to be liked by the other students. You don't think you get special privileges in class except what you deserve because of your hard work.

Background Information

You like school a lot, and you work hard. You think others could do just as well as you if they would work instead of clowning around. One reason you work hard in school is that the teacher rewards you with special privileges when your work is good and when you finish before the others. You don't have many friends in the class.

Creating the Peaceable School (2nd ed.) © 2002 by R. L. Bodine, D. K. Crawford, and F. Schrumpf. Research Press (800) 519-2707.

STUDENT A

Situation

You and Student B were yelling and screaming in the rest room. The custodian walked in and found you pushing each other around the room, then took you back to class. Your teacher has asked you to try to work it out.

Your Point of View

You and Student B were just messing around, having a little fun throwing spitballs at the mirror in the rest room, when Student B purposely hit you with a big wad. You got a little mad and started yelling and chasing Student B around the room. You and Student B were pushing each other a little when the custodian came in and got all upset. You weren't mad enough at Student B to fight.

Background Information

You and Student B are best friends because you do wild and crazy things together. You especially like to roughhouse with Student B and often get into wild play.

STUDENT B

Situation

You and Student A were yelling and screaming in the rest room. The custodian walked in and found you pushing each other around the room, then took you back to class. Your teacher has asked you to try to work it out.

Your Point of View

You and Student A were have fun throwing spitballs at the mirror in the rest room. You were trying to see who could get the biggest one to stick. You made a real big one, and when you threw it, it slipped out of your hand and hit Student A. Student A got upset and started yelling at you and chasing you. Student A caught you and started pushing you, so you pushed back.

Background Information

You and Student A are good friends, and you like to do wild things together. You don't have many other friends, so Student A is important to you, even though he/she often gets you into trouble. You would especially like it if Student A would not be so rough all the time.

SIMULATION 12 — STUDENT A

Situation

You and Student B got into an argument about who owns some colored pencils. You have decided to try to work it out before you get into trouble with the teacher and miss free time.

Your Point of View

Your colored pencils are missing, and you think Student B took them because you see Student B using colored pencils. Student B claims the colored pencils are not yours. You get mad and shove Student B's stuff off the table onto the floor.

Background Information

You often cannot find things that are yours. You have a hard time remembering to put things back into your storage area. You and Student B are buddies.

SIMULATION 12 — STUDENT B

Situation

You and Student A got into an argument about who owns some colored pencils. You have decided to try to work it out before you get into trouble with the teacher and miss free time.

Your Point of View

Student A is always accusing someone of taking his/her things. You just got new colored pencils from your aunt, and you are sure those are the ones you are using. Student A knocked your stuff off the table, so you pulled the chair out from under him/her.

Background Information

Your storage area is always next to Student A's, and the two of you often share things in the classroom. Student A always seems to have new stuff—whenever Student A loses something, his/her mom replaces it. You usually don't have new things, so you often borrow from Student A. You and Student A are best buddies.

TABLE 19   Request for Mediation Information: Simulations 13–20

Simulation 13	Your name: *Principal*
	
	Names and grade levels of students in conflict:
	
	    Name: *Student A*
	
	    Name: *Student B*
	
	Where conflict occurred: *Hall*
	
	Briefly describe the problem: *These two students were pushing and seemed ready to fight in the hallway outside the gym. They are isolated until a mediation is scheduled.*

Simulation 14	Your name: *Student A*
	
	Names and grade levels of students in conflict:
	
	    Name: *Student A*
	
	    Name: *Student B*
	
	Where conflict occurred: *Other (specify)—Library*
	
	Briefly describe the problem: *I loaned _____ a library book, and she/he lost it. Now I'm supposed to pay for it.*

Simulation 15	Your name: *Teacher*
	
	Names and grade levels of students in conflict:
	
	    Name: *Student A*
	
	    Name: *Student B*
	
	Where conflict occurred: *Other (specify)—On a field trip to the skating rink*
	
	Briefly describe the problem: *Student A and Student B were disruptive during the field trip and had to be placed in time-out at the skating rink. Their behavior was embarrassing to the rest of the group.*

Simulation 16	Your name: *Student A*
	
	Names and grade levels of students in conflict:
	
	    Name: *Student A*
	
	    Name: *Student B*
	
	Where conflict occurred: *Hall*
	
	Briefly describe the problem: *Student B and his/her friends have been harassing me, and after I told the teacher about an incident today outside of class, the teacher suggested I submit a request for mediation.*

TABLE 19   (continued)

Simulation 17	Your name: *Homeroom teacher*
	Names and grade levels of students in conflict:
	Name: *Student A*
	Name: *Student B*
	Where conflict occurred: *Other (specify)—All over the school*
	Briefly describe the problem: *After I received several reports that Students A and B have been in loud disagreements throughout the school, I suggested that they request a mediation.*
Simulation 18	Your name: *Student A*
	Names and grade levels of students in conflict:
	Name: *Student A*
	Name: *Student B*
	Where conflict occurred: *Lunchroom*
	Briefly describe the problem: *Student B made upsetting comments about how I dress to a friend.*
Simulation 19	Your name: *Outside grounds supervisor*
	Names and grade levels of students in conflict:
	Name: *Student A*
	Name: *Student B*
	Where conflict occurred: *Outside grounds*
	Briefly describe the problem: *Students A and B were scuffling just outside the school doors, and I sent them to the office. They agreed to mediation.*
Simulation 20	Your name: *Assistant principal*
	Names and grade levels of students in conflict:
	Name: *Student A*
	Name: *Student B*
	Where conflict occurred: *Hall*
	Briefly describe the problem: *Students A and B were in the hall outside the art room, surrounded by a group of students. A and B were in the center of the group and were shouting racial slurs at each other. I separated them just as they were about to start swinging their fists. Students A and B are in the in-school suspension room until there can be a mediation.*

SIMULATION 13

STUDENT A

Situation

You and Student B were scuffling in the hall near the gym when the principal intervened. The principal isolated the two of you in the office and requested that you work it out. You both agreed.

Your Point of View

You and Student A were playing around between classes in the hallway, and suddenly Student A got mad and started yelling at you and shoving you. The principal heard Student A yelling. He sent the two of you to the office. You still don't know why Student A got so mad.

Background Information

You and Student B have been good friends the last 2 years. Joking around and play fighting is how you often act toward each other. You really like that. Play fighting is how you and your friends show you are friends. Student B is a good friend, but you think she/he is too serious and gets upset easily. You didn't mean any harm.

SIMULATION 13

STUDENT B

Situation

Student A and you were scuffling in the hall near the gym when the principal intervened. The principal isolated the two of you in the office and requested that you work it out. You both agreed.

Your Point of View

You have gotten very tired of the way Student A has been treating you. Student A can be such a jerk. Student A is always putting you down and using you as a play punching bag. Student A is always clowning around and roughhousing. It's time Student A got some of her/his own medicine.

Background Information

You feel everyone is on your case. Your grades were low this semester; you were cut from the basketball team; and your father might be taking a job in another town, so your family might have to move again.

SIMULATION 14

Situation

You are very mad at Student B because of a lost library book. You have requested the peer mediation/negotiation.

Your Point of View

You and Student B are arguing because she/he lost a library book. You were working together on a report, and Student B borrowed the book from you and never returned it. You got an overdue notice from the library. If you don't find the book, you're going to have to pay for it.

Background Information

You don't have the money to pay for the book. You and Student B have been good friends, but you feel you've been taken advantage of because you did most of the work on the report. Losing the book is the "last straw."

SIMULATION 14

Situation

Student A is very mad at you because of a lost library book. Student A has requested the peer mediation/negotiation.

Your Point of View

Student A is saying that you lost the library book. However, you are sure that you returned it to Student A before the due date. You feel as though Student A is unfairly putting the blame of losing the book on you. You've already got enough problems without being blamed for something that is not your fault.

Background Information

Student A has been a good friend and because she/he is a really good student, you were happy to work on the report with her/him. You have a history of losing and forgetting things, and sometimes you don't work very hard at school. However, this time you are sure it isn't your fault the book is missing.

SIMULATION 15   STUDENT A

Situation

Student B and you are members of the Student Helpers Club. During an end-of-the-month appreciation field trip to the skating rink, Student B yelled at you. You yelled back at Student B, and an argument occurred. A teacher-sponsor sent you both to time-out at the rink and did not allow either of you to continue skating.

Your Point of View

You are upset with Student B because you think she/he stole your new sneakers during the trip. You left your new sneakers on the bench next to Student B while you went to the rest room. When you returned, both Student B and the sneakers were gone. You caught up to Student B and yelled at her/him, demanding she/he return your sneakers.

Background Information

Your parents worked hard to give you those sneakers for your birthday. You think that Student B is jealous because you have some expensive sneakers that her/his parents cannot afford.

SIMULATION 15   STUDENT B

Situation

Student A and you are members of the Student Helpers Club. During an end-of-the-month appreciation field trip to the skating rink, Student A yelled at you. You yelled back at Student A, and an argument occurred. A teacher-sponsor sent you both to time-out at the rink, and neither of you was allowed to continue skating.

Your Point of View

After Student A left her/his sneakers on the bench, you got on the ice to skate. You don't know who took the sneakers, but it wasn't you.

Background Information

You are upset with Student A because she/he was really rude to you. You think Student A could've asked you in a way about the sneakers different from yelling at you and accusing you in front of your friends while you were skating. You have no patience or respect for people you think are rude.

SIMULATION 16 — STUDENT A

Situation

You were walking down the hallway after class when Student B walked in front of you and Student B then bumped into you. You think the bump was intentional.

Your Point of View

You hate all the racial jokes and comments made about you. You are sick of Student B and his/her friends making your time in school so hard to get through.

Background

You are one of the only members of your race in your class, and you are a race different from Student B. You feel that Student B is trying to make his/her friends dislike you because you are from a different ethnic group. Besides the problems with Student B and his/her small group of friends, you have had no problems with other people in class, including those of Student B's race. You have had problems with Student B's friends making racial comments to you in class. You think Student B bumped you in the hallway because he/she doesn't like you because of your race, just like his/her friends. You also are upset because Student B's girlfriend/boyfriend is one of very few close friends you have at school, and this problem might make it difficult to keep that friendship going.

SIMULATION 16 — STUDENT B

Situation

Student A was walking down the hallway after class when you walked in front of him/her and then bumped into him/her. Student A thinks it was intentional.

Your Point of View

You don't like Student A's talking to your girlfriend/boyfriend in class because you feel it's disrespectful. You also don't like it when Student A tells other people that you are trying to get him/her jumped by your friends. You want this gossip to stop because it gives you a bad reputation in the school.

Background

You have had problems with Student A ever since school started. Although all of your friends are the same race as you, you have a couple of acquaintances who are the same race as Student A. You have no problem with Student A because he/she is a different race. You are angry with Student A because he/she has been talking to your girlfriend/boyfriend too much. You think Student A talks to your girlfriend/boyfriend to make you look bad to your friends or he/she is trying to cut you out of that special relationship.

SIMULATION 17   STUDENT A

Situation

You and Student B are members of the same homeroom. Your homeroom teacher urged you to request mediation/negotiate after the teacher heard that you had been in several arguments throughout the school.

Your Point of View

Student B has been spreading rumors that you are gay and that your mother is gay. You want the rumors stopped.

Background Information

You think that Student B has a big mouth and loves to gossip about things he/she doesn't really know. Your mother is gay, but you are not. You don't think being gay is a problem, and it isn't anyone else's business if your mother is gay.

SIMULATION 17   STUDENT B

Situation

Student A and you are members of the same homeroom. Your homeroom teacher urged you to request mediation/negotiate after the teacher heard that you had been in several arguments throughout the school.

Your Point of View

You did tell someone about Student A's mother being gay but only one person. You never told anyone that Student A was gay, but you have heard this rumor around the school.

Background Information

You have no problem with homosexuals and don't know what the problem is with other students who tease Student A or talk behind his/her back. Student A shouldn't be so sensitive and overreactive. He/she should be able to get over it and go on with life.

Situation

You overheard Student B make a comment to a mutual friend that you wear the same old clothes every week.

Your Point of View

You are fed up with this type of comment. You think Student B is a bit stupid or bored if all he/she can do is spend time talking about you. You want Student B to leave you alone and stop talking about you to others.

Background

You come from a poor family and are trying hard to do well in school. You and your mother are living on her disability checks, and you cannot afford to wear many new things. You have no problem coming to school dressed as you do as long as no one makes any comments about the way you are dressed. You're there to learn, and how you look has nothing to do with whether you can learn or not. You aren't really friends with Student B, but you have some of the same people as friends. You don't want to upset them by fighting with Student B, and you also don't want to get in trouble with the school. You don't want to be embarrassed because of Student B's opinion of your clothes.

Situation

Student A overheard you make a comment to a mutual friend that Student A wears the same old clothes every week.

Your Point of View

You can understand why Student A is upset after hearing the comment about his/her dress. But you weren't talking to Student A, and you are free to talk about the way people dress in school.

Background

You always try to wear nice clothes because you take pride in how you look. You know you are lucky because you have a family who helps you buy new clothes, but you also do a lot of work at home, including taking care of your brother and sister, as payment for those clothes. You think that everyone in school should dress well and make the best appearance possible. Walking in with dirty hats and the same dingy jeans every week is disrespectful. You make comments about the way everyone is dressed, not just Student A. Student A just happened to hear a comment only about the way he/she was dressed. You and Student A share some of the same friends, but you aren't friends, and you don't want to be friends. You don't want some of the friends you share getting angry at you for arguing with Student A, so you are willing to find some type of solution.

SIMULATION 19   STUDENT A

Situation

You and Student B have agreed to try mediation/negotiation when you were sent to the office by the outside grounds supervisor for getting into an argument and shoving match while surrounded by a group of students.

Your Point of View

You were showing pictures to some of your friends when Student B tried to grab them from you. You told Student B to wait, but he/she grabbed the pictures. Some of the pictures ripped in half, and those that didn't were wrinkled. You became upset and starting yelling at and shoving Student B. You want Student B to pay for the pictures to be redeveloped.

Background Information

The pictures mean a lot to you. They are of your family from last summer's family reunion, the first in 5 years, and of your new baby brother.

SIMULATION 19   STUDENT B

Situation

Student A and you have agreed to try mediation/negotiation when you were sent to the office by the outside grounds supervisor for getting into an argument and shoving match while surrounded by a group of students.

Your Point of View

When Student A said he/she had some pictures to show, he/she told you that you could see them also. You were holding some of the pictures when Student A started yelling at you about getting fingerprints on them. Student A tried to grab them from you. Some pictures were ripped when Student A tried to get them away from you.

Background Information

You think that Student A has a problem sharing things with you because he/she thinks that he/she is better than you. This is just another time that Student A is trying to get you in trouble.

SIMULATION 20

STUDENT A

Situation

You and Student B were in the hallway outside the art room, shouting racial slurs at each other. You were about to start fighting when the assistant principal broke it up.

Your Point of View

Student B has been making racial slurs about you for some time. You think Student B feels superior to you because he/she has nicer things, gets better grades, and plays on the soccer team. You suspect that Student B is upset because you are dating classmates of Student B's race.

Background Information

You are from a different ethnic group than Student B. You come from a poor neighborhood, and you receive average to poor grades. You resent Student B because he/she flaunts expensive clothes and has expensive possessions. Aside from the problems with Student B, you are popular and influential with friends and classmates.

SIMULATION 20

STUDENT B

Situation

Student A and you were in the hallway outside the art room, shouting racial slurs at each other. You were about to start fighting when the assistant principal broke it up.

Your Point of View

Student A and you have had ongoing problems. You think Student A is jealous and is always competing with you. Student A puts you down and tries to take over your friends, especially those of the opposite sex.

Background Information

You are from a different ethnic group than Student A. Your parents work hard to provide you with advantages, such as nice clothes and a cell phone, which your more affluent classmates also have. You receive better than average grades, and you play on the soccer team. Aside from the problems with Student A, you are popular and influential with friends and classmates, although you have no other friends from other ethnic groups.

Program Forms
and Assessment Measures

Mediator Application Form

As a mediator, I understand my role is to help students resolve conflicts peaceably. As a mediator, I will do my best to respect the participants of mediation, remain neutral, and keep the mediation confidential.

As a mediator, I agree to the following terms:

> To complete all mediation training sessions
>
> To maintain confidentiality in all mediations
>
> To responsibly conduct general duties of a mediator, including conducting mediations, completing all necessary forms, and promoting the program
>
> To maintain satisfactory school behavior (this includes requesting mediation before taking inappropriate action if I become involved in a conflict)
>
> To satisfactorily complete all class assignments and to make up any class work missed because of mediation training or conducting mediations

If these responsibilities are not met, I understand that I will lose the privilege of being a mediator. I accept these responsibilities for the school year.

Student signature _____ Date _____

Please write an answer to the following questions to share with your parent(s) or guardian(s).

1. I want to be a mediator because:

2. I think I will be a good mediator because (name some qualities you have that you think will make you a good mediator):

Creating the Peaceable School (2nd ed.) © 2002 by R. L. Bodine, D. K. Crawford, and F. Schrumpf. Research Press (800) 519-2707.

Mediator Student Nomination

I would like to nominate the following students to be peer mediators because I would respect and trust them to help me resolve a conflict:

1. _____

2. _____

Signature _____ Date _____

Mediator Staff Nomination

I would like to nominate the following students to be peer mediators:

1. _____

2. _____

Signature _____ Date _____

Conflict Resolution Record Form

Room no. _____ Month _____ Year _____ Page _____ of _____

Conflict resolution process	Date day/mo.	Disputants' names (first only)	Disputants' sex M/F	Disputants' race	Referral source	Type of dispute	Created agreement Y/N	Satisfied with process Y/N	Satisfied with outcome next day Y/N	Satisfied with outcome next mo. Y/N

Key

Conflict resolution process
N = Negotiation
M = Mediation
GPS = Group problem solving

Race
AA = African American
A = Asian
C = Caucasian
HL = Hispanic/Latino
O = Other

Referral source
D = Disputant
S = Student
T = Teacher
C = Counselor
SW = Social Worker
DAP = Dean/assistant principal
P = Principal
O = Other

Type of dispute
R = Rumor
H = Harrassment
T = Threats
N = Name-calling
F = Fights or hitting
B = Bias or prejudice
RL = Relationship
P = Property
O = Other

Creating the Peaceable School (2nd ed.) © 2002 by R. L. Bodine, D. K. Crawford, and F. Schrumpf. Research Press (800) 519-2707.

461

Preprogram Student Assessment

Date _____

Circle the number that best corresponds to how you think the school staff should respond to conflict between students in the school or classroom.

	Always	Often	Sometimes	Never
1. Tell the students to "knock it off."	1	2	3	4
2. Try to smooth over the situation.	1	2	3	4
3. Help students understand different points of view.	1	2	3	4
4. Separate students and keep them away from each other.	1	2	3	4
5. Send students to the principal's office.	1	2	3	4
6. Determine who started it.	1	2	3	4
7. Try to find the cause of the problem.	1	2	3	4
8. Ask students to apologize to each other.	1	2	3	4
9. Ask students to mediate or negotiate.	1	2	3	4
10. Assign a punishment or consequence.	1	2	3	4
11. Let students have it out, as long as no one gets physically hurt.	1	2	3	4
12. Tell students to settle it after class.	1	2	3	4

Circle the number that best describes how much you agree or disagree with each of the following statements.

	Strongly agree	Agree somewhat	Disagree somewhat	Strongly disagree
1. Conflict should not happen in school.	1	2	3	4
2. Group problem solving is not a good way to resolve conflicts affecting everyone in the classroom.	1	2	3	4
3. Disputants must change or align their values to resolve conflicts over values.	1	2	3	4
4. When students fight over property, an equal distribution is always an effective solution.	1	2	3	4
5. There is always someone who is right and someone who is wrong in a dispute.	1	2	3	4
6. Avoiding conflict helps students build productive relationships.	1	2	3	4

Creating the Peaceable School (2nd ed.) © 2002 by R. L. Bodine, D. K. Crawford, and F. Schrumpf. Research Press (800) 519-2707.

	Strongly agree	Agree somewhat	Disagree somewhat	Strongly disagree
7. Arguing over positions to find a compromise prevents disputants from finding solutions that address their interests and needs.	1	2	3	4
8. Students can peacefully resolve conflicts involving bias and prejudice.	1	2	3	4
10. Conflict is a natural part of life and is an opportunity to learn.	1	2	3	4
11. Students are effective negotiators.	1	2	3	4
12. Mediation is a process that could be used to resolve disputes between teachers and students.	1	2	3	4

Postprogram Student Assessment

Date _____

Circle the number that best corresponds to how you think the school staff should respond to conflict between students in the school or classroom.

	Always	Often	Sometimes	Never
1. Tell the students to "knock it off."	1	2	3	4
2. Try to smooth over the situation.	1	2	3	4
3. Help students understand different points of view.	1	2	3	4
4. Separate students and keep them away from each other.	1	2	3	4
5. Send students to the principal's office.	1	2	3	4
6. Determine who started it.	1	2	3	4
7. Try to find the cause of the problem.	1	2	3	4
8. Ask students to apologize to each other.	1	2	3	4
9. Ask students to mediate or negotiate.	1	2	3	4
10. Assign a punishment or consequence.	1	2	3	4
11. Let students have it out, as long as no one gets physically hurt.	1	2	3	4
12. Tell students to settle it after class.	1	2	3	4

Circle the number that best describes how much you agree or disagree with each of the following statements.

	Strongly agree	Agree somewhat	Disagree somewhat	Strongly disagree
1. Conflict should not happen in school.	1	2	3	4
2. Group problem solving is not a good way to resolve conflicts affecting everyone in the classroom.	1	2	3	4
3. Disputants must change or align their values to resolve conflicts over values.	1	2	3	4
4. When students fight over property, an equal distribution is always an effective solution.	1	2	3	4
5. There is always someone who is right and someone who is wrong in a dispute.	1	2	3	4
6. Avoiding conflict helps students build productive relationships.	1	2	3	4

Creating the Peaceable School (2nd ed.) © 2002 by R. L. Bodine, D. K. Crawford, and F. Schrumpf. Research Press (800) 519-2707.

	Strongly agree	Agree somewhat	Disagree somewhat	Strongly disagree
7. Arguing over positions to find a compromise prevents disputants from finding solutions that address their interests and needs.	1	2	3	4
8. Students can peacefully resolve conflicts involving bias and prejudice.	1	2	3	4
9. Conflict is a natural part of life and is an opportunity to learn.	1	2	3	4
10. Students are effective negotiators.	1	2	3	4
11. Mediation is a process that could be used to resolve disputes between teachers and students.	1	2	3	4

Answer the following questions.

1. I have participated in group problem solving sessions. ☐ yes ☐ no

   If yes, were agreements reached ☐ most of the time ☐ sometimes ☐ almost never

   If yes, were agreements honored ☐ most of the time ☐ sometimes ☐ almost never

2. Number of group problem solving sessions in which you participated ☐ fewer than 10 ☐ 10–20 ☐ more than 20

3. I have participated as a disputant in negotiation sessions. ☐ yes ☐ no

   If yes, were agreements reached ☐ most of the time ☐ sometimes ☐ almost never

   If yes, were agreements honored ☐ most of the time ☐ sometimes ☐ almost never

4. Number of negotiation sessions in which you participated: ☐ fewer than 10 ☐ 10–20 ☐ more than 20

5. I have participated as a disputant in mediation sessions. ☐ yes ☐ no

   If yes, were agreements reached ☐ most of the time ☐ sometimes ☐ almost never

   If yes, were agreements honored ☐ most of the time ☐ sometimes ☐ almost never

6. Number of mediation sessions in which you participated as a disputant: ☐ fewer than 10 ☐ 10–20 ☐ more than 20

7. I have served as a mediator using the six-step mediation process. ☐ yes ☐ no

   Number of mediation sessions in which you served as a mediator: ☐ fewer than 10 ☐ 10–20 ☐ more than 20

Preprogram Staff Assessment

Date _____

Circle the number that best corresponds to your response to conflict between students in the school or classroom.

	Always	Often	Sometimes	Never
1. Tell the students to "knock it off."	1	2	3	4
2. Try to smooth over the situation.	1	2	3	4
3. Help students understand different points of view.	1	2	3	4
4. Separate students and keep them away from each other.	1	2	3	4
5. Send students to the principal's office.	1	2	3	4
6. Determine who started it.	1	2	3	4
7. Try to find the cause of the problem.	1	2	3	4
8. Ask students to apologize to each other.	1	2	3	4
9. Ask students to mediate or negotiate.	1	2	3	4
10. Assign a punishment or consequence.	1	2	3	4
11. Let students have it out, as long as no one gets physically hurt.	1	2	3	4
12. Tell students to settle it after class.	1	2	3	4

Circle the number that best describes how much you agree or disagree with each of the following statements.

	Strongly agree	Agree somewhat	Disagree somewhat	Strongly disagree
1. Conflict should not happen in school.	1	2	3	4
2. Group problem solving is not a good way to resolve conflicts affecting everyone in the classroom.	1	2	3	4
3. Disputants must change or align their values to resolve conflict over values.	1	2	3	4
4. When students fight over property, an equal distribution is always an effective solution.	1	2	3	4
5. There is always someone who is right and someone who is wrong in a dispute.	1	2	3	4
6. Avoiding conflict helps students build productive relationships.	1	2	3	4

	Strongly agree	Agree somewhat	Disagree somewhat	Strongly disagree
7. Arguing over positions to find a compromise prevents disputants from finding solutions that address their interests and needs.	1	2	3	4
8. Students can peacefully resolve conflicts involving bias and prejudice.	1	2	3	4
9. Conflict is a natural part of life and is an opportunity to learn.	1	2	3	4
10. Students are effective negotiators.	1	2	3	4
11. Negotiation is a process that could be used to resolve disputes between teachers and students.	1	2	3	4
12. Mediation is a process that could be used to resolve problems between adults in school.	1	2	3	4
13. Managing student behavior without punishment is crucial to the development of cooperative and responsible students.	1	2	3	4

Postprogram Staff Assessment

Date _____

Circle the number that best corresponds to your response to conflict between students in the school or classroom.

	Always	**Often**	**Sometimes**	**Never**
1. Tell the students to "knock it off."	1	2	3	4
2. Try to smooth over the situation.	1	2	3	4
3. Help students understand different points of view.	1	2	3	4
4. Separate students and keep them away from each other.	1	2	3	4
5. Send students to the principal's office.	1	2	3	4
6. Determine who started it.	1	2	3	4
7. Try to find the cause of the problem.	1	2	3	4
8. Ask students to apologize to each other.	1	2	3	4
9. Ask students to mediate or negotiate.	1	2	3	4
10. Assign a punishment or consequence.	1	2	3	4
11. Let students have it out, as long as no one gets physically hurt.	1	2	3	4
12. Tell students to settle it after class.	1	2	3	4

Circle the number that best describes how much you agree or disagree with each of the following statements.

	Strongly agree	**Agree somewhat**	**Disagree somewhat**	**Strongly disagree**
1. Conflict should not happen in school.	1	2	3	4
2. Group problem solving is not a good way to resolve conflicts affecting everyone in the classroom.	1	2	3	4
3. Disputants must change or align their values to resolve conflicts over values.	1	2	3	4
4. When students fight over property, an equal distribution is always an effective solution.	1	2	3	4
5. There is always someone who is right and someone who is wrong in a dispute.	1	2	3	4
6. Avoiding conflict helps students build productive relationships.	1	2	3	4

	Strongly agree	Agree somewhat	Disagree somewhat	Strongly disagree
7. Arguing over positions to find a compromise prevents disputants from finding solutions that address their interests and needs.	1	2	3	4
8. Students can peacefully resolve conflicts involving bias and prejudice.	1	2	3	4
9. Conflict is a natural part of life and is an opportunity to learn.	1	2	3	4
10. Students are effective negotiators.	1	2	3	4
11. Negotiation is a process that could be used to resolve disputes between teachers and students.	1	2	3	4
12. Mediation is a process that could be used to resolve problems between adults in school.	1	2	3	4
13. Managing student behavior without punishment is crucial to the development of cooperative and responsible students.	1	2	3	4

Answer the following questions.

1. I have participated in group problem solving sessions. ☐ yes ☐ no

    If yes, were agreements reached ☐ most of the time ☐ sometimes ☐ almost never

    If yes, were agreements honored ☐ most of the time ☐ sometimes ☐ almost never

2. Number of group problem solving sessions in which you participated ☐ fewer than 10 ☐ 10–20 ☐ more than 20

3. I have participated as a disputant in negotiation sessions. ☐ yes ☐ no

    If yes, were agreements reached ☐ most of the time ☐ sometimes ☐ almost never

    If yes, were agreements honored ☐ most of the time ☐ sometimes ☐ almost never

4. Number of negotiation sessions in which you participated: ☐ fewer than 10 ☐ 10–20 ☐ more than 20

5. I have participated as a disputant in mediation sessions. ☐ yes ☐ no

    If yes, were agreements reached ☐ most of the time ☐ sometimes ☐ almost never

    If yes, were agreements honored ☐ most of the time ☐ sometimes ☐ almost never

6. Number of mediation sessions in which you participated as a disputant: ☐ fewer than 10 ☐ 10–20 ☐ more than 20

7. I have served as a mediator using the six-step mediation process. ☐ yes ☐ no

    Number of mediation sessions in which you served as a mediator: ☐ fewer than 10 ☐ 10–20 ☐ more than 20

Parent/Guardian Permission Letter

Dear Parent or Guardian:

Your daughter or son has applied to be trained as a peer mediator. Peer mediators are students who, with adult supervision, mediate disputes between fellow students. As a result of their training, mediators are known to be fair, reliable, and good communicators. They become peacemakers.

Conflicts between students are a part of daily life in schools. Common conflicts include name-calling, rumors, threats, and friendships gone amiss. Mediation is a conflict resolution approach in which disputants have the chance to sit face-to-face and talk, uninterrupted, so each side of the dispute is heard. After the problem is defined, solutions are created and then evaluated. When an agreement is reached, it is ratified by the disputants.

The trained peer mediator is the outside third person who leads this process. The mediator does not take sides and keeps all information confidential. Mediation is a skill that involves good communication, problem solving, and critical thinking.

Interested students will be selected to participate in the mediation training. The number of peer mediators will be limited, and the group selected will be balanced by race and gender.

Mediators will participate in _____ days of training to be scheduled on _____.

Your child has indicated an interest in being a peer mediator. If you support your child's desire to become a mediator, please sign this form and have your son or daughter return it to

_____ by _____.

If you grant your permission, your child will become eligible to be selected for mediation training. If you have any questions, please call:

_____ at _____.

Sincerely,

I give my permission for _____ to participate in mediation training and to become a peer mediator. I understand that my child is responsible for all school-work missed because of the training or because of the mediation service.

Parent or guardian signature _____ Date _____

Request for Mediation

Your name _____ Date _____

Names of students in conflict (first name and last name of each):

_____

_____

Where conflict occurred (check one):

☐ Bus ☐ Classroom ☐ Rest room ☐ Outside grounds ☐ Lunchroom

☐ Hall ☐ Other (specify) _____

Briefly describe the problem:

_____

_____

_____

_____

Mediation Schedule Notice

_____
(student's name)

You are to serve as a co-mediator for a mediation scheduled at

_____
(time)

on _____
(date)

at _____.
(location)

Creating the Peaceable School (2nd ed.) © 2002 by R. L. Bodine, D. K. Crawford, and F. Schrumpf. Research Press (800) 519-2707.

Mediation Reminder/Pass

_____
(student's name)

This is to remind you that a mediation between you and

_____
(other student's name)

has been scheduled for _____
(time)

on _____
(date)

at _____.
(location)

Creating the Peaceable School (2nd ed.) © 2002 by R. L. Bodine, D. K. Crawford, and F. Schrumpf. Research Press (800) 519-2707.

Mediation Agreement

Date _____

We participated in a mediation on this date and reached an agreement that we believe is fair and that solves the problem between us.

Name _____   Name _____

I agree to: I agree to:

_____   _____

_____   _____

_____   _____

Signature _____   Signature _____

Mediators' signatures _____

_____

Mediation Report Form

Mediator(s) _____

_____

Date of mediation _____ Room number_____

Persons involved in the conflict:

_____

_____

_____

_____

What is the conflict about?

_____

_____

_____

_____

Was the conflict resolved?   ☐ yes   ☐ no

Creating the Peaceable School (2nd ed.) © 2002 by R. L. Bodine, D. K. Crawford, and F. Schrumpf. Research Press (800) 519-2707.

Negotiation Agreement

Date _____

We participated in a negotiation on this date and reached an agreement that we believe is fair and that solves the problem between us.

Name _____   Name _____

I agree to: I agree to:

_____   _____

_____   _____

_____   _____

_____   _____

_____   _____

_____   _____

_____   _____

_____   _____

_____   _____

_____   _____

Signature _____   Signature _____

References

Aber, J. L., Jones, S. M., Brown, J. L., Chaudry, N., & Samples, F. (1998). Resolving conflict creatively: Evaluating the developmental effects of a school-based violence prevention program in neighborhood and classroom context. *Development and Psychopathology, 10*(2), 187–213.

Aber, J. L., Jones, S. M., Brown, J. L., Samples, F., & Chaudry, N. (1996). The evaluation of the Resolving Conflict Creatively Program: An overview. *American Journal of Preventive Medicine, 12*(Suppl.), 82–90.

Bodine, R. J., & Crawford, D. K. (1998). *The handbook of conflict resolution education: A guide to building quality programs in schools.* San Francisco: Jossey-Bass.

Bodine, R. J., & Crawford, D. K. (1999). *Developing emotional intelligence: A guide to behavior management and conflict resolution in schools.* Champaign, IL: Research Press.

Bodine, R. J., Crawford, D. K., & Schrumpf, F. (1994). *Creating the peaceable school: A comprehensive program for teaching conflict resolution* (1st ed.). Champaign, IL: Research Press.

Crawford, D. K., Bodine, R. J., & Hoglund, R. G. (1993). *The school for quality learning: Managing the school and classroom the Deming way.* Champaign, IL: Research Press.

Creating the Peaceable School: A Comprehensive Program for Teaching Conflict Resolution [Video]. (1995). Champaign, IL: Research Press.

Davis, A., & Porter, K. (1985). Dispute resolution: The fourth "R". *Journal of Dispute Resolution, Spring,* 121–139.

Deutsch, M. (1973). *The resolution of conflict: Constructive and restrictive processes.* New Haven, CT: Yale University Press.

Fearn, L. (1974). *Individual development: Creativity.* San Diego: Education Improvement Associates.

Fisher, R., & Ury, W. (1981). *Getting to yes: Negotiating agreement without giving in* (1st ed.). Boston: Houghton Mifflin.

Fisher, R., Ury, W., & Patton, B. (1991). *Getting to yes: Negotiating agreement without giving in* (2nd ed.). Boston: Houghton Mifflin.

Gentry, D. B., & Benenson, W. A. (1992). School-age peer mediators transfer knowledge and skills to home setting. *Mediation Quarterly, 10*(1), 101–109.

Ginott, H. (1972). *Teacher and child: A book for parents and teachers.* New York: Macmillan.

Girard, K., & Koch, S. J. (1996). *Conflict resolution in the schools: A manual for educators.* San Francisco: Jossey-Bass.

Glasser, W. (1969). *Schools without failure.* New York: Harper & Row.

Glasser, W. (1984). *Control theory.* New York: Harper & Row.

Hanson, M. K. (1994). A conflict resolution/student mediation program: Effects on student attitudes and behaviors. *E.R.S. Spectrum, 12*(4), 9–14.

Hessler, R. M., Hollis, S., & Crowe, C. (1998). Peer mediation: A qualitative study of youthful frames of power and influence. *Mediation Quarterly, 15*(3), 187–198.

Johnson, D. W. (1971). Role reversal: A summary and review of the research. *International Journal of Group Tensions, 1,* 318–334.

Johnson, D. W., & Johnson, R. T. (1975). *Learning together and alone: Cooperation, competition, and individualization.* Englewood Cliffs, NJ: Prentice Hall.

Johnson, D. W., & Johnson, R. T. (1993). Cooperative learning and conflict resolution. *The Fourth R, 42,* 1, 4, 8.

Johnson, D. W., & Johnson, R. T. (1994). *Teaching students to be peacemakers: Results of five years of research.* Minneapolis: University of Minnesota.

Jones, T. S. (1998). Research supports effectiveness of peer mediation. *The Fourth R, 82,* 1, 10–12, 18, 21, 25, 27.

Kreidler, W. J. (1984). *Creative conflict resolution: More than 200 activities for keeping peace in the classroom—K-6.* Glenview, IL: Scott Foresman.

Kreidler, W. J. (1990). *Elementary perspectives 1: Teaching concepts of peace and conflict.* Cambridge, MA: Educators for Social Responsibility.

Lindsey, P. (1998). Conflict resolution and peer mediation in public schools: What works? *Mediation Quarterly, 16*(1), 86–89.

Lyon, G. E. (1992). Gifts, not stars. *Horn Book, September–October,* 553.

Metis Associates, Inc. (1990). *Resolving Conflict Creatively Program: 1988–1989 summary of significant findings.* New York: Author.

Ohio Commission on Dispute Resolution and Conflict Management & Ohio Department of Education. (1997). *Conflict management programs in Ohio elementary schools: Case studies and evaluation* (Annual Report). Columbus: Author.

Pruitt, D. (1981). *Negotiation behavior.* New York: Academic.

Roush, G., & Hall, E. (1993). Teaching peaceful conflict resolution. *Mediation Quarterly, 11*(2), 185–191.

Scholes, K. (1990). *Peace begins with you.* San Franciso: Little, Brown.

Schrumpf, F., Crawford, D. K., & Bodine, R. J. (1997). *Peer mediation: Conflict resolution in schools* (Rev. ed.). Champaign, IL: Research Press.

Schrumpf, F., Crawford, D. K., & Usadel, H. C. (1991). *Peer mediation: Conflict resolution in schools.* Champaign, IL: Research Press.

Sharan, Y., & Sharan, S. (1990). Group investigation expands cooperative learning. *Educational Leadership, 47*(4), 17–21.

Slavin, R. (1987). *Cooperative learning: Student teams* (2nd ed.). Washington, DC: National Education Association.

Stevahn, L., Johnson, D. W., Johnson, R. T., Laginski, A. M., & O'Coin, I. (1996). Effects on high school students of integrating conflict resolution and peer mediation training into an academic unit. *Mediation Quarterly, 14*(1), 21–36.

Tschannen-Moran, M. (1991). *Seeds of peace: Ohio's school conflict management grant program.* Columbus: Ohio Commission on Dispute Resolution and Conflict Management and Ohio Department of Education.

Index

Note: Page numbers indicating activities appear in boldface type.

About the Authors

RICHARD J. BODINE co-founded the National Center for Conflict Resolution Education in 1995. He holds an undergraduate degree in teaching of mathematics and chemistry and has taught at the elementary, middle school, high school, and junior college levels. He has a master's degree in special education, specializing in gifted children, and an advanced certificate of education in administration from the University of Illinois at Urbana-Champaign. He has been a secondary school administrator and director of special regional education programs. Richard has consulted with numerous schools on gifted education, individualized learning programs, behavior management, and administrative issues and has directed teacher-training institutes on innovative practice. In the past 8 years, he has trained over 5,000 adults and over 1,200 youths in conflict resolution processes. He has taught graduate-level courses in administration at the University of Illinois, including a course on principalship. For 20 years, he served as principal of Leal Elementary School in Urbana, Illinois. In 1992, he received the Illinois State Board of Education's "Those Who Excel" award as an outstanding administrator. He holds training certificates from CDR Associates of Boulder, Colorado, for mediation, dispute management systems design, and conflict resolution in organizations.

Currently, Richard is training director of the National Center for Conflict Resolution Education and president of Conflict Resolution Education, Inc. He is coauthor of the books *The School for Quality Learning* (1993), the first edition of *Creating the Peaceable School* (1994), the revised edition of *Peer Mediation* (1991, 1997), and *Developing Emotional Intelligence* (1999), all published by Research Press. He has also coauthored *Conflict Resolution Education* (U.S. Department of Justice & U.S. Department of Education, 1996) and *The Handbook for Conflict Resolution Education* (Jossey-Bass, 1998).

DONNA K. CRAWFORD co-founded the Illinois Institute for Dispute Resolution in 1992 and the National Center for Conflict Resolution Education in 1995. A former public school educator, Donna taught in and served as principal of an early childhood center and worked as a district special education administrator with supervisory responsibility for a regional program for students with emotional and behavioral disorders. She is an experienced mediator, reality therapist, and dispute resolution trainer. She holds a master's degree in special education and an advanced certificate of education in administration from the University of Illinois at Urbana-Champaign. Her training in alternative dispute resolution methods includes work with the Justice Center of Atlanta and the Harvard University Negotiation Project. Donna has also served as a practicum supervisor for the Institute for Reality Therapy, Los Angeles, California.

Currently, Donna is executive director of the National Center for Conflict Resolution Education and CEO of Conflict Resolution Education, Inc. She is coauthor of the books *The School for Quality Learning* (1993), the first edition of *Creating the Peaceable School* (1994), *Peer Mediation* (1991, 1997), and *Developing Emotional Intelligence* (1999), all published by Research Press. She also coauthored *Conflict Resolution Education* (U.S. Department of Justice & U.S. Department of Education, 1996), *The Handbook for Conflict Resolution Education* (Jossey-Bass, 1998), and *Take a Stand: Stop the Violence* (a multimedia CD-ROM and video produced by Leo Media, 1999).

FRED SCHRUMPF has practiced school social work for 20 years with children in prekindergarten through twelfth grades. At the university level, Fred has taught courses at both the University of Illinois at Urbana-Champaign and Washington State University. He holds master's degrees in both social work and educational administration from the University of Illinois. In 1990 he was named Social Worker of the Year by the Illini chapter of the National Association of Social Workers. He has been a trainer and consultant for the Illinois Institute for Dispute Resolution and the National Center for Conflict Resolution Education since 1992. He has given many workshops and presentations throughout the United States, Canada, and the Netherlands on peer mediation, the teacher as adviser, creating peaceable schools, and collaboration and team building.

Currently, Fred is student services coordinator for Spokane public schools, Spokane, Washington. He is coauthor of *Life Lessons for Young Adolescents: An Advisory Guide for Teachers* (1993), *Peer Mediation* (1991, 1997), and the first edition of *Creating the Peaceable School,* published by Research Press.